Microsoft® Windows® 7 Administration

Instant Reference

William Panek

D0003694

WILEY

Wiley Publishing, Inc.

Acquisitions Editor: Agatha Kim
Development Editor: M.E. Schutz
Technical Editor: Tylor Wentworth
Production Editor: Christine O'Connor
Copy Editor: Elizabeth Welch
Editorial Manager: Pete Gaughan
Production Manager: Tim Tate
Vice President and Executive Group Publisher: Richard Swadley
Vice President and Publisher: Neil Edde
Book Designer: Maureen Forys
Compositor: Jeff Lytle, Happenstance Type-O-Rama
Proofreader: Publication Services, Inc.
Indexer: Robert Swanson
Project Coordinator, Cover: Lynsey Stanford
Cover Designer: Ryan Sneed

Library of Congress Cataloging-in-Publication Data
Panek, William, 1970-
  Microsoft Windows 7 administration instant reference / William Panek. — 1st ed.
    p. cm.
  ISBN 978-0-470-65047-9 (paper/website)
  ISBN 978-1-118-00094-6 (ebk.)
  ISBN 978-1-118-00096-0 (ebk.)
  ISBN 978-1-118-00095-3 (ebk.)
  1. Microsoft Windows (Computer file)—Handbooks, manuals, etc. 2. Operating systems (Computers)—Handbooks, manuals, etc. 3. Software maintenance—Handbooks, manuals, etc. I. Title.
  QA76.76.O63P3366 2011
  005.4'46—dc22
                            2010032264

Dear Reader,

Thank you for choosing *Microsoft Windows 7 Administration: Instant Reference*. This book is part of a family of premium-quality Sybex books, all of which are written by outstanding authors who combine practical experience with a gift for teaching.

Sybex was founded in 1976. More than 30 years later, we're still committed to producing consistently exceptional books. With each of our titles, we're working hard to set a new standard for the industry. From the paper we print on, to the authors we work with, our goal is to bring you the best books available.

I hope you see all that reflected in these pages. I'd be very interested to hear your comments and get your feedback on how we're doing. Feel free to let me know what you think about this or any other Sybex book by sending me an email at nedde@wiley.com. If you think you've found a technical error in this book, please visit http://sybex.custhelp.com. Customer feedback is critical to our efforts at Sybex.

Best regards,

Neil Edde
Vice President and Publisher
Sybex, an Imprint of Wiley

Acknowledgments

I would like to thank my wife Crystal and my two daughters, Alexandria and Paige, for all of their love and support during the writing of all my books. They make it all worthwhile.

I want to thank my family and especially my brothers Rick, Gary, and Rob. They have always been there for me.

I would like to thank Jeremy Hodgson, my training partner, who spends more time with me on the road than anyone else. His sense of humor keeps me smiling—even when I am homesick.

Finally, I want to thank everyone from Sybex who backed me up on this book: especially Mary Ellen Schutz, developmental editor, who helped me make this the best book possible; Tylor Wentworth, who was my technical editor and has co-authored multiple books with me; Christine O'Connor, who did a great job keeping all the edits organized; Pete Gaughan; Liz Welch; and finally, Agatha Kim, who was the lead for the entire book. She was always there for me and she was great to write for. Thanks to you all and everyone else behind the scenes on this book.

About the Author

Wﬁlliam Panek, (MCP®, MCP+I®, MCSA®, MCSA® W/
SECURITY & MESSAGING, MCSE – NT (3.51 & 4.0)®,
MCSE — 2000 & 2003®, MCSE W/SECURITY & MESSAGING,
MCDBA®, MCT®, MCTS®, MCITP®, CCNA®, CHFI®)

After many successful years in the computer industry and a degree in
computer programming, William Panek decided that he could better use
his talents and his personality as an instructor. He started teaching for
such schools as Boston University, Clark University, and GlobalNet, just
to name a few.

In 1998, Panek started Stellacon Corporation. Stellacon has become
one of New England's most respected training companies. Stellacon
is also a two-time winner of the Best Computer School award in
Portsmouth, New Hampshire.

William brings years of real-world expertise to the classroom and
strives to ensure that each and every student has an understanding of
the course material.

William currently lives in New Hampshire with his wife and two
girls. In his spare time he likes to golf, ski, and snowmobile. William is
also a commercially rated helicopter pilot.

Contents

Introduction

This book was written with over 20 years of IT experience. The author has taken that experience and translated it into a Windows 7 book that will help you develop a clear understanding of how to install and configure Windows 7 while avoiding the possible configuration pitfalls.

Many Microsoft books just explain the Windows operating system, but with this *Administrative Instant Reference*, the author takes it a step further, with many in-depth, step-by-step procedures together with the explanations of how the operating system performs at its best.

Microsoft Windows 7 is the newest version of Microsoft's client operating system software. Microsoft has taken the best of Windows XP and Windows Vista and combined them into their latest creation, Windows 7. Along with the best of Windows XP and Vista, Microsoft has added several new features to Windows 7 to make the more functionality available the users from one location such as Device Stage.

Windows 7 eliminates many of the problems that plagued Windows Vista, and includes a much faster boot time and shutdown. It is also easier to install and configure, and barely stops to ask the user any questions during installation. I will show you what features are installed during the automated installation and where you can make changes if you need to be more in charge of your operating system and its features.

This book takes you through all the ins and outs of Windows 7, including installation, configuration, Group Policy Objects, auditing, backups, Windows Server 2008, and so much more.

Windows 7 has improved on Microsoft's desktop environment, made home networking easier, enhanced searchability, improved performance, built in wireless support, and even built-in touchscreen capabilities—and that's only scratching the surface.

There have been several enhancements that allow Windows 7 to better serve the end user in terms of getting Remote Assistance from others. Windows 7 even adds a simple Easy Connect feature. I will show you the enhancements to Remote Desktop, making the user experience even better than it was before.

When all is said and done, this is a technical book for IT professionals who want to take Windows 7 to the next step. Most IT people just get a copy of Windows 7 and try to learn it. With this book, not only will you learn Windows 7, but you will also become a Windows 7 Master.

Who Should Read This Book

This book is intended for mid- to high-level administrators of networks that use Microsoft operating systems. Such people probably fall into a few basic groups:

- Administrators who are responsible for client operating systems and are looking to implement the Microsoft Windows 7 operating system

- Server administrators or IT managers who are responsible for deciding which operating systems to use and what functionality they need

- Help desk administrators who are responsible for supporting the Windows 7 operating system

This book will help anyone who has to administer Windows 7 in a corporate environment, but it will also help anyone who wants to learn the real ins and outs of the Windows 7 operating system.

What's Inside

Here is a glance at what's in each chapter:

Chapter 1: Installing Windows 7 I take you through the requirements and multiple ways to install the Windows 7 operating system in this chapter.

Chapter 2: Automating a Windows 7 Installation This chapter shows you how to install Windows 7 without the need of user intervention and also how to install multiple copies of Windows 7 quickly and easily.

Chapter 3: Configuring Disks In this chapter you are taken through the process of configuring and managing your physical disks.

Chapter 4: Managing the Desktop I show you how to manage your desktop environment, including customizing the taskbar and Start Menu, creating shortcuts, setting display properties for themes, and configuring Windows Gadgets.

Chapter 5: Managing the Interface I examine the process of configuring the Windows 7 environment in this chapter, including an overview of the main configuration utilities, including Control Panel and the Registry.

Chapter 6: Remote Desktop and Remote Assistance   This chapter explains the new features and benefits to using Remote Assistance and Remote Desktop within Windows 7, how to support end users, and implement Group Policy and scripting.

Chapter 7: Configuring Users and Groups   I take you through the various ways to create and manage your users and groups on the Windows 7 operating system.

Chapter 8: Managing Security   You will see how to configure different types of security on Windows 7, including Local Group Policy Objects (LGPOs), shared permissions, and NTFS security.

Chapter 9: Configuring Hardware and Printing   This chapter explains how to install and configure new hardware, drivers, and printers by using the different installation applets. A discussion of the new Device Stage feature is included as well.

Chapter 10: Configuring Network Connectivity   I explain in this chapter how to set up hardware to provide network connectivity, connect to network devices, set up peer-to-peer networking, and configure network protocols.

Chapter 11: Configuring Internet Explorer 8   You will see how to configure Internet Explorer 8, including Accelerators and Web Slices, pop-up blockers, InPrivate Security features, and security for Internet Explorer 8.

Chapter 12: Installing and Configuring Applications   This chapter shows you how to add and configure many applications that are installed on Windows 7, together with how to install new applications on the Windows 7 operating system. A discussion of Live Mail and Calendar from the online Live Essentials download is also included.

Chapter 13: Maintaining and Optimizing Windows 7   In this exciting chapter you will learn how to monitor, maintain, troubleshoot, and optimize Windows 7 using Performance Monitor, Reliability Monitor, System Information, Task Manager, System Tool, System Configuration, Task Scheduler, and Event Viewer.

The Pocket Reference Series

The *Pocket Reference* series from Sybex provides outstanding instruction for readers with intermediate and advanced skills, in the form of top-notch training and development for those already working in their field and clear, serious education for those aspiring to become pros. Every *Pocket Reference* book includes:

- Skill-based instruction, with chapters organized around real tasks rather than abstract concepts or subjects

- Step-by-step procedures showing you how to install and configure Windows 7 properly

How to Contact Sybex

Sybex strives to keep you supplied with the latest tools and information you need for your work. Please check their website at www.sybex.com, where I'll post additional content and updates that supplement this book should the need arise. Enter **Windows 7** in the Search box (or type the book's ISBN—**9780470650479**), and click Go to access the book's update page.

PART I

Installation

IN THIS PART ▶

1

Installing Windows 7

IN THIS CHAPTER, YOU WILL LEARN TO:

There is an old saying: "To build a good house, you must have a good foundation." Well, that's what this chapter is all about. You'll learn how to properly install Windows 7. We'll show you how to install Windows 7 on one machine and then install Windows 7 on multiple machines using various installation techniques and tools.

With each release of Microsoft Windows, Microsoft tries to take the best of the previous Windows versions and add even better functionality. This is no different with Windows 7. Let's start by looking at some of the features in Windows 7.

Understand Windows 7's New Features

Windows 7 has resolved many of the problems that plagued Windows Vista. Windows 7 has a much faster boot time and shutdown compared to Windows Vista. It is also easier to install and configure.

The Windows 7 operating system functions are also faster than its previous counterparts. Opening, moving, extracting, compressing, and installing files and folders are more efficient than previous versions of Microsoft's client operating systems.

Let's take a look at some of the improvements and features of Windows 7. This is just an overview of some of its benefits.

> **Windows 7 Taskbar**   In the previous versions of Windows, you had a Quick Launch bar on the left side and on the right side you could see which programs were loaded and running. The Quick Launch bar has been replaced by the Windows 7 Taskbar and Jump List. The Taskbar is shown in Figure 1.1.

Figure 1.1: Windows 7 Taskbar

The Windows Taskbar allows users to quickly access the programs they use the most. One advantage to having the applications on the Windows 7 Taskbar is that you have fewer icons on the Desktop, thus allowing for a more manageable desktop environment.

Jump Lists   Jump Lists are a new feature to the Windows lineup. They allow you to quickly access files that you have been working on. For example, if you have the Microsoft Word icon in the Taskbar, you can right-click it and it will show you all the recent files that you have been working with.

Another advantage to using Jump Lists is that you can preset certain applications, like Windows Media Player. For Internet Explorer, you could view all the recent websites that you have visited.

New Preview Pane   Windows XP and Windows Vista have a Preview pane, but Windows 7 has improved on the Preview pane by allowing you to view text files, music files, pictures files, HTML files, and videos. Another new advantage is if you have installed Microsoft Office and Adobe Acrobat Reader, you also have the ability to view Office and PDF files.

Windows Touch   Windows Touch is one of the coolest features included with Windows 7. It allows you to control the operating system and its applications by using a touchscreen.

For example, you can open a picture and then move it around, make it larger or smaller, or place it anywhere on the Desktop—all with the touch of your fingertips on the screen.

Touchscreens are included on laptops, tabletops, GPS devices, phones, and now on the Windows 7 operating system.

Windows XP Mode   Microsoft realizes that many organizations are running Windows XP. Also, many of these same organizations run older applications on these Windows XP systems. This is where Windows XP Mode comes into play. Windows XP Mode gives an organization that chooses to upgrade to Windows 7 the ability to run older Windows XP applications on their new system.

To run Windows XP Mode, Windows 7 uses virtualized technology to run a virtual XP operating system to allow the organization to use the older applications.

HomeGroup Networking   Windows 7 networking has been made easier with the improvement of HomeGroups. HomeGroups are an easy way to set up a network using Windows 7. Windows 7 searches for your home network, and if one is found, it connects after you enter the HomeGroup password.

If a home network is not found, a networking wizard automatically creates a password for the HomeGroup. This password lets you

Installation

PART I

connect all your other computers to the same network. The password can be changed any time after you install Windows 7.

Device Stage   Device Stage is new to the Windows operating systems family. Device Stage enables you to connect a compatible device to your PC and a picture of the device appears. Device Stage allows you to easily share files between devices and computers.

Before Windows 7 Device Stage, when you connected a device to the PC, you might have seen multiple devices appear. For example, when you added a multifunction printer (printer, scanner, and copier), the device might have been added as three separate devices. Device Stage helps resolve this issue.

Another feature of Device Stage is that the device vendors can customize the icons for Device Stage, so that the same multifunction printer can have the ability to order ink from Device Stage.

View Available Networks (VAN)   If you have used a laptop, you have used this feature. When you use a wireless network adapter and you right-click the icon in the system tray, you can choose the wireless network that you want to connect to. You connect to a wireless network through the wireless network adapter. Now that same functionality is built into the Windows 7 operating system.

Windows Internet Explorer 8   Windows 7 includes the newest version of Internet Explorer (IE8). IE8, as shown in Figure 1.2, allows a user to work faster and more efficiently on the Internet due to new search features, address bars, and favorites.

Figure 1.2: Internet Explorer 8 lets you work faster and more efficiently.

Some of the new features of IE8 include:

Instant Search   This feature lets you quickly access search requests without typing the entire search criteria. As you start typing in the search request, you'll see suggestions for your search.

The advantage to Instant Search is that it will also use your browsing history to narrow down the suggestions. After you see what you're looking for, you can make your selection without having to finish the query.

Accelerators   This new feature allows you to accelerate actions on Internet services and applications. For example, if you are looking for a street address and you click the blue Accelerator icon, a map will appear right there on the screen.

Microsoft Accelerators can be used for email, searching, and so forth. Also, other websites like eBay and Facebook offer Accelerators for their services.

Web Slices   Web Slices are instances on a website that you want to access without accessing the site. For example, say you want to get stock quotes, sports scores, or auction items without visiting the sites; this is the advantage of using Web Slices. As the information that you are watching changes, the updates will show immediately.

Understand Windows 7 Architecture

Windows 7 is built on the Windows Vista core, but Windows 7 has limited the files that load at startup to help with the core performance of the operating system. They have also removed many of the fluff items that Windows Vista used, thus allowing for better performance.

When Microsoft first released Windows 7 as a beta, there was a 64-bit version but no 32-bit version. This did not go over well with the Internet bloggers. I even saw a petition online to have a 32-bit version released.

The funny thing is that I also saw a petition asking Microsoft not to release a 32-bit version. The logic behind this was it would force users and manufacturers to upgrade everything to 64-bit. In response, Microsoft has released Windows 7 as both a 32-bit and a 64-bit version.

Installation

PART I

Microsoft could not just release a 64-bit version of Windows 7. This would alienate many users with 32-bit computer systems, and it would cost Microsoft a large share of the client-side software market. Users already have to deal with the PC versus Mac commercials! So Windows 7 users have a choice of either 32-bit or 64-bit.

32-bit vs. 64-bit

When you hear the terms *32-bit* and *64-bit*, this is referring to the CPU, or processor. The number represents how the data is processed. It is processed either as 2^32 or as 2^64. The larger the number, the larger the amount of data that can be processed at any one time.

Think of a large highway that has 32 lanes. Vehicles can travel on those 32 lanes only. When traffic gets backed up, they can only use these lanes, and this can cause traffic delays. But now think of a 64-lane highway and how many more vehicles can travel on that highway. This is an easy way of thinking of how 32-bit and 64-bit processors operate.

The problem here is that if you have a 32-lane highway, you can't just set up 64 vehicles on this highway and let them go. You need to have the infrastructure to allow for 64 vehicles by having 64 lanes. This is the same with computers. Your computer has to be configured to allow you to run a 64-bit processor.

So what does all of this mean to the common user or administrator? Well, it's all about RAM. A 32-bit operating system can handle up to 4 GB of RAM and a 64-bit processor can handle up to 16 exabytes of RAM. The problem here is that Windows and most motherboards can't handle this much RAM.

None of this is new—64-bit is just starting to become accepted with Windows, but other operating systems, like Apple, have been using 64-bit processors for many years.

So should you switch all of your users to 64 bit? The answer is no. Most users do not need to have large amounts of RAM, and the real problem here is that many manufacturers do not have 64 bit–compliant components.

For example, I am writing this book on a 64-bit computer, but if I open Internet Explorer and go to any website that uses Adobe Flash Player, it will not work. Currently, Adobe does not have a 64-bit Flash Player.

NOTE Computer processors are typically rated by speed. The speed of the processor, or CPU, is rated by the number of clock cycles that can be performed in one second. This measurement is typically expressed in gigahertz (GHz). One GHz is one billion cycles per second. Keep in mind that processor architecture must also be taken into account when considering processor speed. A processor with a more efficient pipeline will be faster than a processor with a less efficient pipeline at the same CPU speed.

Prepare to Install Windows 7

Installing Windows 7 is simple, thanks to the installation wizard. The wizard walks you through the entire installation of the operating system.

The hardest part of installing Windows 7 is preparing and planning for the installation. One saying that I teach to IT professionals is "An hour of planning will save you days of work." Planning a Windows 7 rollout is one of the most important tasks that you will perform when you install Windows 7.

You must make many decisions before you insert the Windows 7 media into your machine. The first decision is which edition of Windows 7 you want to install.

The user's job function or requirements may determine which edition of Windows 7 you should use. Do they need their computer for home use or just work? These are some of the factors that you'll take into account when deciding which edition of Windows 7 to install. Let's take a look at the various editions of Windows 7.

Windows 7 Editions

Microsoft offers six editions of the Windows 7 operating system. This allows an administrator to custom-fit a user's hardware and job function to the appropriate edition:

- Windows 7 Starter
- Windows 7 Home Basic
- Windows 7 Home Premium

- Windows 7 Professional
- Windows 7 Enterprise
- Windows 7 Ultimate

Many times Microsoft releases multiple editions of the operating system contained within the same Windows 7 media disk. You can choose to unlock the one that you want based on the product key that you have.

Table 1.1 compares all the Windows 7 editions and lists what they include. We compiled this information from Microsoft's website and TechNet. This table is only a partial representation of all the features and applications that are included.

Table 1.1: Windows 7 Edition Comparison

	Starter Edition	Home Basic Edition	Home Premium Edition	Professional Edition	Enterprise and Ultimate Editions
Processor (32-bit or 64-bit)	Both	Both	Both	Both	Both
Multiprocessor support	No	No	Yes	Yes	Yes
32-bit maximum RAM	4 GB	4 GB	4 GB	4 GB	4 GB
64-bit maximum RAM	8 GB	8 GB	16 GB	192 GB	192 GB
Windows HomeGroup	Yes	Yes	Yes	Yes	Yes
Jump Lists	Yes	Yes	Yes	Yes	Yes
Internet Explorer 8	Yes	Yes	Yes	Yes	Yes
Media Player 12	Yes	Yes	Yes	Yes	Yes
System Image	Yes	Yes	Yes	Yes	Yes
Device Stage	Yes	Yes	Yes	Yes	Yes
Sync Center	Yes	Yes	Yes	Yes	Yes
Windows Backup	Yes	Yes	Yes	Yes	Yes

Table 1.1: Windows 7 Edition Comparison *(continued)*

	Starter Edition	Home Basic Edition	Home Premium Edition	Professional Edition	Enterprise and Ultimate Editions
Remote Desktop	Yes	Yes	Yes	Yes	Yes
ReadyDrive	Yes	Yes	Yes	Yes	Yes
ReadyBoost	Yes	Yes	Yes	Yes	Yes
Windows Firewall	Yes	Yes	Yes	Yes	Yes
Windows Defender	Yes	Yes	Yes	Yes	Yes
Taskbar previews	No	Yes	Yes	Yes	Yes
Mobility Center	No	Yes	Yes	Yes	Yes
Easy user switching	No	Yes	Yes	Yes	Yes
Windows Aero Glass	No	No	Yes	Yes	Yes
Multi-touch	No	No	Yes	Yes	Yes
DVD playback	No	No	Yes	Yes	Yes
Windows Media Center	No	No	Yes	Yes	Yes
XP Mode	No	No	No	Yes	Yes
Encrypting File System (EFS)	No	No	No	Yes	Yes
BitLocker	No	No	No	No	Yes
AppLocker	No	No	No	No	Yes
BranchCache	No	No	No	No	Yes
DirectAccess	No	No	No	No	Yes

Now that you have seen what each edition of Windows 7 can accomplish, let's take a look at the hardware requirements needed to install Windows 7.

Hardware Requirements

Before you can insert the Windows 7 DVD and install the operating system, you first must make sure that the machine's hardware can handle the Windows 7 operating system.

To install Windows 7 successfully, your system must meet or exceed certain hardware requirements. Table 1.2 lists the requirements for a Windows 7–compatible PC.

Table 1.2: Hardware Requirements

Component	Requirements
CPU (processor)	1 GHz 32-bit or 64-bit processor
Memory (RAM)	1 GB of system memory
Hard disk	16 GB of available disk space
Video adapter	Support for DirectX 9 graphics with 128 MB of memory (to enable the Aero theme)
Optional drive	DVD-R/W drive
Network device	Compatible network interface card

> **NOTE** The hardware requirements listed in Table 1.2 were those specified as of this writing. Always check Microsoft's website at www.microsoft.com/windows7 for the most current information.

The Windows 7–compatible PC must meet or exceed the basic requirements to deliver the core functionality of the Windows 7 operating system. These requirements assume that you're installing only the operating system without any premium functionality. For example, you may be able to get by with the minimum requirements if you're installing the operating system just to learn the basics of the software. Remember, the better the hardware, the better the performance.

Besides the basic hardware requirements that are needed to install Windows 7, the requirements for the graphic card depend on the resolution at which you want to run. The required amount of memory is as follows:

- 64 MB is required for a single monitor at a resolution of 1,310,720 pixels or less, which is equivalent to a 1280×1024 resolution.

- 128 MB is required for a single monitor at a resolution of 2,304,000 pixels or less, which is equivalent to a 1920×1200 resolution.

- 256 MB is required for a single monitor at a resolution larger than 2,304,000 pixels.

In addition, the graphics memory bandwidth must be at least 1,600 MB per second, as assessed by the Windows 7 Upgrade Advisor.

Setting the hardware requirements for Windows 7 on your machine can sometime be a difficult task. You may ask yourself, "Does the hardware you currently have support Windows 7?" Microsoft understands this concern and has a tool called the Hardware Compatibility List to help you figure out whether your machines will work with Windows 7.

The Hardware Compatibility List

Along with meeting the minimum requirements, your hardware should appear on the Hardware Compatibility List (HCL). The HCL (also referred to as the Windows Logo'd Products List) is an extensive list of computers and peripheral hardware that have been tested with the Windows 7 operating system.

The Windows 7 operating system requires control of the hardware for stability, efficiency, and security. The hardware and supported drivers on the HCL have been put through rigorous tests to ensure their compatibility with Windows 7. Microsoft guarantees that the items on the list meet the requirements for Windows 7 and do not have any incompatibilities that could affect the stability of the operating system.

If you call Microsoft for support, the first thing a Microsoft support engineer will ask about is your configuration. If you have any hardware that is not on the HCL, you may not be able to get support from Microsoft.

To determine if your computer and peripherals are on the HCL, check the most up-to-date list at `http://winqual.microsoft.com/HCL/Default.aspx`.

Installation

PART I

The HCL will let you know if your hardware is compatible with Windows 7. Besides the basic RAM, video, hard drive, and CPU requirements, there are some other areas of the computer that you should examine for compatibility.

BIOS Compatibility

Before you install Windows 7, verify that your computer has the most current BIOS (Basic Input/Output System). This is especially important if your current BIOS doesn't include support for Advanced Configuration and Power Interface (ACPI) functionality. ACPI functionality is required for Windows 7 to function properly. Check the computer's vendor for the latest BIOS version information.

Driver Requirements

To successfully install Windows 7, you must have the critical device drivers for your computer, such as the hard drive device driver. The Windows 7 media comes with an extensive list of drivers. If your computer's device drivers are not on the Windows 7 installation media, check the device manufacturer's website. If you can't find the device driver on the manufacturer's website and no other compatible driver exists, you are out of luck. Windows 7 won't recognize devices that don't have Windows 7 drivers.

If your hardware does not have drivers for Windows 7, be sure to check the hardware manufacturers' websites often because new drivers for Windows 7 are released frequently.

After you have made sure that the hardware for your machine is compatible for Windows 7, the next decision to make is how you're going to install the operating system.

New Install or Upgrade?

When installing Windows 7, you have two choices: you can install a fresh copy of Windows 7 or you can upgrade from Windows Vista.

An upgrade allows you to retain your existing operating system's applications, settings, and files. If you currently have a computer with Windows Vista, you are eligible to use an upgrade copy of Windows 7.

However, the bad news is you must always perform a clean install with Windows XP or earlier editions of Windows. You can, however, use the Windows Easy Transfer utility to migrate files and settings from Windows XP to Windows 7 on the same computer.

Another possibility is to upgrade your Windows XP machine to Windows Vista and then upgrade the new Vista operating system to Windows 7.

You can perform an upgrade to Windows 7 if the following conditions are true:

- You are running Windows Vista.

- You want to keep your existing applications and preferences.

- You want to preserve any local users and groups you've created.

You must perform a clean install of Windows 7 if any of the following conditions are true:

- There is no operating system currently installed.

- You have an operating system installed that does not support an in-place upgrade to Windows 7 (such as DOS, Windows 9*x*, Windows NT, Windows Me, Windows 2000 Professional, or Windows XP).

- You want to start from scratch, without keeping any existing preferences.

- You want to be able to dual-boot between Windows 7 and your previous operating system.

Table 1.3 shows the Vista operating systems that can be upgraded and to which edition of Windows 7 each should be updated to.

Table 1.3: Windows Vista Upgrade Options

Windows Vista Edition	Windows 7 Edition
Home Basic Edition	Home Basic Edition
Home Premium Edition	Home Premium Edition
Business Edition	Professional Edition
Ultimate Edition	Ultimate Edition

Before you decide if you should upgrade or install a clean Windows 7 operating system, let's take a look at some of the things you need to consider about upgrades.

Upgrade Considerations

Almost all Windows Vista applications should run with the Windows 7 operating system. However, there are a few possible exceptions to this statement:

- Applications that use file system filters, such as antivirus software, may not be compatible.

- Custom power-management tools may not be supported.

Before you upgrade to Windows 7, be sure to stop any antivirus scanners, network services, or other client software. These software packages may see the Windows 7 install as a virus and cause installation issues.

If you're performing a clean install to the same partition as an existing edition of Windows, the contents of the existing Users (or Documents and Settings), Program Files, and Windows directories will be placed in a directory named Windows.old, and the old operating system will no longer be available.

Hardware Compatibility Issues

Ensure that you have Windows 7 device drivers for your hardware. If you have a video driver without a Windows 7–compatible driver, the Windows 7 upgrade will install the Standard VGA driver, which will display the video with an 800×600 resolution. After you get the Windows 7 driver for your video, you can install it and adjust video properties accordingly.

Application Compatibility Issues

Not all applications that were written for earlier editions of Windows will work with Windows 7. After the upgrade, if you have application problems, you can address the problems as follows:

- If the application is compatible with Windows 7, reinstall the application after the upgrade is complete.

- If the application uses dynamic link libraries (DLLs) and there are migration DLLs for the application, apply the migration DLLs.

- Use the Microsoft Application Compatibility Toolkit (ACT) to determine the compatibility of your current applications with Windows 7. ACT will determine which applications are installed, identify any applications that may be affected by Windows updates, and identify any potential compatibility problems with User Account Control (UAC) and Internet Explorer. Reports can be exported for detailed analysis.

- If applications were written for earlier editions of Windows but are incompatible with Windows 7, use the Windows 7 Program Compatibility Wizard. From Control Panel click the Programs icon and then click the Run Programs From Previous Versions link to start the Program Compatibility Wizard.

- If the application is not compatible with Windows 7, upgrade your application to a Windows 7–compliant version.

Windows 7 Upgrade Advisor

To assist you in the upgrade process, the Windows 7 Setup program can check the compatibility of your system, devices, and installed applications and then provide the results to you. You can then analyze these results to determine whether your hardware or software applications will port properly from the Windows Vista edition to Windows 7.

You can download the Windows 7 Upgrade Advisor from Microsoft's website at www.microsoft.com/downloads. The Windows 7 Upgrade Advisor is compatible with Windows 7, Windows Vista, and Windows XP with Service Pack 2 or higher.

When you're running the Upgrade Advisor on a machine running Windows XP, if you do not have .NET Framework 2.0, you are asked to download and install it. After the .NET Framework is installed, you can restart the Upgrade Advisor installation.

After your computer is scanned, the Upgrade Advisor determines whether any incompatibilities exist between your computer and Windows 7. It also tells you which edition of Windows 7 seems to be best for your computer. However, you are by no means limited to upgrading to the recommended edition. The Upgrade Advisor Compatibility reports are broken up into the following three categories:

System Requirements   The System Requirements report alerts you to any shortcomings your system might have when running certain editions of Windows Vista. For example, our lab computer should have no problems accessing all the features of Windows Vista Business, but it won't be able to access all the features of Windows Vista Home Premium or Windows Vista Ultimate because it doesn't have a TV tuner card.

Devices   The Devices report alerts you to any potential Windows Vista driver issues. Each device in your system will be listed in this section either as a device to be reviewed or as a device that should automatically work after Windows 7 is installed. You will need a driver for the network card after Windows 7 is installed.

Programs   The Programs report alerts you to any potential application compatibility issues.

You can also save or print a task list that tells you the most compatible Windows 7 edition, your current system configuration, and the steps you need to take before and after you install Windows 7.

Perform the following steps to download and run the Windows 7 Upgrade Advisor:

1. Go to www.microsoft.com/downloads and download the Windows 7 Upgrade Advisor.

2. After the download is complete, run the .msi installation.

3. The Windows 7 Upgrade Advisor Setup Wizard starts, as shown in Figure 1.3. Click the Next button.

Figure 1.3: Upgrade Advisor Setup Wizard

4. Accept the licensing terms and click Next.

5. At the Select Installation Folder screen, accept the defaults or choose a directory location where you want this program installed, as shown in Figure 1.4. Click Install.

Figure 1.4: The Select Installation Folder screen

6. At the Installation Complete screen, click the Close button.

7. On the desktop, double-click the Windows 7 Upgrade Advisor icon.

8. When the Windows 7 Upgrade Advisor starts, click the Start Check button to start the scan of the machine.

9. After the system scan is complete, the Upgrade Advisor gives you the results. You can print or save these results. Close the Upgrade Advisor.

An Upgrade Checklist

After you make the decision to upgrade, you should develop a plan of attack. The following upgrade checklist (valid for upgrading from Windows Vista) will help you plan and implement a successful upgrade strategy:

- Verify that your computer meets the minimum hardware requirements for Windows 7.

- Be sure that your hardware is on the HCL.

- Make sure you have the Windows 7 drivers for the hardware. You can verify this with the hardware manufacturer.

- Run the Windows 7 Upgrade Advisor tool from the Microsoft website, which also includes documentation on using the utility, to audit the current configuration and status of your computer. It will generate a report of any known hardware or software compatibility issues based on your configuration. You should resolve any reported issues before you upgrade to Windows 7.

- Make sure that your BIOS is current. Windows 7 requires that your computer has the most current BIOS. If it does not, the computer may not be able to use advanced power-management features or device-configuration features. In addition, your computer may cease to function during or after the upgrade. Use caution when performing BIOS updates, as installing the incorrect BIOS can cause your computer to fail to boot.

- Take an inventory of your current configuration. This inventory should include documentation of your current network configuration, the applications that are installed, the hardware items and their configuration, the services that are running, and any profile and policy settings.

- Back up your data and configuration files. Before you make any major changes to your computer's configuration, you should back up your data and configuration files and then verify that you can successfully restore your backup. Chances are if you have a valid backup, you won't have any problems.

- Delete any unnecessary files or applications, and clean up any program groups or program items you don't use. Theoretically, you want to delete all the junk on your computer before you upgrade. Think of this as the spring-cleaning step.

- Verify that there are no existing problems with your drive prior to the upgrade. Perform a disk scan, a current virus scan, and defragmentation. These, too, are spring-cleaning chores. This step just prepares your drive for the upgrade.

- Perform the upgrade.

- Verify your configuration. After Windows 7 has been installed, use the inventory to compare and test each element that was previously inventoried prior to the upgrade to verify that the upgrade was successful.

When you install Windows 7, you must decide how you want to partition the disk drive that the Windows 7 operating system will reside on.

Disk Space Partitioning

Disk partitioning is the act of taking the physical hard drive and creating logical partitions. A logical drive is how space is allocated to the drive's primary and logical partitions. For example, if you have a 500 GB hard drive, you might partition it into three logical drives: a C drive, which might be 200 GB; a D drive, which might be 150 GB; and an E drive, which might be 150 GB.

Some of the major considerations for disk partitioning are as follows:

- The amount of space required
- The location of the system and boot partition
- Any special disk configurations you will use
- The utility you will use to set up the partitions

Partition Size   One important consideration in your disk-partitioning scheme is determining the partition size. You need to consider the amount of space taken up by your operating system, the applications that will be installed, and the amount of stored data. It is also important to consider the amount of space required in the future.

Microsoft recommends that you allocate at least 16 GB of disk space for Windows 7. This allows room for the operating system files and for future growth in terms of upgrades and installation files that are placed with the operating system files.

System and Boot Partitions   When you install Windows 7, files will be stored in two locations: the system partition and the boot partition. The system partition and the boot partition can be the same partition.

The system partition contains the files needed to boot the Windows 7 operating system. The system partition contains the Master Boot Record (MBR) and boot sector of the active drive partition. It is often the first physical hard drive in the computer and normally contains the necessary files to boot the computer. The files stored on the system partition do not take any significant disk space. The active partition is the system partition that is used to start your computer. The C drive is usually the active partition.

The boot partition contains the Windows 7 operating system files. By default, the Windows operating system files are located in a folder named `Windows`.

Installation

PART I

Special Disk Configurations Windows 7 supports several disk configurations. Options include simple, spanned, and striped volumes.

Disk Partition Configuration Utilities If you are partitioning your disk prior to installation, you can use several utilities, such as the DOS or Windows Fdisk program or a third-party utility such as Norton's Partition Magic. You can also configure the disks during the installation of the Windows 7 operating system.

You might want to create only the first partition where Windows 7 will be installed. You can then use the Disk Management utility in Windows 7 to create any other partitions you need.

Another configuration option that you must set when you install Windows 7 is where the computer system files will reside after the install is complete.

Install Windows 7

You can install Windows 7 either from the bootable DVD or through a network installation using files that have been copied to a network share point. You can also launch the setup.exe file from within the Windows Vista operating system to upgrade your operating system.

The Windows 7 DVD is bootable. To start the installation, simply restart your computer and boot to the DVD. The installation process begins automatically. I will walk you through the steps of installing Windows 7 later in this chapter.

If you are installing Windows 7 from the network, you need a distribution server and a computer with a network connection. A distribution server is a server that has the Windows 7 distribution files copied to a shared folder.

Perform the following steps to install Windows 7 over the network:

1. Boot the target computer.

2. Attach to the distribution server and access the share that has the files copied to it.

3. Launch setup.exe.

4. Complete the Windows 7 installation using either the clean install method or the upgrade method.

These methods are discussed in detail in the following sections.

Performing a Clean Install of Windows 7

On any installation of Windows 7, there are three phases to the installation. First you have the Collecting Information phase, then the Installing Windows phase, and finally the Setting Up Windows phase.

Collecting Information   During the collection phase of the installation, Windows 7 gathers the information necessary to complete the installation. This is where Windows 7 gathers your local time, location, keyboard, license agreement, installation type, and installation disk partition information.

Installing Windows   This section of the installation is where your Windows 7 files are copied to the hard disk and the installation is completed. This phase takes the longest as the files are installed.

Setting Up Windows   This phase of the setup is where you set up a username, computer name, and password; enter the product key and security settings; and review your date and time settings. After this is finished, your installation will be complete.

You can run the installation from the optical media or over a network. The only difference in the installation procedure is your starting point: from your optical drive or from a network share. The steps in the following sections assume you are using the Windows 7 DVD to install Windows 7.

When you boot to the Windows 7 installation media, the Setup program automatically starts the Windows 7 installation.

Before you begin any of the procedures, verify that you have access to Windows 7 Ultimate; other editions might vary slightly. You can also download an evaluation edition of Windows 7 from Microsoft's website at www.microsoft.com/windows7.

Perform the following steps for a clean install of Windows 7:

1. Insert the Windows 7 DVD into the machine and start the computer.

2. If you are asked to Hit Any Key to start the DVD, press Enter.

3. The first screen asks you to select your language, local time, and keyboard. After filling in these fields, click Next, as shown in Figure 1.5.

Figure 1.5: Windows 7 Installation screen

4. At the next screen, click the Install Now button, as shown in Figure 1.6.

Figure 1.6: Windows 7 Install Now screen

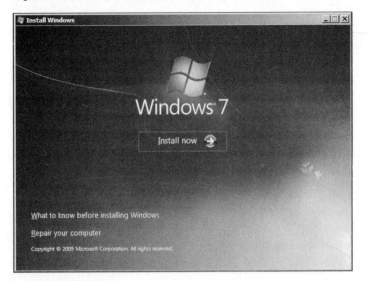

5. A message shows you that Setup is starting. The licensing screen will be first. Read and accept the license agreement and then click Next.

6. A screen asking you "Which type of installation do you want?" is next, as shown in Figure 1.7. Click Custom (Advanced).

Figure 1.7: Choosing the Windows 7 installation type

7. The next screen asks you where you want to install Windows 7, as shown in Figure 1.8. Choose an unformatted free space or a partition (the partition will be erased) with at least 16 GB available. You can also click the Drive Options (Advanced) link to create your own partition. After you choose your partition, click Next.

8. After your partition is set, the installation starts. You see the progress of the installation during the entire process. After the installation is complete, the machine reboots.

9. After the installation is complete, the username and computer name screen appears, as shown in Figure 1.9. Type in your username and computer name and click Next.

Figure 1.8: Specify a location for installing Windows 7.

Figure 1.9: Adding a username and computer name

10. Next, set your password and password hint, as shown in Figure 1.10. Enter your password twice and enter your hint. Click Next.

Figure 1.10: Password screen

11. The next screen asks you to enter your 25-digit product key. Enter your product key and make sure the check box to automatically register your machine when you're online is selected. Click Next.

12. Settings related to Windows Update and security appear, as shown in Figure 1.11. You can select Use Recommended Settings or Install Important Updates For Windows Only, or have the computer ask you later. If you select the option to use the recommended settings, the following settings are configured:

   - Windows Update will be enabled and updates will automatically install.

   - Windows Defender will be installed and any collected information will be sent to Microsoft.

   - Errors will automatically be sent to Microsoft.

   - The latest drivers for your hardware will automatically be downloaded from Windows Update.

Figure 1.11: Specify settings related to Windows Update and security.

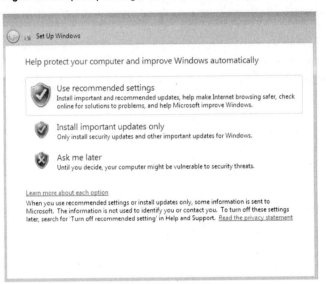

13. You are now able to verify your time and date settings. Configure your time, time zone, and date. Click Next.

14. You then set your computer's current location. You have the ability to choose from a home, work, or public location. Choose where your computer is located, as shown in Figure 1.12.

Figure 1.12: Choosing a network location

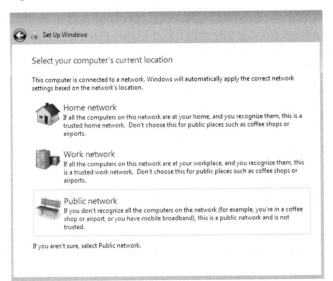

15. Windows will finalize your setup and the installation will be complete.

As you can see, installing Windows 7 is an easy process on a new computer system. But what if the system already has Windows Vista? Let's take a look at how to perform an installation of Windows 7 onto a machine with Windows Vista.

Performing an Upgrade to Windows 7

If your machine has Windows Vista already installed, you have the ability to upgrade the machine to Windows 7.

Similar to a clean install, you can run the installation from the installation DVD or over a network. The only difference in the installation procedure is your starting point: from your optical drive or from a network share. The following steps assume that you are using the Windows 7 DVD to install the Windows 7 operating system.

> **NOTE** You can't upgrade Windows XP to Windows 7 directly. I will discuss the tools used to install a Windows 7 operating system on a Windows XP machine later in this chapter.

Perform the following steps to go through the process of installing Windows 7 by upgrading Windows Vista:

1. Insert the Windows 7 DVD.

2. If Autorun does not start, go to the DVD drive and click `setup.exe`. After the setup starts (by the `setup.exe` or Autorun), click Install Windows 7.

3. You are prompted to update your current operating system. If you choose not to update, the installation might fail. You can also choose to send information to Microsoft during this process.

4. The Microsoft Windows 7 license terms will appear. The installation does not allow you to click Next until you have accepted the license terms.

5. You are prompted to select the type of installation you want to perform. Choose the Upgrade link.

6. You will see a compatibility report that alerts you of any applications or drivers that are not supported in Windows 7. Click Next.

During the Installing Windows Upgrade phase, all the files required by the Setup program are copied to the hard drive. During the process, the computer automatically reboots. This process takes several minutes and proceeds automatically without user intervention. The following process information messages appear on the screen along with a completion percentage for each:

1. Copying Windows files

2. Gathering files, settings, and programs

3. Expanding Windows files

4. Installing features and updates

5. Transferring files, settings, and programs

After your computer finishes copying files and reboots, you will be in the Setting Up Windows phase of the installation. Perform the following steps to complete the upgrade:

1. The first screen asks for your Windows product key. Type your 25-digit product key and click Next.

2. Settings related to Windows Update and security appear next. You can use the recommended settings, install important updates only, or have the computer ask you later.

3. On the next screen, you review your time and date settings. Set up your local time and date and choose if you want daylight savings time. Click Next.

4. The installation completes.

When you install Windows 7, you might run into setup problems or errors. Let's take a look at the troubleshooting process involved with Windows 7 installations.

Troubleshooting Installation Problems

The Windows 7 installation process is designed to be as simple as possible. The chances for installation errors are greatly minimized through the use of wizards and the step-by-step process. However, errors may occur.

Identifying Common Installation Problems

As most of you are aware, installations seldom go off without a hitch. Some of the possible installation errors that you might encounter are listed in Table 1.4.

Table 1.4: Troubleshooting Common Installation Problems

Error	Explanation/Possible Solutions
Media Errors	Media errors are caused by defective or damaged DVDs. To check the disc, put it into another computer and see if you can read it. Also check your disc for scratches or dirt—it might just need to be cleaned.
Insufficient Disk Space	Windows 7 needs at least 16 GB of free space for the installation program to run properly. If the Setup program cannot verify that this space exists, the program will not let you continue.
Not Enough Memory	Make sure that your computer has the minimum amount of memory required by Windows 7 (1 GB). Having insufficient memory might cause the installation to fail or blue-screen errors to occur after installation.
Not Enough Processing Power	Make sure that your computer has the minimum processing power required by Windows 7 (1 GHz). Having insufficient processing power might cause the installation to fail or blue-screen errors to occur after installation.
Hardware That Is Not on the HCL	If your hardware is not listed on the HCL, Windows 7 might not recognize the hardware or the device might not work properly.
Hardware with No Driver Support	Windows 7 will not recognize hardware without driver support.
Hardware That Is Not Configured Properly	If your hardware is Plug and Play–compatible, Windows 7 should configure it automatically. If your hardware is not Plug and Play–compatible, you need to manually configure the hardware per the manufacturer's instructions.
Incorrect Product Key	Without a valid product key, the installation will not go past the Product Key screen. Make sure that you have not typed an incorrect key (check your Windows 7 installation folder or your computer case for this key).

Installation

PART I

Table 1.4: Troubleshooting Common Installation Problems *(continued)*

Error	Explanation/Possible Solutions
Failure to Access TCP/IP Network Resources	If you install Windows 7 with typical settings, the computer is configured as a DHCP client. If there is no DHCP server to provide IP configuration information, the client will still generate an autoconfigured IP address but will be unable to access network resources through TCP/IP if the other network clients are using DHCP addresses.
Installing Nonsupported Hard Drives	If your computer is using a hard disk that does not have a driver included on the Windows 7 media, you will receive an error message stating that the hard drive cannot be found. You should verify that the hard drive is properly connected and functional. Obtain a driver for Windows 7 from the manufacturer and then specify the driver location by selecting the Load Driver option during partition selection.

Troubleshooting with Installation Log Files

When you install Windows 7, the Setup program creates several log files. You can view these logs files to check for any problems during the installation process. The following two log files are particularly useful for troubleshooting:

setupact.log   The action log includes all the actions that were performed during the setup process and a description of each action. These actions are listed in chronological order. The action log is stored as \Windows\setupact.log.

setuperr.log   The error log includes any errors that occurred during the installation. For each error, there is a description and an indication of the severity of the error. This error log is stored as \Windows\setuperr.log.

In the following steps you will view the Windows 7 setup logs to determine whether there were any problems with your Windows 7 installation.

Follow these steps to troubleshoot failed installations with setup logs:

1. Select Start ➤ Computer.

2. Double-click Local Disk (C:).

3. Double-click Windows.

4. In the Windows folder, double-click the setupact.log file to view your action log in Notepad. When you finish viewing this file, close Notepad.

5. Double-click the setuperr.log file to view your error file in Notepad. If no errors occurred during installation, this file will be empty. When you finish viewing this file, close Notepad.

6. Close the directory window.

After you install Windows 7 and look at the setup logs, it might be necessary to transfer user's data from one system to another or migrate data from the same computer. Let's take a look at the migration process.

Migrating Files and Settings

Rather than perform an in-place upgrade, you can choose to migrate your files and settings from an existing installation. In this case, you can use the User State Migration Tool (USMT) or Windows Easy Transfer.

User State Migration Tool

You can download a utility called the User State Migration Tool (USMT) that administrators use to migrate large numbers of users over automated deployments. The USMT for Windows 7 is now part of Windows Automated Installation Kit (Windows AIK). The USMT is similar to Windows Easy Transfer with the following differences:

- The USMT is more configurable and can use XML files to specify which files and settings are transferred.

- The USMT is scriptable and uses command-line utilities to save and restore user files and settings.

The USMT consists of two executable files, ScanState.exe and LoadState.exe, and three migration rule information files, Migapp.xml, Migsys.xml, and Miguser.xml. You can create a Config.xml file that specifies what should and should not be migrated. The purposes of these files are as follows:

ScanState.exe collects user data and settings information based on the configuration of the Migapp.xml, Migsys.xml, and Miguser.xml files and stores it as an image file.

`LoadState.exe` deposits the information that is collected to a computer running a fresh copy of Windows 7.

The information that is migrated includes the following:
From each user:

- Documents
- Video
- Music
- Pictures
- Desktop files
- Start Menu
- Quick Launch toolbar
- Internet Explorer Favorites

From the All Users profile:

- Shared Documents
- Shared Video
- Shared Music
- Shared Desktop files
- Shared Pictures
- Shared Start Menu
- Shared Internet Explorer Favorites
- Files with certain file types, including `.doc`, `.docx`, `.dot`, `.rtf`, `.txt`, `.wps`, `.wri`, `.xls`, `.csv`, `.wks`, `.ppt`, `.pps`, `.pot`, `.pst`, and more
- Access control lists (ACLs)

The USMT will not migrate hardware settings, drivers, passwords, application binaries, synchronization files, DLL files, or other executables.

Using the USMT

The USMT is downloadable software from Microsoft's website. In its simplest form, you use the USMT in the following manner:

1. Run `ScanState.exe` on the source computer. `ScanState.exe` will copy the user state data to an intermediate store. The intermediate

store (for example, a CD-RW) must be large enough to accommodate the data that will be transferred. Scanstate.exe would
commonly be executed as a shortcut sent to users that they would
deploy in the evening or through a scheduled script.

2. Install a fresh copy of Windows 7 on the target computer.

3. Run LoadState.exe on the target computer. LoadState.exe will
access the intermediate store to restore the user settings.

When you use the USMT, you can create a script that can be run
manually or can be used as an automated process at a scheduled time.
Table 1.5 defines the options for the Scanstate.exe and Loadstate.exe
commands.

Table 1.5: Options for scanstate.exe and loadstate.exe

Option	Description
/config	Specifies the config.xml file that should be used
/encrypt	Encrypts the store (scanstate.exe only)
/decrypt	Decrypts the store (loadstate.exe only)
/nocompress	Disables data compression
/genconfig	Generates a config.xml file but does not create a store
/targetxp	Optimizes ScanState for use with Windows XP
/all	Migrates all users
/ue	User exclude: excludes the specified user
/ui	User include: includes the specified user
/uel	Excludes user based on last login time
/v verboselevel	Used to identify what verbosity level will be associated with the log file on a scale of 0–13, with 0 the least verbose

Windows Easy Transfer

Windows 7 ships with a utility called Windows Easy Transfer that is
used to transfer files and settings from one computer to another. You

can transfer some or all of the following files and settings from a computer running Windows XP with Service Pack 2 or Windows Vista:

- User accounts
- Folders and files
- Program settings
- Internet settings
- Favorites
- Email messages, contacts, and settings

You can transfer the migrated files and settings using the following methods:

- Easy Transfer Cable, which is a USB cable that connects to the source and destination computers
- CD or DVD
- Removable media, such as a USB flash drive or a removable hard drive
- Network share
- Direct network connection

You can password-protect the migrated files and settings if you use CDs, DVDs, removable media, or a network share. Now let's take a look at how to upgrade a Windows XP machine to Windows 7.

Upgrading from Windows XP to Windows 7

Because the upgrade option from Windows XP to Windows 7 is not available, you can use Windows Easy Transfer to integrate settings from Windows XP to Windows 7 on the same computer.

The first step in this migration process is to copy your files to a removable media such as an external hard drive or thumb drive or to a network share. After the installation of the Windows 7 operating system, you can then migrate these files onto the Windows 7 system.

Perform the following steps to migrate from Windows XP to Windows 7:

1. Insert the Windows 7 DVD while running Windows XP. If the Windows 7 installation window opens automatically, close it.

2. Open Windows Explorer by right-clicking the Start menu and then clicking Explore.

3. Browse to the DVD drive on your computer and click `migsetup.exe` in the `Support\Migwiz` directory.

4. When the Windows Easy Transfer window opens, click Next.

5. Select an external hard disk or USB flash drive.

6. Click This Is My Old Computer. Windows Easy Transfer scans the computer.

7. Click Next. You can also determine which files should be migrated by selecting only the user profiles you want to transfer or by clicking Customize.

8. Enter a password to protect your Easy Transfer file, or leave the box blank, and then click Save.

9. Browse to the external location on the network or to the removable media where you want to save your Easy Transfer file and then click Save.

10. Click Next. Windows Easy Transfer displays the filename and location of the Easy Transfer file you just created.

Perform the following steps to use the Windows 7 DVD to install the operating system:

1. Start Windows 7 Setup by browsing to the root folder of the DVD in Windows Explorer and then double-clicking `setup.exe`.

2. Click Go Online To Get The Latest Updates (Recommended) to retrieve any important updates for Windows 7. This step is optional. If you choose not to check for updates during Setup, click Do Not Get The Latest Updates.

3. Read and accept the Microsoft Software License Terms and then click Next. If you decline, Windows 7 Setup will exit.

4. Click Custom to perform an upgrade to your existing Windows installation.

5. Select the partition where you would like to install Windows. To move your existing Windows installation into a `Windows.old` folder and replace the operating system with Windows 7, select the partition where your current Windows installation is located.

6. Click Next and then click OK.

7. Windows 7 Setup will proceed without further interaction.

Now, perform the following steps to migrate files to the destination computer:

1. If you saved your files and settings in an Easy Transfer file on a removable media such as a universal flash device (UFD) rather than on a network share, insert the removable media into the computer.

2. Select Start ➢ All Programs ➢ Accessories ➢ System Tools ➢ Windows Easy Transfer.

3. When the Windows Easy Transfer window opens, click Next.

4. Click An External Hard Disk Or USB Flash Drive.

5. Click This Is My New Computer.

6. Click Yes, Open The File.

7. Browse to the location where the Easy Transfer file was saved. Click the filename, and then click Open.

8. Click Transfer to transfer all files and settings. You can also determine which files should be migrated by selecting only the user profiles you want to transfer, or by clicking Customize.

9. Click Close after Windows Easy Transfer has completed moving your files.

Once the migration process is complete, you should regain the disk space used by the Windows XP system by using the Disk Cleanup tool to delete the `Windows.old` directory.

Perform the following steps to use the Disk Cleanup tool:

1. Open Disk Cleanup by selecting Start ➢ All Programs ➢ Accessories ➢ System Tools ➢ Disk Cleanup.

2. Click Clean Up System Files.

3. Previous installations of Windows are scanned. After they are scanned, select Previous Windows Installation(s) and any other categories of files you want to delete.

4. Click OK and then click Delete Files.

An important decision that you should consider is whether to upgrade your Windows XP clients to Windows Vista first and then upgrade the machine to Windows 7.

As you have seen, you can migrate your users' data, but let's say you have software installed and you can't locate the CD/DVD for that software package. It might be beneficial to a user or organization to upgrade the Windows XP machine to Windows Vista. After that installation is complete, upgrade the Vista machine to Windows 7.

This is just another option that is available to you when you migrate your users to the Windows 7 operating system.

Another option you may choose is to run two different operating systems on the same computer system. Called dual-booting, this approach gives you the choice of which operating system you want to boot into when the system starts. Installing multiple operating systems onto the same computer is called dual-booting or multibooting.

Supporting Multiboot Options

You might want to install Windows 7 but still be able to run other operating systems. Dual-booting or multibooting allows your computer to boot multiple operating systems. Your computer will be automatically configured for dual- or multibooting if there was a supported operating system on your computer prior to the Windows 7 installation, you didn't upgrade from that operating system, and you installed Windows 7 into a different partition.

One reason for multibooting is to test various systems. If you have a limited number of computers in your test lab and you want to be able to test multiple configurations, you should multiboot. For example, you might configure one computer to multiboot with Windows XP Professional, Windows Vista, and Windows 7.

Here are some keys to successful multiboot configurations:

- Make sure you have plenty of disk space.

- Windows 7 must be installed on a separate partition in order to dual- or multiboot with other operating systems.

- If you want to support dual- or multibooting with Windows XP and Windows 7, Windows XP must be installed first. If you install Windows 7 first, you cannot install Windows XP without ruining your Windows 7 configuration. This requirement also applies to Windows 9x, Windows 2000, and Windows Vista.

- Never, ever upgrade to Windows 7 dynamic disks. Dynamic disks are seen only by Windows 2000, Windows XP Professional, Windows Server 2003, Windows Vista, and Windows 7, and are not recognized by any other operating system, including Windows NT and Windows XP Home Edition.

- Only Windows NT 4.0 (with Service Pack 4), Windows 2000, Windows XP, Windows Vista, Windows 7, Windows Server 2003, and Windows Server 2008 can recognize NTFS file systems. Other Windows operating systems use FAT16 or FAT32 and cannot recognize NTFS. All Windows-based operating systems can recognize FAT partitions.

- If you will dual- or multiboot with Windows 9x, you must turn off disk compression or Windows 7 will not be able to read the drive properly.

- Do not install Windows 7 on a compressed volume unless the volume was compressed using NTFS compression.

- Files that are encrypted with Windows 7 will not be available to Windows NT 4.

After you install each operating system, you can choose the operating system that you will boot to during the boot process. You will see a boot selection screen that asks you to choose which operating system you want to boot.

The Boot Configuration Data (BCD) store contains boot information parameters that were previously found in boot.ini in older versions of Windows. To edit the boot options in the BCD store, use the bcdedit utility, which can be launched only from a command prompt.

Perform the following steps to open a command prompt window:

1. Launch \Windows\system32\cmd.exe.

2. Open the Run command by pressing Windows key+R.

3. Type cmd.exe in the Search Programs And Files box and press Enter.

After the command prompt window is open, type **bcdedit** to launch the bcdedit utility. You can also type **bcdedit/?** to see all the various bcdedit commands.

After the Windows 7 installation is complete, it's time to do some general housekeeping. The first thing you need to do is activate the Windows 7 operating system.

Using Windows Activation

Windows Activation is Microsoft's way of reducing software piracy. Unless you have a corporate license for Windows 7, you will need to perform postinstallation activation. You can do this online or by phoning Microsoft. Windows 7 will attempt automatic activation three days after you log on to Windows 7 for the first time. There is a grace period when you will be able to use the operating system without activation. After the grace period expires, you will not be able to create new files or save changes to existing files until Windows 7 is activated. When the grace period runs out, the Windows Activation Wizard automatically starts; it walks you through the activation process.

Using Windows Update

Windows Update, as shown in Figure 1.13, is a utility that connects to Microsoft's website and checks to ensure that you have the most up-to-date version of Microsoft products.

Figure 1.13: Windows Update

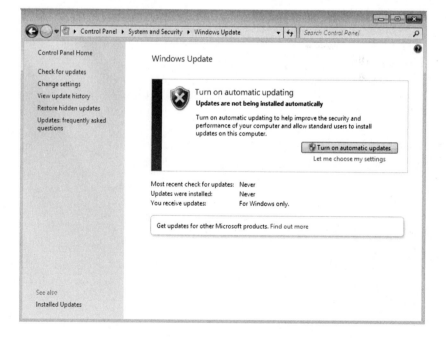

Here are some of the common update categories associated with Windows Update:

- Critical updates
- Service packs
- Drivers

Perform the following steps to configure Windows Update:

1. Select Start ➢ Control Panel.

   - From Windows Icons View, select Windows Update.

   - From Windows Category View, select System And Security, Windows Update.

2. Configure the options you want to use for Windows Update, and click OK.

You can access the following options from Windows Update:

Check For Updates When you click Check For Updates, Windows Update retrieves a list of available updates from the Internet. You can then click View Available Updates to see what updates are available. Updates are marked as Important, Recommended, or Optional. Figure 1.14 shows a sample list of updates.

Figure 1.14: Checking for updates

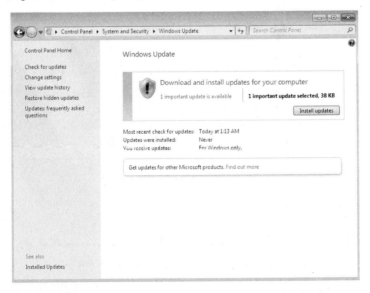

Change Settings   Clicking Change Settings allows you to customize how Windows can install updates.

You can configure the following options:

- Install Updates Automatically (Recommended)
- Download Updates But Let Me Choose To Install Them
- Download Updates But Let Me Choose Whether To Download And Install Them
- Never Check For Updates (Not Recommended)

Figure 1.15 shows the settings that you can configure for Windows Update.

Figure 1.15: Changing settings in Windows Update

View Update History   View Update History, as shown in Figure 1.16, is used to view a list of all the installations that have been performed on the computer. You can see the following information for each installation:

- Update Name
- Status (Successful, Unsuccessful, Or Canceled)
- Importance (Important, Recommended, Or Optional)
- Date Installed

Figure 1.16: Windows Update: View Update History

Restore Hidden Updates With Restore Hidden Updates, you can list any updates that you have hidden from the list of available updates. You might hide updates that you don't want users to install.

Sometimes it is important for you to test and verify the updates before your users can install the updates. This area allows you to see hidden updates so that they can be tested before deployment.

Updates: Frequently Asked Questions The Updates: Frequently Asked Questions link will bring up a help screen about updates. Common questions and answers are listed in this window.

Installed Updates Installed Updates allows you to see the updates that are installed and to uninstall or change them if necessary. The Installed Updates feature is a part of the Programs and Features applet in Control Panel, which allows you to uninstall, change, and repair programs.

Updates are important to keep your Windows 7 operating system current, but when Microsoft has many updates or security patches, they release service packs.

Installing Windows Service Packs

Service packs are updates to the Windows 7 operating system that include bug fixes and product enhancements. Some of the options that might be included in service packs are security fixes or updated versions of software, such as Internet Explorer.

Perform the following steps prior to installing a service pack:

1. Back up your computer.

2. Check your computer to ensure that it is not running any malware or other unwanted software.

3. Check with your computer manufacturer to see whether there are any special instructions for your computer prior to installing the service pack.

You can download service packs from Microsoft's website, receive service packs via Windows Update, or pay for a copy of the service pack to be mailed to you on disk. Before you install a service pack, read the Release Note that is provided for each service pack on Microsoft's website.

Installation

PART I

2

Automating a Windows 7 Installation

Installation

PART I

A s you noticed in the previous chapter, installing Windows 7 is a quick and easy process. But as an IT manager or professional, you might have to install hundreds of copies of Windows 7 at one time. You wouldn't want to do the installation of Windows 7 one machine at a time.

In this chapter we will discuss the different ways to automate the installation process of Windows 7.

Use the Microsoft Deployment Toolkit 2010

Microsoft has released a program called the Microsoft Deployment Toolkit (MDT) 2010. This toolkit is a way of automating desktop and server deployment. The MDT offers you the following benefits:

- Administrative tools that allow for the deployment of desktops and servers through the use of a common console, as shown in Figure 2.1

- Quicker deployments and the capability to have standardized desktop and server images and security

- Zero Touch deployments of Windows 7, Windows Server 2008, Windows Vista, Windows Server 2003, and Windows XP

Figure 2.1: The MDT console

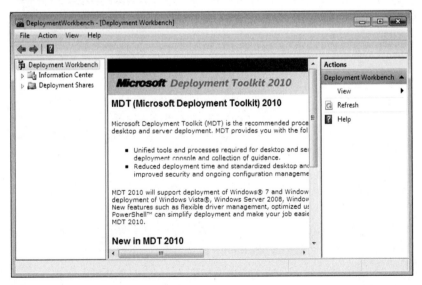

To install the MDT 2010 package onto your computer (regardless of the operating system being deployed), you must first meet the minimum requirements. These requirements need to be met only on the computer where MDT 2010 is being installed:

- Microsoft Management Console (MMC) 3.0
- Microsoft .NET Framework 2.0 or higher
- Windows PowerShell command-line interface, version 1.0 or 2.0
- Community Technology Preview (CTP) 3 or higher
- Windows Automated Installation Kit (Windows AIK) for Windows 7

Installing MDT 2010

You can install MDT 2010 without installing the Windows AIK first, but you won't be able to use the package fully until the Windows AIK is installed.

For Zero Touch deployments, MDT 2010 requires the following components:

- If deploying Windows 7 or Windows Server 2008, System Center Configuration Manager (SCCM) 2007 Service Pack 2 (SP2) is required.

- If you want to deploy previous versions of Windows using MDT 2010, SCCM 2007 Service Pack 1 (SP1) can be used, but you can't use Deployment Workbench in this configuration to maintain an MDT database. If you're using an MDT database with SCCM, you should use SCCM 2007 SP2.

You can install MDT 2010 on the Windows 7 operating system machine that we installed in Chapter 1, "Installing Windows 7." If you decide to install the MDT onto a server or production machine, we recommend that you perform a full backup before you complete these steps. Installing MDT 2010 will replace any previous version of MDT that the machine is currently using.

Perform these steps to download and install MDT 2010:

1. Download the MDT 2010 utility from Microsoft's website.

2. Double-click `MicrosoftDeploymentToolkit_x86.exe` to start the installation. If you downloaded the 64-bit version, click that version.

Installation

PART I

3. At the Welcome screen, click Next.

4. At the License screen, accept the license agreement and click Next.

5. At the Custom Setup screen, shown in Figure 2.2, click the down arrow next to the Microsoft Deployment Toolkit and choose "Entire feature will be installed on local hard drive." Click Next.

Figure 2.2: MDT's Custom Setup screen

6. At the Ready To Install screen, click Install.

7. When the installation completes, click Finish.

Configuring MDT 2010

Once you've installed MDT 2010, follow these steps to configure it and set up a distribution share and database:

1. Create a shared folder on your network called **Distribution** and give the Everyone group full control for this exercise.

2. Open the MDT workbench by clicking Start ➢ All Programs ➢ Microsoft Development Toolkit ➢ Deployment Workbench.

3. If the User Account Control box appears, click Yes.

4. In the left pane, right-click Deployment Shares and choose New Deployment Share, as shown in Figure 2.3.

Figure 2.3: Select New Deployment Share from this menu.

5. The New Deployment Share Wizard begins. At the first screen, choose the directory where the deployments will be stored. Click the Browse button and choose the distribution share that you created in step 1. Then, click Next.

6. At the Share Name screen, accept the default, of distribution. Click Next.

7. At the Deployment Share Description screen, accept the default description name and click Next.

8. At the Allow Image Capture screen, make sure the "Ask if an image should be captured" check box is selected, as shown in Figure 2.4. Images can be captured after they're deployed to a domain. By checking this box, you have the option to either capture or not capture the image after deployment. Click Next.

9. At the Allow Admin Password screen, check the box that allows the user to set the admin password for the local machine. If the box is not checked, you can preset the password before deployment.

10. At the Allow Product Key screen, select the option "Ask users to enter a product key at time of installation." You also can preset

the product key and then the user would not be required to supply the product key. Many organizations have site licenses and the user would not be required to enter a product key. Click Next.

Figure 2.4: The Allow Image Capture screen

11. At the Summary screen, verify all your settings and click Next.

12. Once the installation is complete, a confirmation screen appears. Click Finish. Close the MDT Workbench.

Now that you have seen how to install the MDT 2010 utility, let's look at other ways to automatically install Windows 7.

Perform Unattended Installations

Unattended installation is a practical method of automatic deployment when you have a large number of clients to install and the computers require different hardware and software configurations. Unattended installations utilize an answer file called `Autounattend.xml` to provide configuration information during the unattended installation process. Recall the Windows 7 installation from the previous chapter: it asks you for your locale, type of installation, and so forth. The answer file enables these questions to be answered without user intervention.

With an unattended installation, you can use a distribution share to install Windows 7 on the target computers. You can also use a Windows 7 DVD with an answer file located on the root of the DVD, on a floppy disk, or on a universal flash device (UFD), such as an external USB flash drive.

Unattended installations allow you to create customized installations that are specific to your environment. Custom installations can support custom hardware and software installations. Because the answer file for Windows 7 is in XML format, all custom configuration information can be contained within the `Autounattend.xml` file. This is different from past versions of Windows where creating automated installation routines for custom installations required that multiple files be used. In addition to providing standard Windows 7 configuration information, you can use the answer file to provide installation instructions for applications, additional language support, service packs, and device drivers.

If you use a distribution share, it should contain the Windows 7 operating system image and the answer file to respond to installation configuration queries. The target computer must be able to connect to the distribution share over the network. After the distribution share and target computers are connected, you can initiate the installation process. Figure 2.5 illustrates the unattended installation process.

Figure 2.5: Unattended installation with a distribution share and a target computer

Distribution Share

Stores:
Windows 7 Image File
Answer File (Autounattend.xml)

Target

Requires:
Network Connection

The Advantages of an Unattended Installation

In a mid-sized or large organization, it just makes sense to use automated setups. As stated earlier, it's impossible to install hundreds of Windows 7 machines one at a time. There are many advantages to using unattended installations as a method for automating Windows 7 installation. Here are some of the advantages:

- An unattended install saves time and money because users do not have to interactively respond to each installation query.

- The process can be configured to provide automated query response, while still selectively allowing users to provide specified input during installations.

- An unattended install can be used to install clean copies of Windows 7 or upgrade an existing operating system (providing it is on the list of permitted operating systems) to Windows 7.

- An unattended install can be expanded to include installation instructions for applications, additional language support, service packs, and device drivers.

- The physical media for Windows 7 does not need to be distributed to all computers that will be installed.

The Disadvantages of an Unattended Installation

A client operating system is one of the most important items that you'll install onto a machine. You probably feel better installing a client operating system when you're physically doing it. That way, if there's a glitch, you can spot it and deal with it immediately.

This method is not practical for mass installations. But one of the biggest disadvantages to using an unattended installation is that an administrator does not physically walk through the installation of Windows 7. If something happens during the install, you might never know it, but the end user might experience small issues throughout the entire lifetime of the machine.

Here are two other disadvantages to using unattended installations as a method for automating Windows 7 installations:

- They require more initial setup than a standard installation of Windows 7.

- Someone must have access to each client computer and must initiate the unattended installation process on the client side.

In the next section we'll look at the Windows Deployment Services utility.

Using Windows Deployment Services

Windows Deployment Services (WDS) is an updated version of Remote Installation Services (RIS). WDS is a suite of components that allows you to remotely install Windows 7 on client computers.

A WDS server installs Windows 7 on the client computers, as shown in Figure 2.6. The WDS server must be configured with the Preboot Execution Environment (PXE) boot files, the images to be deployed to the client computers, and the answer file. WDS client computers must be PXE capable. PXE is a technology that's used to boot to the network when no operating system or network configuration has been installed and configured on a client computer.

Figure 2.6: WDS uses a WDS server and WDS clients.

WDS Server

WDS Client

Stores:
PXE Boot Files and Boot Images
Windows 7 Boot Images
Answer File(s)

Requires:
PXE-Compatible Boot

The WDS clients access the network with the help of a Dynamic Host Configuration Protocol (DHCP) server. This allows the WDS client to remotely install the operating system from the WDS server. The network environment must be configured with a DHCP server, a Domain Name System (DNS) server, and an Active Directory to connect to the WDS server. No other client software is required to connect to the WDS server. Remote installation is a good choice for automatic deployment when you need to deploy to large numbers of computers and the client computers are PXE compliant.

Installation

PART I

Advantages of Using WDS

The advantages of using WDS as a method for automating Windows 7 installations are as follows:

- You can standardize Windows 7 installations across a group or organization.

- You do not need to distribute the physical media for Windows 7 to all computers that will be installed.

- You can control end-user installation deployment through the Group Policy utility. For example, you can configure which choices a user can access and which are automatically specified through the end-user Setup Wizard.

Now that we've listed the advantages of WDS, let's take a look at the disadvantages.

Disadvantages of Using WDS

The disadvantages of using WDS as a method for automating Windows 7 installations include the following:

- You can use it only if your network is running Windows Server 2003 or Windows Server 2008 with Active Directory installed.

- The clients that use WDS must be PXE capable.

Next let's look at the System Preparation Tool.

Using the System Preparation Tool and Disk Imaging

The System Preparation Tool (sysprep.exe) is used to prepare a computer for disk imaging, which can then be captured using ImageX (a new imaging management tool included with Windows 7) or third-party imaging software.

Disk imaging is the process of taking a snapshot of a computer and then using that snapshot to create new computers, allowing for automated deployments. The reference, or source, computer has Windows 7 installed and is configured with the settings and applications that should be installed on the target computers. The image (snapshot) is then created and that image can be transferred to other computers, thus installing the operating system, settings, and applications that were defined on the reference computer.

Advantage of Imaging

Using the System Preparation Tool and disk imaging is a good choice (and the most commonly used in the real world) for automatic deployment when you have a large number of computers with similar configuration requirements or machines that need to be rebuilt frequently.

For example, Stellacon Training Center, a Microsoft education center that I work for, reinstalls the same software every week for new classes. Imaging is a fast and easy way to simplify the deployment process.

Using imaging software can save time and money. It saves time because you do not have to rebuild machines from scratch, and saving time in turn saves an organization money.

In the real world, imaging software is the most common way to install or reinstall corporate computers. The reason that most organizations use images is not only to create new machines quickly and easily, but also to re-image end users' machines that crash.

In most companies, end users will have space on a server (home folders) that allow them to store data. The reason I give my end users space on the server is because this way, at night we only need to back up the servers and not the end users' machines. If my end users place all their important documents on the server, it gets backed up.

Now if you also use images and an end user's machine crashes, you just reload the image and the user is back up and running in minutes. Because their documents are saved on the server, users don't lose any of their information.

Many organizations use third-party imaging software instead of using sysprep.exe and ImageX. This is another good way of imaging your Windows 7 machines. Just make sure that your third-party software supports the Windows 7 operating system.

The System Preparation Tool prepares the reference computer by stripping away any computer-specific data, such as the security identifier (SID), which is used to uniquely identify each computer on the network, any event logs, and any other unique system information. The System Preparation Tool also detects any Plug and Play devices that are installed and can adjust dynamically for any computers that have different hardware installed.

When the client computer starts an installation using a disk image, you can customize what is displayed on the Windows Welcome screen and the options that are displayed through the setup process. You can also fully automate when and how the Windows Welcome screen is displayed during the installation process by using the /oobe (out-of-the-box experience) switch with the System Preparation Tool and an answer file named oobe.xml.

The System Preparation Tool is a utility that's good only for setting up a new machine. You do not use it to image a computer for upgrading a current machine. There are a few switches that you can use in conjunction with sysprep.exe to configure the tool for your specific needs. Table 2.1 shows you some of the sysprep.exe switches and what they can do for you.

Table 2.1: sysprep.exe Switches

Switch	Explanation
/pnp	Forces a mini-setup wizard to start at reboot so that all Plug and Play devices can be recognized.
/generalize	Allows Sysprep to remove all system-specific data from the Sysprep image. If you're running the GUI version of Sysprep, this is a check box.
/oobe	Initiates the Windows Welcome screen at the next reboot.
/audit	Initiates Sysprep in Audit mode.
/nosidgen	Forces a mini-setup on restart. Sysprep does not generate new SIDs upon restart.
/reboot	Stops and restarts the computer system.
/quiet	Runs without displaying any confirmation dialog messages.
/mini	Tells Sysprep to run the mini-setup on the next reboot.

The Windows System Preparation tool is a free utility that comes on all Windows operating systems. By default, the Sysprep utility can be found on the Windows Server 2008 and Windows 7 operating systems in \Windows\system32\sysprep.

When you decide to use Sysprep to set up your images, you must follow a few rules in order for the utility to work properly:

- You can use images to restart the Windows activation clock. The Windows activation clock starts to decrease as soon as Windows starts for the first time. You can only restart the Windows activation clock three times using Sysprep.

- The computer you're running Sysprep on has to be a member of a workgroup. The machine can't be part of a domain. If the computer is a member of the domain, when you run Sysprep the computer is automatically removed from the domain.

- When you install the image, the system prompts you for a product key. You can use an answer file during the install, which will have all the information needed for the install and you won't be prompted for any information.

- A third-party utility or ImageX is required to deploy the image that is created from Sysprep.

- If you're using Sysprep to capture an NTFS partition, any files or folders that are encrypted will become corrupted and unreadable.

One advantage to Sysprep and Windows 7 is that you can use Sysprep to prepare a new machine for duplication. You can use Sysprep to take an image from one machine and then a third-party application can use that image to create another machine. The steps needed to image a new machine are as follows:

1. Install the Windows 7 operating system.

2. Install all components on the OS.

3. Run sysprep/generalize to create the image.

When you image a computer using the Windows Sysprep utility, a Windows image (.wim) file is created. Most third-party imaging software products can work with the Windows image file.

Advantages of Using the System Preparation Tool

The advantages of using the System Preparation Tool as a method for automating Windows 7 installations include the following:

- For large numbers of computers with similar hardware, it greatly reduces deployment time by copying the operating system, applications, and Desktop settings from a reference computer to an image, which can then be deployed to multiple computers.

- Using disk imaging facilitates the standardization of Desktops, administrative policies, and restrictions throughout an organization.

- Reference images can be copied across a network connection or through DVDs that are physically distributed to client computers.

Disadvantages of Using the System Preparation Tool

The disadvantages of using the System Preparation Tool as a method for automating Windows 7 installations include the following:

- You must use ImageX, third-party imaging software, or hardware disk-duplicator devices for an image-based setup.

- You must use the version of the System Preparation Tool that shipped with Windows 7. You cannot use an older version of Sysprep on a Windows 7 image.

- Sysprep cannot detect any hardware that is non–Plug and Play compliant.

Using the Windows AIK

Another way to install Windows 7 is to use the Windows AIK. The Windows AIK is a set of utilities and documentation that allows you to configure and deploy Windows operating systems. You can use the Windows AIK to accomplish the following:

- Capture Windows images with ImageX.

- Configure and edit your images by using the Deployment Image Servicing and Management (DISM) utility.

- Create Windows PE images.

- Migrate user data and profiles using the User State Migration Tool (USMT).

- Centrally manage volume activations by using the Volume Activation Management Tool (VAMT).

You can install and configure the Windows AIK on the following operating systems:

- Windows 7

- Windows Server 2008

- Windows Server 2003 with SP3

- Windows Vista with SP1

The Windows AIK is a good solution for organizations that need to customize the Windows deployment environments. The Windows AIK gives you the flexibility needed for mass deployments of Windows operating systems. Because every organization's needs are different, the Windows AIK allows you to use all or just part of the deployment tools available. The Windows AIK allows you to manage deployments by using some additional tools:

Microsoft Deployment Toolkit   The tools included with this part of the Windows AIK allow you to easily deploy and configure Windows operating systems and images.

Application Compatibility Toolkit   When you're installing new Windows operating systems, applications that ran on the previous version of Windows might not work properly. The Application Compatibility Toolkit helps solve these issues before they occur.

Microsoft Assessment and Planning (MAP) Toolkit   The MAP toolkit is a utility that will locate computers on a network and then perform a thorough inventory of these computers. This inventory can then be used to determine which machines can have Windows 7 installed.

Summarizing Windows 7 Deployment Tools

Table 2.2 summarizes the installation tools for Windows 7 and lists the client hardware and server requirements, and indicates whether the option supports a clean install or an upgrade.

Installation

PART I

Table 2.2: Summary of Windows 7 Installation Tools

Tool	Required Client Hardware	Required Server Hardware and Services	Clean Install or Upgrade Only
MDT 2010	PC that meets the Windows 7 requirements; access to the network	Network installation, distribution server.	Clean install
Windows AIK	PC that meets the Windows 7 requirements	None. The Windows AIK can be installed on any compatible machine.	Clean install
Unattended installation	PC that meets the Windows 7 requirements; access to the network	None with DVD; if using network installation, distribution server with pre-configured client images.	Clean install or upgrade
WDS	PC that meets the Windows 7 requirements and that is PXE compliant	Windows Server 2003 with SP1 or Windows Server 2008 to act as a WDS server with image files, Active Directory, DNS server, and DHCP server.	Clean install
System Preparation Tool	Reference computer with Windows 7 installed and configured; PC that meets the Windows 7 requirements; ImageX, third-party disk imaging software, or hardware disk-duplicator device	None.	Clean install

Table 2.3 summarizes the unattended installation tools and files that are used with automated installations of Windows 7, the associated installation method, and a description of each tool.

Table 2.3: Summary of Windows 7 Unattended Deployment Utilities

Tool or File	Automated Installation Tool	Description
setup.exe	Unattended installation	Program used to initiate the installation process

Table 2.3: Summary of Windows 7 Unattended Deployment Utilities *(continued)*

Tool or File	Automated Installation Tool	Description
`Autounattend.xml`	Unattended installation	Answer file used to customize installation queries
Windows System Image Manager	Unattended installation	Program used to create answer files to be used for unattended installations
`imageX.exe`	Sysprep	Command-line utility that works in conjunction with Sysprep to create and manage Windows 7 image files for deployment
`sysprep.exe`	Sysprep	System Preparation Tool, which prepares a source reference computer that is used in conjunction with a distribution share or with disk duplication through ImageX, third-party software, or hardware disk-duplication devices

The Windows 7 installation utilities and resources relating to automated deployment are found in a variety of locations. Table 2.4 provides a quick reference for each utility or resource and its location.

Table 2.4: Location of Windows 7 Deployment Utilities and Resources

Utility	Location
`sysprep.exe`	Included with Windows 7; installed to `%WINDIR%\system32\sysprep`
ImageX	Installed with the Windows AIK; installed to `C:\Program Files\Windows AIK\Tools\x86\imagex.exe`
Windows System Image Manager	Installed with the Windows AIK; installed to `C:\Program Files\Windows AIK\Tools\Image Manager\ImgMgr.exe`

Now that you have seen some of the ways you can install Windows 7, let's take a more detailed look at each one.

Deploy Unattended Installations

You can deploy Windows 7 installations or upgrades through a
Windows 7 distribution DVD or through a distribution server that
contains Windows 7 images and associated files, such as Autounattend
.xml for unattended installations. Using a DVD can be advantageous if
the computer on which you want to install Windows 7 is not connected
to the network or is connected via a low-bandwidth network. It is also
typically faster to install a Windows 7 image from DVD than to use a
network connection.

Unattended installations rely on options configured in an answer file
that is deployed with the Windows 7 image. Answer files are XML files
that contain the settings that are typically supplied by the installer during attended installations of Windows 7. Answer files can also contain
instructions on how programs and applications should be run.

The Windows Setup program is run to install or upgrade to
Windows 7 from computers that are running compatible versions of
Windows, as discussed in Chapter 1. In fact, Windows Setup is the
basis for the other types of installation procedures that we discuss in
this chapter, including unattended installations, WDS, and image-based
installations.

The Windows Setup program (setup.exe) replaces winnt32.exe and
winnt.exe, which are the setup programs used in versions of Windows
prior to Windows Vista. Although a graphical tool, Windows Setup can
be run from the command line. For example, you can use the following
command to initiate an unattended installation of Windows 7:

    setup.exe/unattend:answerfile

The Windows Setup program has several command-line options that
can be applied, as you can see in Table 2.5.

Table 2.5: setup.exe Command-Line Options and Descriptions

setup.exe Option	Description
/1394debug:*channel* [baudrate:*baudrate*]	Enables kernel debugging over a FireWire (IEEE 1394) port for troubleshooting purposes. The [*baudrate*] optional parameter specifies the baud rate for data transfer during the debugging process.

Table 2.5: setup.exe Command-Line Options and Descriptions *(continued)*

setup.exe **Option**	**Description**
/debug:*port* [baudrate:*baudrate*]	Enables kernel debugging over the specified port for troubleshooting purposes. The [*baudrate*] optional parameter specifies the baud rate for data transfer during the debugging process.
/dudisable	Prevents a dynamic update from running during the installation process.
/emsport:{com1|com2| usebiossettings|off} [/emsbaudrate:*baudrate*]	Configures EMS to be enabled or disabled. The [*baudrate*] optional parameter specifies the baud rate for data transfer during the debugging process.
/m:*folder_name*	Used with Setup to specify that replacement files should be copied from the specified location. If the files are not present, Setup will use the default location.
/noreboot	Specifies that the computer should not restart so that you can execute another command prior to the restart. Normally, when the down-level phase of setup.exe is complete, the computer restarts.
/tempdrive:*drive letter*	Specifies the location that will store the temporary files for Windows 7 and the installation partition for Windows 7.
/unattend:[*answerfile*]	Specifies that you'll be using an unattended installation for Windows Vista. The *answerfile* variable points to the custom answer file you'll use for installation.

Next we'll look at the System Preparation tool (Sysprep), which is one of many ways to install Windows 7 automatically.

Using the System Preparation Tool to Prepare an Installation for Imaging

You can use disk images to install Windows 7 on computers that have similar hardware configurations. Also, if a computer is having technical difficulties, you can use a disk image to quickly restore it to a baseline configuration.

To create a disk image, you install Windows 7 on the source computer with the configuration that you want to copy and use the System Preparation Tool to prepare the installation for imaging. The source computer's configuration should also include any applications that should be installed on target computers.

After you prepare the installation for imaging, you can use imaging software such as ImageX to create an image of the installation.

The System Preparation Tool (sysprep.exe) is included with Windows 7, in the %WINDIR%\system32\sysprep directory. When you run this utility on the source computer, it strips out information from the master copy that must be unique for each computer, such as the SID. Table 2.6 defines the command options that you can use to customize the sysprep.exe operation.

Table 2.6: System Preparation Command-Line Options

Switch	Description
/audit	Configures the computer to restart in Audit mode, which allows you to add drivers and applications to Windows or test the installation prior to deployment
/generalize	Removes any unique system information from the image, including the SID and log information
/oobe	Specifies that the Windows Welcome screen should be displayed when the computer reboots
/quiet	Runs the installation with no user interaction
/quit	Specifies that the System Preparation tool should quit after the specified operations have been completed
/reboot	Restarts the target computer after the System Preparation Tool completes
/shutdown	Specifies that the computer should shut down after the specified operations have completed
/unattend	Indicates the name and location of the answer file to use

In the following sections, you'll learn how to create a disk image and how to copy and install from a disk image.

Preparing a Windows 7 Installation

Follow these steps to run the System Preparation Tool and prepare an installation for imaging:

1. Install Windows 7 on a source computer. The computer should have a similar hardware configuration to the destination computer(s). The source computer should not be a member of a domain. (See Chapter 1 for instructions on installing Windows 7.)

2. Log on to the source computer as Administrator and, if desired, install and configure any applications, files (such as newer versions of Plug and Play drivers), or custom settings (for example, a custom Desktop) that will be applied to the target computer(s).

3. Verify that your image meets the specified configuration criteria and that all applications are properly installed and working.

4. Select Start ➢ Computer, and navigate to C:\%WINDIR%\System32\sysprep. Double-click the Sysprep application icon.

5. The Windows System Preparation Tool dialog box appears. Select the appropriate options for your configuration.

6. If configured to do so, Windows 7 is rebooted into Setup mode, and you are prompted to enter the appropriate setup information.

7. You are now able to use imaging software to create an image of the computer to deploy to other computers.

Perform the following steps to use the System Preparation Tool to prepare the computer for disk imaging. The Sysprep utility must be run on a machine with a clean version of Windows 7. If you upgraded a Windows Vista machine to Windows 7, you won't be able to run Sysprep.

1. Log on to the source computer as Administrator and install and configure any applications that should also be installed on the target computer.

2. Select Start ➢ Computer, and navigate to C:\%WINDIR%\System32\sysprep. Double-click the Sysprep application icon.

3. In the System Preparation Tool dialog box, select Enter System Out-of-Box Experience (OOBE) in the system cleanup action.

4. Under the Shutdown options, depending on the options selected, you can specify whether the System Preparation Tool will quit,

the computer will shut down, or the computer will be rebooted into Setup mode (and you'll need to configure the setup options). Choose the Reboot option. Click OK.

5. Configure the Sysprep utility and name the image `image.wim`.

After creating the Sysprep image, you need to use some type of third-party software to install the image. Windows includes a utility called ImageX for just that purpose.

Using ImageX to Create a Disk Image

After you've run the System Preparation Tool on the source computer, you can create an image from the installation, and you can then install the image on target computers.

To create an image, you can use ImageX, which is a command-line utility that lets you create and manage Windows Image (.wim) files.

Before you can create your disk image using ImageX, you must first build a Windows Preinstallation Environment (PE) disk so you can boot into the Windows PE environment.

Windows AIK

To complete the following steps, you must have the Windows AIK utility installed. If the Windows AIK is not installed, you can install it by following the installation steps in the section "Using Windows System Image Manager to Create Answer Files" later in this chapter.

To create the Windows PE boot DVD:

1. Click Start ➢ All Programs ➢ Windows AIK ➢ Deployment Tools Command Prompt.

2. At the command prompt, run

    ```
    Copype.cmd <architecture> <destination>
    ```

    where *<architecture>* is **x86**, **amd64**, or **ia64**, and *<destination>* is a path to a local directory.

For example:

```
copype.cmd x86 c:\winpe_x86)
```

will create the following directories:

```
\winpe_x86
\winpe_x86\ISO
\winpe_x86\mount
```

3. On the same computer, create your .iso file using the following command:

```
oscdimg -n -bc:\winpe_x86\etfsboot.com c:\winpe_x86\ISO
c:\winpe_x86\winpe_x86.iso
```

4. Burn the .iso image to a DVD.

Now that you have created the Windows PE disk, you'll run the ImageX utility to create a disk image of a Windows 7 installation:

1. Boot the computer into Windows PE.

2. Type the following command, assuming that your DVD\CD drive is configured as drive D:

```
D:\ImageX.exe /capture C: C:\Images\image.wim "Windows
7" /verify
```

3. Copy the new image to a network share at \\Server\Images by using these commands:

```
net use z: \\Server\Images
copy C:\Images\image.wim z:
```

After you create the disk image, the next step is to install the disk image. In the next section, you'll learn to install the disk image to a new machine.

Installing from a Disk Image

Now that you've run the System Preparation Tool and ImageX on the source computer, you can copy the image and install it on the target computer.

After the image is copied, you should boot the destination computer into Windows PE. If the computer has been used previously, it may be necessary to reformat the hard drive (which you can do using the diskpart utility in Windows PE).

The Diskpart Utility

Diskpart is a command-line utility that allows you to manage and configure your hard disks, volumes, or partitions. To learn more about how to use this utility, check Microsoft's website at www.microsoft.com.

If the image is stored over the network, you should then copy the image to the destination computer by using the net use [dir] [network share] and copy [file] [dir] commands. Then, use the /apply option of the ImageX utility to apply the image to the local computer. If an answer file has not been deployed along with the image, you might have to supply such information as regional settings, the product key, the computer name, and the password to the new computer after the destination computer is rebooted.

Next, you'll install Windows 7 from a disk image. You'll use the stripped image that you created in the previous section to simulate the process of continuing an installation from a disk image.

1. Boot the target computer into the Windows PE environment.

2. Copy the image you created in the previous section to the local computer by using these commands:

```
net use z: \\Server\Images
copy Z:\Images\image.wim C:
```

3. Apply the image to the target computer using the following ImageX command:

```
D:\ImageX.exe /apply C:\Images\image.wim C:
```

There are some switches that you can use with ImageX to help you configure your Windows 7 images. Table 2.7 shows you some of the switches available for ImageX. They are configured alphabetically in the table and not based on importance of the switch.

Table 2.7: ImageX Switches

ImageX Switch	Description
Imagex /append	Allows you to append an image to a preexisting image.
Imagex /apply	Applies an image to a specific drive on a machine.
ImageX /capture	Captures an image from the drive and creates a new Windows Image File (.wim) file.
ImageX /delete	Allows you to delete a volume image from a WIM file with multiple images.
ImageX /dir	Allows you to see the files and folders of an image.
ImageX /export	Gives you the ability to export a WIM file to another WIM file.
ImageX /info	Allows you to gather data about a WIM file. Among the data that you can gather are file size, image index number, file count, and a description.
ImageX /mount	Allows a Windows XP with SP2, Windows Server 2003 with SP1, Windows Vista, Windows 7, or Windows Server 2008 read-only WIM file to be mounted.
ImageX /split	Allows a WIM file to be split by size onto multiple media. For example, if you have a 2 GB image, you can use the split switch to place the files onto multiple CDs instead of one DVD.
ImageX /unmount	Unmounts a mounted image.
ImageX /verify	Verifies the data integrity of the WIM image.

Installation

PART I

When you install Windows 7, the installation wizard asks you questions such as your username and computer name. There is a way to answer these questions without actually being in front of the computer. As you'll see in the next section, you can do this by using an answer file.

Using Windows System Image Manager to Create Answer Files

Answer files are automated installation scripts used to answer the questions that appear during a normal Windows 7 installation. You can use answer files with Windows 7 unattended installations, disk image installations, or WDS installations. Setting up answer files allows you to easily deploy Windows 7, with little or no user intervention, to computers that might not be configured in the same manner. Because answer files are associated with image files, you can validate the settings in an answer file against the image file.

You can create answer files by using the Windows System Image Manager (SIM) utility. There are several advantages to using Windows SIM to create answer files:

- You can easily create and edit answer files through a graphical interface, which reduces syntax errors.

- It simplifies the addition of user-specific or computer-specific configuration information.

- You can validate existing answer files against newly created images.

- You can include additional application and device drivers to the answer file.

In the following sections, you'll learn about options that you can configure through Windows SIM, how to create answer files with Windows SIM, how to format the answer file, and how to manually edit answer files.

Configuring Components Through Windows SIM

You can use Windows SIM to configure a wide variety of installation options. The following list defines what components you can configure through Windows SIM and gives a short description of each component.

auditSystem   Adds additional device drivers, specifies firewall settings, and applies a name to the system when the image is booted into Audit mode. Audit mode is initiated by using the sysprep/audit command.

auditUser   Executes RunSynchronous or RunAsynchronous commands when the image is booted into Audit mode. Audit mode is initiated by using the sysprep /audit command.

generalize   Removes system-specific information from an image so that the image can be used as a reference image. The settings specified in the generalize component will only be applied if the sysprep /generalize command is used.

offlineServicing Specifies the language packs and packages to apply to an image prior to the image being extracted to the hard disk.

oobeSystem Specifies the settings to apply to the computer the first time that the computer is booted into the Windows Welcome screen, which is also known as the out-of-the-box experience (OOBE). To boot to the Welcome screen, use the sysprep /oobe command.

Specialize Configures the specific settings for the target computer, such as network settings and domain information. This configuration pass is used in conjunction with the generalize configuration pass.

Windows PE Sets the Windows PE–specific configuration settings, as well as several Windows Setup settings, such as partitioning and formatting the hard disk, selecting an image, and applying a product key.

Now let's take a look at how you can create answer files using Windows SIM.

Creating Answer Files with Windows SIM

To create an answer file with Windows SIM, the first thing you must do is install the Windows AIK.

Perform the following steps to download and install the Windows Automated Installation Kit. The Windows AIK is a free download from Microsoft's website.

1. Download the Windows AIK ISO file from Microsoft's website.

2. Transfer the ISO file to a DVD.

3. Insert the DVD into your Windows 7 machine.

4. When Autoplay starts, select Run StartCD.exe. If Autorun does not appear, open Windows Explorer and click startCD.exe under the DVD drive.

5. At the User Account Control screen, click Yes.

6. The Welcome To Windows Automated Installation Kit screen appears, as shown in Figure 2.7. Click the Windows AIK Setup link on the left.

7. When you see the Welcome screen, click Next.

Figure 2.7: The Windows AIK installation screen

8. At the License Terms screen, click the I Agree radio button and click Next.

9. At the Select Installation Folder screen (see Figure 2.8), choose where you want to install the Windows AIK files. You can also choose who has the rights to use the Windows AIK. For this exercise, choose Everyone and then click Next.

Figure 2.8: The Select Installation Folder screen

10. At the Confirmation screen, verify your settings and click Next.

11. At the Installation Complete screen, verify that there are no errors and click Close.

12. Close the Windows AIK installation screen.

After you install the Windows AIK, you can run the Windows SIM utility to create a new answer file or edit existing answer files.

Perform the following steps to create a new answer file using Windows SIM:

1. Select Start ➤ All Programs ➤ Microsoft Windows AIK, and click Windows System Image Manager.

2. Windows System Image Manager displays an empty screen with five panes, as shown in Figure 2.9: a pane for selecting distribution shares, a pane for selecting Windows image files, the answer file pane, a properties pane, and a pane for displaying validation messages.

Figure 2.9: The Windows SIM screen

3. Select the Windows 7 image file for which a new answer file should be created by clicking File ➤ Select A Windows Image Or Catalog File or by right-clicking the Windows Image pane in Windows SIM and clicking Select Windows Image (see Figure 2.10).

Figure 2.10: Select Windows Image option

4. Select File ➤ New Answer File or right-click the Answer File pane and select New Answer File from the context menu to generate the structure of the new answer file.

5. Right-click each component as desired to modify the configuration pass options that are specific to the new environment. You can drill down within a component to provide specific customizations, or you can modify parent-level components.

6. When you have finished customizing the answer file for the desired environment, click File ➤ Save Answer File to save the answer file.

You can use an answer file to provide automated answers for a DVD-based installation. Simply create a new answer file named **Autounattend.xml** and copy it to the root of the DVD. Insert the Windows 7 DVD and set the BIOS to boot from the DVD drive. As the installation begins, Windows Setup will implicitly search for answer files in a number of locations, including the root of removable media drives.

In the next section you'll see how to install Windows 7 remotely through the use of Windows Deployment Services.

Using Windows Deployment Services

In earlier Windows versions, another method that many IT departments used to deploy operating systems was Remote Installation Services (RIS). RIS was a utility that allowed you to deploy an operating system remotely. On the client machine that was receiving the operating system, you'd use a set of disks (RIS client disks) that would automatically initiate a network card, connect to the RIS server, and download the operating system.

For Windows 7 and Windows Server 2008, a new version of RIS has been developed that's called Windows Deployment Services (WDS). WDS (see Figure 2.11) allows you to install a Windows operating system without using an installation CD or DVD. Using WDS enables you to deploy the operating system through a network installation. WDS can deploy Windows XP, Windows Server 2003, Microsoft Vista, Windows 7, and Microsoft Windows Server 2008.

Figure 2.11: Windows Deployment Services

Here are some of the advantages of using WDS for automated installation:

- You can remotely install Windows 7.

- The procedure simplifies management of the server image by allowing you to access Windows 7 distribution files from a distribution server.

- You can quickly recover the operating system in the event of a computer failure.

The basic steps of the WDS process from a PXE-enabled WDS client are as follows:

1. The WDS client initiates a special boot process through the PXE network adapter (and the computer's BIOS configured for a network boot). On a PXE client, the client presses F12 to start the PXE boot process and to indicate that you want to perform a WDS installation.

2. A list of available Windows PE boot images displays. Select the appropriate Windows PE boot image from the menu.

3. The Windows Welcome screen displays. Click Next.

4. Enter your credentials for accessing and installing images from the WDS server.

5. A list of available operating system images displays. Select the appropriate image file to install.

6. At the next screen, enter the product key for the selected image.

7. The Partition And Configure The Disk screen displays. You can install a mass storage device driver, if needed, by pressing F6.

8. The image copy process is initiated, and the selected image is copied to the WDS client computer.

The following sections describe how to set up the WDS server and the WDS clients and how to install Windows 7 through WDS.

Preparing the WDS Server

With the WDS server, you can manage and distribute Windows 7 operating system images to WDS client computers. The WDS server contains any files necessary for PXE booting, Windows PE boot images, and the Windows 7 images to be deployed.

The following steps for preparing the WDS server are discussed in the upcoming sections:

1. Make sure the server meets the requirements for running WDS.

2. Install WDS.

3. Install the WDS Server components.

4. Configure and start WDS.

5. Configure the WDS server to respond to client computers (if this was not configured when WDS was installed).

For WDS to work, the server on which you'll install WDS must meet the requirements for WDS and be able to access the required network services. Now let's take a look at the requirements needed for WDS.

WDS Server Requirements

The WDS server must meet the following requirements:

- The computer must be a domain controller or a member of an Active Directory domain.

- At least one partition on the server must be formatted as NTFS.

- WDS must be installed on the server.

- The computer must be running the Windows Server 2003 or Windows Server 2008 operating system.

- A network adapter must be installed.

Network Services Requirements

The following network services must be running on the WDS server or be accessible to the WDS server from another network server:

- TCP/IP (installed and configured)

- A DHCP server, which is used to assign DHCP addresses to WDS clients (ensure that your DHCP scope has enough addresses to accommodate all the WDS clients that will need IP addresses)

- A DNS server, which is used to locate the Active Directory controller

- Active Directory, which is used to locate WDS servers and WDS clients, as well as to authorize WDS clients and manage WDS configuration settings and client installation options

In the next section you'll see how to install the WDS server components.

Installing the WDS Server Components

You can configure WDS on a Windows Server 2003 or Windows Server 2008 computer by using the Windows Deployment Services Configuration Wizard or by using the wdsutil command-line utility. Table 2.8 describes the options for the wdsutil command.

Table 2.8: wdsutil Command-Line Options

Option	Description
/initialize	Initializes the configuration of the WDS server
/uninitialize	Undoes any changes made during the initialization of the WDS server
/add	Adds images and devices to the WDS server
/convert	Converts Remote Installation Preparation (RIPrep) images to WIM images
/remove	Removes images from the server
/set	Sets information in images, image groups, WDS servers, and WDS devices
/get	Gets information from images, image groups, WDS servers, and WDS devices
/new	Creates new capture images or discover images
/copy	Copies images from the image store
/export	Exports to WIM files images contained within the image store
/start	Starts WDS services
/stop	Stops WDS services
/disable	Disables WDS services
/enable	Enables WDS services
/approve	Approves Auto-Add devices
/reject	Rejects Auto-Add devices

Table 2.8: wdsutil Command-Line Options *(continued)*

Option	Description
/delete	Deletes records from the Auto-Add database
/update	Uses a known good resource to update a server resource

The first step in setting up WDS to deploy operating systems to the clients is to install the WDS role. You do this by using Server Manager. You must make sure that DNS, DHCP, and Active Directory are installed before completing the following steps.

Network Infrastructure

DNS and DHCP are discussed in detail in *MCTS: Windows Server 2008 Network Infrastructure Configuration Study Guide* by William Panek, Tylor Wentworth, and James Chellis (Sybex, 2008).

To install WDS on Windows Server 2008:

1. Start Server Manager by clicking Start ➤ Administrative Tools ➤ Server Manager.

2. On the left-hand side, click Roles.

3. In the right-hand window pane, click the Add Roles link, which launches the Add Roles Wizard.

4. Click Next at the Before You Begin screen.

5. Click the Windows Deployment Services check box. Click Next.

6. At the Overview screen, click Next.

7. At the Select Role Services screen, make sure both check boxes (Deployment Server and Transport Server) are selected, and then click Next.

8. At the Confirmation screen, verify the installation selections and click Install.

9. At the Installation Results screen, click Close.

10. Close Server Manager.

The next step is to configure the WDS server to respond to the WDS clients.

Configuring the WDS Server to Respond to Client Requests

Perform these steps to configure the WDS server:

1. Start WDS by clicking Start ➢ Administrative Tools ➢ Windows Deployment Services.

2. In the left-hand window pane, expand the Servers link. Click the name of your server, and then right-click it and choose Configure Server.

3. The Welcome screen appears explaining that you need an Active Directory Domain Services, DHCP, DNS, and an NTFS partition. If you meet these minimum requirements, click Next.

4. The Remote Installation Folder Location screen appears. Accept the defaults by clicking Next.

5. When you see the System Volume Warning dialog box, click Yes.

6. The DHCP Option 60 screen is next, as shown in Figure 2.12. Select both check boxes and click Next.

Figure 2.12: The DHCP Option 60 screen

7. The PXE Server Initial Settings screen (see Figure 2.13) asks you to choose how PXE will respond to clients. Choose the "Respond to all (known and unknown) client computers" radio button. Click Finish.

Figure 2.13: The PXE Server Initial Settings screen

8. At the Configuration Complete screen, make sure the Add Image To The Windows Deployment Server Now check box is deselected. Click Finish.

One of the advantages of using WDS is that it can work with Windows image (.wim) files. As you learned earlier, you can create Windows image files by using the Windows Sysprep utility.

One component that you need to pay attention to when using WDS is the Preboot Execution Environment (PXE) boot device. PXE boot devices are network interface cards (NICs) that can talk to a network without the need for an operating system because they have a set of pre-boot commands within the boot firmware.

PXE boot adapters connect to a WDS server and request the data needed to load the operating system remotely. Since most of the machines that you're using WDS for do not have an operating system on the computer, you must have NIC adapters that can connect to a network without an operating system in order for WDS to work properly.

For the same reason, you must set up DHCP to accept PXE machines. Those machines need a valid TCP/IP address so that they can connect to the WDS server.

The WDS server side is now installed and configured. The next step involves setting up the WDS client side.

Preparing the WDS Client

The WDS client is the computer on which Windows 7 will be installed. WDS clients rely on a technology called PXE, which allows the client computer to remotely boot and connect to a WDS server.

To act as a WDS client, the computer must meet all the hardware requirements for Windows 7 (see Chapter 1) and have a PXE-capable network adapter installed. Also, a WDS server must be present on the network. Additionally, the user account used to install the image must be a member of the Domain Users group in Active Directory.

After you install and configure the WDS server, you can install Windows 7 on a WDS client that uses a PXE-compliant network card.

To install Windows 7 on the WDS client:

1. Start the computer. When prompted, press F12 for a network service boot.

2. The Windows PE displays. When you see the Windows Welcome screen, click Next to start the installation process.

3. Enter the username and password of an account that has permissions to access and install images from the WDS server.

4. A list of available operating system images stored on the WDS server appears. Select the image to install and click Next.

5. Enter the product key for the selected Windows 7 image and click Next.

6. At the Partition And Configure the Disk screen, select the desired disk partitioning options, or click OK to use the default options.

7. Click Next to initiate the image-copying process. The Windows Setup process begins after the image is copied to the WDS client computer.

Now you know all the different ways to install Windows 7. Next let's look at a tool that can help you determine which machines can install Windows 7.

Use the Microsoft Assessment and Planning Toolkit

This chapter is about installing Windows 7 on multiple computers. One utility that you can use to help design your network is the

Microsoft Assessment and Planning (MAP) Toolkit. MAP is a utility that will locate computers on a network and then perform a thorough inventory of these computers. To obtain this inventory, MAP uses multiple utilities like the Windows Management Instrumentation (WMI), the Remote Registry Service, or the Simple Network Management Protocol (SNMP).

Having this information will allow you to determine if the machines on your network will be able to load Windows 7, Windows Vista, Windows Server 2008, Microsoft Office 2007, and Microsoft Application Virtualization. One advantage of using MAP when determining the requirements for Windows 7 is that MAP will also advise you of any hardware upgrades needed for a machine or device driver availability.

Anyone who has been in the industry for a while can see the potential of using MAP. A utility that goes out and discovers your network hardware and then advises you of needed resources to allow the operating system to operate properly is a tool that should be in every administrator's arsenal.

When deciding to locate the computers on your network, you have several approaches. The following list shows your discovery options and how they try to discover the computers:

Use Active Directory Domain Services   Select this check box to find computer objects in Active Directory.

Use The Windows Networking Protocols   Select this check box to find computers in workgroups and Windows NT 4.0 domains.

Import Computer Names From A File   Select this check box to import computer names from a file.

Scan An IP Address Range   Select this check box to find computers within a specified IP address range.

Manually Enter Computer Names And Credentials   Select this check box to enter computer names individually.

You'll probably find it challenging to determine how many servers are needed for Windows 7 end users and where to place them on your network. A useful feature included with MAP is the ability to obtain performance metric data from the computers. MAP will also generate a report that recommends which machines can be used for Windows 7.

MAP generates your report in both Microsoft Excel and Word. These reports can provide information to you in summary and full detail modes. MAP can generate reports for you for some of the following scenarios:

- Identify currently installed client operating systems and their requirements for migrating to Windows 7.

- Identify currently installed Windows Server systems and their requirements for migrating to Windows Server 2008.

- Identify currently installed Microsoft Office software and their requirements for migrating to Office 2007.

- Access server performance by using the Performance Metrics Wizard.

- Perform Hyper-V or Virtual Server 2005 server consolidation and placement.

- Assess machines (clients, servers) for installation of Microsoft Application Virtualization (formerly known as SoftGrid).

To install MAP, you must first take a look at the system requirements.

MAP System Requirements

MAP is a free utility that you can download from Microsoft. But before you can install MAP, you must verify that the computer that MAP will be installed on meets minimum requirements. The minimum requirements to install MAP are as follows:

Supported Operating Systems   The supported operating systems include Windows 7, Windows Server 2008, Windows Server 2003, Windows Vista with Service Pack 1, and Windows XP Professional Edition.

CPU Architecture   MAP can be installed on both the 32-bit and 64-bit versions of any of the listed operating systems.

Hardware Requirements   Hardware requirements include: 1.6 GHz or faster processor minimum or dual-core for Windows 7; 1.5 GB of RAM minimum, 2 GB recommended for Windows 7 or Windows Vista; minimum of 1 GB of available hard disk space; and a network card that supports 10/100 Mbps.

Additional Requirements   Some additional requirements are Microsoft SQL Server 2005 Express Edition, Microsoft Word (2003 with SP2 or 2007), and Microsoft Excel (2003 with SP2 or 2007).

Installing MAP

Follow these steps to install MAP from the Windows AIK installation utility that you downloaded previously in this chapter:

1. Insert the Windows AIK DVD into your machine.

2. When Autoplay starts, click Run StartCD.exe. If Autorun does not display, open Windows Explorer and click startCD.exe under the DVD drive.

3. At the User Account Control screen, click Yes.

4. The Welcome To Windows Automated Installation Kit screen appears, as shown in Figure 2.14. Click the MAP Download link on the left. This takes you to the Microsoft website where you can download MAP.

Figure 2.14: The Windows AIK installation screen

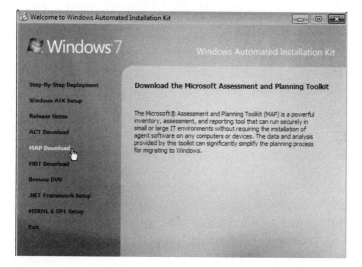

5. Scroll down to the bottom of the page and click the download button for Microsoft_Assessment_and_Planning_Solution_Setup .x64.exe or x86.exe.

6. Click Save. Save the file to your hard drive.

7. After the file is downloaded to your hard drive, click Run.

8. The Microsoft Assessment and Planning Solution Accelerator Setup Wizard appears, as shown in Figure 2.15. Make sure the

option to automatically check for device compatibility is checked and click Next.

Figure 2.15: The MAP setup screen

9. The License Agreement screen appears next. Click the "I accept the terms of the license agreement" radio button and click Next.

10. At the Installation Folder screen, accept the default location by clicking Next.

11. A screen appears asking about SQL Server 2005 Express. If you have a previous version of SQL Server 2005 Express on your machine, click the radio button "Install from previous downloaded installation files." If you do not have a previous copy of SQL, make sure that the radio button Download And Install is checked. After your selection, click Next.

12. The SQL Server 2005 Express License Agreement screen appears next. Click the "I accept the terms of the license agreement" radio button and click Next.

13. At the Ready To Install screen, click Install. The Installing The Microsoft Assessment And Planning Solution Accelerator status screen appears and shows you the status of the installation process. Once the installation is complete, the Installation Successful screen appears.

Configuring and Testing the Server

Now that you have installed MAP, it's time to configure and test the server. Perform the following steps to create your database for testing:

1. Start MAP by clicking Start ➤ All Programs ➤ Microsoft Planning And Assessment Solution Accelerator, and then clicking Microsoft Planning And Assessment Solution.

2. The first thing you need to do is select your database. You are going to create your database at this time. To accomplish this, click Select A Database in either the center or right window pane, as shown in Figure 2.16.

Figure 2.16: Click Select A Database in either the center or right window pane.

3. The Create Or Select A Database screen appears. Make sure that you click the Create An Inventory Database radio button. In the Name field, type **Windows 7** and click OK.

Once your database is created, you'll have the ability to run the various options to test the machines and servers. At this point, you decide which scenario you'd like to test for your network.

It's useful to have a utility like MAP to help you detect not only your network and its operating systems, but also recommend enhancements.

Work with Windows PE

Windows PE is the new Windows Preinstallation Environment that replaces the Microsoft DOS environment. It is used in Windows Vista, Windows Server 2008 R2, and Windows 7 environments.

The Windows PE environment is included with multiple Microsoft tools for Windows Server 2008 and Windows 7. These tools include the Windows Automated Installation Kit (Windows AIK), Windows PE Kit, and the Windows OEM Preinstallation Kit (Windows OPK).

NOTE The Windows Automated Installation Kit (Windows AIK) is discussed earlier in this chapter.

Using Windows PE Tools

Because Windows PE is used for Windows 7 and Windows Server 2008 R2, there are many tools that can be used with the Windows PE environment. Table 2.9 shows a few of the tools available with Windows PE.

Table 2.9: Windows PE Tools

Tool	Description
Bcdedit	Boot configuration data (BCD) files uses a store to define the boot applications and boot application settings. This store replaces the `boot.ini` file.
Bootsect	Bootsect allows you to update the master boot code; it lets you restore the boot sector on your Windows 7 computer.
Diskpart	Diskpart allows you to manage your disks, partitions, or volumes.
DISM	The Deployment Image Servicing and Management (DISM) utility is an advanced set of tools that allows you to install, uninstall, configure, and update the features for offline Windows image files and offline Windows PE images.
ImageX	ImageX allows you to capture and install Windows 7 images.

Table 2.9: Windows PE Tools *(continued)*

Tool	Description
Oscdimg	Oscdimg is a utility that is used for creating an image file (`.iso`) of a 32-bit or 64-bit Windows PE version.
PEImg	PEImg is a utility used for creating and modifying offline Windows PE images.
Wpeinit	Wpeinit is a utility that initializes Windows PE each time it boots.

One of the advantages of using Windows PE is that you can include Windows PE within the Windows 7 disk image. Normally when you want to place a Windows 7 image on a machine, you must use a third-party imaging tool or use ImageX to transfer the image to the new machine. If Windows PE is included within the image, the machine can boot into the Windows PE environment to install the image.

When working with the Windows PE environment, you must follow these rules:

- All hardware devices need to be Plug and Play (PnP) compatible.

- You must be using TCP/IP (either IPv4 or IPv6).

- Your machine must have a minimum of 254 MB of RAM.

- The video must be VESA compatible.

Configuring a Windows PE Environment

There are a few files that you can manipulate when configuring the Windows PE environment. Table 2.10 explains these configurable files and what they do for the Windows PE environment.

Table 2.10: Windows PE Configuration Files

Files	Description
`winpeshl.ini`	This is the Windows PE shell file. This file allows you to customize your Windows PE shell environment.
BCD store file	The BCD store allows you to configure your Boot Configuration Data (BCD). You can use the `bcdedit` command to configure the BCD store.

Table 2.10: Windows PE Configuration Files *(continued)*

Files	Description
Autounattend.xml	This file allows you to provide answers to the questions that are asked during the installation process. Using this file allows you to automate the installation process without user intervention.
startnet.cmd	This script allows you to configure your network setup for the Windows PE environment.

Setting Up a Windows PE Bootable Media Device

If you want to set up a Windows PE bootable media device, complete the following steps:

1. Click Start ➤ All Programs ➤ Microsoft Windows AIK.

2. Right-click on the Deployment Tools command prompt and choose Run As Administrator.

3. Enter one of three commands (depending on your system):

   - Copype x86 C:\winpe_x86 (x86 32-bit machines)

   - Copype amd64 C:\winpe_x64 (x64-bit machines)

   - Copype ia64 C:\winpe_ia64 (Itanium-based machines)

The Windows PE files are stored under the winpe directory. You have the ability to change the winpe directory to another location or directly to a media file. After the files are created, you can add them to an image or bootable media. You also have the ability to edit the different files at this time to customize the Windows PE environment for your organization.

3

Configuring Disks

IN THIS CHAPTER, YOU WILL LEARN TO:

D uring the installation of Windows 7, you have the chance to designate the initial configuration for your disks. After Windows 7 is installed, you can use many of the Windows 7's utilities and features to change these configurations and perform disk management tasks.

For file system configuration, you can use NTFS or FAT32. You can also change FAT32 partitions to NTFS after the initial configuration. This chapter covers the features of each file system and how to use the Convert utility to upgrade to NTFS.

Windows 7 supports basic, dynamic, and the GUID partition table (GPT) disks. When you install Windows 7, the drives are configured as basic disks.

Dynamic disks are supported by Windows 7, Windows Vista, Windows XP Professional, Windows 2000 (all versions), Windows Server 2003, and Windows Server 2008 and allow you to create simple volumes, spanned volumes, and striped volumes.

This chapter also covers other disk management features such as data compression, data encryption, disk defragmentation, disk cleanup, and disk error checking.

Configure File Systems

Each partition (each logical drive that is created on a hard drive) you create under Windows 7 must have a file system associated with it.

When you select a file system, you can select FAT32 or NTFS. You typically select file systems based on the features you want to use and whether you will need to access the file system using other operating systems. If you have a FAT32 partition and want to update it to NTFS, you can use the Convert utility. The features of each file system and the procedure for converting file systems are covered in the following sections.

Selecting a File System

Your file system is used to store and retrieve the files stored on your hard drive. One of the most fundamental choices associated with file management is the choice of your file system's configuration. Microsoft recommends that you use NTFS with Windows 7, because doing so will allow you to take advantage of features such as local security, file compression, and file encryption. You should choose FAT32 if you want to dual-boot your computer with a version of Windows that does not support NTFS because these file systems are backward compatible with other operating systems.

Table 3.1 summarizes the capabilities of each file system, and they are described in more detail in the following sections.

Table 3.1: File System Capabilities

Feature	FAT32	NTFS
Supporting operating systems	Windows 95 OSR2, Windows 98, Windows Me, Windows 2000, Windows XP, Windows Server 2003, Windows Server 2008, Windows Vista, and Windows 7	Windows NT, Windows 2000, Windows XP, Windows Server 2003, Windows Vista, and Windows 7
Long filename support	Yes	Yes
Efficient use of disk space	Yes	Yes
Compression support	No	Yes
Encryption support	No	Yes
Support for local security	No	Yes
Support for network security	Yes	Yes
Maximum volume size	32 GB	16 TB with 4 KB clusters or 256 TB with 64 KB clusters

Installation

PART I

Let's start looking at the supported file systems.

FAT32

FAT32 is an updated version of FAT. FAT32 was first shipped with Windows 95 OSR2 (Operating System Release 2), and can be used by Windows 7.

One of the main advantages of FAT32 is its support for smaller cluster sizes, which results in more efficient space allocation than was possible with FAT16. Files stored on a FAT32 partition can use 20 to 30 percent less disk space than files stored on a FAT16 partition. FAT32 supports drive sizes from 512 MB up to 2 TB, although if you create and format a FAT32 partition through Windows 7, the FAT32 partition can only be up to 32 GB. Because of the smaller cluster sizes, FAT32 can also load programs up to 50 percent faster than programs loaded from FAT16 partitions.

The main disadvantages of FAT32 compared to NTFS are that it does not provide as much support for larger hard drives and it does not provide very robust security options. It also offers no native support for disk compression. Now that you understand FAT32, let's take a look at NTFS.

NTFS

NTFS, which was first used with the NT operating system, offers the highest level of service and features for Windows 7 computers. NTFS partitions can be up to 16 TB with 4 KB clusters or 256 TB with 64 KB clusters.

NTFS offers comprehensive folder- and file-level security. This allows you to set an additional level of security for users who access the files and folders locally or through the network. For example, two users who share the same Windows 7 computer can be assigned different NTFS permissions, so that one user has access to a folder but the other user is denied access to that folder.

NTFS also offers disk management features—such as compression and encryption services—and data recovery features.

You should also be aware that there are several versions of NTFS. Every version of Windows 2000 uses NTFS 3.0. Windows 7, Windows Vista, Windows XP, Windows Server 2003, and Windows Server 2008 use NTFS 3.1. NTFS versions 3.0 and 3.1 use similar disk formats, so Windows 2000 computers can access NTFS 3.1 volumes and Windows 7 computers can access NTFS 3.0 volumes.

NTFS 3.1 includes the following features:

- When files are read or written to a disk, they can be automatically encrypted and decrypted.

- Reparse points are used with mount points to redirect data as it is written or read from a folder to another volume or physical disk.

- There is support for sparse files, which are used by programs that create large files but allocate disk space only as needed.

- Remote storage allows you to extend your disk space by making removable media (for example, external tapes) more accessible.

- You can use recovery logging on NTFS metadata, which is used for data recovery when a power failure or system problem occurs.

Now that you have seen the differences between FAT32 and NTFS, let's discuss how to change a FAT32 drive to an NTFS drive.

Converting a File System

In Windows 7, you can convert FAT32 partitions to NTFS. File system conversion is the process of converting one file system to another without the loss of data. If you format a drive as another file system, as opposed to converting that drive, all the data on that drive will be lost.

To convert a partition, use the Convert command-line utility. The syntax for the `Convert` command is as follows:

```
Convert [drive:] /fs:ntfs
```

For example, if you wanted to convert your D drive to NTFS, you'd type the following command from a command prompt:

```
Convert D: /fs:ntfs
```

When the conversion process begins, it will attempt to lock the partition. If the partition cannot be locked—perhaps because the partition contains the Windows 7 operating system files or the system's page file—the conversion won't take place until the computer is restarted.

Using the *Convert* Command

You can use the /v switch with the `Convert` command. This switch specifies that you want to use verbose mode, and all messages will be displayed during the conversion process. You can also use the /NoSecurity switch that specifies that all converted files and folders will have no security applied by default so they can be accessed by anyone.

In the following steps, you convert your D drive from FAT32 to NTFS. These steps assume that you have a D drive that is formatted with the FAT32 file system.

Perform the following steps to convert a FAT32 partition to NTFS:

1. Copy some folders to the D drive.

2. Select Start, then type **cmd** into the Search box to open a command prompt.

3. In the Command Prompt dialog box, type **Convert D: /fs:ntfs** and press Enter.

4. After the conversion process is complete, close the Command Prompt dialog box.

5. Verify that the folders you copied in step 1 still exist on the partition.

Stopping a Conversion

If you choose to convert a partition from FAT32 to NTFS, and the conversion has not yet taken place, you can cancel the conversion by editing the Registry with the regedit command. The key that needs to be edited is HKEY_LOCAL_MACHINE\System\ CurrentControlSet\Control\SessionManager. The BootExecute value should be changed from autoconv \DosDevices\x: / FS:NTFS to autocheck autochk*.

After you decide which file system you want to use, you need to decide what disk storage type you want to configure. Let's take a look at some of the disk storage options that you have.

Configure Disk Storage

Windows 7 supports three types of disk storage: basic, dynamic, and GUID partition table (GPT). Basic storage is backward compatible with other operating systems and can be configured to support up to four partitions. Dynamic storage is supported by Windows 2000, Windows XP, Windows Server 2003, Windows Server 2008, Windows Vista, and Windows 7, and allows storage to be configured as volumes. GPT storage allows you to configure volume sizes larger than 2 TB and up to 128 primary partitions. The following sections describe the basic storage, dynamic storage, and GPT storage configurations.

Basic Storage

Basic storage consists of primary and extended partitions and logical drives. The first partition that is created on a hard drive is called a primary partition and is usually represented as drive C. Primary partitions use all the space that is allocated to each partition and use a single drive letter to represent the partition. Each physical drive can be partitioned as follows:

- As a single partition
- As four primary partitions
- As three primary partitions and one extended partition

With an extended partition, you can allocate the space however you like, and each suballocation of space (called a logical drive) is represented by a different drive letter. For example, a 500 GB extended partition could have a 250 GB D partition and a 250 GB E partition.

At the highest level of disk organization, you have a physical hard drive. You cannot use space on the physical drive until you have logically partitioned the physical drive. A partition is a logical definition of hard drive space.

One of the advantages of using multiple partitions on a single physical hard drive is that each partition can have a different file system. For example, the C drive might be FAT32 and the D drive might be NTFS. Multiple partitions also make it easier to manage security requirements.

Basic storage is the default setting, and this is the type that many users continue to use. But what if you want some additional functionality from your storage type? Let's take a look at some of the more advanced disk storage options.

Dynamic Storage

Dynamic storage is a Windows 7 feature that consists of a dynamic disk divided into dynamic volumes. Dynamic volumes cannot contain partitions or logical drives.

Dynamic storage supports three dynamic volume types: simple volumes, spanned volumes, and striped volumes. Dynamic storage also supports software-based Redundant Array of Inexpensive Disks (RAID).

To set up dynamic storage, you create or upgrade a basic disk to a dynamic disk. When you convert a basic disk to dynamic, you do not lose any of your data. After the disk is converted, you can then create dynamic volumes within the dynamic disk.

You create dynamic storage with the Windows 7 Disk Management utility, which I will explore following the descriptions of the dynamic volume types. Let's take a closer look at the various types of dynamic volumes.

Simple Volumes

A simple volume contains space from a single dynamic drive. The space from the single drive can be contiguous or noncontiguous. Simple volumes are used when you have enough disk space on a single drive to hold your entire volume. Figure 3.1 shows two simple volumes on a physical disk.

Figure 3.1: Two simple volumes

Simple Volume C:\
10GB

Simple Volume D:\
10GB

Physical Disk 0
20GB

Spanned Volumes

A spanned volume consists of disk space on two or more dynamic drives; up to 32 dynamic drives can be used in a spanned volume configuration. Spanned volume sets are used to dynamically increase the size of a dynamic volume. When you create spanned volumes, the data is written sequentially, filling space on one physical drive before writing to space on the next physical drive in the spanned volume set. Typically, administrators use spanned volumes when they are running out of disk space on a volume and want to dynamically extend the volume with space from another hard drive.

You do not need to allocate the same amount of space to the volume set on each physical drive. This means you could combine a 500 GB partition on one physical drive with two 750 GB partitions on other dynamic drives, as shown in Figure 3.2.

Figure 3.2: A spanned volume set

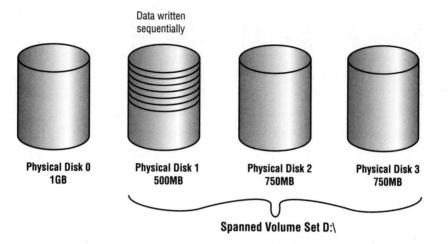

Data written
sequentially

Physical Disk 0
1GB

Physical Disk 1
500MB

Physical Disk 2
750MB

Physical Disk 3
750MB

Spanned Volume Set D:\

Because data is written sequentially, you do not see any performance enhancements with spanned volumes as you do with striped volumes (which we discuss next). The main disadvantage of spanned volumes is that if any drive in the spanned volume set fails, you lose access to all the data in the spanned set.

Striped Volumes

A striped volume stores data in equal stripes between two or more (up to 32) dynamic drives, as shown in Figure 3.3. Because the data is written sequentially in the stripes, you can take advantage of multiple I/O performances and increase the speed at which data reads and writes take place. Typically, administrators use striped volumes when they want to combine the space of several physical drives into a single logical volume and increase disk performance.

The main disadvantage of striped volumes is that if any drive in the striped volume set fails, you lose access to all the data in the striped set.

In the last few years a new storage type has emerged in the Microsoft computer world. As with most new technologies, it also has some advantages over the previous technologies. Let's take a look at the newest advantage to storage types.

Figure 3.3: A striped volume set

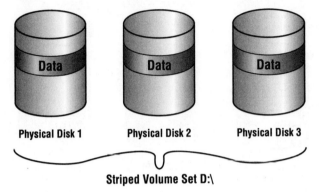

GUID Partition Table

The GUID Partition Table (GPT) is available for Windows 7 and was first introduced as part of the Extensible Firmware Interface (EFI) initiative from Intel. Basic and dynamic disks use the Master Boot Record (MBR) partitioning scheme that all operating systems have been using for years. Basic and Dynamic disks use Cylinder-Head-Sector (CHS) addressing with the MBR scheme.

The GPT disk partitioning system uses the GUID Partition Table to configure the disk area. GPT uses a newer addressing scheme called Logical Block Addressing (LBA). Another advantage is that the GPT header and partition table are written to both the front and the back end of the disk, which in turn provides for better redundancy.

The GPT disk partitioning system gives you many benefits over using the MBR system, including the following:

- Allows a volume size larger than 2 TB

- Allows up to 128 primary partitions

- Used for both 32-bit or 64-bit Windows 7 editions

- Includes Cyclical Redundancy Check (CRC) for greater reliability

There is one disadvantage to using the GPT drives: you can only convert a GPT drive if the disk is empty and not partitioned.

To convert any disk or format any volume or partition, you can use the Disk Management utility. Let's take a look at how to manage your disks using the Disk Management utility.

Access and Manage the Disk Management Utility

The Disk Management utility is a Microsoft Management Console (MMC) snap-in that gives administrators a graphical tool for managing disks and volumes within Windows 7. In this section, you'll learn how to access the Disk Management utility and use it to manage basic tasks, basic storage, and dynamic storage. You will also learn about troubleshooting disks through disk status codes.

But before I dive into the Disk Management utility, let's first take a look at the Microsoft Management Console (MMC). It is important to understand the MMC because Disk Management (like many other tools) is an MMC snap-in.

Using the MMC

The MMC is the console framework for application management. The MMC provides a common environment for snap-ins. Snap-ins are administrative tools developed by Microsoft or third-party vendors. Some of the MMC snap-ins that you may use are Computer Management, Active Directory Users and Computers, Active Directory Sites and Services, Active Directory Domains and Trusts, and DNS Management.

Knowing how to use and configure the MMC snap-ins allows you to customize your work environment. For example, if you are in charge of Active Directory Users and Computers and DNS, you can add both of these snap-ins into the same window. This would then allow you to just open one application to configure all your tasks.

The MMC offers many other benefits, including the following:

- The MMC is highly customizable—you add only the snap-ins you need.

- Snap-ins use a standard, intuitive interface, so they're easier to use than previous versions of administrative utilities.

- You can save and share MMC consoles with other administrators.

- You can configure permissions so that the MMC runs in authoring mode, which an administrator can manage, or in user mode, which limits what users can access.

- You can use most snap-ins for remote computer management.

By default, the MMC contains three panes: a console tree on the left, a details pane in the middle, and an optional Actions pane on the right, as shown in Figure 3.4. The console tree lists the hierarchical structure of all snap-ins that have been loaded into the console. The details pane contains a list of properties or other items that are part of the snap-in that is highlighted in the console tree. The Actions pane provides a list of actions that the user can access depending on the item selected in the details pane.

Figure 3.4: The MMC console tree, details pane, and Actions pane

Accessing the MMC

On a Windows 7 computer, to open the MMC click Start and type **MMC** in the Search dialog box. When you first open the MMC, it contains only the Console Root folder, as shown in Figure 3.4 earlier. The MMC does not have any default administrative functionality. It is simply a framework used to organize administrative tools through the addition of snap-in utilities.

The first thing that you should decide when you use the MMC is which of the different administrative mode types is best suited for your organization.

Configuring MMC Modes

You can configure the MMC to run in author mode, for full access to the MMC functions, or in one of three user modes, which have more limited access to the MMC functions. To set a console mode, while in the MMC editor select File ➤ Options to open the Options dialog box. In this dialog box, you can select from the console modes listed in Table 3.2.

Installation

PART I

Table 3.2: MMC Console Modes

Console Mode	Description
Author mode	Allows use of all the MMC functions.
User mode—full access	Gives users full access to window management commands, but they cannot add or remove snap-ins or change console properties.
User mode—limited access, multiple window	Allows users to create new windows but they cannot close any existing windows. Users can access only the areas of the console tree that were visible when the console was last saved.
User mode—limited access, single window	Allows users to access only the areas of the console tree that were visible when the console was last saved, and they cannot create new windows.

After you decide which administrative role you are going to run, it's time to start configuring your MMC snap-ins.

Adding Snap-Ins

The biggest advantage of using the MMC is to add snap-ins the way your organization needs them. Adding snap-ins is a simple and quick procedure.

Perform the following steps to add snap-ins to the MMC and save it:

1. To start the MMC editor, click Start, type MMC in the Search box, and press Enter.

2. From the main console window, select File ➤ Add/Remove Snap-in to open the Add Or Remove Snap-ins dialog box.

3. Highlight the snap-in you want to add and click Add, as shown in Figure 3.5.

Figure 3.5: The MMC Add Or Remove Snap-ins dialog box

4. If prompted, specify whether the snap-in will be used to manage the local computer or a remote computer, as shown in Figure 3.6. Then click Finish.

5. Repeat steps 2 and 3 to add each snap-in you want to include in your console.

Figure 3.6: Choose between a local or remote computer.

6. When you finish adding snap-ins, click OK.

7. Click OK to return to the main console screen.

8. After you have added snap-ins to create a console, you can save it by selecting File ➤ Save As and entering a name for your console.

You can save the console to a variety of locations, including a program group or the Desktop. By default, custom consoles have an .msc extension.

Many applications that are MMC snap-ins, including Disk Management, are already configured for you under the administrative tools section of Windows 7. Now that you have looked at the MMC editor, let's take a look at the Disk Management utility.

Accessing the Disk Management Utility

The Disk Management utility, located under the Computer Management snap-in by default, is a one-stop shop for configuring your disk options.

First, to have full permissions to use the Disk Management utility, you must be logged on with Administrative privileges. You can access the Disk Management utility a few different ways. You can right-click Computer from the Start menu and select Manage, and then in Computer Management, select Disk Management. You could also choose Start ➤ Control Panel ➤ Administrative Tools ➤ Computer Management.

The Disk Management utility's opening window, shown in Figure 3.7, shows the following information:

- The volumes that are recognized by the computer

- The type of disk: basic, dynamic, or GPT

- The type of file system used by each partition

- The status of the partition and whether the partition contains the system or boot partition

- The capacity (amount of space) allocated to the partition

- The amount of free space remaining on the partition

- The amount of overhead associated with the partition

Installation

PART I

Figure 3.7: The Disk Management window

Windows 7 also includes a command-line utility called diskpart, which you can use as a command-line alternative to the Disk Management utility. You can view all the options associated with the diskpart utility by typing **diskpart** at a command prompt, and then typing **?** at the diskpart prompt.

The Disk Management utility allows you to configure and manage your disks. Let's take a look at some of the tasks that you can perform in Disk Management.

Managing Administrative Hard Disk Tasks

The Disk Management utility allows you to perform a variety of hard drive administrative tasks. These tasks are discussed in the sections that follow:

- Viewing disk properties
- Viewing volume and local disk properties
- Adding a new disk
- Creating partitions and volumes
- Upgrading a basic disk to a dynamic or GPT disk

- Changing a drive letter and path
- Deleting partitions and volumes

Viewing Disk Properties

To view the properties of a disk, right-click the disk number in the lower panel of the Disk Management main window and choose Properties from the context menu. This brings up the disk's Properties dialog box. Click the Volumes tab, as shown in Figure 3.8, to see the volumes associated with the disk, which contains the following disk properties:

- The disk number
- The type of disk (basic, dynamic, CD-ROM, removable, DVD, or unknown)
- The status of the disk (online or offline)
- Partition style (MBR or GPT)
- The capacity of the disk
- The amount of unallocated space on the disk
- The logical volumes that have been defined on the physical drive

Figure 3.8: The Volumes tab of a disk's Properties dialog box

Disk Properties

If you click the General tab of a disk's Properties dialog box, the hardware device type, the hardware vendor that produced the drive, the physical location of the drive, and the device status are displayed.

Viewing Volume and Local Disk Properties

On a dynamic disk, you manage volume properties. On a basic disk, you manage partition properties. Volumes and partitions perform the same function, and the options discussed in the following sections apply to both. (The examples here are based on a dynamic disk using a simple volume. If you're using basic storage, you'll view the local disk properties rather than the volume properties.)

To see the properties of a volume, right-click the volume in the upper panel of the Disk Management main window and choose Properties. This brings up the volume's Properties dialog box. Volume properties are organized on seven tabs: General, Tools, Hardware, Sharing, Security, Previous Versions, and Quota. The Security and Quota tabs appear only for NTFS volumes. Let's explore all these tabs in detail:

General   The information on the General tab of the volume's Properties dialog box, as shown in Figure 3.9, gives you an idea of how the volume is configured. This dialog box shows the label, type, file system, used and free space, and capacity of the volume. The label is shown in an editable text box, and you can change it if desired. The space allocated to the volume is shown in a graphical representation as well as in text form.

The label on a volume or local disk is for informational purposes only. For example, depending on its use, you might give a volume a label such as APPS or ACCTDB.

The Disk Cleanup button starts the Disk Cleanup utility, with which you can delete unnecessary files and free disk space.

This tab also allows you to configure compression for the volume and to indicate whether the volume should be indexed.

Figure 3.9: General properties for a volume

Tools   The Tools tab of the volume's Properties dialog box, shown in Figure 3.10, provides access to three tools, as follows:

- Click the Check Now button to run the Error-Checking utility to check the volume for errors. You'd do this if you were experiencing problems accessing the volume or if the volume had been open during a system restart that did not go through a proper shutdown sequence.

- Click the Defragment Now button to run the Disk Defragmenter utility. This utility defragments files on the volume by storing the files contiguously on the hard drive.

- Click the Back Up Now button to open the Backup Status and Configuration dialog box, which allows you to configure backup procedures.

Figure 3.10: The Tools tab of the volume's Properties dialog box

Hardware The Hardware tab of the volume's Properties dialog box, shown in Figure 3.11, lists the hardware associated with the disk drives that are recognized by the Windows 7 operating system. The bottom half of the dialog box shows the properties of the device that's highlighted in the top half of the dialog box.

For more details about a hardware item, highlight it and click the Properties button in the lower-right corner of the dialog box. This brings up a Properties dialog box for the item. Your Device Status field should report that "This device is working properly." If that's not the case, you can click the Troubleshoot button to open a troubleshooting wizard that will help you discover what the problem is.

Sharing On the Sharing tab of the volume's Properties dialog box, shown in Figure 3.12, you can specify whether or not the volume is shared. Volumes are not shared by default. To share a volume, click the Advanced Sharing button, which lets you specify whether the volume is shared and, if so, what the name of the share should be. You can also specify who will have access to the shared volume.

Security The Security tab of the volume's Properties dialog box, shown in Figure 3.13, appears only for NTFS volumes. Use the Security tab to set the NTFS permissions for the volume.

Figure 3.11: The Hardware tab of the volume's Properties dialog box

Figure 3.12: The Sharing tab of the volume's Properties dialog box

Figure 3.13: The Security tab of the volume's Properties dialog box

Previous Versions   The Previous Versions tab displays shadow copies of the files that are created by System Restore, as shown in Figure 3.14. Shadow copies of files are backup copies created by Windows in the background in order to enable you to restore the system to a previous state. On the Previous Versions tab, you can select a copy of the volume and either view the contents of the shadow copy or copy the shadow copy to another location. If System Restore is not enabled, then shadow copies of a volume will not be created.

Quotas   Quotas give you the advantage of limiting the amount of hard disk space that a user can have on a volume or partition, as shown in Figure 3.15. There are a few options that you can configure when you enable quotas. By default, quotas are disabled. To enable quotas, check the Enable Quota Management check box.

The "Deny disk space to users exceeding quota limit" check box is an option. With this box enabled, you can:

- Deny disk storage to users who exceed their quota limit
- Monitor quotas
- Set the size of quota limits and warnings
- Log quota events

Figure 3.14: The Previous Versions tab of the volume's Properties dialog box

Figure 3.15: The Quota tab of the volume's Properties dialog box

Adding a New Disk

You can add new hard disks to a system in order to increase the amount of disk storage you have. This is a fairly common task that you'll need to perform as your application programs and files grow larger.

How you add a disk depends on whether your computer supports hot swapping of drives. Hot swapping is the process of adding a new hard drive while the computer is turned on. Most desktop computers do not support this capability. Remember, your user account must be a member of the Administrators group in order to install a new drive. The following list specifies configuration options:

Computer Doesn't Support Hot Swapping   If your computer does not support hot swapping, you must first shut down the computer before you add a new disk. Then add the drive according to the manufacturer's directions. When you finish, restart the computer. You should find the new drive listed in the Disk Management utility.

Computer Supports Hot Swapping   If your computer does support hot swapping, you don't need to turn off your computer first. Just add the drive according to the manufacturer's directions. Then open the Disk Management utility and select Action ➤ Rescan Disks. You should find the new drive listed in the Disk Management utility.

After you add a new disk, the next step is to create a partition (on a basic disk) or a volume (on a dynamic disk). Partitions and volumes fill similar roles in the storage of data on disks, and the processes for creating them are the same.

Creating a Volume or a Partition

Creating a volume or partition is a fairly easy process. To create the new volume or partition, right-click the unformatted free space and start the wizard. The New Volume Wizard guides you through the process of creating a new volume, as follows:

1. In the Disk Management utility, right-click an area of free storage space and choose the type of volume to create. If only one drive is installed, you'll only be able to create a simple volume. You can click New Simple Volume to create a new simple volume.

2. The Welcome To The New Simple Volume Wizard screen appears. Click Next.

3. The Select Volume Size screen appears. Select the size of the volume that you want to create and then click Next.

4. Next you see the Assign Drive Letter Or Path screen, as shown in Figure 3.16. You can specify a drive letter, mount the volume as an empty folder, or choose not to assign a drive letter or drive path. If you choose to mount the volume as an empty folder, you can have an unlimited number of volumes, negating the drive-letter limitation. If you choose not to assign a drive letter or path, users will not be able to access the volume. Make your selections and click Next.

Figure 3.16: The Assign Drive Letter Or Path screen

5. The Format Partition screen appears, as shown in Figure 3.17. This screen allows you to choose whether you will format the volume. If you choose to format the volume, you can format it as FAT32 or NTFS. You can also select the allocation block size, enter a volume label (for information only), specify a quick format, or choose to enable file and folder compression. After you've made your choices, click Next.

6. The Completing The New Volume Wizard screen appears next. Verify your selections. If you need to change any of them, click the Back button to reach the appropriate screen. When everything is correctly set, click Finish.

Now that we created a new volume or partition, let's take a look at how to convert a basic disk to dynamic or GPT.

Figure 3.17: The Format Partition screen

Upgrading a Basic Disk to a Dynamic or GPT Disk

When you install a fresh installation of Windows 7, your drives are configured as basic disks. To take advantage of the features offered by Windows 7 dynamic or GPT disks, you must upgrade your basic disks to either dynamic or GPT disks.

Upgrading Disks

Upgrading basic disks to dynamic disks is a one-way process as far as preserving data is concerned and a potentially dangerous operation. Before you perform this upgrade (or make any major change to your drives or volumes), create a new backup of the drive or volume and verify that you can successfully restore the backup.

You can convert any basic partition to a dynamic disk, but you can only convert unformatted free space to a GPT disk.

Perform the following steps to convert a drive to a GPT:

1. If the volume or partition that you want to convert has data, first delete the partition or volume.

2. Open the Disk Management utility by clicking the Start button, right-click Computers, and choose Manage.

3. Click Disk Management in the lower-left section.

4. Right-click the drive letter and choose Convert To GPT Disk, as shown in Figure 3.18.

5. After the disk converts, you can right-click the disk and see that the Convert To MBR Disk option is now available.

Figure 3.18: Choosing Convert To GPT Disk

Converting to a GPT Disk

There are a few other methods for converting a basic disk to a GPT disk. You can use the diskpart utility and type the **Convert GPT** command. You can also create a GPT disk when you first install a new hard drive. After you install the new hard drive, during the initialization phase you can choose GPT Disk.

Another type of conversion that you might need to perform is converting a basic disk to a dynamic disk. Follow these steps:

1. In the Disk Management utility, right-click the disk you want to convert and select the Convert To Dynamic Disk option.

2. In the Convert To Dynamic Disk dialog box, check the disk that you want to upgrade and click OK.

3. In the Disks To Convert dialog box, click Convert.

4. A confirmation dialog box warns you that you will no longer be able to boot previous versions of Windows from this disk. Click Yes to continue to convert the disk.

Benefits of Converting Disks

For many years, IT managers used just basic disks. There's a huge disadvantage to just using basic disks. Basic disks can't be extended without the use of a third-party utility. One problem that many IT managers ran into related to home folder storage. Home folders are storage areas on the server for your users. Users store data on the home folders and that data can then be backed up.

The main issue with home folders is that the space you give your users is never enough. The home folders tend to fill up your hard drive or partition. With basic disks, you could not extend the partition. But one of the advantages of dynamic disks is that they can be extended (as long as they are formatted with NTFS). Now if the hard disk or volume fills up, just extend the volume to a free area on the hard disk or add another hard drive. This is a huge advantage to anyone who has dealt with hard drives or partitions filling up.

As you are configuring the volumes or partitions on the hard drive, another thing that you might need to configure is the drive letter and paths.

Changing the Drive Letter and Path

There might be times when you need to change drive letters and paths when you add new equipment. Let's suppose that you have a hard drive with two partitions; drive C is assigned as your first partition and drive D as your second partition. Your DVD-ROM is assigned the drive letter of E. You add a new hard drive and partition it as a new volume. By default, the new partition is assigned as drive F. If you want your logical drives to appear listed before the DVD-ROM drive, you can use the Disk Management utility's Change Drive Letter And Paths option to rearrange your drive letters.

When you need to reassign drive letters, right-click the volume for which you want to change the drive letter and choose Change Drive Letter And Paths. This brings up the dialog box shown in Figure 3.19.

Click the Change button to access the Change Drive Letter Or Path dialog box, as shown in Figure 3.20. Use the drop-down list next to the Assign The Following Drive Letter option to select the drive letter you want to assign to the volume.

TIP   If a drive letter is already assigned, then you can't use it. It won't come up in the list.

Installation

PART I

Figure 3.19: The dialog box for changing a drive letter or path

Figure 3.20: Editing the drive letter

Perform the following steps to edit the drive letter of the partition you created:

1. Select Start ➤ Control Panel ➤ System And Maintenance ➤ Administrative Tools. Double-click Computer Management; then expand Storage and then Disk Management.

2. Right-click a drive that you have created and select Change Drive Letter And Paths.

3. In the Change Drive Letter And Paths dialog box, click Change.

4. In the Change Drive Letter Or Path dialog box, select a new drive letter and click OK.

5. In the dialog box that appears, click Yes to confirm that you want to change the drive letter.

Another task that you might need to perform is deleting a partition or volume that you have created. The next section looks at these tasks.

Deleting Partitions and Volumes

When you configure your hard disks, there may be a time that you want to reconfigure your drive by deleting the partitions or volumes on the hard drive. You may also want to delete a volume so that you can extend another volume. You can configure these tasks in Disk Management.

When you delete a volume or partition, you see a warning that all the data on the partition or volume will be lost. You have to click Yes to confirm that you want to delete the volume or partition. This confirmation is important because after you delete a partition or volume, it's gone for good.

In the following steps, you will delete a partition that you have created. When you delete a partition or volume, make sure that it's an empty partition or volume or back up all the data before the deletion.

1. In the Disk Management utility, right-click the volume or partition that you want to remove and choose Delete Volume.

2. A warning box appears stating that after this volume is deleted, all data will be lost. Click Yes. The volume will be removed and the area will be returned as unformatted free space.

Now that we've looked at some of the basic tasks of Disk Management, let's explore how to manage storage.

Manage Dynamic Storage

The Disk Management utility offers support for managing storage. You can create, delete, and format partitions or volumes on your hard drives. You can also extend or shrink volumes on dynamic disks. Additionally, you can delete volume sets and striped sets. The first section I will cover is dynamic storage and volumes.

As noted previously in this chapter, a dynamic disk can contain simple, spanned, or striped volumes. With the Disk Management utility you can create volumes of each type. You can also create an extended volume, which is the process of adding disk space to a single simple volume. The following sections describe these disk management tasks.

Creating Simple, Spanned, and Striped Volumes

As explained previously, you use the New Volume Wizard to create a new volume. To start the New Volume Wizard, in the Disk Management utility right-click an area of free space where you want to create the volume. Then you can choose the type of volume you want to create: Simple, Spanned, or Striped.

When you choose to create a spanned volume, you are creating a new volume from scratch that includes space from two or more physical drives, up to a maximum of 32 drives.

When you choose to create a striped volume, you are creating a new volume that combines free space from two to 32 drives into a single logical partition. The free space on all drives must be equal in size. Data in the striped volume is written across all drives in 64 KB stripes. (Data in spanned and extended volumes is written sequentially.)

Striped volumes are RAID 0 because striped volumes do not offer any type of redundancy. Striped volumes offer you better performance and are normally used for temporary files or folder. The problem with a striped volume is if you lose one of the drives in the volume, the entire striped volume is lost.

Another option that you have with volumes is extending the volumes to create a larger storage area, which I discuss in the next section.

Creating Extended Volumes

When you create an extended volume, you are taking a single, simple volume (maybe one that is almost out of disk space) and adding more disk space to it, using free space that exists on the same physical hard drive. When the volume is extended, it is seen as a single drive letter. To extend a volume, the simple volume must be formatted as NTFS. You cannot extend a system or boot partition.

An extended volume assumes that you are using only one physical drive. A spanned volume assumes that you are using two or more physical drives.

Perform the following steps to create an extended volume:

1. In the Disk Management utility, right-click the volume you want to extend and choose Extend Volume.

2. The Extend Volume Wizard starts. Click Next.

3. The Select Disks screen appears, as shown in Figure 3.21. You can specify the maximum size of the extended volume. The maximum size you can specify is determined by the amount of free space that exists in all of the dynamic drives on your computer. Click Next.

Figure 3.21: The Select Disks screen

4. The Completing The Extend Volume Wizard screen appears. Click Finish.

After a volume is extended, no portion of the volume can be deleted without losing data on the entire set. (However, you can shrink a volume without losing data by using the Shrink Volume option in Disk Management.)

One issue that you might run into with hard drives is that they go bad from time to time. In case you have never heard a hard drive fail, there is a distinct clicking. Once you experience it, you will never forget it. When drives go bad, Disk Management can help determine which drive is experiencing the problem and what the issue might be. In the next section, we'll look at hard disk errors.

Troubleshoot with Disk Management

You can use the Disk Management utility to troubleshoot disk errors through a set of status codes; however, if a disk will not initialize, no status code is displayed. Disks will not initialize if there is no valid disk signature.

The problem with disk errors is that you don't know when a disk fails or which disk failed. Disk Management can help you with this. When disks have problems or errors, status codes get assigned. Knowing what these codes mean will help you determine what the problem is but, more importantly, what steps you need to take to fix the problem.

In the troubleshooting section I will discuss many of the error codes that Disk Management can issue to the disk, volume, or partition.

Using Disk Management Status Codes

The main window of the Disk Management utility displays the status of disks and volumes. Table 3.3 contains the possible status codes and a description of each code; these are very useful in troubleshooting disk problems.

Table 3.3: Disk and Volume Status Codes

Status Code	Description
Online	Indicates that the disk is accessible and that it is functioning properly. This is the normal disk status.
Online (Errors)	Indicates that I/O errors have been detected on the dynamic disk. Only used with dynamic disks. One possible fix for this error is to right-click the disk and select Reactivate Disk to attempt to return the disk to Online status. This fix will work only if the I/O errors were temporary. You should immediately back up your data if you see this error and suspect that the I/O errors are not temporary.
Healthy	Specifies that the volume is accessible and functioning properly.
Healthy (At Risk)	Indicates that a dynamic volume is currently accessible but I/O errors have been detected on the underlying dynamic disk. This option is usually associated with Online (Errors) for the underlying disk.

Table 3.3: Disk and Volume Status Codes *(continued)*

Status Code	Description
Offline or Missing	Indicates that the disk is not accessible. Used only with dynamic disks This error can occur if the disk is corrupted or the hardware has failed. If the error is not caused by hardware failure or major corruption, you may be able to re-access the disk by using the Reactivate Disk option to return the disk to Online status. If the disk was originally offline and then the status changed to Missing, it indicates that the disk has become corrupted, has been powered down, or was disconnected.
Unreadable	Indicates that the disk is inaccessible and might have encountered hardware errors, corruption, or I/O errors or that the system disk configuration database is corrupted. This can occur on basic or dynamic disks. This message may also appear when a disk is spinning up while the Disk Management utility is rescanning the disks on the computer.
Failed	Specifies that the volume can't be started. Can be seen with basic or dynamic volumes. This error can occur because the disk is damaged or the file system is corrupted. If this message occurs with a basic volume, you should check the underlying disk hardware. If the error occurs on a dynamic volume, verify that the underlying disks are Online.
Unknown	Occurs if the boot sector for the volume becomes corrupted—for example, from a virus. Used with basic and dynamic volumes. This error can also occur if no disk signature is created for the volume.
Incomplete	Occurs when you move some, but not all, of the disks from a multidisk volume. If you do not complete the multivolume set, the data will be inaccessible.
Foreign	Occurs if you move a dynamic disk from a computer running Windows 2000 (any version), Windows XP Professional, Windows Vista, Windows Server 2003, or Windows Server 2008 to a Windows 7 computer. This error is caused because configuration data is unique to computers where the dynamic disk was created. You can correct this error by right-clicking the disk and selecting the option Import Foreign Disks. Any existing volume information will then be visible and accessible.

Besides knowing the error codes, you might face other issues that can arise when installing or configuring disks. One issue that might occur is that a disk fails to initialize when installed.

Troubleshooting Disks That Fail to Initialize

When you add a new disk to your computer in Windows 7, the disk does not initially contain a disk signature, which is required for the disk to be recognized by Windows. Disk signatures are at the end of the sector marker on the Master Boot Record (MBR) of the drive.

When you install a new drive and run the Disk Management utility, a wizard starts and lists all new disks that have been detected. The disk signature is written through this process. If you cancel the wizard before the disk signature is written, you see the disk status Not Initialized. To initialize a disk, right-click the disk you want to initialize and select the Initialize Disk option.

As you have seen, Disk Management can be a useful tool in your computer management arsenal. If you decide to format your partition or volume using NTFS, you then receive added benefits like compression, encryption, quotas, and security. In the next section, I will look at some of these benefits.

Installation

PART I

Manage Data Compression

One of the advantages of using NTFS over FAT32 is the ability to compress data. I teach IT administrators data compression, and I like to refer to a well-known infomercial where people put all of their blankets into a large bag—and then they hook a vacuum to the bag and suck all the air out. This is a great example of how compression works. Data compression is the process of storing data in a form that takes less space than uncompressed data.

If you have ever "zipped" or "packed" a file, you have used a form of data compression. The compression algorithms support cluster sizes only up to 4 KB, so if you are using larger cluster sizes, NTFS compression support is not available. If you have permission to modify an NTFS volume, you can manage data compression through Windows Explorer or the Compact command-line utility.

Files and Folders   Files as well as folders in an NTFS file system can be either compressed or uncompressed. Files and folders are managed independently, which means that a compressed folder can contain uncompressed files, and an uncompressed folder can contain compressed files.

Transparency   Access to compressed files by applications is transparent. For example, if you access a compressed file through Microsoft Word, the file will be uncompressed automatically when it is opened and then automatically compressed again when it is closed.

Lag Time   Compression happens quickly, but if, for example, you compress a 500 GB hard drive, you can't guarantee that there won't be any lag time on your machine or server.

FAT32   Data compression is available only on NTFS partitions. Because of this, if you copy or move a compressed folder or file to a FAT32 partition, Windows 7 automatically uncompresses the folder or file.

System Files   Certain system files (for example, `pagefile.sys`) can't be compressed.

Color Coding   You also have the ability to show compressed files and folders with an alternate color.

Perform the following steps to compress and uncompress folders and files:

1. Select Start ➤ Run; then type **Explorer** and click OK.

2. In Windows Explorer, find and select Computer, a Local Disk (C:), and then a folder on that drive. The folder you select should contain files.

3. Right-click the folder and select Properties. On the General tab of the folder's Properties dialog box, note the value listed for Size On Disk. Then click Advanced.

4. In the Advanced Attributes dialog box, check the Compress Contents To Save Disk Space option, as shown in Figure 3.22. Then click OK.

Figure 3.22: Advanced Attributes screen

5. In the Confirm Attribute Changes dialog box, select the option Apply Changes To This Folder, Subfolders And Files. (If this confirmation dialog box does not appear, you can display it by clicking the Apply button in the Properties dialog box.) Click OK to confirm your changes.

6. On the General tab of the folder's Properties dialog box, note the value that now appears for Size On Disk. This size should have decreased because you compressed the folder.

To uncompress folders and files, repeat the steps of this exercise and uncheck the Compress Contents To Save Disk Space option in the Advanced Attributes dialog box.

As I said previously, you can specify that compressed files be displayed in a different color from the uncompressed files. To do so, in Windows Explorer select Organize ➢ Folder And Search Options ➢ View. Under Files And Folders, check the Show Encrypted Or Compressed NTFS Files In Color option.

Besides compressing files and folders in Windows Explorer, you can also compress the files and folders using the Compact command-line utility.

Using the Compact Command-Line Utility

The command-line options for managing file and folder compression are Compact and Expand. You can access these commands from a command prompt. Using the Compact utility offers you more control over file and folder compression than Windows Explorer. For example, you can use the Compact command with a batch script or to compress only files that meet a specific criterion (for example, all the DOC files in a specific folder). Some of the options that you can use with the Compact command are shown in Table 3.4.

Table 3.4: Compact and Expand Commands

Option	Purpose
/C	Compresses the specified file or folder
/U	Uncompresses the specified file or folder
/S:dir	Specifies which folder should be compressed or uncompressed

Installation

PART I

Table 3.4: Compact and Expand Commands *(continued)*

Option	Purpose
/A	Displays any files that have hidden or system file attributes
/I	Indicates that any errors should be ignored
/F	Forces a file to be compressed
/Q	Reports only critical information, when used with reporting
/?	Displays help

Compression is a nice advantage to using NTFS but another advantage is data encryption. In the following section I discuss the benefits of using data encryption.

Manage Data Encryption with EFS

Data encryption is a way to increase data security. Encryption is the process of translating data into code that is not easily accessible to users other than the person who encrypted the data. After data has been encrypted, you must have the correct key (SID number) to decrypt the data. Unencrypted data is known as plain text, and encrypted data is known as cipher text.

The Encrypting File System (EFS) is the Windows 7 technology that is used to store encrypted files on NTFS partitions. Encrypted files add an extra layer of security to your file system. A user with the proper key can transparently access encrypted files. A user without the proper key is denied access. If the user who encrypted the files is unavailable, you can use the data recovery agent (DRA) to provide the proper key to decrypt folders or files.

The EFS features included with Windows 7 include some of the following:

- The ability to automatically color-code encrypted files in green text, so you can easily identify files that have been encrypted

- Support so that offline folders can also be encrypted

- A shell user interface (UI) that is used to support encrypted files for multiple users

- Control over who can read the encrypted files

In the following sections you'll learn how to encrypt and decrypt data, create and manage DRAs, recover encrypted files, share encrypted files, and use the Cipher utility.

Encrypting and Decrypting Folders and Files

To use EFS, a user specifies that a folder or file on an NTFS partition should be encrypted. The encryption is transparent to users. However, when other users try to access the file, they will not be able to unencrypt the file—even if those users have Full Control NTFS permissions. Instead, they receive an error message.

Compression and Encryption

Windows 7 does not allow you to have a folder or file compressed and encrypted at the same time. Windows Server 2003 and Windows Server 2008 do support concurrent compression and encryption.

Perform the following steps to learn to use EFS to encrypt a folder. For this exercise, before you encrypt any data you must create a new user.

1. To create a new user, select Start ➤ Control Panel ➤ System And Maintenance ➤ Administrative Tools. Under System Tools, expand Local Users And Groups and right-click the Users folder. Choose New User.

2. Create a new user named Paige and make her password P@ssw0rd. Deselect the User Must Change Password At Next Logon option for this user. Click Create.

3. Close Computer Management.

4. Select Start and type Explorer in the Search box.

5. In Windows Explorer, find and select a folder on the C drive. The folder you select should contain files. Right-click the folder and select Properties.

6. On the General tab of the folder's Properties dialog box, click Advanced.

7. In the Advanced Attributes dialog box, check the Encrypt Contents To Secure Data option. Then click OK.

8. In the Confirm Attribute Changes dialog box (if this dialog box does not appear, click the Apply button in the Properties dialog box to display it), select Apply Changes To This Folder, Subfolders And Files. Then click OK.

9. Log off as Administrator and log on as Paige.

10. Open Windows Explorer and attempt to access one of the files in the folder you encrypted. You should receive an error message stating that the file is not accessible.

11. Log off as Paige and log on as Administrator.

To decrypt folders and files, repeat these steps, but uncheck the Encrypt Contents To Secure Data option in the Advanced Attributes dialog box.

The problem with encryption is that no one but the user who encrypts the data can open the files. But the owner of the data can share the encrypted files with other users. In the next section, I'll show you at how to share your encrypted data with other users.

Managing EFS File Sharing

In Windows 7, it is possible to share encrypted files with another person or between two computers. To share encrypted files, you must have a valid EFS certificate for the user who should have access to the file. By implementing EFS file sharing, you provide an additional level of recovery in the event that the person who encrypted the files is unavailable.

Perform the following steps to implement EFS file sharing:

1. Encrypt the file if it is not already encrypted (see the previous section for the steps involved).

2. Through Windows Explorer, access the encrypted file's properties. At the bottom of the dialog box, click Advanced.

3. The Advanced Attributes dialog box appears. In the Compress Or Encrypt Attributes section of the Advanced Attributes dialog box, click the Details button.

4. When the Encryption Details dialog box opens, click the Add button to add any additional users (provided they have a valid

certificate for EFS in Active Directory or that you have imported a valid certificate from the server side onto the local computer) who should have access to the encrypted file.

5. Close the Properties box for the folder.

Once files or folders are encrypted, you might run into difficulties when the data must be accessed and the user who encrypted it is not available. There are a few ways to unencrypt the data. In the next section I will show you how to recover encrypted data.

Using the DRA to Recover Encrypted Data

You can use the data recovery agent (DRA) to access the encrypted files. DRAs are implemented differently depending on the version of your operating system and the configuration of your computer.

- For Windows 7 computers that are a part of a Windows Server 2008 Active Directory domain, the domain Administrator user account is automatically assigned the role of DRA.

- For Windows 7 computers that are installed as stand-alone computers or if the computer is a part of a workgroup, no default DRA is assigned.

WARNING You should use extreme caution when using EFS on a stand-alone Windows 7 computer. If the key used to encrypt the files is lost, there is no default recovery process, and all access to the files will be lost.

Creating a DRA on a Stand-Alone Windows 7 Computer

If you install Windows 7 on a stand-alone computer or on a computer that is part of a workgroup, then no DRA is created by default. To manually create a DRA, use the Cipher command-line utility as follows:

```
Cipher /R:filename
```

The /R switch is used to generate two files, one with a .pfx extension and one with a .cer extension. The PFX file is used for data recovery, and the CER file includes a self-signed EFS recovery agent certificate.

The CER file (self-signed public key certificate) can then be imported by an administrator into the local security policy, and the PFX file (private key) can be stored by an administrator in a secure location. Cipher is explained further in the next section.

After you create the public and private keys to be used with EFS, perform the following steps to specify the DRA through Local Security Policy:

1. Through Local Security Policy, which you can access through Administrative Tools or the Local Computer Policy MMC snap-in, expand Public Key Policies and then Encrypting File System, as shown in Figure 3.23.

Figure 3.23: Encrypting File System in Local Policies

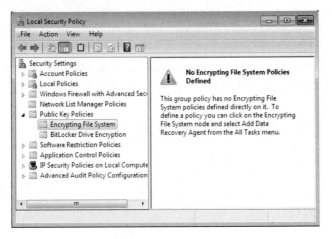

2. Right-click Encrypting File System and select Add Data Recovery Agent.

3. The Add Recovery Agent Wizard starts. Click Next to continue.

4. The Select Recovery Agents screen appears, as shown in Figure 3.24. Click the Browse Folders button to access the CER file you created with the Cipher /R:*filename* command. Select the certificate and click Next.

Figure 3.24: The Select Recovery Agents screen of the Add Recovery Agent Wizard

5. The Completing The Add Recovery Agent Wizard screen appears. Confirm that the settings are correct and click Finish.

You will see the data recovery agent listed in the Local Security Settings dialog box, under Encrypting File System. Let's continue encryption with recovering encrypted files in the next section.

Recovering Encrypted Files

If the DRA has the private key to the DRA certificate (that was created through Cipher /R:*filename*), the DRA can decrypt files in the same manner as the user who originally encrypted the file. After the encrypted files are opened by a DRA, they are available as unencrypted files and can be stored as either encrypted or unencrypted files.

Using the Cipher Utility

Cipher is a command-line utility that you can use to encrypt files on NTFS volumes. The syntax for the Cipher command is as follows:

```
Cipher /[command parameter] [filename]
```

Table 3.5 lists common command parameters associated with the Cipher command. This list is only a partial representation of all the Cipher commands.

Table 3.5: Cipher Command Parameters

Parameter	Description
/E	Specifies that files or folders should be encrypted. Any files that are subsequently added to the folder will be encrypted.
/D	Specifies that files or folders should be decrypted. Any files that are subsequently added to the folder will not be encrypted.
/S:dir	Specifies that subfolders of the target folder should also be encrypted or decrypted based on the option specified.
/I	Causes any errors that occur to be ignored. By default, the Cipher utility stops whenever an error occurs.
/H	Specifies that hidden and system files should be displayed. By default, files with hidden or system attributes are omitted from display.
/K	Creates a new certificate file and certificate key.
/R	Generates a recovery agent key and certificate for use with EFS.
/X	Backs up the EFS certificate and keys into the specified file name.

Perform the following steps to use the Cipher utility to encrypt files. Make sure that you have encrypted a folder on the C drive before you complete these steps.

1. Select Start ➢ All Programs ➢ Accessories ➢ Command Prompt.

2. In the Command Prompt dialog box, type **C:** and press Enter to access the C drive.

3. At the C:\> prompt, type **cipher**. You'll see a list of folders and files and the state of encryption. The folder you encrypted should be indicated by an E.

4. Type **MD TEST** and press Enter to create a new folder named Test.

5. Type **cipher /e test** and press Enter. You'll see a message verifying that the folder was encrypted.

By now you have seen many of the advantages of using NTFS to format your volumes and partitions. Next, I look at how to keep these volumes and partitions running at peak performance.

Use Disk Maintenance Tools

As IT professionals, part of our job is to keep our systems running the best way that they can. Most of us have seen machines running quickly when they are new, but then they start to slow down over time—even when we do not install any new software.

Microsoft Windows 7 includes a few utilities that you can run to help keep your system running efficiently. In the next sections I discuss three of these utilities—Disk Defragmenter, Disk Cleanup, and Check Disk.

Running the Disk Defragmenter Utility

Data is normally stored sequentially on the disk as space is available. Fragmentation naturally occurs as users create, delete, and modify files. The access of noncontiguous data is transparent to the user; however, when data is stored in this manner, the operating system must search through the disk to access all the pieces of a file. This slows down data access.

Disk defragmentation rearranges the existing files so they are stored contiguously, which optimizes access to those files. In Windows 7, you use the Disk Defragmenter utility to defragment your disk.

In the Disk Defragmenter window, shown in Figure 3.25, you can schedule when the Disk Defragmenter should run or run the Disk Defragmenter tool immediately.

Figure 3.25: The Disk Defragmenter window

You can also defragment disks through the command-line utility, defrag. The disk needs to have at least 15 percent free space for defrag to run properly. You can analyze the state of the disk by using Defrag VolumeName /a.

Perform the following steps to defragment your Windows 7 machine:

1. Start the Disk Defragmenter utility by opening Computer Management.

2. Right-click the C drive and choose Properties.

3. Click the Tools tab.

4. Click the Defragment Now button.

5. Either schedule a defragment or click the Defragment Disk button to start the defragment immediately.

It is a good practice to run Disk Defragmenter at least once a week on a Windows 7 machine that is constantly being used. If the machine is not used that often, you can space out how often you defrag the machine.

In the next section I discuss another tool that is included with Windows 7: the Disk Cleanup utility.

Running the Disk Cleanup Utility

One concern that most IT professionals face is how to conserve hard disk space for users. Hard drives continue to get larger and larger but so do applications. This is where the Disk Cleanup utility can help.

When the Disk Cleanup utility runs, it calculates the amount of disk space you can free up. Perform the following steps to run the Disk Cleanup utility:

1. Select Start ➢ Control Panel ➢ System And Maintenance ➢ Administrative Tools ➢ Computer Management.

2. Right-click the drive and choose Properties.

3. On the General tab, click the Disk Cleanup button. The Disk Cleanup utility will start to calculate the system data.

4. After the analysis is complete, you will see the Disk Cleanup dialog box, as shown in Figure 3.26, which lists files that are suggested for deletion and shows how much space will be gained by deleting those files. Click OK.

Figure 3.26: The Disk Cleanup utility

5. When you are asked to confirm that you want to delete the files, click Yes. The Disk Cleanup utility deletes the files and automatically closes the Disk Cleanup dialog box.

Another issue that you might run into is bad sectors on your hard disk. Windows 7 also includes a utility to help you troubleshoot disk devices and volumes.

Running the Check Disk Utility

If you are having trouble with your disk devices or volumes, you can use the Windows 7 Check Disk utility. This utility detects bad sectors, attempts to fix errors in the file system, and scans for and attempts to recover bad sectors. To use Check Disk, you must be logged in as a member of the Administrators group.

File system errors can be caused by a corrupted file system or by hardware errors. If you have software errors, the Check Disk utility might help you find them. There is no way to fix hardware errors through software, however. If you have excessive hardware errors, you should replace the disk drive.

Perform the following steps to run the Check Disk utility:

1. Select Start ➤ Control Panel ➤ System And Maintenance ➤ Administrative Tools.

2. Double-click Computer Management and then expand Storage and select Disk Management.

3. Right-click the drive you wish to check and choose Properties.

4. Click the Tools tab and then click the Check Now button.

5. In the Check Disk dialog box, you can choose one or both of the options to automatically fix file system errors and to scan for and attempt recovery of bad sectors, as shown in Figure 3.27. For this exercise, check both of the disk options check boxes. Then click Start.

Figure 3.27: The Check Disk utility

Another way to run the Check Disk utility is from the command line, using the command Chkdsk. Chkdsk is used to create and display a status report, which is based on the file system you are using.

PART II

Configuration

IN THIS PART ▶

Configuration

PART II

4

Managing the Desktop

IN THIS CHAPTER, YOU WILL LEARN TO:

Configuration

PART II

The Windows 7 operating system allows you to configure the Windows 7 Desktop to suit your own personal preferences. Some of these options include customizing the Taskbar and Start menu, creating shortcuts, setting display properties for user themes, and configuring Windows gadgets.

You have the ability to configure the accessibility options. Accessibility options support users with limited sight. You can configure the Desktop and use Windows 7 utilities to provide a higher degree of accessibility.

You can also configure the Power button to make it easier for your users. Its default setting is Shut Down, but you can change that. Finally, I will look at using a machine with multiple users and how to configure the options to customize these users.

Configure Desktop Settings

The Windows 7 Desktop is the visual setting that appears when a user logs into the operating system. The Desktop includes the wallpaper, Start menu, and icons, as shown in Figure 4.1. When administrators install Windows 7 from a clean install, they will notice that the Desktop contains no icons except for the Recycle Bin.

The Windows 7 Default Desktop appears (on a clean install only) after a user has logged on to a Windows 7 computer for the first time. Users can then configure their Desktops to suit their personal preferences and to work more efficiently. One of the advantages to the Windows 7 Desktop is that administrators can configure the Desktop the way they like it. Microsoft includes premade Desktops called themes. Administrators can set Windows 7 to use the Windows 7 Aero theme, the Windows 7 Standard theme, the Windows 7 Basic theme, the Windows Classic theme, or any customized theme that they want.

The following list shows the common default options that appear on the Start menu and All Programs section:

Getting Started   Use Getting Started to access preset tasks, as shown in Figure 4.2. Some of these tasks include Discover Windows 7, Personalize Windows, Transfer Your Files, Back Up Your Files, and Add New Users.

Windows Media Center   This shortcut starts the Windows Media Center that is used to play the multimedia files.

Calculator   This shortcut starts the Calculator program.

Figure 4.1: Default Windows 7 Desktop and Start menu from a clean install

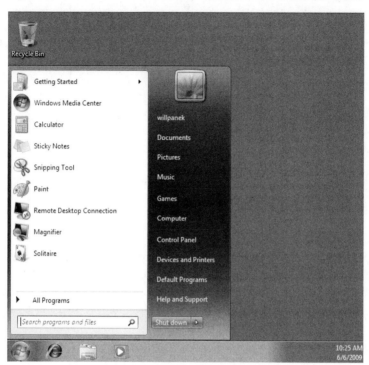

Figure 4.2: Getting Started tasks

Sticky Notes This application places a Sticky Note on the Desktop, like the one shown in Figure 4.3. You can then type a message or reminder onto the Sticky Note. The note remains on the Desktop until you remove it.

Figure 4.3: Sticky Notes

Snipping Tool This tool allows a user to capture an item on the Desktop, as shown in Figure 4.4. The user clicks the Snipping Tool and then drags the cursor around an area that will then be captured. The captured area can be drawn on, highlighted, or saved as a file.

Figure 4.4: Snipping Tool

Paint This shortcut starts the Paint program, an application that allows you to change or manipulate graphic files.

Remote Desktop Connection This program allows a user to connect remotely to another machine. To connect to another computer, the Remote Desktop Connection must be enabled on the receiving computer.

Magnifier The Magnifier utility is one of the Ease of Access utilities. The Ease of Access utilities are included with Windows 7 to allow limited-sight users to experience Windows 7 more easily. Some of these tools include the Magnifier, Narrator, and On-Screen Keyboard.

Solitaire   This shortcut starts the Solitaire game. You can also access this game from the Games section of the Start menu.

All Programs   The Windows 7 Desktop default settings also include the default All Programs section, as shown in Figure 4.5.

Figure 4.5: Default All Programs section

Default Programs   When choosing the Default Programs shortcut, you can access four different configuration items: Set Your Default Programs, Associate A File Type Or Protocol With A Program, Change Autoplay Settings, and Set Program Access And Computer Defaults.

Default Gadget Gallery   This shortcut opens the default Gadget Gallery. Gadgets are mini-applications that can be placed on the Desktop. Gadgets are explained in detail later in this chapter in the section "Configuring Windows Gadgets."

Internet (Internet Explorer 8)   This shortcut starts the built-in web browser. When used with an Internet connection, Internet Explorer 8 provides an interface for accessing the Internet or a local intranet.

Windows DVD Maker   This application is used to view and edit photo and video files to create your own personal DVDs.

Windows Fax And Scan   This application allows the user to create and manage scans and faxes. Windows Fax And Scan allows users to send or receive faxes from their workstation.

Windows Media Center   Windows Media Center lets you watch TV on your computer or laptop. When you start the Media Center for the first time, a wizard walks you through the TV setup. Windows Media Center also allows you to play DVD movies and music.

Windows Media Player   The Windows Media Player allows a user to play all your media files. Windows Media Player allows you to play videos, music, pictures, and recorded TV.

Windows Update   This shortcut allows users to receive updates from either Microsoft's web server or from a Windows Server Update Services (WSUS) machine. Windows Updates allows you to receive updates and security patches for the Windows 7 operating system.

XPS Viewer   The XPS viewer is a new application that allows you to view Microsoft XML Paper Specification (XPS) files. The XPS viewer also allows you to print these files.

Accessories   The Accessories section includes many Windows 7 tools such as Calculator, Command Prompt, Windows PowerShell, Ease Of Use, Run, Paint, Notepad, and so forth, as shown in Figure 4.6.

Figure 4.6: Accessories section of Start menu

Games   This section opens up the games that are included with Windows 7, among them Chess Titans, FreeCell, Games Explorer, Hearts, Internet Backgammon, Internet Checkers, Internet Spades, Mahjong Titans, Minesweeper, Purble Place, Solitaire, and Spider Solitaire.

Maintenance   The Maintenance section includes important maintenance utilities like Backup And Restore, Create A System Repair Disk, Help And Support, and Windows Remote Assistance.

Startup   The Startup section allows you to place application shortcuts in the Startup section. After these shortcuts are placed in the Startup section, the application automatically starts when the system user logs in.

User Documents   This shortcut (shown as willpanek in Figure 4.1) opens the user's personnel folders.

Documents   By default, the Documents folder stores the documents that the user creates. Each user has a unique Documents folder, so even if a computer is shared, individual users have unique personal folders.

Pictures   This application displays any pictures that are in the user's Pictures folder.

Music   This shortcut displays any music that is in the My Music folder.

Computer   This shortcut allows users to centrally manage your computer's files, hard drives, and devices with removable storage. It also allows you to manage system tasks and other places (such as other computers on the network) and to view details about your computer.

Control Panel   Control Panel holds many utilities and tools that allow you to configure your computer. We discuss Control Panel in greater detail in Chapter 5, "Managing the Interface."

Devices And Printers   This shortcut opens the Devices And Printers section. Here you can add or configure any of your hardware devices or printers.

Help And Support   This shortcut is used to access the Windows 7 Help And Support resources. Users can also access Windows 7 online help from this utility.

Search　This feature searches for pictures, music, video, documents, files and folders, computers, or people.

Shut Down Button　This button, also known as the Power button, is used to shut down the computer. There is an arrow next to the button that allows your machine to Switch User, Log Off, Lock, Restart, or Sleep.

Complete the following steps to change the Power button options:

1. Click the Start button and then right-click on the Power button.

2. Choose Properties.

3. On the Power Button Action pull-down menu, choose which action you want to perform when the button is used.

When you configure the Desktop, you have the ability to switch between background and Desktop themes. To switch between these different themes, right-click an area of open space on the Desktop and select Personalize. In the Theme Settings section, you can then select the theme you want to use.

The Desktop also includes the Recycle Bin. The Recycle Bin is a special folder that holds the files and folders that have been deleted, assuming that your hard drive has enough free space to hold the deleted files. If the hard drive is running out of disk space, the files that were deleted first will be copied over. You can retrieve and clear files (for permanent deletion) from the Recycle Bin.

Administrators or users can configure the Desktop by customizing the Taskbar and Start menu, adding shortcuts, and setting display properties. You'll learn about these configurations in the following sections. Let's start with the Desktop themes.

Configuring Windows Aero

Windows Aero is the user interface component of Windows 7. When the Windows Aero theme is configured, open windows are displayed with a transparent glass effect and subtle animations.

To enable Windows Aero, you must first ensure that the Windows 7 theme is selected. This can be accomplished through the Personalization Control Panel option. You can open this Control Panel option by right-clicking the Desktop and selecting Personalize; then choose the Windows 7 theme by clicking the theme you want in the Aero Theme (7) section.

After you choose the Windows 7 theme, you can configure the theme's background picture, color, sounds, and screen savers. To configure the theme's background picture, click the Background link on the bottom and then choose the picture you like. To configure the Windows Aero color scheme, just click the Color link below and then select the color you want from the Color Scheme list.

You do the same for sounds and screen saver. Just click the link below the Themes box and select the sounds and screen saver that you want to use with your theme.

After you specify your Desktop theme, it's time to configure your Taskbar and Start menu.

Perform the following steps to configure your Windows 7 themes:

1. Right-click an open area of the desktop and choose Personalize.

2. Scroll down to the Aero Themes (7) section and choose a theme.

The Personalization dialog box also includes several configurable options that control various aspects of your theme:

Desktop Background   This option lets you pick your Desktop background, which uses a picture or an HTML document as wallpaper.

Windows Color And Appearance   This option allows you to fine-tune the color and style of your windows.

Sounds   This option lets you choose the sounds that will be played based on the action taken. Each action can have its own sound.

Screen Saver   This option lets you select a screen saver that starts after the system has been idle for a specified amount of time. You can also specify a password that must be used to re-access the system after it has been idle. When the idle time has been reached, the computer will be locked, and the password of the user who is currently logged on must be entered to access the computer. You can also adjust monitor power settings.

Windows 7 includes many screen saver options that can be used and configured. Some of these screen saver options are:

- None
- 3D Text
- Blank
- Bubbles

Configuration

PART II

- Mystify
- Photos
- Ribbons

Change Desktop Icons   This option allows users to customize the Desktop icons. Users also have the ability to change shortcut icons.

Change Mouse Pointers   This option allows users to customize the appearance of the mouse pointers.

Change Your Account Picture   This option lets users change their account picture. The account picture is the picture next to your account name when you log on.

Perform the following steps to configure your theme options:

1. Right-click an unoccupied area on the Desktop and select Personalize to open the Personalization dialog box.

2. Select Desktop Background and then select the Picture Library option from the pull-down menu. Click the Clear All box. Then put a check in the picture that you want to use for your Desktop background. In the Picture Position box, choose Fill. Click Save Changes.

3. Click Screen Saver, select the 3d Text, and specify a wait of five minutes. Click OK.

Perform the following steps to change your account picture:

1. Right-click your Desktop and choose Personalize.

2. Click the Change Your Account Picture link in the upper-left corner.

3. Choose a new picture for your account.

4. Click the Change Picture button.

Now that you have seen how to configure your Desktop theme, let's take a look at how to configure your Taskbar and Start menu.

Customizing the Taskbar and Start Menu

Users can customize the Taskbar and Start menu using the Properties dialog box shown in Figure 4.7. The easiest way to access this dialog box is to right-click a blank area in the Taskbar and choose Properties from the context menu.

Figure 4.7: The Taskbar tab of the Taskbar And Start Menu Properties dialog box

The Taskbar And Start Menu Properties dialog box has three tabs: Taskbar, Start Menu, and Toolbars. Let's look at each one.

Configuring Taskbar Properties

On the Taskbar tab of the Taskbar And Start Menu Properties dialog box, you can specify Taskbar features, such as whether the Taskbar is always visible and its location on the screen. Table 4.1 lists the properties on the Taskbar tab.

Table 4.1: Taskbar Properties

Property	Description
Lock The Taskbar	Locks the Taskbar into the current position so it cannot be moved around the Desktop and locks the size of the Taskbar. This option is enabled by default.
Auto-Hide The Taskbar	Hides the Taskbar. This option is disabled by default. When it is enabled, you show the Taskbar by clicking the area of the screen where the Taskbar appears.

Table 4.1: Taskbar Properties *(continued)*

Property	Description
Use Small Icons	Allows the use of small icons on the desktop. This is disabled by default.
Taskbar Location On Screen	Allows you to choose where the Taskbar location will be on your Desktop. The four choices are Bottom, Left, Right, and Top.
Taskbar Buttons	Allows an administrator to decide what to do with the Taskbar buttons. There are three choices: Always Combine And Hide Labels, Combine When Taskbar Is Full, and Never Combine.
Notification Area	Allows you to customize which icons and notifications appear in the notification area.
Preview Desktop With Aero Peek	Allows you to temporarily view the Desktop when you move your mouse to show desktop buttons at the end of the Taskbar.

Next let's look at the second tab and see how to configure the Start menu properties.

Configuring Start Menu Properties

The Start Menu tab of the Taskbar And Start Menu Properties dialog box allows you to customize your Start menu. By selecting this tab, you can customize many of the Windows 7 Start menu options and even configure the Power button.

Users or administrators can add or remove items from the Start menu, remove records of recently accessed items, and specify which Start menu options are configured by clicking the Customize button. Figure 4.8 shows the options for customizing the Start menu for Windows 7.

The Customize Start Menu dialog box shows a list of options that administrators or users can enable or disable to change the look and feel of the Start menu. Table 4.2 lists some of the options that you can configure using the Customize Start Menu dialog box.

Figure 4.8: Customize Start Menu dialog box

Table 4.2: The Start Menu Customizable Options

Option	Settings
Computer	The Computer icon can be configured to be displayed as a link, as a menu, or not displayed at all.
Connect To	The Connect To option can be enabled or disabled.
Control Panel	The Control Panel icon can be configured to be displayed as a link, as a menu, or not displayed at all.
Default Programs	The Default Programs option can be enabled or disabled.
Devices And Printers	Enabled by default. Shows the Devices And Printers shortcut on the Start menu.
Documents	The Documents icon can be configured to be displayed as a link, as a menu, or not displayed at all.
Downloads	This option shows the Downloads folder on the Start menu. The three choices are Display As Link, Display As A Menu, and Don't Display This Item (the default setting).
Enable Context Menus And Dragging And Dropping	The Enable Context Menus And Dragging And Dropping option can be enabled or disabled.

Table 4.2: The Start Menu Customizable Options   *(continued)*

Option	Settings
Favorites Menu	The Favorites menu can be enabled or disabled.
Games	The Games icon can be configured to be displayed as a link, as a menu, or not displayed at all.
Help	The Help option can be enabled or disabled.
Highlight Newly Installed Programs	The Highlight Newly Installed Programs option can be enabled or disabled.
Homegroup	This option displays the Homegroup shortcut on the Start menu. It is not enabled by default.
Music	The Music icon can be configured to be displayed as a link, as a menu, or not displayed at all.
Network	The Network option can be enabled or disabled.
Open Submenus When I Pause On Them With The Mouse Pointer	The Open Submenus When I Pause On Them With The Mouse Pointer option can be enabled or disabled.
Personal Folder	The Personal Folder icon can be configured to be displayed as a link, as a menu, or not displayed at all.
Pictures	The Pictures icon can be configured to be displayed as a link, as a menu, or not displayed at all.
Printers	The Printers option can be enabled or disabled.
Recent Items	This option shows Recent Items on the Start menu. It is not enabled by default.
Recorded TV	This option shows the Recorded TV folder on the Start menu. The three choices are Display As Link, Display As A Menu, and Don't Display This Item (the default setting).
Run Command	The Run Command option can be enabled or disabled.
Search	The Search option can be enabled or disabled.
Search Communications	The Search Communications option can be enabled or disabled.
Search Favorites And History	The Search Favorites And History option can be enabled or disabled.
Search Files	The Search Files icon can be configured to search the user's files, search the entire index, or to not search for files.

Figure 4.9:: The Start Menu Customizable Options *(continued)*

Option	Settings
Search Programs	The Search Programs option can be enabled or disabled.
Sort All Programs Menu By Name	The Sort All Programs Menu By Name option can be enabled or disabled.
System Administrative Tools	The System Administrative Tools icon can be configured to be displayed on the All Programs menu, on the All Programs menu and the Start menu, or not displayed at all.
Use Large Icons	The Use Large Icons option can be enabled or disabled.
Videos	This option shows the Videos folder on the Start menu. The three choices are Display As Link, Display As A Menu, and Don't Display This Item (the default setting).

The final tab in the Taskbar And Start Menu Properties dialog box is Toolbars. Let's take a look.

Configuring Toolbar Options

The Toolbars tab of the Taskbar And Start Menu Properties dialog box allows you to configure which toolbars will be displayed on the Taskbar, as shown in Figure 4.9. The toolbars that can be displayed include the Address, Links, Tablet PC Input Panel, and Desktop toolbars. None of the toolbars are enabled by default.

Figure 4.9: Toolbars tab of the Taskbar And Start Menu Properties dialog box

Perform the following steps to check your current Taskbar and Start menu configuration and then configure Taskbar and Start menu properties:

1. Select Start ➣ All Programs. Note the size of the icons in the Start menu. There is no Programs menu item for Administrative Tools.

2. Right-click an empty space on the Taskbar and choose Properties.

3. Click the Start Menu tab and then click the Customize button.

4. In the Customize Start Menu dialog box, scroll down to System Administrative Tools, click Display On The All Programs Menu And Start Menu, and then click OK twice.

5. Select Start ➣ All Programs and note that the All Programs menu lists Administrative Tools.

6. Edit the Taskbar and Start Menu properties as you like or return them to their default settings.

Knowing how to configure your Start menu allows you to customize the user's environment. Now let's look at how to set up and configure shortcuts.

Configuring Shortcuts

As you know, shortcuts are links to objects that are easily accessible from your computer. You can use a shortcut to quickly access a file, program, folder, printer, or computer from your Desktop. Shortcuts can exist in various locations, including on the Desktop, on the Start menu, and within folders.

To create a shortcut from Windows Explorer, just right-click the item for which you want to create a shortcut, and select Send To ➣ Desktop (Create Shortcut) from the context menu. Then you can click the shortcut and drag it where you want it to appear.

Perform the following steps to create a shortcut and place it on the Desktop:

1. Select Start ➣ All Programs ➣ Accessories ➣ Windows Explorer to start Windows Explorer.

2. Expand Computer, then Local Disk, then Windows, and then System32. Right-click System32 and choose Send To ➣ Desktop (Create Shortcut).

3. In the System32 folder, scroll down until you see Calc. Right-click Calc and select Send To ➤ Desktop (Create Shortcut). A shortcut to calc.exe will be placed on the Desktop.

4. View the Desktop and verify that both shortcuts are present.

After you set up your shortcuts, you can configure how your display will look by adding gadgets. Let's look at how to set up and configure gadgets.

Configure Windows Gadgets

Windows gadgets were first introduced in Windows Vista Sidebar. Windows 7 has removed the Sidebar but still allows you to add gadgets. Windows gadgets are programs that provide quick, visual representations of information, such as the weather, RSS (web) feeds, your calendar, and the current time.

Windows gadgets are installed by default on Windows 7, but they have to be added to the Windows 7 Desktop, as shown in Figure 4.10.

Figure 4.10: Windows gadgets

Administrators or users can add or remove gadgets on the Windows Desktop. To remove a gadget, click the gadget and choose Remove.

To add a gadget, right-click the Desktop and choose Gadgets, choose the gadget that you want by right-clicking the gadget, and click the Add link.

Perform the following steps to add the Windows 7 gadgets to your Desktop:

1. Right-click the desktop and choose Gadgets to open the Add Gadgets screen.

2. Right-click the gadget that you would like to install and choose Add.

3. Close the Add Gadgets screen.

After you have added the gadget to the Desktop, you can configure the gadget. To do so, mouse over the gadget and a small picture of a wrench appears, as shown in Figure 4.11. Click the wrench to configure the gadget.

Figure 4.11: Configuring the gadget

Administrators or users can also remove gadgets at any time by closing the gadget. Again when you mouse over the gadget, you can click the X above the wrench to close the gadget (see Figure 4.11 earlier). You can also add other gadgets by going to the Internet and viewing and adding other gadgets.

Perform the following steps to add other gadgets from the Internet:

1. Right-click the desktop and choose Gadgets.

2. Click the Get More Gadgets Online link.

3. Find the gadget you want to install and choose Download, as shown in Figure 4.12.

Figure 4.12: Installing a new gadget from the Internet

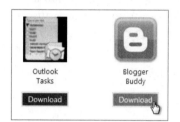

4. After you click the Download link, it will take you to another website where you click the Download link again.

5. The File Download box appears. Click the Save button.

6. Save the file to a folder on your machine.

7. After the download is complete, click the Open button.

8. On the Desktop Gadgets screen, click the Install button.

   After the installation is complete, the new gadget appears on the Desktop.

Now that you know how to add and configure gadgets to your desktop, you'll learn how to set your regional settings and multiple language settings.

Manage Multiple Languages and Regional Settings

In addition to configuring your Desktop, you can configure the language and regional settings that are used on your computer Desktop. Windows 7 supports multiple languages through the use of multilanguage technology. Multilanguage technology is designed to meet the following needs:

- Provide support for multilingual editing of documents
- Provide support for various language interfaces in your environment
- Allow users who speak various languages to share the same computer

In the following sections, you will learn about multilingual technology, what options are available for Windows 7 multilingual support, and how to enable and configure multilingual support.

Configuring Multilingual Technology

Windows 7 is built on Microsoft's Multilingual User Interface (MUI) technology and thus supports user options to view, edit, and process documents in a variety of languages. These options are provided through Unicode support, the National Language Support API, the Multilingual API, language files, and Multilingual Developer Support. Let's discuss each in turn:

Unicode   This is an international standard that allows character support for the common characters used in the world's most common languages.

National Language Support API   This is used to provide information for locale, character mapping, and keyboard layout. Locale settings are used to set local information such as date and time format, currency format, and country names. Character mapping arranges the mapping of local character encodings to Unicode. Keyboard layout settings include character typing information and sorting information.

Multilingual API   This is used to set up applications to support keyboard input and fonts from various language versions of applications. For example, Japanese users will see vertical text, and Arabic users will see right-to-left ligatures. This technology allows users to create mixed-language documents.

Language Files   These are files in which Windows 7 stores all language-specific information, such as text for help files and dialog boxes. They are separate from the operating system files. System code can thus be shared by all language versions of Windows 7, which allows modular support for different languages.

Multilingual Developer Support   This is a special set of APIs that enables developers to create generic code and then provide support for multiple languages.

Configuring Windows 7 Multilanguage Support

Multilanguage support is implemented using MUI technology, which allows the Windows 7 user interface to be presented in different languages and for applications to be viewed and edited in different languages based on the language file selected.

Depending on the level of language support required by your environment, you may use either a localized version of Windows 7 or install language files to support multiple languages. In this section we'll describe these versions and show you how to configure multilanguage support.

Using Localized Versions of Windows 7

Microsoft provides localized editions of Windows 7. For example, users in the United States will most likely use the English version, and users in Japan will most likely use the Japanese version. Localized versions of Windows 7 include fully localized user interfaces for the language that was selected. In addition, localized versions allow users to view, edit, and print documents in many different languages.

Installing the localized version of Windows 7 is important, but what if you have users who speak multiple languages? Let's take a look at Windows 7 language packs.

Installing Windows 7 Language Packs

Windows 7 MUI support provides user interfaces in several languages. Language packs are useful in multinational corporations where users speak several languages and must share computers. It is also appropriate when administrators want to deploy a single image of Windows 7 worldwide. You can manage multiple users who share a single computer and speak different languages through user profiles (covered in Chapter 7, "Configuring Users and Groups") or through Group Policies (covered in Chapter 8, "Managing Security").

Configuration

PART II

To implement multilanguage support, the appropriate language files to be implemented must be installed on the computer. There are two types of languages files in Windows 7:

Multilingual User Interface Pack (MUI)   This type of language file provides a translated version of the majority of the user interface. A license is required to use MUIs.

Language Interface Pack (LIP)   LIP language files consist of freely available files that provide a translated version of the most popular aspects of the user interface. LIPs require a parent language because LIP files do not translate all components of the user interface.

Now that you have seen what the multilanguage options are, let's take a look at how to configure and enable multilingual support.

Enabling and Configuring Multilingual Support

On the Windows 7 operating system, you can enable and configure multilingual editing and viewing by choosing Start ➤ Control Panel ➤ Regional And Language Options. This opens the Region And Language dialog box, as shown in Figure 4.13.

Figure 4.13: The Region And Language dialog box

Through Region and Language Options, you can configure formats, location, keyboards and languages, and administrative settings. We'll look at each of these in the following sections.

Formats Tab   The Formats tab of the Region And Language dialog box enables you to configure how numbers, currencies, dates, and times are displayed on the screen. You can change the current format using the Current Format drop-down list, which provides many different format options such as English (United States), German (Germany), and Chinese (Singapore). The Customize This Format button provides the ability to customize how numbers, currencies, times, and dates are displayed based on user or corporate preferences.

On the Formats tab, you can click the Additional Settings button to configure the rest of your options, as shown in Figure 4.14.

Figure 4.14: Additional Settings screen

Location Tab   The Location tab of the Region And Language dialog box, as shown in Figure 4.15, enables you to specify the current location to use in software that provides localized information, such as news and weather information. The Current Location drop-down list provides you with a list of locations that can be selected.

Figure 4.15: Location tab

Keyboards And Languages Tab The Keyboards And Languages tab of the Region And Language dialog box enables you to configure the input and keyboard language, and allows you to install or uninstall language packs, as shown in Figure 4.16. This tab also provides the ability to configure the language bar options and advanced keyboard settings. Click the Install/Uninstall Languages button to open the Install Or Uninstall Display Languages Wizard, which lets you select the languages to install or uninstall on your computer.

Administrative Tab The Administrative tab, as shown in Figure 4.17, allows you to support languages for non-Unicode programs. This enables non-Unicode programs to display menus and dialog boxes in the user's native language. This tab also allows you to copy the current settings to reserved accounts, such as the default user account or to system accounts.

Figure 4.16: Keyboards And Languages tab

Figure 4.17: Administrative tab

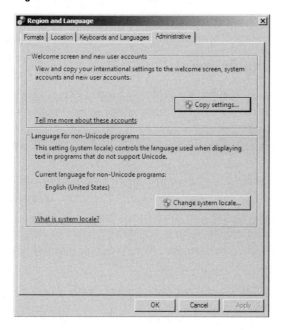

Perform the following steps to configure the locale settings on your computer:

1. Select Start ≻ Control Panel ≻ Regional And Language Options.

2. One by one, click the Formats, Location, Keyboards And Languages, and Administrative tabs and note the configurations on each tab.

3. Click the Formats tab and select the Danish (Denmark) option from the Current Format drop-down list. Then click the Apply button.

4. In the Number, Currency, Time, and Date fields, note the changed configurations.

5. Reset your locale to the original configuration and click Apply.

After configuring your multilingual support, another feature that can be configured is your accessibility features. The next section focuses on configuring the accessibility options.

Configure Accessibility Features

Windows 7 allows you to configure the Desktop so those users with special accessibility needs can use the Windows 7 Desktop more easily. Through its accessibility options and utilities, Windows 7 supports users with limited sight, hearing, or mobility. This section describes how to use these accessibility features.

Setting Accessibility Options

Through the Ease of Access Center available in Control Panel, you can configure keyboard, sound, display, mouse, and general properties of Windows 7 for users with special needs. To access the accessibility options screen, as shown in Figure 4.18, select Control Panel ≻ Ease Of Access Center.

The Ease of Access Center provides several options for customizing the computer to make it easier to use. Some commonly configured accessibility options include magnifying the text on the screen, configuring the text on the screen to be narrated, configuring an onscreen keyboard, and configuring a high-contrast desktop environment. Here are some other settings that can be modified for improved accessibility:

Use The Computer Without A Display   These options allow the computer to be optimized for visually impaired users, as shown in

Figure 4.19. You can turn on the Narrator, turn on audio descriptions, and turn off animations.

Figure 4.18: The Ease of Access Center

Control Panel Home	Make your computer easier to use
Change administrative settings	

Quick access to common tools

You can use the tools in this section to help you get started.

Windows can read and scan this list automatically. Press the SPACEBAR to select the highlighted tool.

☐ Always read this section aloud   ☑ Always scan this section

Start Magnifier   Start Narrator

Start On-Screen Keyboard   Set up High Contrast

Not sure where to start? Get recommendations to make your computer easier to use

Explore all settings
When you select these settings, they will automatically start each time you log on.

Use the computer without a display
Optimize for blindness

Make the computer easier to see
Optimize visual display

Use the computer without a mouse or keyboard
Set up alternative input devices

Make the mouse easier to use
Adjust settings for the mouse or other pointing devices

Make the keyboard easier to use
Adjust settings for the keyboard

Use text or visual alternatives for sounds
Set up alternatives for sounds

Make it easier to focus on tasks
Adjust settings for reading and typing

Configuration

PART II

Figure 4.19: Use The Computer Without A Display options

Use the computer without a display
When you select these settings, they will automatically start each time you log on.

Hear text read aloud ————————————————————————————

☐ Turn on Narrator

Narrator reads aloud any text on the screen. You will need speakers.

☐ Turn on Audio Description

Hear descriptions of what's happening in videos (when available).

Set up Text to Speech

Adjust time limits and flashing visuals ——————————————————

☐ Turn off all unnecessary animations (when possible)

How long should Windows notification dialog boxes stay open?

5.0 seconds ▼

See also ——————————————————————————————————

Audio Devices and Sound Themes

Learn about additional assistive technologies online

Make The Computer Easier To See   These options allow the display to be optimized for users with sight impairments, as shown in Figure 4.20. You can select a high-contrast color scheme, turn on the Narrator and audio descriptions, turn on the screen magnifier, and fine-tune display effects.

Figure 4.20: Make The Computer Easier To See options

Use The Computer Without A Mouse Or Keyboard   These options allow the computer to use an alternative input device. You can configure the onscreen keyboard to be displayed, or you can configure speech recognition.

Make The Mouse Easier To Use   These options adjust the appearance of the mouse pointer, whether the keyboard should be used to move the mouse around, and whether hovering over a window will activate the window, as shown in Figure 4.21.

Figure 4.21: Mouse options

Make The Keyboard Easier To Use   These options optimize the keyboard configuration, as shown in Figure 4.22. This contains settings for using Sticky Keys, Filter Keys, and Toggle Keys. Sticky Keys allows the Shift, Ctrl, Alt, or Windows key to be used in conjunction with another key by pressing the keys separately rather than simultaneously. Filter Keys ignores brief or repeated keystrokes and slows the repeat rate. Toggle Keys makes a noise whenever you press the Caps Lock, Num Lock, or Scroll Lock key.

Use Text Of Visual Alternatives For Sounds   These options let you specify whether you want to use Sound Sentry, which generates a visual warning whenever the computer makes a sound, and whether to display captions for speech and sounds on your computer.

Make It Easier To Focus On Tasks   These options allow you to configure settings for optimizing reading and typing settings as well as animations. Some of the settings are Turn On Narrator, Turn On Sticky Keys, Turn On Toggle Keys, and Turn On Filter Keys.

Figure 4.22: Keyboard accessibility options

Make the keyboard easier to use
When you select these settings, they will automatically start each time you log on.

Control the mouse with the keyboard

☐ Turn on Mouse Keys

Use the numeric keypad to move the mouse around the screen.

Set up Mouse Keys

Make it easier to type

☐ Turn on Sticky Keys

Press keyboard shortcuts (such as CTRL+ALT+DEL) one key at a time.

Set up Sticky Keys

☐ Turn on Toggle Keys

Hear a tone when you press CAPS LOCK, NUM LOCK, or SCROLL LOCK.

☑ Turn on Toggle Keys by holding down the NUM LOCK key for 5 seconds

☐ Turn on Filter Keys

Ignore or slow down brief or repeated keystrokes and adjust keyboard repeat rates.

Set up Filter Keys

Make it easier to use keyboard shortcuts

☐ Underline keyboard shortcuts and access keys

Make it easier to manage windows

☐ Prevent windows from being automatically arranged when moved to the edge of the screen

See also

Add a Dvorak keyboard and change other keyboard input settings

| OK | Cancel | Apply |

Now that you have an understanding of the different accessibility options, let's take a look at how to use some of the accessibility utilities.

Configuring Accessibility Utilities

Windows 7 provides several accessibility utilities, including the Magnifier, Narrator, and the On-screen Keyboard. Let's take a look at these options in more detail.

Using the Magnifier Utility   The Magnifier utility creates a separate window to magnify a portion of your screen, as shown in Figure 4.23. This option is useful for users who have poor vision. To access Magnifier, select Start ➤ All Programs ➤ Accessories ➤ Ease Of Access ➤ Magnifier. As you can see in Figure 4.23, when you place your mouse over an object, it magnifies the object.

Figure 4.23: The Magnifier utility

Using the Narrator Utility The Narrator utility can read aloud onscreen text, dialog boxes, menus, and buttons. This utility requires that you have some type of sound output device installed and configured. To access Narrator, select Start ➤ All Programs ➤ Accessories ➤ Ease Of Access ➤ Narrator. This brings up the dialog box shown in Figure 4.24.

Configuration

PART II

Figure 4.24: The Microsoft Narrator dialog box

Using the On-screen Keyboard The On-screen Keyboard displays a keyboard on the screen, as shown in Figure 4.25. Users can use the On-screen Keyboard keys through a mouse or another input device as an alternative to the keys on the regular keyboard. To access the On-screen Keyboard, select Start ➢ All Programs ➢ Accessories ➢ Ease Of Access ➢ On-screen Keyboard.

Figure 4.25: The On-screen Keyboard

Perform these steps to configure the Windows 7 accessibility features:

1. Select Start ➢ All Programs ➢ Accessories ➢ Ease Of Access ➢ Magnifier.

2. Experiment with the Magnifier utility. When you finish, click the Exit button in the Magnifier Settings dialog box.

3. Select Start ➢ All Programs ➢ Accessories ➢ Ease Of Access ➢ On-screen Keyboard.

4. Select Start ➢ All Programs ➢ Accessories ➢ Notepad to open Notepad.

5. Create a text document using the On-screen Keyboard. When you finish, close the Notepad document without saving it.

6. Close the On-screen Keyboard.

Two other Desktop options that you can use are Shut Down and Switch Users. Let's take a look at these features.

Configure the Power Button

Unless you decide to run your computer 24 hours a day, you will eventually want to shut down. By default on the Start menu, you have a Shut Down button (also called the Power button). By clicking this button, your machine will power off. But the Power button does not have to be set to the Shut Down option. You can configure this button to Switch User, Log Off, Lock, Restart, or Shut Down, as shown in Figure 4.26.

Figure 4.26: Shut Down button options

You may have a machine that is shared by multiple users, and it may be better for you to have the Switch User button on the Start menu instead of the Shut Down button. Configuring the Switch User option would make it easier on your users.

Perform the following steps to configure the Power button to Switch User:

1. Right-click the Shut Down button and choose Properties.

2. The Taskbar And Start Menu Properties dialog box appears. Make sure that you are working on the Start Menu tab.

3. From the Power Button Action drop-down list, choose Switch User.

4. Click OK.

5. Click the Start menu and verify that the Power button is now set to Switch User.

If you have a machine that has multiple users, these users might be working on the machine at different times. Let's talk about how to configure your machine for multiple users.

Manage a Multiple-User Environment

Many organizations have machines that multiple users must work on. As an administrator, you can configure a Windows 7 machine for multiple users.

When a user first logs on to a Windows 7 computer, the user will have a generic default Desktop and generic default settings. You can configure the machine so that a preset Desktop and preset configuration takes effect, as shown in Figure 4.27.

Figure 4.27: Configuring the Welcome screen and new user account settings

Creating Default Settings for New Users

As you can see in Figure 4.27, there are two check boxes in the Copy Your Current Settings To section. These two check boxes allow you to copy your current settings to the Welcome screen, system accounts, and a new user.

Perform the following steps to make your administrative account the default settings for all new users:

1. Click Start ➢ Control Panel ➢ Region And Language.
2. Click the Administrative tab.
3. Click the Copy Settings button.
4. Check the New User Accounts check box.
5. Click OK.

Another task that you can complete is to allow the users' Desktop to follow them anywhere on the network. Let's now look at roaming profiles.

Managing User Profiles

User profiles are the Desktop settings that a user currently uses. When a user logs on to Windows 7 and sets up their Desktop, this is called a local user profile.

As an administrator, you can set it up so that the user's local profile can become a roaming profile. A roaming profile is a user profile that follows the user to any machine that they log into.

To set up a roaming profile, you must first be connected to a domain. Then you have to set up a shared folder on a server and copy the user's profile to that folder. The user's domain account properties will need to point to the roaming profile, and you are all set.

Perform the following steps to copy the Windows 7 user's profile to a server location. Your Windows 7 computer must be part of a domain to complete these steps. On the domain you must have a shared folder that you can place the profile into.

1. Click Start ➢ Control Panel ➢ System.
2. Click the Advance System Settings link in the upper-left corner.
3. In the System Properties dialog box, click the Advanced tab.
4. On the Advanced tab, click the Settings button in the User Profiles section, as shown in Figure 4.28.

Configuration

PART II

Figure 4.28: Click Settings in the User Profiles section.

5. Choose a profile and click the Copy To button.

6. Copy the profile to one of your servers.

User profiles are an easy way to make your users feel comfortable no matter what computer they log on to. Knowing how to configure a Desktop from start to finish is a great way to personalize any Windows 7 computer.

5

Managing the Interface

Configuration

PART II

N ow that you have configured the Windows 7 Desktop, you need to configure the Windows 7 interface. In this chapter, I examine the process of configuring the Windows 7 environment, beginning with an overview of the main configuration utilities.

The Control Panel is one of the most important configuration areas of Windows 7. The Control Panel includes many items that can help you optimize, maintain, and personalize the operating system. One of the most important items in Control Panel is the System item. The System icon has operating system information, and you can configure Devices, Remote Settings, and System Protection here as well.

Another important component that you need to manipulate and configure is the video adapter. Many users have moved to multiple adapters to make their working environment more customizable. The user may have an application running on one monitor and email open on another.

If you use Windows 7 on a laptop computer, it is important to properly configure your power options. Configuring the power options on a laptop will allow you to get the most life from your laptop batteries. You can choose among many power options to customize laptops for each of your users.

I will examine how services operate and how to configure your services to start manually or automatically. I also explore how to configure services in the event of a service error.

Configure the Windows 7 Operating System

Windows 7 includes several utilities for managing various aspects of the operating system configuration. In the following sections, you will learn how to configure your operating system using Control Panel and the Registry Editor.

Let's start with Control Panel and the various utilities included within it.

Using Control Panel

Control Panel is a set of GUI utilities that allow you to configure Registry settings without using a Registry editor. The Registry is a database used by the operating system to store configuration information.

Let's take a closer look at the utilities that are available through Control Panel:

Action Center   The Action Center has two configurable sections: Security and Maintenance. The Security section allows you to configure four options:

- Virus Protection, which allows you to install and configure virus protection
- Windows Update, which allows you to update Windows 7
- Check For Solutions To Unreported Problems, which allows you to report and check for unreported problems
- Set Up Backup, which allows you to configure a backup

The Maintenance section allows you to set up a backup. Backups and Windows Update are explained later in this section.

Administrative Tools   By clicking this icon, you can access multiple administrative tools that can help you configure and monitor the Windows 7 operating system. These tools include

- Computer Services
- Computer Management
- Data Sources (ODBC)
- Event Viewer
- iSCSI Initiator
- Local Security Policy
- Performance Monitor
- Print Management
- Services
- System Configuration
- Task Scheduler
- Windows Firewall with Advanced Security
- Windows Memory Diagnostics
- Windows PowerShell Modules

Configuration

PART II

AutoPlay AutoPlay lets you configure media disks that will automatically start when inserted into the Media Player, as shown in Figure 5.1. Each of the media you use has different configuration settings, but the basic choices are as follows:

- Play Media Using The Windows Media Player
- Open The Folder To View Files Using Windows Explorer
- Take No Action
- Ask Me Every Time

Figure 5.1: AutoPlay options

Backup And Restore Backup And Restore allows you to install and configure your backup media. Backups allow a user to make a copy of all important data on their machine in the event of a hardware failure or disaster.

BitLocker Drive Encryption BitLocker Drive Encryption helps prevent unauthorized users from accessing files stored on the hard drives. The user is able to use the computer as normal but unauthorized users cannot read or use any of their files. BitLocker encryption is covered in greater detail in Chapter 8, "Managing Security."

Color Management   Color Management allows you to configure some of the video adapter settings, as shown in Figure 5.2. You can configure the Windows Color System Defaults, ICC Rendering Intent To WCS Gamut Mapping, and Display Calibration, as well as change the system defaults.

Figure 5.2: Color Management

Credential Manager   You use the Credential Manager to store credentials such as usernames and passwords. These usernames and passwords are stored in vaults so that you can easily log on to computers or websites.

There are three credential sections: Windows Credentials, Certificate-Based Credentials, and Generic Credentials. You can add credentials by clicking the Add Credentials link next to each of the three sections, as shown in Figure 5.3.

Figure 5.3: Credential Manager

Date And Time   Click the Date And Time icon to configure the local date and time for your Windows 7 machine. You also have the ability to synchronize your clock with the Internet, as shown in Figure 5.4.

Figure 5.4: Time synchronization

Default Programs   Click the Default Programs icon to choose the programs that Windows uses by default. For example, you can set Internet Explorer 8 (IE8) to be the default Internet browser, as shown in Figure 5.5.

Figure 5.5: Setting default programs

Desktop Gadgets   Click the Desktop Gadgets icon to set up various gadgets for your Windows 7 Desktop. Configuring gadgets was covered in Chapter 4, "Managing the Desktop."

Device Manager   Click the Device Manager icon to configure the devices on your Windows 7 machine. You can configure such devices as disk drives, display adapters, DVD/CD-ROM drives, monitors, and network adapters.

Devices And Printers   Click the Devices And Printers icon to add or configure the devices on your machine and your printers. Adding and configuring devices is covered in greater detail in Chapter 9, "Configuring Hardware and Printing."

Display   Click the Display icon to configure your display properties, as shown in Figure 5.6. You can change the size of the text and other items on your screen. You also have the ability to change the resolution, calibrate colors, change display settings, adjust ClearType text, and change custom text size.

Ease Of Access Center   The Ease Of Access Center enables you to set up your accessibility options.

Folder Options   Click the Folder Options icon to configure how you can view the folders on your Windows 7 machine by default.

You can configure how you browse and navigate folders, which files and folders you can view, and how folders are searched, as shown in Figure 5.7.

Figure 5.6: Display options

Figure 5.7: View Folder options

Fonts   Click the Fonts icon to install, preview, delete, show, hide, and configure the fonts that the applications on your Windows 7 operating system can use; get fonts online; adjust ClearType text; find a character; and change font size.

Getting Started   The Getting Started item allows you to learn about and configure your Windows 7 operating system. By clicking this icon, you can do the following:

- Go online to find out what's new in Windows 7
- Personalize Windows
- Transfer files and settings from another computer
- Use a HomeGroup to share with other computers in your home
- Choose when to be notified about changes to your computer
- Go online to get Windows Live Essentials
- Back up your files
- Add new users to your computer
- Change the size of the text on your screen

HomeGroup   The HomeGroups item gives you the ability to create and configure your HomeGroup. HomeGroups are small local networks that you can easily configure at home and work.

When you install HomeGroups on your first computer, a password is assigned so that you can connect other computers to this HomeGroup. You can change the password by clicking the HomeGroup icon.

Indexing Options   Windows uses the Indexing feature to perform very fast searches of common files on your computer. Index Settings give you the ability to configure which files and applications are indexed, as shown in Figure 5.8.

Internet Properties   Click the Internet Properties icon to configure how the Internet will operate. From this item you can configure your home page, browsing history, tabs, security, privacy, content, connections, and programs, as shown in Figure 5.9.

Configuration

PART II

Figure 5.8: The Index Settings tab of Advanced Options

Figure 5.9: Internet Properties

Keyboard   In Keyboard Properties, you configure how the keyboard will react when used. You can set the character repeat speed (how fast the keyboard will repeat what you are typing) and the cursor speed. You can also configure the keyboard drivers in this properties window.

Location And Other Sensors   Sensors are either software or hardware devices that pick up information from the surrounding area for your computer. Windows 7 supports both hardware sensors, like motion detectors, and software sensors, like those that permit your computer to react to an incoming network packet. Windows 7 supports the following list of the sensors:

- GPS
- Accelerometer
- Proximity
- Light
- RFID (radio frequency identification)
- Compass
- Camera
- Microphone
- Temperature
- Moisture
- Motion detector
- Traffic
- Weather station

Mail   Mail Properties allows you to set up your client-side mail. In the Mail Properties window, you can set up different user profiles (mailboxes) and specify connections to specific local mail servers or Internet mail servers.

Mouse   The Mouse item gives you the ability to configure how the mouse will operate, as shown in Figure 5.10. You can configure the buttons, click speed, the ClickLock feature, pointer type, pointer options, center wheel, and hardware properties.

Figure 5.10: Configuring the mouse properties

Network And Sharing Center   The Network And Sharing Center allows you to configure your Windows 7 machine to connect to a local network or the Internet. You can configure TCP/IP, set up a new network, connect to a network, choose a HomeGroup, and configure the network adapter.

Notification Area   The Notification Area is the area where icons and other notifications are displayed in the lower-right window (next to the time) of the Windows 7 taskbar. The Notification Area item in Control Panel allows you to configure which icons appear on the Taskbar and which notifications are shown.

Parental Controls   Parental Controls allow you to manage how children can use a Windows 7 computer. With Parental Controls, you can set the hours that children can use the computer, the programs that they can access, and the type of games that they can play.

When children try to access an application or game that they are not allowed to use, a notification will let them know that the application or game is restricted. The child can click a link that will then ask for access to the application or game, and the parent can accept or decline the request.

Performance Information And Tools   The Performance Information And Tools item gives you the ability to run a Windows Experience Index measurement, as shown in Figure 5.11. The Windows Experience Index measures the performance of the computer system.

The results will be issued as a base score. The higher the base score, the better your machine will perform. Performance Information And Tools also shows you how you can improve the performance of your machine.

Figure 5.11: Performance Information And Tools

Personalization   Personalization allows you to set up your desktop environment. Chapter 4 gives more details about the Personalization item.

Phone And Modem   The Phone And Modem Properties window allows you to set up your local dialing properties and modem options, as shown in Figure 5.12. You can specify your dialing location, modem properties, and telephone providers.

Figure 5.12: Phone And Modem Properties window

Power Options   Power plans allow a user to maximize their Windows 7 machine's performance and/or conserve energy. You have the ability to enter your own power restrictions to customize your machine. Power options are important settings when dealing with laptops. Because many users of laptops use batteries, power options allow you to get the most time from their batteries. There is more information about power management later in this chapter.

Programs And Features   Clicking the Programs And Features icon opens the old Add/Remove Programs item from Windows XP. Programs And Features allows you to uninstall, change, or repair programs and features, as shown in Figure 5.13.

Programs And Features also allows you to choose which Windows 7 features you want installed on your machine, as shown in Figure 5.14. Some of the features that you can enable are games, Indexing Services, Telnet Client, and Telnet Server.

Recovery   The Recovery item allows a user or administrator to recover the Windows 7 system to a previously captured restore point. System Restore is one of the first recovery options when your Windows 7 system experiences problems.

Figure 5.13: Programs And Features

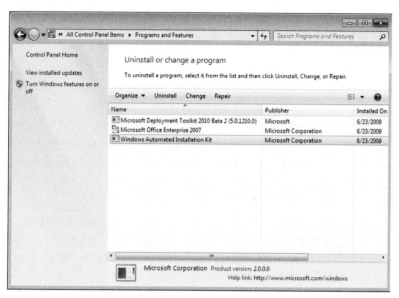

Figure 5.14: To turn on a feature, select its check box.

Region And Language   The Region And Language item allows you to configure your local regional settings. Chapter 4 discusses the Region And Language item in detail.

RemoteApp And Desktop Connections   Click the RemoteApp And Desktop Connections icon to access programs and desktops on your network. To connect to these resources (Remote Applications and Desktops), you must have the proper permissions to access these resources.

The RemoteApp and Desktop Connections item allows you to connect to either a remote computer or a virtual computer. To create a new connection, use the Set Up A New Connection Wizard included with the RemoteApp And Desktop Connections item.

Sound   The Sound item allows you to configure your machine's audio. You can configure output (speakers and audio drivers) and you can configure your input devices (microphones).

Speech Recognition   The Speech Recognition item allows you to configure your speech properties. Using Speech Recognition, you speak into the computer and that speech is displayed in text on the system. Many programs like Microsoft Office can type in the words as you speak them into the system. With Speech Recognition, you can complete the following items:

- Start Speech Recognition
- Set Up Microphone
- Take Speech Tutorials
- Train Your Computer To Better Understand You
- Open The Speech Reference Card

Sync Center   The Sync Center allows you to configure synchronization between the Windows 7 machine and a network server. The Sync Center also enables you to see when the synchronization occurred, if the synchronization was successful, and if there were any errors.

System   System is one of the most important features in Control Panel. It allows you to view which operating system the machine is using, check system resources (Processor, RAM), change the computer name/domain/workgroup, and activate Windows 7. By clicking the System icon you can also access the following items:

- Device Manager
- Remote Settings
- System Protection
- Advanced Settings

Taskbar And Start Menu   The Taskbar And Start Menu item allows you to configure how the Taskbar, Start Menu, and toolbars will operate. Chapter 4 discusses the Taskbar And Start Menu item in detail.

Troubleshooting   The Troubleshooting item in Control Panel allows you to troubleshoot common Windows 7 problems, as shown in Figure 5.15. You can troubleshoot the following:

- Programs
- Hardware And Sound
- Network And Internet
- Appearance And Personalization
- System And Security

Figure 5.15: Troubleshooting options

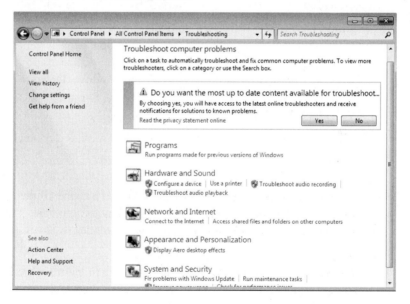

User Accounts   The User Accounts item allows you to create and modify user accounts. By clicking User Accounts, you can do the following:

- Change user passwords
- Remove passwords

- Change the account picture
- Change the account name
- Change the account type
- Manage accounts
- Change User Account Control settings

Windows CardSpace   Windows CardSpace is a new way for you to interact with websites and online services. Windows CardSpace allows you to replace the username and passwords that you currently use with online services. Using Windows CardSpace allows you to do the following:

- Review the identity of the site
- Manage your information by using information cards
- Review card information before you send it to a site
- Allow sites to request information from you

Windows Defender   Windows Defender is a built-in Windows 7 spyware protector. It is included free with the operating system and starts automatically protecting your system after you turn it on. Chapter 8 provides more information about Windows Defender. Windows Defender can operate in the following two modes:

Real-Time Protection   Real-Time Protection allows Windows Defender to run in the background and protect your system as you are working live on the Internet or network.

Scanning Options   The Scanning Options mode allows you to run a system scan at any time to check for spyware. This mode does not require the Windows Defender to always be running.

Windows Firewall   Windows Firewall, as shown in Figure 5.16, helps prevent unauthorized users or hackers from accessing your Windows 7 machine from the Internet or the local network. Chapter 8 provides more information about Windows Firewall.

Windows Update   Windows Update allows you to configure how the Windows 7 operating system receives updates from

Microsoft's website. Chapter 1, "Installing Windows 7," explains Windows Update.

Figure 5.16: Windows Firewall

Now that you have an understanding of the items available through Control Panel, let's take a look at the procedures for performing several useful tasks.

Installing a Telnet Client

Perform the following steps to install the Telnet client on the Windows 7 operating system:

1. Open the Programs And Features utility by clicking Start ➤ Control Panel ➤ Programs And Features.

2. Click the Turn Windows Features On Or Off link in the upper-left corner.

3. Scroll down the features list and check the Telnet Client check box.

4. Click OK.

Running Performance Information And Tools

Perform the following steps to run Performance Information And Tools to receive your baseline performance score:

1. Open the Performance Information And Tools utility by clicking Start ≻ Control Panel ≻ Performance Information And Tools.

2. If the computer has not been rated yet, click the Rate This Computer button. If the computer has a rating, click the Update My Score link.

3. The computer will take a few minutes and test your hardware. After your score appears, close the Performance Information And Tools window.

Configuring Windows Defender

Now let's take a look at how to work with the Windows Defender. Perform the following steps to configure the Windows Defender:

1. Open Windows Defender by clicking Start ≻ Control Panel ≻ Windows Defender.

2. Click the Check For Updates Now button, as shown in Figure 5.17.

Figure 5.17: Windows Defender

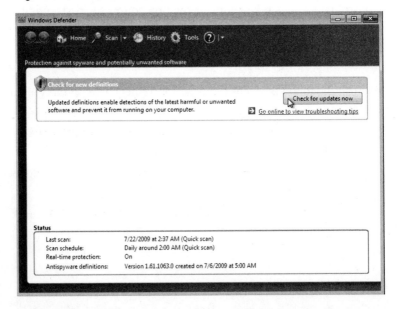

3. The Checking For Updates screen appears. This process may take a few minutes. After the update is complete, a message should state the status of the machine. If no unwanted software is detected, close Windows Defender. If unwanted software is detected, remove the unwanted software and then close Windows Defender.

Now that we have looked at all the icons in Control Panel, let's now look at the System utility in greater detail.

Understanding the System Utility

Clicking the System icon in Control Panel lets you access a useful set of utilities and tasks that allow you to configure remote access, system devices, system protection, and the computer name, just to name a few.

Let's look at the information that can be viewed and the tasks that can be configured in Control Panel:

Windows Edition The Windows Edition section shows you which edition of Windows the machine is currently using. The Windows Edition section also shows whether service packs are installed.

System The System section shows information about the system hardware. The System sections also shows:

- Rating
- Processor
- Installed Memory (RAM)
- System Type
- Pen and Touch

Computer Name/Domain Changes In the Computer Name, Domain, and Workgroup setting section, you can change the name of the computer system and also change the workgroup or domain, as shown in Figure 5.18.

Windows Activation The Windows Activation section allows you to activate your Windows 7 operating system. The Windows Activation section also allows you to change your product key before activating.

Figure 5.18: You can change the computer name, domain, or workgroup.

Remote Settings   The Remote Settings section allows you to set the Remote Assistance and Remote Desktop properties for the Windows 7 system, as shown in Figure 5.19. Windows Remote Assistance allows you to connect to a machine and control the mouse and keyboard while the user is on with you. This option can be enabled or disabled.

Figure 5.19: Remote Settings screen

Remote Desktop allows you to have your own session on the Windows 7 operating system. While you are logged on to the Windows 7 operating system through Remote Desktop, the user of the machine can't view the session. You can choose from the following three Remote Desktop options:

Don't Allow Connections From This Machine   Choosing this option prevents anyone from connecting to this machine through Remote Desktop.

Allow Connections From Computers Running Any Version Of Remote Desktop (Less Secure)   This setting allows any computer running Remote Desktop to connect to this Windows 7 machine. These machines do not need to use network-level authentication, and that makes this connection type less secure.

Allow Connections Only From Computers Running Remote Desktop With Network Level Authentication (More Secure)   Network-level authentication is a new method used for Remote Desktop (Windows Vista and higher). It allows Remote Desktop users to connect to the Windows 7 operating system securely.

You also have the ability in Remote Desktop to specify which users have access to the Windows 7 machine through the use of Remote Desktop.

System Protection   The System Protection tab allows you to configure restore points and recoverability for the Windows 7 operating system, as shown in Figure 5.20. You can also manage disk space and manage all your restore points on the System Protection tab.

Advanced System Settings   The Advanced System Settings tab allows you to set up such items as visual effects, processor scheduling, memory usage, virtual memory, desktop settings, system startup, and recoverability, as shown in Figure 5.21.

There are three main sections on the Advanced System Settings tab:

Performance   The Performance section allows you to configure the Visual Effects, the virtual memory, processor scheduling, and data execution prevention for the Windows 7 operating system.

The virtual memory is a section of the hard drive that is used by the system and RAM. Think of RAM as a pitcher of water. As the water fills up the pitcher, the pitcher fills. Once full, the water would overflow. The virtual memory is the overflow for RAM. When RAM fills up, the oldest data in the RAM gets put into the virtual memory. This way, the system does not need to look at an entire hard drive for that data. It finds it in the virtual memory.

The Data Execution Prevention section helps protect against damage from viruses and other security threats.

Figure 5.20: System Protection tab

Figure 5.21: Advanced System Settings

User Profiles   The User Profiles section allows you to copy, delete, or move a user's desktop profile to another location or user account.

Startup And Recovery   The Startup And Recovery section, as shown in Figure 5.22, allows you to configure which operating system will be booted by default (important for dual-booting machines) and what should happen when the system gets a startup error.

Figure 5.22: Startup And Recovery options

You can also configure the Device Manager from the System item. Let's now take a look at configuring some of the options using the System utility.

Changing a Computer Name

Perform the following steps to change the computer name:

1. Open the System utility by clicking Start ➤ Control Panel ➤ System.

2. In the resulting window, in the Computer Name, Domain and Workgroup section, click the Change Settings link.

3. Click the Change button in the To Rename This Computer section.

4. In the Computer Name field, enter a new name for your computer. Click OK.

5. A dialog box asking to reboot the machine appears. Click OK.

6. Click Close. Click the Restart Now button.

Now that we have renamed the computer, let's take a look at how to configure performance options.

Manipulating Virtual Memory

Perform the following steps to manipulate your system's virtual memory:

1. Open the System utility by clicking Start ➤ Control Panel ➤ System.

2. In the left-hand side, click the Advanced System Settings link.

3. In the Performance section, click the Settings button.

4. When the Performance screen appears, click the Advanced tab.

5. In the Virtual Memory section, click the Change button.

6. Deselect the Automatically Manage Paging File Size For All Drives check box.

7. Click the Custom Size radio button.

8. Set the Minimum and Maximum settings to one and half times RAM. For example, if your RAM is 1024 MB, change both settings to 1536 MB.

9. Click the Set button.

10. Click OK. Click OK at the Performance screen.

11. Close the System Properties window.

Setting Up Recoverability Options

Now let's see how to set up some recoverability options for your operating system.

Perform the following steps to create a restore point:

1. Open the System utility by clicking Start ➤ Control Panel ➤ System.

2. In the left-hand side, click the System Protection link.

3. When the System Protection screen appears, click the Create button in the Create A Restore Point Right Now section.

4. A dialog box asks you to type in a description to help identify which restore point it is. Type in today's date and click the Create button.

5. After it finishes, a dialog box stating that the restore was created successfully appears. Click the Close button.

6. Click the System Restore button.

7. At the System Restore screen, click Next.

   At the "Restore your computer to the state it was in before the selected event" screen, you should see the restore point that you just created.

8. If the restore that you created is there, click Cancel. If the restore is not there, repeat steps 2 through 5.

Enabling Remote Desktop Connections

Another task that we will complete is allowing Remote Desktop connections. Perform the following steps to enable Remote Desktop connections:

1. Open the System utility by clicking Start ➤ Control Panel ➤ System.

2. In the left-hand side, click the Remote Settings link.

3. In the Remote Desktop section, click the Allow Connections From Computers Running Any Version Of Remote Desktop (Less Secure) radio button.

4. Make sure that the Allow Remote Assistance Connections To This Computer check box is selected.

5. Click OK.

6. Close the System Properties window.

Another way to configure options within the Windows 7 operating system is to configure the settings directly in the Registry. In the next section you'll learn how to use the Registry Editor.

Using the Registry Editor

You use the Registry Editor program to edit the Registry. This utility is designed for advanced configuration of the system. Usually when you make changes to your configuration, you use other utilities, such as those available in Control Panel, which we discussed in the previous section.

WARNING   Only experienced administrators should use the Registry Editor. It is intended for making configuration changes that can be made directly through the Registry only. For example, you might edit the Registry to specify an alternate location for a print spool folder. Improper changes to the Registry can cause the computer to fail to boot. Use the Registry Editor with extreme caution.

Windows 7 uses the REGEDIT program as the primary utility for Registry editing in Windows 7. This program supports full editing of the Registry. To use REGEDIT, select Start and type **REGEDIT** in the Search dialog box.

The Registry is organized in a hierarchical tree format of keys and subkeys that represent logical areas of computer configuration. By default, when you open the Registry Editor, you see five Registry key listings, as shown in Figure 5.23 and described in Table 5.1.

Figure 5.23: The Registry Editor window

Table 5.1: Registry Keys

Registry Key	Description
HKEY_CLASSES_ROOT	Configuration information that Windows Explorer uses to properly associate file types with applications.
HKEY_CURRENT_USER	Configuration information for the user who is currently logged on to the computer. This key is a subkey of the HKEY_USERS key.
HKEY_LOCAL_MACHINE	Computer hardware configuration information. This computer configuration is used regardless of the user who is logged on.
HKEY_USERS	Configuration information for all users of the computer.
HKEY_CURRENT_CONFIG	Configuration of the hardware profile that is used during system startup.

Another configuration that you can set is the display devices. Let's take a look at how to configure them.

Manage Display Devices

When you configure display devices, most users think you are speaking of just the monitors. But the display device is attached to a video adapter and that is actually what you are configuring.

A video adapter is the device that outputs the display to your monitor. You install a video adapter in the same way that you install other hardware. If it is a Plug and Play device, all you need to do is shut down your computer, add the video adapter, and turn on your computer. Windows 7 automatically recognizes the new device.

You can configure several options for your video adapters, and if you have multiple monitors with their own video adapters, you can configure multiple-display support. The following sections describe video adapter configuration and how to configure your computer to support multiple monitors.

Configuring Video Adapters

The options for video settings are on the Monitor tab of the Display Settings dialog box, as shown in Figure 5.24. To access this dialog box, select Control Panel ➤ Appearance and Personalization ➤ Personalization ➤ Display Settings. Alternatively, you could right-click an empty area on your Desktop, select Personalize from the pop-up menu, and then select Display.

Figure 5.24: The Monitor tab of the Display Settings dialog box

Within the Display properties you can configure the resolution, calibrate the colors, change display settings, adjust ClearType text, and set the custom DPI.

To configure advanced settings for your video adapter, click the Advanced button in the lower-right corner of the Display properties. This button opens the Properties dialog box for the display monitor, as shown in Figure 5.25.

You'll see the following four tabs with options for your video adapter and monitor:

Adapter   Allows you to view and configure the properties of your video adapter. In the Adapter section, there is a Properties button. The Properties button allows you to configure the graphic adapter properties, including drivers.

Monitor   Allows you to view and configure the properties of your monitor, including the refresh frequency (how often the screen is redrawn) and colors shown (High Color 16 or True Color 32).

Troubleshooter Allows you to configure how Windows 7 uses your graphics hardware. For example, you can configure hardware acceleration settings, as shown in Figure 5.26.

Figure 5.25: The Properties dialog box for a display monitor and graphics adapter

Figure 5.26: Display Adapter Troubleshooter

Configuration

PART II

Color Management Allows you to select color profiles (the colors that are displayed on your monitor), calibrate your display, and change system setting defaults, as shown in Figure 5.27.

Figure 5.27: Color Management, Advanced tab

Perform the following steps for viewing and documenting your video adapter settings:

1. Right-click an empty area on the Desktop, choose Personalize, and select Display Settings.

2. Click the Change Display Settings link.

3. Click the Advanced Settings link.

4. Click the Monitor tab. Make a note of your current settings.

5. Click the Troubleshoot tab. Make a note of your current settings.

6. Click OK to close the monitor Properties dialog box.

7. Click OK to close the Display Settings dialog box.

Using Multiple-Display Support

Windows 7 allows you to extend your Desktop across multiple monitors. This means you can spread your applications across multiple monitors.

Using multiple monitors is becoming a common practice in the corporate environment. Many programmers use multiple monitors while coding, and many like to have multiple monitors so that they can work and monitor email at the same time.

Setting Up Multiple-Display Support

To set up multiple-display support, you must have a video adapter installed that supports multiple monitors or a separate video adapter installed for each monitor.

TIP   If your computer has the video adapter built into the system board, you should install Windows 7 before you install the second video adapter because Windows 7 will disable the video adapter that is built into the system board if it detects a second video adapter. When you add a second video adapter after Windows 7 is installed, it automatically becomes the primary video adapter.

Perform the following steps to configure multiple-display support:

1. Turn off your computer and install the new video adapters, if needed. Plug your monitors into the video adapters and turn on your computer. Assuming that the adapters are Plug and Play–compatible, Windows 7 automatically recognizes your new adapters and loads the correct drivers.

2. Open the Display Settings dialog box (right-click an empty area on your Desktop, select Personalize, and click Display Settings). You should see an icon for each of the monitors.

3. Click the number of the monitor that will act as your additional display. Then select the Extend the Desktop Onto This Monitor check box. Repeat this step for each additional monitor you want to configure. You can change the order in which the displays are arranged by dragging and dropping the monitor icons in the Monitor tab of the Display Settings dialog box.

4. When you finish configuring the monitors, click OK to close the dialog box.

Troubleshooting Multiple-Display Support

If you are having problems with multiple-display support, use the troubleshooting guidelines listed in Table 5.2.

Configuration

PART II

Table 5.2: Troubleshooting Multiple Display Problems

Symptom	Possible Solutions
The Extend The Desktop Onto This Monitor option isn't available.	If the Monitor tab of the Display Settings dialog box doesn't give you the option Extend The Desktop Onto This Monitor, confirm that your secondary adapter is supported for multiple-display support. Confirm that you have the most current drivers (that are Windows 7–compliant and support dual-mode capabilities) loaded. Confirm that Windows 7 is able to detect the secondary video adapter. Try selecting the secondary adapter rather than the primary adapter in the Display Settings dialog box.
No output appears on the secondary display.	Confirm that your secondary adapter is supported for multiple-display support, especially if you are using a built-in motherboard video adapter. Confirm that the correct video driver has been installed for the secondary display. Restart the computer to see if the secondary video driver is initialized. Check the status of the video adapter in Device Manager. Try switching the order of the video adapters in the computer's slots. See if the system will recognize the device as the primary display.
An application is not properly displayed.	Disable the secondary display to determine if the problem is specific to multiple-display support. Run the application on the primary display. If you are running MS-DOS applications, try running the application in full-screen mode. For Windows applications, try running the application in a maximized window.

Now that you have configured Control Panel and the display adapters, let's look at how to configure your power options for mobile computers.

Use Power Management for Mobile Computer Hardware

Windows 7 includes several features that are particularly useful for laptop computers. For example, through Power Options in Control Panel, you can select a power plan and enable power-management features with Windows 7.

Recognizing the Improvements to Power Management

Windows 7 builds on the power-management features that were introduced with Windows XP with the following enhancements:

- Battery meter, which provides a notification icon in the system tray that details the computer's battery power

- Power plans, which are collections of hardware and software settings optimized for a specific function

- Sleep power state, which combines the speed of standby with the features of hibernate mode

- ReadyDrive, which provides faster booting and resume times when used in conjunction with ReadyDrive-capable hard drives

After exploring some of the features of Windows 7 Power Management, let's look at managing the various power options.

Managing Power States

In Windows 7, the Advanced Configuration Power Interface (ACPI) specifies the following different levels of power states:

- Fully active PC

- Sleep

- Hibernation

- Complete shutdown of PC

The sleep power state is a new power state introduced with Windows 7 that combines the features of hibernate and standby. When a computer enters the sleep power state, data including window locations and running applications is saved to the hard disk, and that session is available within seconds when the computer wakes. This allows the computer to be put into a power-saving state when not in use but provides quick access to the in-process user session, thus enabling the user to begin working more quickly than if the computer were shut down or put into hibernation.

Hibernation falls short of a complete shutdown of the computer. With hibernation, the computer saves all of your Desktop state as well as any open files. To use the computer again, press the power button. The computer should start more quickly than from a complete shutdown because it does not have to go through the complete startup process. You will have to again log on to the computer. Similar to when the computer is put into Sleep mode, all the documents that were open when the computer went into hibernation are still available. With hibernation you can easily resume work where you left off. You can configure your computer to hibernate through Power Options or by choosing Start, and then clicking the arrow and selecting Hibernate from the drop-down menu. This option appears only if hibernation has been enabled through Power Options.

> **NOTE**   The Hibernation mode might not be available on your Windows 7 laptop by default. You must make sure that your firmware can support Hibernation.

If the Hibernation mode does not appear by default and your system can support Hibernation, perform the following steps to enable the Hibernate function:

1. Open an elevated command prompt. (Right-click the command prompt and choose Run As Administrator, as shown in Figure 5.28.)

Figure 5.28: Running an elevated command prompt

2. Click Yes at the dialog box.

3. At the prompt, type **powercfg -h on** and press Enter. Entering the same command and using the off switch would disable Hibernate on the machine.

4. Close the command prompt.

Now let's look at the various types of power options that you can configure.

Managing Power Options

You configure power options through the Power Options Properties dialog box. To access this dialog box, open Control Panel and click Power Options. The Power Options dialog box provides the ability to manage power plans and to control power options, such as when the display is turned off, when the computer sleeps, and what the power button does.

Configuring Power Plans

Windows 7 includes three configurable power plans: Balanced, Power Saver, and High Performance. Power plans control the trade-off between quick access to an existing computer session and energy savings. In Windows 7, each power plan contains default options that you can customize to meet the needs of various scenarios.

> **Balanced**   The Balanced power plan, as its name suggests, provides a balance between power savings and performance. By default, this plan is configured to turn off the display after 20 minutes, and to put the computer to sleep after one hour of idle time. These times can be modified as needed. Other power options that can be modified include Wireless Adapter settings and Multimedia settings. You can configure wireless adapters for maximum power saving or maximum performance. By default, the Balanced power plan configures wireless adapters for maximum performance. You can configure the Multimedia settings so that the computer will not be put into Sleep mode when sharing media from the computer. For example, if the computer is acting as a Media Center device, you can configure the computer to remain on by setting the Prevent Idling To Sleep option so that other computers can connect to it and stream media from it even when the computer is not being used for other purposes.

Configuration

PART II

Power Saver   The Power Saver power plan is optimized for power savings. By default, the display is configured to be turned off after 20 minutes of inactivity, and the computer is put into Sleep mode after one hour of inactivity. Additionally, this power plan configures hard disks to be turned off after 20 minutes of inactivity.

High Performance   The High Performance power plan is configured to provide the maximum performance for portable computers. By default, the computer will never enter Sleep mode, but the display will be turned off after 20 minutes. When this setting is configured, by default, the Multimedia settings are configured with the Allow The Computer To Enter Away Mode option, which allows the computer to enter into a new power state called Away mode. Away mode configures the computer to appear off to users but remain accessible for media sharing. For example, the computer can record television shows when in Away mode.

You can modify the existing power plans to suit your needs by clicking Change Plan Settings, or you can use the preconfigured power plans listed in Table 5.3.

Table 5.3: Windows 7 Power Plans

Power Plan	Turn Off Display	Put the Computer to Sleep
Balanced	After 20 minutes	1 hour
Power Saver	After 20 minutes	1 hour
High Performance	After 20 minutes	Never

After you decide which power plan is going to be used, you might want to configure some of the advanced power options. In the next section we'll discuss the various power options.

Configure Advanced Power Settings

Each power plan contains advanced settings that can be configured, such as when the hard disks will be turned off and whether a password is required on wakeup. To configure these advanced settings, open Control Panel, click Power Options, and select the power plan you want to use. Then, click Change Advanced Power Settings to open the Advanced Settings tab of the Power Options dialog box, shown in Figure 5.29.

Figure 5.29: Advanced power settings

You can then modify the settings as desired or restore the plan defaults. For example, one option that you might want to change if you are using a mobile computer is the Power Buttons And Lid option, which configures what happens when you press the power button or close the lid of the mobile computer. When either of these actions occurs, the computer can be configured to do nothing, shut down, go into Sleep mode, or go into Hibernate mode.

Configuring Hibernation

Although Sleep is the preferred power-saving mode in Windows 7, Hibernation mode is still available for use. Hibernation for a computer means that anything stored in memory is also stored on your hard disk. This ensures that when your computer is shut down, you do not lose any of the information that is stored in memory. When you take your computer out of hibernation, it returns to its previous state.

To configure your computer to hibernate, access the Advanced Settings tab of the Power Options dialog box. The Hibernate option appears under the Sleep option.

Perform the following steps to configure a power plan for your computer. If the Hibernate option is not present, perform the steps in the previous section to enable hibernation.

1. Select Start ➤ Control Panel and click the Power Options icon.

2. Select a power plan to modify from the Preferred Plans list and click Change Plan Settings.

3. Configure the power plan options for your computer based on your personal preferences. Click Change Advanced Power Settings to modify advanced power settings. When all changes are made, click Save Changes.

4. Close Control Panel.

One advantage when you use a laptop on the battery is that you can see how much time you have left until the battery dies. Let's take a look at the battery meter.

Managing Power Consumption Using the Battery Meter

Windows 7 includes a battery meter that you can use to monitor the battery power consumption on your computer. The battery meter also provides notification on what power plan is being used.

The battery meter appears in the Notification Area of the Windows Taskbar and indicates the status of the battery, including the percentage of battery charge. As the battery charge gets lower, the battery meter provides a visual indication of the amount of charge left. For example, when the battery charge reaches the low-battery level, a red circle with a white X is displayed.

The battery meter also provides a quick method for changing the power plan in use on the computer. By clicking the battery meter icon, you can select between the three preferred power plans available with Windows 7.

Using Windows ReadyBoost and Windows 7

With Windows Vista, Microsoft introduced several new technologies to help boost operating system performance. Windows ReadyBoost is a technology introduced with Windows Vista that is also available in Windows 7.

Windows ReadyBoost allows for the use of multiple nonvolatile flash memory devices as an additional memory cache. When the physical memory devices become full on a computer with Windows ReadyBoost configured, data is written to the flash device instead of to the hard drive. This improves performance because data can be read more quickly from the flash drive than from the hard drive.

When a compatible device is installed on a Windows 7 computer, a ReadyBoost tab is displayed on the device's properties page that can be used to configure Windows ReadyBoost.

To use a flash memory device with Windows ReadyBoost, the device must meet the following specifications:

- It must have a storage capacity of at least 256 MB.

- It must support USB 2.0.

- It must support a throughput of 2.5 MBps for 4 K random reads and 1.75 MBps for 512 K random writes.

Configuring Advanced Settings

ReadyDrive is also a technology included with Windows 7 that you can use to speed up the boot process, resume from a hibernation state faster, and conserve battery power for mobile computers. ReadyDrive relies on new hybrid hard disks, which use flash memory technology in conjunction with mechanical hard disk technology.

When you use ReadyDrive, data is written to flash memory instead of to the mechanical hard disk. This saves battery power because the mechanical hard disk does not need to perform as many read/write actions. Additionally, read/write times with flash memory are quicker than with traditional hard disk media, so resuming from hibernation occurs faster.

Configuring the power options on a laptop can help save energy and extend battery life. Another important item to take into account when configuring Windows 7 is how you are managing your Windows services.

Manage Windows 7 Services

A service is a program, routine, or process that performs a specific function within the Windows 7 operating system. You can manage services through the Services window, as shown in Figure 5.30, which can be accessed in a variety of ways. If you go through the Computer Management utility, right-click Computer, select Manage, expand Services And Applications, and then expand Services. You can also go through Administrative Tools or set up Services as a Microsoft Management Console (MMC) snap-in.

Configuration

PART II

Figure 5.30: The Services window

For each service, the Services window lists the name, a short description, the status, the startup type, and the logon account that is used to start the service. To configure the properties of a service, double-click the service name to open its Properties dialog box, as shown in Figure 5.31.

Figure 5.31: The Properties dialog box for a service

Service Properties

The Service Properties dialog box contains the following four tabs of options for services: General, Log On, Recovery, and Dependencies.

General   The General tab allows you to view and configure the following options:

- The service display name

- A description of the service

- The path to the service executable

- The startup type, which can be Automatic, Manual, or Disabled

- The current service status

- Start parameters that can be applied when the service is started

In addition, the buttons across the lower part of the dialog box allow you to change the service status to start, stop, pause, or resume the service.

Log On   The Log On tab, as shown in Figure 5.32, allows you to configure the logon account that is used to start the service. Choose the local system account or specify another logon account.

Figure 5.32: The Log On tab of a service's
Properties dialog box

Configuration

PART II

Recovery   The Recovery tab, as shown in Figure 5.33, allows you to designate what action will be taken if the service fails to load. For the first, second, and subsequent failures, you can select from the following actions:

- Take No Action
- Restart The Service
- Run A Program
- Restart The Computer

If you choose Run A Program, specify any command-line parameters along with it. If you choose Restart The Computer, you can configure a message that will be sent to users who are connected to the computer before it is restarted. You can also specify how long until a machine is restarted if an error occurs.

Figure 5.33: The Recovery tab of a service's Properties dialog box

Dependencies   The Dependencies tab, shown in Figure 5.34, lists any services that must be running in order for the specified service to start. If a service fails to start, you can use this information to examine the dependencies and then make sure each one is running. In the bottom panel, you can verify whether any other services depend on this service before you decide to stop it.

Figure 5.34: The Dependencies tab of a service's Properties dialog box

Perform the following steps to configure services in the Windows 7 operating system:

1. Start Computer Management by clicking Start and then right-clicking Computer. Choose Manage from the context menu.

2. In the Computer Management MMC, expand the Services And Applications section.

3. Click the Services link.

4. Scroll down the list and double-click Remote Desktop Configuration.

5. Under Startup Type, choose Automatic.

6. On the Log On tab, click the This Account radio button.

7. Click the Browse button and choose the local administrator account, as shown in Figure 5.35. Click OK.

Figure 5.35: Select User screen

8. In the Password boxes, type and verify the Administrator password.

9. In the Recovery tab, make sure the following settings are configured, as shown in Table 5.4.

Table 5.4: Recovery Tab Options

Action	Response
First Failure	Restart The Service
Second Failure	Restart The Service
Subsequent Failures	Take No Action
Reset Fail Count After	1 Day
Restart Service After	10 Minutes

10. Click OK.

11. Close the Computer Management MMC.

Services are just another troubleshooting and configuring tool that is part of your arsenal of troubleshooting techniques. Properly working services allow your Windows 7 operating system to work properly.

6

Remote Desktop and Remote Assistance

Configuration

PART II

E nd-user support for most IT departments is a major concern and time-consuming endeavor. Anything we can do to provide a more efficient solution to user issues is a major benefit. Basic telephone or chat support works in many cases, but imagine you could see what the end user sees or even interface with them...enter Remote Assistance and Remote Desktop. If you've been using them with XP and Vista, you're going to be pleased with Windows 7.

Remote assistance in Windows Vista provided many enhancements over previous versions, including improved security, performance, and usability. Windows 7 goes even further: it adds Easy Connect to make it even easier for novice users to request help from expert users; Group Policy support has been increased; and it provides command-line functionality (meaning you can add scripting), bandwidth optimization, logging, and more.

Remote Desktop is a tool that allows you to take control of a remote computer's keyboard, video, and mouse. This tool does not require someone collaborating with you on the remote computer. Remote Desktop is used to access applications on remote machines, troubleshoot issues, as well as take complete control of a remote machine to meet an end user's needs.

In this chapter, I will explain some of the new features and benefits to using Remote Assistance and Remote Desktop within Windows 7 and how to support end users, implement Group Policy, and use scripting. I will explain the integration of the previous operating system Remote Assistance and Remote Desktop with Windows.

Use Remote Assistance

Remote Assistance provides a method for inviting help by instant message, email, a file, or (new to Windows 7) an Easy Connect option. To use Remote Assistance, the computer requesting help and the computer providing help must have Remote Assistance capabilities, and both computers must have network connectivity (they have to be able to talk to each other).

Remote Assistance is designed to allow an expert user to provide assistance to a novice user. The terms expert and novice are used to describe the assistor (expert) and assistee (novice). When assisting a novice user, the expert can use the text-based chat built into Remote

Assistance. The expert can also take control of a novice user's desktop (with permission). Common examples of when you would use Remote Assistance include the following:

- Diagnosing problems that are difficult to explain or reproduce. Remote Assistance can allow an expert to remotely view the computer and the novice user can show the expert an error or problem.

- Guiding a novice user through a complex set of instructions. The expert can also take control of the computer and complete the tasks if necessary.

New/Updated Features

The Windows 7 Remote Assistance feature builds on the implementations in previous versions of Windows. Multiple sessions over a shared network are now reliable using the connectivity improvement of network address translation (NAT) traversal using IPv6 and Teredo tunneling. A stand-alone executable is made available (msra. exe) that will accept several options, allowing script options to be available. Performance improvements optimizing bandwidth, connect time, and improved startup times have also been added. Group Policy settings have been added for improved manageability. The new Easy Connect feature for soliciting Remote Assistance will provide one more level of simplicity for the end users—always a huge benefit to any IT infrastructure.

Easy Connect

The Easy Connect method for accessing a Remote Assistance session is new for Windows 7. Easy Connect uses the Peer Name Resolution Protocol (PNRP) to set up direct peer-to-peer transfer using a central machine in the Internet to establish the connection. PNRP uses IPv6 and Teredo tunneling to register a machine as globally unique. You're not using IPv6? You are with PNRP; Windows 7 (as well as Vista and Server 2008) has IPv6 turned on natively as well as the currently used standard of IPv4. You will, however, only be able to use Easy Connect with Windows 7 and beyond. I'll discuss more about IPv6 in a later chapter, but to give you an idea, you can see the structure of the PNRP Teredo IPv6 packet in Figure 6.1.

Configuration

PART II

Figure 6.1: Teredo and IPv6 PNRP structure

Time	Source	Destination	Protocol	Info
88 15.301866	2001:0:4137:9e50:2810	2001:0:4137:9e50:1864	IPv6	IPv6 no next header
89 15.310901	2001:0:4137:9e50:2810	2002:d093:467d::d093:	ICMPv6	Echo request
90 15.321489	192.168.1.124	70.41.124.129	UDP	Source port: 59021 Des
91 15.321832	2001:0:4137:9e50:2810	2001:0:4137:9e50:205c	IPv6	IPv6 no next header
92 15.330986	65.55.129.172	192.168.1.124	UDP	Source port: pnrp-port
93 15.331472	65.55.129.172	192.168.1.124	UDP	Source port: pnrp-port

⊞ User Datagram Protocol, Src Port: 59021 (59021), Dst Port: teredo (3544)
  Teredo IPv6 over UDP tunneling

To establish a Remote Assistance session with a user using Easy Connect, the novice (the user being helped) should open the Windows Remote Assistance screen. This is done by selecting Start ➤ All Programs ➤ Maintenance ➤ Windows Remote Assistance (see Figure 6.2).

Figure 6.2: Accessing Remote Assistance

End users can also access the Remote Assistance feature by choosing Start ➤ Help And Support and choosing More Support options in the lower left of the Windows Help and Support window. Some users may be used to going to the Windows Help and Support window from previous operating system versions. It looks different, but it's still there. You can also launch the Windows Remote Assistance screen by typing **msra** in the Start menu Search box (Figure 6.3).

Figure 6.3: Using the Search box to launch Remote Assistance

Whichever way the novice or the expert launches the feature, the Windows Remote Assistance screen will become available. To get the novice user started using Easy Connect, the user must select Invite Someone You Trust To Help You. The initial Remote Assistance window where the novice will initiate an invitation is shown in Figure 6.4.

Figure 6.4: Remote Assistance initial screen

TIP Windows 7 is configured by default to allow Remote Assistance. If this has been disabled in the configuration, an error will be generated here and you must enable Remote Assistance. To enable a remote computer to allow Remote Desktop access, select Start ➤ Control Panel ➤ System And Security ➤ System. Click Remote Settings in the left pane. Select the Allow Remote Assistance Connections To This Computer check box and click OK. This will create an exception in Windows Firewall to allow Remote Assistance.

The Windows Remote Assistance screen (Figure 6.5) will ask "How do you want to invite your trusted helper?" and will offer the user the option to use Easy Connect.

Figure 6.5: Remote Assistance Invite screen

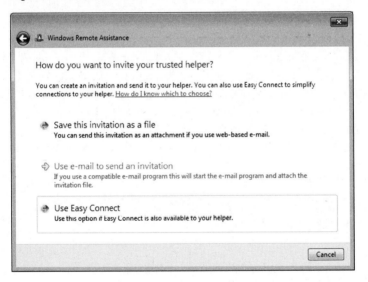

One nice feature of Easy Connect is that if the novice user has already established an Easy Connect session previously with an expert user, the screen after selecting Use Easy Connect will offer the novice the ability to connect to the same expert. The novice user can also choose to invite someone new and/or delete the old contact if necessary (Figure 6.6). The expert user will have the same option after choosing Use Easy Connect from the machine used for a previous Easy Connect session.

Figure 6.6: Remote Assistance Easy Re-Connect

After you select the Use Easy Connect option, Windows 7 will verify network connectivity briefly. This is the point at which the PNRP actions take place and the novice user's information is added to a cloud in the Internet space. The cloud is the group of machines holding little pieces of information, the identifiers of users needing connectivity, set up in a peer-to-peer sharing environment. PNRP uses this distributed infrastructure for its peer-to-peer name resolution. The novice user's contact information is entered into the PNRP cloud and an associated password is created (Figure 6.7) and displayed to the novice user.

Figure 6.7: Remote Assistance password

The novice user can now relay the password to the expert by text message, telephone, or any convenient conversation method. The novice will simply have to wait for the expert to initiate their part. The novice user will still have to accept the connection once the expert starts the Remote Assistance session.

The expert user needs to start a Remote Assistance session the same way the novice did. However, the expert will choose Help Someone Who Has Invited You from the Windows Remote Assistance screen (Figure 6.8).

The expert user will be presented with a dialog box to enter the password given by the novice user (Figure 6.9) who is initiating the Remote Assistance session.

After a few moments of querying the PNRP cloud and finding the connection path back to the novice user, the novice user is presented with a confirmation box (Figure 6.10) verifying that they want to allow help from the expert.

Figure 6.8: Choose Help Someone Who Has Invited You.

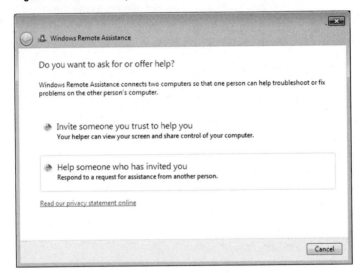

Figure 6.9: Entering the Easy Connect password

Figure 6.10: Click Yes at this screen to allow help.

The novice user will now have a control bar on their screen indicating the Remote Assistance session is active, as seen in Figure 6.11. From this control bar the novice can initiate a chat session with the expert and modify some general session settings (bandwidth, logging, contact information exchange, and sharing control).

Figure 6.11: Remote Assistance control bar

The expert user will be shown the novice user's desktop within a separate Remote Assistance window. The expert user will also have some general configuration setting capabilities as well as an option to request control (see Figure 6.12) of the novice user's desktop. The novice user will be allowed to accept or reject the expert's request.

Figure 6.12: The expert user will be shown the novice user's desktop.

Configuration

PART II

The expert and novice user can now have an interactive session where the necessary assistance can be provided. This method of help takes out the "Can you tell me what you see on your screen?" issues between two users. The Easy Connect feature takes one more problem out of the equation, getting a novice user to send an invitation to another user. The one caveat here is both users must be using Windows 7 for Easy Connect to be an option.

Invitation as a File

Requesting Remote Assistance from Windows 7 and other operating systems can also be initiated using an invitation as a file. The novice user should be instructed to send a file to the expert user providing assistance. The novice will also have to provide the password for the connection to the expert.

Complete the following steps to allow a novice user to generate an invitation file that will be sent to an expert user to initiate a Remote Assistance session. The expert user will then accept the invitation and the novice user will allow the expert to complete the connection.

NOTE   Most exercises presented in this section require two machines (real or virtual) to be connected to provide Remote Assistance novice and Remote Assistance expert functionality.

---

1. Have the novice user generate an invitation file and password. Select Start ➤ All Programs ➤ Maintenance ➤ Windows Remote Assistance.

2. The novice user chooses Invite Someone You Trust To Help You.

3. The novice user chooses Save This Invitation To A File.

4. The novice user will be given the option to save the invitation file. The default location is Libraries/Documents with a filename of Invitation.msrcIncident. The novice user can accept the default location by pressing the Save button.

5. The novice user sees the Windows Remote Assistance window with a password and the instructions to give the expert the invitation file and password. The invitation file must now be delivered to the expert. The expert must also be given the password to complete the Remote Assistance connection.

6. The expert user will save the Invitation file received from the novice user to the machine being used for Remote Assistance. The default location or Documents/Libraries can be used. The expert user should also have the password that was generated by the novice user.

7. The expert user will continue the establishment of the Remote Assistance session by selecting Start ➤ All Programs ➤ Maintenance ➤ Windows Remote Assistance.

8. The expert user chooses Help Someone Who Has Invited You.

9. The expert user chooses Use An Invitation File.

10. The expert user will select the saved invitation file and choose Open.

11. The expert user is presented with a Remote Assistance password dialog box. The password conveyed by the novice user is entered. The expert user's machine is now establishing a connection to the novice user. The expert must still wait for the novice to accept the connection.

12. The novice user will accept the connection and the Remote Assistance session continues as if it was using Easy Connect.

Invitation as E-mail

Requesting Remote Assistance from Windows 7 and other operating systems can also be initiated using an invitation sent by the default email program on the novice user's machine. The novice user should be instructed to email the invitation to the expert user providing assistance as well as provide the password for the connection.

Complete the following steps to have a novice user create an email invitation and send it to an expert user to request Remote Assistance.

1. Have the novice user generate an email invitation file and password. Select Start ➤ All Programs ➤ Maintenance ➤ Windows Remote Assistance.

2. The novice user chooses Invite Someone You Trust To Help You.

3. The novice user chooses Use E-mail To Send An Invitation As A File. If the novice user does not have a default email program set up, this option will be grayed (not available for selection).

4. The novice user's default email application will launch with the invitation file as an attachment and a generic message requesting help. The novice user simply needs to enter the email address of

the expert user who is going to provide Remote Assistance and send the email.

5. The novice user sees the Windows Remote Assistance window with a password and the instructions to tell the helper the connection password. The expert receives the email and must also be given the password to complete the Remote Assistance connection.

6. The expert user opens the email received from the novice user on the machine being used for Remote Assistance. The expert opens the attachment to initiate the connection to the novice. The expert user should also have the password that was generated by the novice user.

7. The expert user is presented a Remote Assistance password dialog box. The password conveyed by the novice user is entered. The expert user's machine is now establishing a connection to the novice user. The expert must still wait for the novice to accept the connection.

8. The novice user will accept the connection and the Remote Assistance session is continuing as if it was using Easy Connect.

Live Messenger Remote Assistance

Using Windows Live Messenger, Remote Assistance can also be initiated. Although you can share an invitation file through Live Messenger, there is a menu item available (as an Action item from the chat window) that allows a simplified Remote Assistance invitation offer. This may be a useful function for users who participate in the Windows Live Messenger experience and who also have the novice user who needs Remote Assistance as a buddy. In the world of IT desktop management, it is usually the case the end (novice) users are not buddies with the desktop support team.

Command-Line Remote Assistance

Windows Remote Assistance is also available from the command line using the Microsoft Remote Assistance executable (msra.exe) in both Windows 7 and Vista. This allows an expert to launch any of the functions of Remote Assistance from the command line. This also allows an IT team to set up a scripted environment for novice users as well. By issuing the msra.exe command without any switches, the initial Windows Remote Assistance screen is available, as shown in Figure 6.13.

Figure 6.13: MSRA novice-initiated Remote Assistance

Remote Assistance can also be incorporated in Group Policy in an enterprise environment by configuring the expert user as a helper for users in the enterprise (by domain or OU). Once configured as a helper, the expert can initiate a Remote Assistance session by issuing the command msra /offerra. This will bring up the Who Do You Want To Help? Remote Assistance screen (Figure 6.14). The expert can also include the novice user's IP address or computer name as an option to the offerRA switch to initiate the Remote Assistance session in one stop (such as **msra /offerra** *ipaddress* | *computername*).

Figure 6.14: MSRA expert-initiated Remote Assistance

```
C:\Windows\system32\cmd.exe
C:\Users\tyloru>msra /offerra
C:\Users\tyloru>
```

Windows Remote Assistance

Who do you want to help?

With the appropriate group policy settings in place you can connect directly using either name or the IP address. What settings are needed?

Type a computer name or IP address:

Or choose from your history:

Several switches are available to enable you to further control the establishment of the Remote Assistance session for both the novice and the expert user. Table 6.1 highlights many of the switches.

Table 6.1: MSRA Command-Line Switches

Switch	OS Availability	Functionality
/?	Vista and Windows 7	Displays the help options
/novice	Vista and Windows 7	Starts Remote Assistance at the Invite screen
/expert	Vista and Windows 7	Starts Remote Assistance at the Help Someone screen
/offerRA *ip* / *computer*	Vista and Windows 7	Starts Remote Assistance at the expert-initiated screen or with the options, by automatically initiating with the novice user (used with Group Policy configured in an Enterprise environment)
/email *password*	Vista and Windows 7	Creates an email invitation to be sent to an expert user to request assistance using the novice's default email program; a random password will be generated and need to be conveyed to the expert, or a password can be specified with the *password* option and conveyed to the expert.
/saveasfile path *password*	Vista and Windows 7	Creates a file invitation to be given to an expert user to request assistance; a random password will be generated, or optionally a password can be specified with the *password* option and conveyed to the expert.
/openfile *path*	Vista and Windows 7	Used to open the invitation file sent to the expert; can be local or on a shared network drive; the expert will enter the password given to the user when the session was initiated.
/geteasyhelp	Windows 7 only	Starts a novice user's Remote Assistance session using Easy Connect; presents the novice with the password to convey to the expert user.

Table 6.1: MSRA Command-Line Switches *(continued)*

Switch	OS Availability	Functionality
/offereasyhelp	Windows 7 only	Starts an expert user's Remote Assistance session using Easy Connect; presents the expert user with the screen to enter the password from the novice user.
/getcontacthelp *address*	Windows 7 only	Reestablishes a Remote Assistance session from a novice user's machine to the address from the previous session. The address is in the RAContactHistory.xml file as a 20-byte hexadecimal string with an .RAContact extension.
/offercontacthelp *address*	Windows 7 only	Reestablishes a Remote Assistance session from an expert user's machine to the address from the previous session. The address is in the RAContactHistory.xml file as a 20-byte hexadecimal string with an .RAContact extension.

Being able to run Windows Remote Assistance from the command line has many benefits to an IT team. Scripting is one benefit of msra.exe as well as simplicity for administrators who are comfortable with command-line utilization. Let's go through the process of establishing an Easy Connect session and a reestablishment of the session using msra.exe.

Establishing a First-Time Remote Assistance Connection

Complete the following steps to allow a first-time Remote Assistance connection establishment:

1. On the novice user's machine, launch Easy Connect from the command line: select Start ➢ All Programs ➢ Accessories ➢ Command Prompt, and type **msra /geteasyhelp**.

2. Note the Easy Connect password and take it (or give it) to the expert user at the expert user's machine.

3. On the expert user's machine, launch Easy Connect from the command line: select Start ➢ All Programs ➢ Accessories ➢ Command Prompt, and type **msra /offereasyhelp**.

PART II

Configuration

4. Enter the Easy Connect password generated from the novice machine for this session.

5. The novice user's machine displays the screen to accept help from the expert user; choose Yes to establish the session.

6. The Remote Assistance session is established and the expert user can help the novice user.

Reconnecting with an Expert

Perform the next set of steps to review the file with the address used to connect a user in a previous session to reconnect to the same party.

1. Acquire the Remote Assistance address for the session that is going to be reestablished from the novice user's machine; this is in the \users*user*\appdata\local directory on the novice user's machine in the file named RAContactHistory.xml. The entry is in the ADDRESS= line near the bottom of the file and is 20 bytes in length.

2. On the novice user's machine, launch Easy Connect from the command line: select Start ➢ All Programs ➢ Accessories ➢ Command Prompt, and type msra /getcontacthelp *address*.

   The novice user's machine is now waiting for the expert user to establish the connection.

3. On the expert user's machine, acquire the Remote Assistance address for the session that is going to be reestablished to the novice user's machine; this is in the \users*user*\appdata\local directory on the expert users machine in the file named RAContactHistory.xml. The entry is in the ADDRESS= line near the bottom of the file and is 20 bytes in length.

4. On the expert user's machine, launch Easy Connect from the command line: select Start ➢ All Programs ➢ Accessories ➢ Command Prompt, and type msra /offercontacthelp *address*.

5. The novice user's machine displays the screen to accept help from the expert user; choose Yes to reestablish the Remote Assistance session.

6. The Remote Assistance session is established and the expert user can help the novice user.

The `msra.exe` command-line options for saving as a file and for emailing an invitation can also be valuable to the IT staff. Scripting to the command line for creating an email invitation can be a timesaver for IT staff. Remember that you can define a password, or it can be randomly generated if the password parameter is not included in the `msra.exe` command. The following procedure uses the `msra.exe` application to create an email Remote Assistance invitation with a predefined password for the expert user to provide.

1. From the novice user's machine select Start ➤ All Programs ➤ Accessories ➤ Command Prompt, and type **msra /email raWillP** (the password is case sensitive). If the password parameter is not entered, a random password is generated.

2. The default email program on the novice user's machine launches with a message stating help is desired; it includes an attachment of the invitation file, `Invitation.msraincident`. Enter the expert user's email address and send the invitation. The password must be conveyed to the expert in order to establish the Remote Assistance session.

3. The expert user receives the email sent by the novice user and opens the attachment, launching the Remote Assistance program, and requests the password for the novice user's session.

4. Enter the password (passwords are case sensitive) and click OK. The novice user accepts the expert user and the Remote Assistance session continues normally.

Creating and Saving Invitation Files

In the following steps, you will create and save an invitation file to be presented to an expert user. This time, though, you will let `msra.exe` generate a random password, which the novice user will convey to the expert.

1. On the novice user's machine, select Start ➤ All Programs ➤ Accessories ➤ Command Prompt, and type **msra /saveasfile** *path*. (The path is an accessible directory and filename for the invitation.) The file is saved with the `.msraincident` extension. Optionally you can add a password parameter to the command to specify that a password be used (passwords are case sensitive).

2. The novice user's machine displays the password to be conveyed to the expert user. The novice user emails the file in the *path* location to the expert user.

3. The expert user receives the file from the novice user and opens it by selecting Start ➢ All Programs ➢ Accessories ➢ Command Prompt and typing `msra /openfile` *path* (the path is an accessible directory and filename for the invitation).

4. The expert user enters the password (which is case sensitive) and clicks OK. The novice user accepts the expert user and the Remote Assistance session continues normally.

Now that we have looked at Remote Assistance, let's see how Remote Desktop works.

Use a Remote Desktop

Remote Desktop is a Windows 7 tool that allows you to take control of a remote computer's keyboard, video, and mouse. When you control a remote computer with this tool, no one needs to be available to collaborate with you. While the remote computer is being accessed, it remains locked and actions that are performed remotely are not visible on the monitor that is attached to the remote computer.

New/Updated Features

Windows 7 Remote Desktop is an enhanced version of the Remote Desktop functionality that has been with us for many of the previous versions of Windows—both client and server operating systems. Remote Desktop uses Remote Desktop Protocol (RDP) to provide the data between a host and a client machine. Windows 7 uses the latest version of RDP, RDP 7.0. Windows 7 Remote Desktop enhancements include:

- RDP Core Performance Enhancements
- True Multi-Monitor Support
- Direct 2D and Direct 3D 10.1 Application Support
- Windows 7 Aero Support
- Bi-directional Audio Support
- Multimedia and Media Foundation support

There are many uses for Remote Desktop. The most common involves an administrator attempting to perform tasks on an end machine or server. This is a valid use, but you can take it further and make it an end-user function as well. Many of you have been using Terminal Servers for a while now, with the end user using a local machine as an extension of the monitor, keyboard, and mouse when the operating system is located anywhere but on the local machine. Often, this function serves end users sitting at a console at work. But consider the case of a user who has the opportunity to work from home as well as at the office. Wouldn't it be nice if you could provide the same environment without having to provide duplicate information (at work and at home)? Remote Desktop for the end user is becoming that solution.

The one remaining caveat is that the end user expects the same functionality and performance regardless of which keyboard they're using—home or office. If you notice the enhancements to Remote Desktop (which are enhancements to RDP), you can see the main goal of enhancing Remote Desktop is to make the user experience as comfortable and seamless as possible. The example here is that of true multimonitor support. In the previous version of RDP, you could span multiple monitors. This did not give you the multiple-monitor functionality end users would have at the local machine (in the case of a laptop with an external monitor). The Windows 7 implementation allows independent multiple-monitor functionality. The end-user experience is also enhanced with the new audio functionality. This also becomes a better environment for the administrator.

Configuring a Computer for Remote Desktop

To enable a remote computer to allow Remote Desktop access:

1. Select Start ➤ Control Panel ➤ System And Security ➤ System.

2. Click Remote Settings in the left pane.

3. On the Remote tab of System Properties, choose either Allow Connections From Computers Running Any Version Of Remote Desktop (Less Secure) or Allow Connections Only From Computers Running Remote Desktop With Network Level Authentication (More Secure).

Don't Allow Connections To This Computer is the default selection. The Allow options create an exception in Windows Firewall to permit Remote Desktop sessions. Figure 6.15 shows the Remote tab of the System Properties dialog box where Remote Desktop access is configured.

Figure 6.15: Remote tab of System Properties

By default, only members of the Administrators group can access a computer that has been configured to use Remote Desktop. To enable other users to access the computer remotely, choose Select Users. The Remote Desktop Users dialog box shown in Figure 6.16 is where users can be added. This dialog box allows you to add a user to the Remote Desktop Users group on the machine.

Figure 6.16: You can add Remote Desktop users on this screen.

You can verify the exceptions in Windows Firewall by choosing Start ➤ Control Panel ➤ System And Security ➤ Windows Firewall. Select Allow A Program Or Feature Through Windows Firewall in the left pane. Remote Desktop should be selected in the Allowed Programs And Features box.

Once the configuration to allow a Remote Desktop session on the computer being accessed remotely (the host) is complete and permission has been granted for the user to access the machine, a Remote Desktop session can be started. Use the following steps to set up a Remote Desktop session:

1. From the machine where the Remote Desktop session is being initiated (the client), choose Start ➤ All Programs ➤ Accessories ➤ Remote Desktop Connection.

2. Enter the computer name or IP address of the host machine where the Remote Desktop session is going to be established. This is a machine that has been configured to accept Remote Desktop connections.

3. Click the Connect button.

4. Enter user credentials with permission to establish a Remote Desktop session on the remote machine and click OK.

5. You might be asked to continue with a certificate that cannot be verified. If you are confident you are connecting to the correct machine, you can click Yes to continue.

6. If a user was logged onto the remote machine, you may continue by clicking Yes, but the user will be disconnected from the terminal. The user will remain logged on the machine but will not have access while the Remote Desktop session is active. The user at the remote machine will be given the opportunity to cancel the connection, but the connection will be established if no intervention occurs.

7. The client machine will now display the Desktop of the host machine. Administrative and/or user functions can be carried out just as if the administrator or user was sitting at the host machine.

8. When the session is complete, the terminal session can be terminated by closing the Remote Desktop window or choosing Start ➤ Logoff Options ➤ Disconnect. This will end the interactive session, but the logon session will remain active on the host machine. To disconnect and log off the Remote Desktop session, choose Start ➤ Logoff.

Configuration

PART II

Remote Desktop Connection Options

When connecting to a Remote Desktop host machine, you have several options for enhancing the client user session. The options allow configuration for general settings, display options, local resource access, programs to be executed on startup, the user experience, and advanced options for security and Remote Desktop gateway access. The options are available by selecting the Options button in the lower left of the initial Remote Desktop Connection screen. Figure 6.17 shows this screen with the options both hidden (left) and displayed (right).

Figure 6.17: Remote Desktop options

From the General tab, you can select the host computer and username. You can choose to save user credentials on this tab as well. The connection settings can be saved to a file, or an existing RDP file can be opened from the General tab.

From the Display tab (Figure 6.18), you can adjust the size of the display screen. This is also where you can select the option to use multiple monitors. The color depth (color quality) appears on the Display tab along with the option to display the connection bar when using full-screen display.

On the Local Resources tab (Figure 6.19), you can configure remote audio settings, keyboard settings, and local device and resources access.

Figure 6.18: Remote Desktop Display options

Figure 6.19: Remote Desktop Local Resources options

The Programs tab (Figure 6.20) for Remote Desktop options allows the selection of a program to run at connection startup. The program name and path are specified as well as a start-up folder if necessary.

Figure 6.20: Remote Desktop Programs options

The end-user experience is important to the overall success of using Remote Desktop in the user environment. Remote Desktop can be used to provide a user with the ability to connect to their machine and "remote in." The most seamless environment from the work to the remote location is desirable, but will be dependent on the bandwidth available. The more bandwidth, the more high-end features can be made available to the end user. OK, this is also nice for the administrator who is working on an end user machine as well. The Experience tab (Figure 6.21) of the options dialog allows the configuration of the "End User Experience."

The behavior of the Remote Desktop connection with regard to security is configured on the Advanced tab of the Remote Desktop options dialog. The Advanced tab also allows the configuration of a Remote Desktop Gateway to allowing Remote Desktop connections to be established from any Internet location through SSL. The user must still be authorized and the Remote Desktop client must still be available.

Figure 6.21: Remote Desktop Experience Options

Saving Remote Desktop Connection Options

A nice feature of Remote Desktop is the ability to save your RDP connection parameters as a file, which can then be opened (as simply as double-clicking the file on a machine with a Remote Desktop client available). Complete the following steps to save an RDP file used to supply preconfigured parameters to a Remote Desktop session establishment:

1. Ensure that the user's host machine is configured to allow Remote Desktop connections. The user should be a member of the Remote Desktop Users group.

2. Launch the Remote Desktop connection dialog box by selecting Start ➤ All Programs ➤ Accessories ➤ Remote Desktop Connection.

3. Click Options in the lower left of the Remote Desktop Connection dialog box to expand the options.

4. Ensure the computer name or IP address and username are entered for the desired connection.

5. Optionally, other options can be configured if desired.

6. Click Save As on the General tab.

7. Enter a filename for the RDP connection file to be saved and choose Save to save the file. Note the default location is Documents from the Libraries parent. You may want to access this file later; it does not need to be run from this directory.

Initiating a Connection with an RDP File

The perfect end to using an .rdp Remote Desktop file is to reestablish a Remote Desktop session using the saved file. The following steps walk you through the process of using the file:

1. Launch the Remote Desktop connection dialog by selecting Start ➤ All Programs ➤ Accessories ➤ Remote Desktop Connection.

2. Click Options in the lower left of the Remote Desktop Connection dialog box to expand the options.

3. On the General tab of the Remote Desktop Connection screen with Options selected, choose Open.

4. The RDP file is opened and the connection parameters are loaded into the Remote Desktop Connection screen. Choose Connect to establish the Remote Desktop session with the configured parameters.

5. A warning message might appear stating the publisher of the remote connections cannot be verified. You can continue if you are confident this is the correct file. From this warning box, you can also open options to allow or /prohibit resource access for this connection.

6. The Remote Desktop session will now begin.

Controlling a Windows Aero Interface

One of the added features of Remote Desktop in Windows 7 is the ability to handle the Windows Aero interface. The Aero interface uses the opaque window borders as well as the flip functionality available since Vista. This experience was not available in previous versions of Remote Desktop. To have the full Windows Aero experience, the Desktop Composition option needs to be selected in the Remote Desktop options. The following procedure will take you through the process of enabling Desktop Composition.

1. Launch the Remote Desktop connection dialog box by selecting Start ➤ All Programs ➤ Accessories ➤ Remote Desktop Connection.

2. Click Options in the lower left of the Remote Desktop Connection dialog box.

3. Click the Experience tab.

4. Select the appropriate bandwidth or type of connection between the client and the host (choose the slowest link between them). Bandwidth-based experience parameters are suggestions and can be modified by choosing the desired (or undesired) experience item. Remember, Desktop Composition is going to present the client user with the Windows Aero experience.

Viewing Advanced Remote Desktop Gateway Options

Windows Server 2008 has the ability to be a Remote Desktop Gateway by adding the TS Gateway role. Once installed, a client can connect to (or through, as the case may be) the host via the Terminal Server. This can be accomplished via Internet Explorer and an HTTPS session (the Remote Desktop client can be automatically installed when connecting) or by configuring a Remote Desktop Gateway within the Remote Desktop Connection Options' Advanced screen. The following steps will take you to the screen to configure Remote Desktop Gateway.

1. Launch the Remote Desktop connection dialog box by selecting Start ➤ All Programs ➤ Accessories ➤ Remote Desktop Connection.

2. Click Options in the lower-left corner of the Remote Desktop Connection window.

3. Click the Advanced tab.

4. In the Connect From Anywhere section, click the Settings button.

5. Review the Remote Desktop Gateway configuration items.

Command-Line Remote Desktop

It is possible to initiate a Remote Desktop session using command-line functionality. This provides you with scripting capabilities for Remote

Configuration

PART II

Desktop. The command line uses the `mstsc.exe` (Microsoft Terminal Server Client) application with optional switches for configuration. Several switches can be included on the same command line if appropriate (screen width and height, for example). The command-line options are shown in Table 6.2.

Table 6.2: MSTSC Command-Line Switches

Switch	Functionality
`/?`	Displays the help options.
`/v:server`	Starts Remote Desktop specifying the server name of the host machine.
`/v:port`	Starts Remote Desktop specifying an IP address (port) for the host machine.
`/admin`	Starts Remote Desktop in admin mode, bypassing TS CAL (Terminal Server Client Access License) requirements and disabling several functions not required for administration services.
`/f`	Starts Remote Desktop in full-screen mode.
`/w:width`	Specifies the width of the Remote Desktop connection window.
`/h:height`	Specifies the height of the Remote Desktop connection window.
`/public`	Starts Remote Desktop in public mode; passwords and bitmaps are not cached.
`/span`	Matches the Remote Desktop width and height with the local virtual desktop. This can span multiple monitors if necessary; monitors must be arranged to form a rectangle.
`/multimon`	Configures the Remote Desktop session to match the client-side configuration for multiple monitors. The layout does not have to be rectangular and can consist of various sizes of monitors.
`/edit filename`	Opens a previously defined RDP file for editing. It opens the file in the Remote Desktop Connection window with options expanded, allowing you to edit the existing parameters in the RDP file. The variable *filename* must include the full path.
`/migrate`	Migrates legacy connection files created with the previous Client Connection Manager to the new RDP connection file format.

Rather than use the menu structure to launch the Remote Desktop Connection screen, you can launch it through the command prompt or from the Start menu Search box.

Launching Remote Desktop

The following procedure guides you through launching Remote Desktop from the command prompt:

1. On the client machine, launch Remote Desktop from the command line: select Start ➤ All Programs ➤ Accessories ➤ Command Prompt and type `mstsc`.

2. Enter the name or IP address of the host machine where the Remote Desktop session is to be established. The host machine must be configured to allow Remote Desktop sessions and the user connecting will need to have authorization to establish a Remote Desktop session.

3. The user on the client machine will enter credentials and the Remote Desktop session will continue normally.

4. When the session is complete, the terminal session can be terminated by closing the Remote Desktop window or by choosing Start ➤ Logoff Options ➤ Disconnect. This ends the interactive session; however, the logon session remains active on the host machine. To disconnect and log off the Remote Desktop session, choose Start ➤ Logoff.

Specifying a Host Machine

If you know the IP address (or name) of the machine you want to establish a Remote Desktop session with, you can include the IP or name as a parameter to the `mstsc.exe` command. Complete the following steps to complete this type of session:

1. On the client machine, launch Remote Desktop from the command line: select Start ➤ All Programs ➤ Accessories ➤ Command Prompt and type `mstsc /v:ip-address` (where the IP address is the host machine). The host machine must be configured to allow Remote Desktop sessions and the user connecting will need to have authorization to establish a Remote Desktop session.

2. The user on the client machine will enter credentials and the Remote Desktop session will continue normally.

3. When the session is complete, the terminal session can be terminated by closing the Remote Desktop window or choosing Start ➤ Logoff Options ➤ Disconnect. This will end the interactive session,

Configuration

PART II

however, the logon session will remain active on the host machine. To disconnect and log off the Remote Desktop session, choose Start ➢ Logoff.

Editing an RDP Configuration File

If you have previously configured a Remote Desktop connection and saved the file, you can open the file for editing using `mstsc.exe`. When you open the file for editing, the file is loaded into the Remote Desktop Connection dialog box without attempting to establish the connection. The Remote Desktop Connection window is opened with the options expanded (you don't have to click the Options button). The following procedure is used to open a previously saved RDP configuration file.

1. On the client machine, launch Remote Desktop from the command line: select Start ➢ All Programs ➢ Accessories ➢ Command Prompt and type `mstsc /edit filename` (where `filename` is the path and filename of a previously defined RDP connection file).

2. The Remote Desktop Connection window will open with the options expanded and the parameters from the previously defined RDP file loaded for editing.

3. Changes can be made (or parameters verified) by viewing the configuration of the various tabs.

4. Changes made can be saved to the RDP file by choosing Save As from the General tab.

5. Use the existing filename or enter a new filename for the RDP connection file to be saved and choose Save to save the file.

Specifying Display Size

You can specify other parameters when launching a Remote Desktop session from the command line. Two more options for `mstsc.exe` are the width and height of the display window on the local machine. The following procedure configures the IP address of the machine you are connecting to as well as the local machine's display size as 640 × 480 for the Remote Desktop:

1. On the client machine, launch Remote Desktop from the command line: select Start ➢ All Programs ➢ Accessories ➢ Command Prompt and type `mstsc /v:ip-address /w:640 /h:480`. The host machine must be configured to allow Remote Desktop

sessions and the user connecting will need to have authorization to establish a Remote Desktop session.

2. The user on the client machine will enter credentials and the Remote Desktop session will continue normally.

3. When the session is complete, the terminal session can be terminated by closing the Remote Desktop window or choosing Start ➤ Logoff Options ➤ Disconnect. This will end the interactive session, but the logon session will remain active on the host machine. To disconnect and log off the Remote Desktop session, choose Start ➤ Logoff.

Remote Assistance and Remote Desktop can be helpful tools in the administrative arsenal. They allow you to help your users without having to be physically present at their location.

Configuration

PART II

PART III

Users and
Security

IN THIS PART ▶

Users and Security

PART III

7

Configuring Users and Groups

IN THIS CHAPTER, YOU WILL LEARN TO:

Users and Security

PART III

O ne task that must be completed before users can access a Windows 7 machine is creating user accounts. Without a user account, a user cannot log on to a computer, server, or network.

When a user logs onto a Windows 7 machine, they must supply a username and password. Then their user accounts are validated by a security mechanism. In Windows 7, users can log on to a computer locally, or they can log on through Active Directory.

When you first create users, you assign them usernames, passwords, and password settings. After a user is created, you can change these settings and select other options for that user through the User Accounts tool in Control Panel.

Group accounts are used to ease network administration by grouping together users who have similar permission requirements. Groups are an important part of network management. Many administrators are able to accomplish the majority of their management tasks through the use of groups; they rarely assign permissions to individual users. Windows 7 includes built-in local groups, such as Administrators and Backup Operators. These groups already have all the permissions needed to accomplish specific tasks. Windows 7 also uses default special groups, which are managed by the system. Users become members of special groups based on their requirements for computer and network access.

You create and manage local groups through the Local Users and Groups tool. With this utility, you can add groups, change group membership, rename groups, and delete groups.

Understand Windows 7 User Accounts

When you install Windows 7, several user accounts are created automatically. You can then create new user accounts. As you already know, these accounts allow users to access resources.

On Windows 7 computers, you can create local user accounts. If your network has a Windows Server 2008, Windows Server 2003, or Windows Server 2000 domain controller, your network can have domain user accounts as well.

One of the features included with Windows 7 is User Account Control (UAC). UAC provides an additional level of security by limiting the level of access that users have when performing normal, everyday tasks. When needed, users can gain elevated access for specific administrative tasks.

In the following sections, you will learn about the default user accounts that are created by Windows 7 and the difference between local and domain user accounts.

Working with Account Types

Windows 7 supports two basic types of user accounts: Administrator and Standard User, as shown in Figure 7.1. Each one of these accounts has a specific purpose:

Figure 7.1: User Types screen

Administrator   The Administrator account provides unrestricted access for performing administrative tasks. As a result, Administrator accounts should be used only for performing administrative tasks and should not be used for normal computing tasks.

Only Administrator accounts can change the Registry. This is important to know because when you install most software onto a Windows 7 machine, the Registry gets changed. This is why you need administrator rights to install most software.

Standard User   You should apply the Standard User account for every user of the computer. Standard User accounts can perform most day-to-day tasks, such as running Microsoft Word, accessing email, using Internet Explorer, and so on. Running as a Standard User increases security by limiting the possibility of a virus or other malicious code from infecting the computer and making systemwide changes, because Standard User accounts are unable to make systemwide changes.

When you install Windows 7, by default premade accounts called built-in accounts are established. Let's look at these account types.

Using Built-in Accounts

Built-in accounts are accounts that are created at the time you install the Windows 7 operating system. Windows 7, when installed into a workgroup environment, has four user accounts, as shown in Figure 7.2.

Figure 7.2: Four default accounts

Administrator The Administrator account is a special account that has full control over the computer. The Administrator account can perform all tasks, such as creating users and groups, managing the file system, and setting up printing. Note that the Administrator account is disabled by default.

Guest The Guest account allows users to access the computer even if they do not have a unique username and password. Because of the inherent security risks associated with this type of user, the Guest account is disabled by default. When this account is enabled, it is usually given limited privileges.

HomeGroup User The HomeGroup user is created by default to allow this machine to connect to other machines within the same HomeGroup network. This account is enabled by default.

Initial User   The initial user account uses the name of the registered user. By default, the initial user is a member of the Administrators group.

These users are considered local users and their permissions are contained within the Windows 7 operating system. You can also have users logging into the Windows 7 computer who are considered domain users. Let's look at the difference between these account types.

Using Local and Domain User Accounts

Windows 7 supports two kinds of users: local users and domain users. A computer that is running Windows 7 has the ability to store its own user accounts database. The users stored at the local computer are known as local user accounts.

Active Directory is a directory service that is available with the Windows Server 2008, Windows Server 2003, and Windows 2000 Server platforms. It stores information in a central database called Active Directory that allows users to have a single user account for the network. The users stored in Active Directory's central database are called domain user accounts.

If you use local user accounts, they must be configured on each computer that the user needs access to within the network. For this reason, domain user accounts are commonly used to manage users on any network with more than 10 users.

On Windows 7, Windows Server 2008, Windows Server 2003, Windows XP, and Windows Vista computers you can create local users through the Local Users and Groups item, as described in the section "Work with User Accounts," later in this chapter. On Windows Server 2008, Windows Server 2003, and Windows 2000 Server domain controllers, you manage users with the Microsoft Active Directory Users and Computers utility.

Users and Security

PART III

NOTE   Active Directory is covered in more detail in Chapter 10, "Configuring Network Connectivity." But if you are looking for a book that covers Active Directory in detail, refer to *MCTS: Windows Server 2008 Active Directory Configuration Study Guide*, by William Panek and James Chellis (Sybex, 2008).

Now that you're familiar with the different types of users, let's see how to use accounts to log on and log off the local machine or domain.

Log On and Log Off

Users and administrators must log on to a Windows 7 computer before they can use that computer. When you create user accounts, you set up the computer to accept the logon information provided by the Windows 7 user. You can log on locally to a Windows 7 computer using a local computer account, or you can log on to a domain using an Active Directory account.

When you install the computer, you specify that it will be a part of a workgroup, which implies a local logon, or that the computer will be a part of a domain, which implies a domain logon.

When users are ready to stop working on a Windows 7 computer, they should log off. Users can log off using the Windows Security dialog box.

In the following sections, you will learn about local user authentication and how a user logs off a Windows 7 computer.

Understanding the Local User Logon Authentication Process

Depending on whether you are logging on to a computer locally or are logging on to a domain, Windows 7 uses two different logon procedures. When you log on to a Windows 7 computer locally, you must present a valid username and password (ones that exist within the local accounts database). As part of a successful authentication, the following steps take place:

1. At system startup, the user is prompted to click their username from a list of users who have been created locally. This is significantly different from the Ctrl+Alt+Del logon sequence that was used by earlier versions of Windows. The Ctrl+Alt+Del sequence is still used when you log on to a domain environment. You can also configure the Ctrl+Alt+Del logon sequence as an option in a local environment.

2. The local computer compares the user's logon credentials with the information in the local security database.

3. If the information presented matches the account database, an access token is created. Access tokens are used to identify the user and the groups of which that user is a member.

TIP   Access tokens are created only when you log on. If you change group memberships, you need to log off and log on again to update the access token.

Other actions that take place as part of the logon process include the following list:

- The system reads the part of the Registry that contains user configuration information.

- The user's profile is loaded. (User profiles are discussed in the section "Setting Up User Profiles, Logon Scripts, and Home Folders," later in this chapter.)

- Any policies that have been assigned to the user through a user or Group Policy are enforced. (Policies for users are discussed later in Chapter 8, "Managing Security.")

- Any logon scripts that have been assigned are executed. (I discuss assigning logon scripts to users in the "Setting Up User Profiles, Logon Scripts, and Home Folders" section.)

- Persistent network and printer connections are restored.

Now that you've seen how a local logon process works, let's explore logging off a Windows 7 machine.

Logging Off Windows 7

To log off Windows 7, click Start, point to the arrow next to the Shutdown button, and then click Logoff. Pressing Ctrl+Alt+Del also presents you with a screen that allows you to select whether to lock the computer, switch users, log off, change the password, or start Task Manager.

At this point you should have a good grasp of the various types of accounts on a Windows 7 computer. Next let's see how to manage these accounts.

Users and Security

PART III

Work with User Accounts

To set up and manage your local user accounts, use the Local Users and Groups or the User Accounts utility in Control Panel. With either option, you can create, disable, delete, and rename user accounts, as well as change user passwords.

Using Local Users and Groups

Here are the two common methods for accessing the Local Users and Groups utility:

- You can load Local Users and Groups as a Microsoft Management Console (MMC) snap-in. (See Chapter 3, "Configuring Disks," for details on the MMC and the purpose of snap-ins.)

- You can access the Local Users and Groups tool through the Computer Management utility.

Perform the following steps to access the Local Users and Groups utility. The steps first add the Local Users and Groups snap-in MMC to the Desktop.

1. Select Start. In the search box, type **MMC,** and then press Enter.

2. If a warning box appears, click Yes.

3. Select File ➢ Add/Remove Snap-in.

4. Scroll down the list, highlight Local Users and Groups, and then click the Add button, as shown in Figure 7.3.

5. In the Choose Target Machine dialog box, click the Finish button to accept the default selection of Local Computer.

6. Click OK in the Add Or Remove Snap-in dialog box.

7. In the MMC window, right-click the Local Users and Groups folder and choose New Window From Here. You will see that Local Users and Groups is now the main window.

8. Click File ➢ Save As. Name the console **Local Users and Groups** and make sure you save it to the Desktop using the Save In drop-down box, as shown in Figure 7.4. Click the Save button.

9. Close the MMC Snap-in.

Figure 7.3: Local Users and Groups snap-in

Figure 7.4: Saving the Local Users and Groups console

You should now see the Local Users and Groups snap-in on your Desktop. You can also open the Local Users and Groups MMC from the Computer Management utility.

Perform the following steps to open the Local Users and Groups utility from the Computer Management utility:

1. Select Start and then right-click My Computer and select Manage.

2. In the Computer Management window, expand the System Tools folder and then the Local Users and Groups folder.

TIP   If your computer doesn't have the MMC configured, the quickest way to access the Local Users and Groups utility is through the Computer Management utility.

Now let's look at another way to configure users and groups: using the User Accounts utility in Control Panel.

Using the User Accounts Item in Control Panel

The User Accounts item in Control Panel provides the ability to manage user accounts, in addition to configuring parental controls. To access this utility, click Start ➢ Control Panel ➢ User Accounts. Table 7.1 shows the configurable options in User Accounts.

Table 7.1: Configurable User Account Options

Option	Explanation
Change Your Password	This allows users to change their password.
Remove Your Password	Allows you to remove a password from a user's account.
Change Your Picture	Allows you to change the account picture.
Change Your Account Name	Allows you to rename the account.
Change Your Account Type	Allows you to change your account type from Standard User to Administrator, or vice versa.
Manage Another Account	Allows you to configure other accounts on the Windows 7 machine.
Change UAC Settings	Allows you to set the level of notification when changes are made to a user's computer. These notifications can prevent potentially hazardous programs from being loaded onto the operating system.

Table 7.1: Configurable User Account Options *(continued)*

Option	Explanation
Manage Your Credentials	Allows you to set up credentials that easily enable you to connect to websites that require usernames and passwords or computers that require certificates.
Create A Password Reset Disk	Allows you to create a disk that users can use when they forget their password.
Link Online IDs	Allows you to link an Online ID with your Windows account. This makes it easier to share files with other computers.
Manage Your File Encryption Certificates	Allows you to manage your file encryption certificates.
Configure Advanced User Profile Properties	This link brings you directly to the User's Profile dialog box in Control Panel ➤ System ➤ Advanced ➤ System Settings.
Change My Environment Variables	Allows you to access the Environment Variables dialog box directly.

After you install Windows 7, you must create user accounts for users who will be accessing the machine. Let's take a look at this process.

Creating New Users

To create users on a Windows 7 computer, you must be logged on as a user with permissions to create a new user, or you must be a member of the Administrators group. In the following sections, you will learn about username rules and conventions, usernames, and security identifiers in more detail.

Username Rules and Conventions

The only requirement for creating a new user is that you must provide a valid username. "Valid" means that the name must follow the Windows 7 rules for usernames. However, it's also a good idea to have your own rules for usernames, which form your naming convention.

The following rules apply to Windows 7 usernames:

- A username must be from 1 to 20 characters.

- The username must be unique to all other user and group names stored on that specified computer.

- The username cannot contain the following characters:
  * / \ [ ] : ; | = , + ? < > " @

- A username cannot consist exclusively of periods or spaces.

Keeping these rules in mind, you should choose a naming convention (a consistent naming format). For example, consider a user named William Panek. One naming convention might use the last name and first initial, for the username WillP or WilliamP. Another naming convention might use the first initial and last name, for the username WPanek.

Other user-naming conventions are based on the naming convention defined for email names, so that the logon name and email name match. You should also provide a mechanism that would accommodate duplicate names. For example, if you had a user named Jane Smith and a user named John Smith, you might use a middle initial for usernames, such as JDSmith and JRSmith.

It is also a good practice to come up with a naming convention for groups, printers, and computers.

TIP It's not a good practice to use the first name and first letter of the user's last name, as in WilliamP. In a mid-sized to large company, there are greater chances of having two WilliamP users' accounts, but the odds that you will have two WPaneks are rare.

If you choose to use the first name and first letter of the last name option, it can be a lot of work to go back and change this format later if the company grows larger. Choose a naming convention that can grow with the company.

Now, let's look at how usernames get a special ID number associated with the account and how that number affects your accounts.

Usernames and Security Identifiers

When you create a new user, a security identifier (SID) is automatically created on the computer for the user account. The username is a property of the SID. For example, a user SID might look like this:

S-1-5-21-823518204-746137067-120266-629-500

It's apparent that using SIDs for user identification would make administration a nightmare. Fortunately, for your administrative tasks, you see and use the username instead of the SID.

SIDs have several advantages. Because Windows 7 uses the SID as the user object, you can easily rename a user while still retaining all the properties of that user. The reason is that all security settings get associated with the SID and not the user account.

SIDs also ensure that if you delete and re-create a user account with the same username, the new user account will not have any of the properties of the old account because it is based on a new, unique SID. Every time you create a new user, a unique SID gets associated. Even if the username is the same as a previously deleted account, the system still sees the username as a new user.

Because every user account gets a unique SID number, it is a good practice to disable accounts for users who leave the company instead of deleting the accounts. If you ever need to access the disabled account again, you can do so. Disabling user accounts and deleting user accounts are discussed in detail in the next two sections.

When you create a new user, there are many options that you have to configure for that user. Table 7.2 describes all the options available in the New User dialog box.

Table 7.2: User Account Options Available in the New User Dialog Box

Option	Description
User Name	Defines the username for the new account. Choose a name that is consistent with your naming convention (for example, WPanek). This is the only required field. Usernames are not case sensitive.
Full Name	Allows you to provide more detailed name information. This is typically the user's first and last names (for example, Will Panek). By default, this field contains the same name as the User Name field.
Description	Typically used to specify a title and/or location (for example, Sales-Nashville) for the account, but it can be used to provide any additional information about the user.
Password	Assigns the initial password for the user. For security purposes, avoid using readily available information about the user. Passwords are case sensitive.
Confirm Password	Confirms that you typed the password the same way two times to verify that you entered the password correctly.
User Must Change Password At Next Logon	If enabled, forces the user to change the password the first time they log on. This is done to increase security. By default, this option is selected.

Users and Security

PART III

Table 7.2: User Account Options Available in the New User Dialog Box *(continued)*

Option	Description
User Cannot Change Password	If enabled, prevents a user from changing their password. It is useful for accounts such as Guest that are shared by more than one user. By default, this option is not selected.
Password Never Expires	If enabled, specifies that the password will never expire, even if a password policy has been specified. For example, you might enable this option if this is a service account and you do not want the administrative overhead of managing password changes. By default, this option is not selected.
Account Is Disabled	If enabled, specifies that this account cannot be used for logon purposes. For example, you might select this option for template accounts or if an account is not currently being used. It helps keep inactive accounts from posing security threats. By default, this option is not selected.

Perform the following steps to create a new local user account. Before you complete these steps, make sure you are logged on as a user with permissions to create new users and have already added the Local Users and Groups snap-in to the MMC.

1. Open the Admin Console MMC desktop shortcut that was created in the previous steps and expand the Local Users and Groups snap-in. If a dialog box appears, click Yes.

2. Highlight the Users folder and select Action ➢ New User. The New User dialog box appears, as shown in Figure 7.5.

Figure 7.5: New User dialog box

3. In the User Name text box, type **CPanek**.

4. In the Full Name text box, type **Crystal Panek**.

5. In the Description text box, type **Operations Manager**.

6. Leave the Password and Confirm Password text boxes empty and accept the defaults for the check boxes. Make sure you deselect the User Must Change Password At Next Logon option. Click the Create button to add the user.

7. Use the New User dialog box to create six more users, filling out the fields as follows:

   - Name: **WPanek**; Full Name: **Will Panek**; Description: **IT Admin**; Password: (blank)

   - Name: **TWentworth**; Full Name: **Tylor Wentworth**; Description: **Cisco Admin**; Password: (blank)

   - Name: **GWashington**; Full Name: **George Washington**; Description: **President**; Password: **P@sswOrD**

   - Name: **JAdams**; Full Name: **John Adams**; Description: **Vice President**; Password: **v!$t@**

   - Name: **BFranklin**; Full Name: **Ben Franklin**; Description: **NH Sales Manager**; Password: **P3@ch** (with a capital P)

   - Name: **ALincoln**; Full Name: **Abe Lincoln**; Description: **Tech Support**; Password: **Bearded1** (capital B)

8. After you finish creating all the users, click the Close button to exit the New User dialog box.

NOTE   You can also create users through the command-line utility NET USER. For more information about this command, type **NET USER /?** at a command prompt.

As we stated earlier, it's a good practice to disable accounts for users who leave the company. Let's look at that process.

Disabling User Accounts

When a user account is no longer needed, the account should be disabled or deleted. After you've disabled an account, you can later enable it again to restore it with all of its associated user properties. An account that is deleted, however, can never be recovered.

Users and Security

PART III

NOTE   User accounts not in use pose a security threat because an intruder could access your network through an inactive account. User accounts that are no longer needed should be disabled immediately.

You might disable an account because a user will not be using it for a period of time, perhaps because that employee is going on vacation or taking a leave of absence. Another reason to disable an account is that you're planning to put another user in that same function.

For example, suppose that Gary, the engineering manager, quits. If you disable his account, when your company hires a new engineering manager, you can simply rename Gary's user account (to the username for the new manager) and enable that account. This ensures that the user who takes over Gary's position will have all the same user properties and own all the same resources.

Disabling accounts also provides a security mechanism for special situations. For example, if your company were laying off a group of people, a security measure would be to disable their accounts at the same time the layoff notices were given out. This prevents those users from inflicting any damage to the company's files after they receive their layoff notice.

Perform the following steps to disable a user account. Before you complete these steps, you should have already created new users, as shown in the previous section.

1. Open the Admin Console MMC desktop shortcut and expand the Local Users and Groups snap-in.

2. Open the Users folder. Double-click user WPanek to open his Properties dialog box.

3. In the General tab, check the Account Is Disabled box. Click OK.

4. Close the Local Users and Groups MMC.

5. Log off and attempt to log on as WPanek. This should fail because the account is now disabled.

6. Log back on using your user account.

TIP   Another option for accessing a user's properties is to highlight the user, right-click, and select Properties.

Now when users have left a company for a long period of time and you know you no longer need the user account, you can delete the account. Let's look at how to delete user accounts.

Deleting User Accounts

As noted in the preceding section, you should disable a user account if you are not sure that the account will ever be needed again. But if the account has been disabled and you know that the user account will never need access again, you should then delete the account.

To delete a user, open the Local Users and Groups utility, highlight the user account you want to delete, and click Action to bring up the menu, as shown in Figure 7.6. Then select Delete. You can also delete an account by clicking the account and pressing the Delete key on the keyboard.

Figure 7.6: Deleting a user account

Because user deletion is a permanent action, you see the dialog box shown in Figure 7.7 that asks you to confirm that you really want to delete the account. After you click the Yes button, you will not be able to re-create or re-access the account (unless you restore your local user accounts database from a backup).

Figure 7.7: Confirming user deletion

Perform the following steps to delete a user account. These steps assume you have completed the previous steps in this chapter.

1. Open the Admin Console MMC Desktop shortcut and expand the Local Users and Groups snap-in.

2. Expand the Users folder and single-click on user JAdams to select his user account.

3. Select Action ➤ Delete. The dialog box for confirming user deletion appears.

4. Click Yes to confirm that you want to delete this user.

5. Close the Local Users and Groups MMC.

Now that we have disabled and deleted accounts, let's see how to rename a user's account.

Renaming User Accounts

After you have created an account, you can rename the account at any time. Renaming a user account allows the user to retain all the associated user properties of the previous username. As noted previously in the chapter, the name is a property of the SID.

You might want to rename a user account because the user's name has changed (for example, the user got married) or because the name was spelled incorrectly. Also, as explained in the "Disabling User Accounts" section, you can rename an existing user's account for a new user, such as someone hired to take an ex-employee's position, when you want the new user to have the same properties.

Perform the following steps to rename a user account. These steps assume you have completed all of the previous steps in this chapter.

1. Open the Admin Console MMC shortcut and expand the Local Users and Groups snap-in.

2. Open the Users folder and highlight user ALincoln.

3. Select Action ➤ Rename.

4. Type the username **RReagan** and press Enter. Notice that the Full Name retained the original property of Abe Lincoln in the Local Users and Groups utility.

5. Double-click RReagan to open their properties and change the user's full name to **Ronald Reagan**.

6. Click the User Must Change Password At Next Logon check box.

7. Click OK.

8. Close the Local Users and Groups MMC.

NOTE Renaming a user does not change any "hard-coded" names, such as the user's home folder. If you want to change these names as well, you need to modify them manually, for example, through Windows Explorer.

Another common task that you must deal with is resetting the user's password. You'll learn how next.

Changing a User's Password

What should you do if a user forgets their password and can't log on? You can't just open a dialog box and see the old password. However, as the administrator, you can change the user's password and then the user can use the new one.

Teach Your Users

It is important as IT managers and IT administrators to teach your users the proper security measures that go along with password protection. As you have all probably seen before, the users who tape their password to their monitors or under the keyboards need to be taught the correct methods for protecting their passwords.

It's our job as IT professionals to teach our users proper security. It always amazes me when I do consulting how many IT departments fail to do this task.

IT personnel should give classes to their users at least once a month on different topics. One of these topics should be proper password security. Teach your users how to protect their passwords and what to do if their passwords get compromised.

Perform the following steps to change a user's password. This exercise assumes you have completed all the previous steps in this chapter.

1. Open the Admin Console MMC Desktop shortcut and expand the Local Users and Groups snap-in.

2. Open the Users folder and highlight user CPanek.

3. Select Action ➤ Set Password. The Set Password dialog box appears.

4. A warning appears that indicates risks are involved in changing the password. Select Proceed.

5. Type the new password and then confirm the password. Click OK.

6. Close the Local Users and Groups MMC.

Now that you have seen how to create users in Windows 7, let's look at configuring and managing your user's properties.

Manage the User's Properties

For more control over user accounts, you can configure user properties. Through the user's Properties dialog box, you can change the original password options, add the users to existing groups, and specify user profile information.

To open a user's Properties dialog box, access the Local Users and Groups utility, open the Users folder, and double-click the user account. The user's Properties dialog box has tabs for the three main categories of properties: General, Member Of, and Profile.

The General tab contains the information you supplied when you set up the new user account, including any Full Name and Description information, the password options you selected, and whether the account is disabled. If you want to modify any of these properties after you've created the user, simply open the user's Properties dialog box and make the changes on the General tab.

You can use the Member Of tab to manage the user's membership in groups. The Profile tab lets you set properties to customize the user's environment. The following sections discuss the Member Of and Profile tabs in detail.

Managing User Group Membership

The Member Of tab of the user's Properties dialog box displays all the groups that the user belongs to, as shown in Figure 7.8. On this tab, you can add the user to an existing group or remove that user from a group. To add a user to a group, click the Add button and select the group that the user should belong to. If you want to remove the user from a group, highlight the group and click the Remove button.

Figure 7.8: The Member Of tab of the user's Properties dialog box

PART III

Users and Security

Perform the following steps to add a user to an existing group. These steps assume you have completed all the previous steps in this chapter.

1. Open the Local Users and Groups MMC Desktop snap-in that you created in the previous steps.

2. Open the Users folder and double-click user WPanek. The WPanek Properties dialog box appears.

3. Select the Member Of tab and click the Add button. The Select Groups dialog box appears.

4. Under Enter The Object Names To Select, type **Backup Operators** and click the Check Names button. After the name is confirmed, click OK.

5. Click OK to close the WPanek Properties dialog box.

The final tab in the user's properties is called the Profile tab. Now let's look at that Profile tab and the options that you can configure within that tab.

Setting Up User Profiles, Logon Scripts, and Home Folders

The Profile tab of the user's Properties dialog box, shown in Figure 7.9, allows you to customize the user's environment. Here, you can specify the following items for the user:

- User profile path
- Logon script
- Home folder

The following sections describe how these properties work and when you might want to use them.

Setting a Profile Path

User profiles contain information about the Windows 7 environment for a specific user. For example, profile settings include the Desktop arrangement, program groups, and screen colors that users see when they log on.

Each time you log on to a Windows 7 computer, the system checks to see if you have a local user profile in the Users folder, which was created on the boot partition when you installed Windows 7.

Figure 7.9: The Profile tab of the user's
Properties dialog box

The first time users log on, they receive a default user profile. A
folder that matches the user's logon name is created for the user in the
Users folder. The user profile folder that is created holds a file called
ntuser.dat, as well as subfolders that contain directory links to the
user's Desktop items.

Perform the following steps to create two new users and set up local
user profiles:

1. Using the Local Users and Groups utility, create two new users:
    APanek and PPanek. Deselect the User Must Change Password At
    Next Logon option for each user.

2. Select Start ➢ All Programs ➢ Accessories ➢ Windows Explorer.
    Expand Computer, then Local Disk (C:), and then Users. Notice
    that the Users folder does not contain user profile folders for the
    new users.

3. Log off and log on as APanek.

4. Right-click an open area on the Desktop and select Personalize.
    In the Personalization dialog box, select a color scheme and click
    Apply, and then click OK.

5. Right-click an open area on the Desktop and select New ➤ Shortcut. In the Create Shortcut dialog box, type **CALC**. Accept CALC as the name for the shortcut and click Finish.

6. Log off as APanek and log on as PPanek. Notice that user PPanek sees the Desktop configuration stored in the default user profile.

7. Log off as PPanek and log on as APanek. Notice that APanek sees the Desktop configuration you set up in steps 3, 4, and 5.

8. Log off as APanek and log on as your user account. Select Start ➤ All Programs ➤ Accessories ➤ Windows Explorer. Expand Computer, then Local Disk (C:), and then Users. Notice that this folder now contains user profile folders for APanek and PPanek.

The drawback of local user profiles is that they are available only on the computer where they were created. For example, suppose all of your Windows 7 computers are a part of a domain and you use only local user profiles.

User Rick logs on at Computer A and creates a customized user profile. When he logs on to Computer B for the first time, he will receive the default user profile rather than the customized user profile he created on Computer A. For users to access their user profile from any computer they log on to, you need to use roaming profiles; however, these require the use of a network server and they can't be stored on a local Windows 7 computer.

In the next sections, you will learn about how roaming profiles and mandatory profiles can be used. To have a roaming profile or a mandatory profile, your computer must be a part of a network with server access.

Using Roaming Profiles

A roaming profile is stored on a network server and allows users to access their user profile, regardless of the client computer to which they're logged on. Roaming profiles provide a consistent Desktop for users who move around, no matter which computer they access. Even if the server that stores the roaming profile is unavailable, the user can still log on using a local profile.

If you are using roaming profiles, the contents of the user's system-drive:\Users\UserName folder will be copied to the local computer each time the roaming profile is accessed. If you have stored large files in any subfolders of your user profile folder, you might notice a significant delay when accessing your profile remotely as opposed to locally.

If this problem occurs, you can reduce the amount of time the roaming profile takes to load by moving the subfolder to another location, such as the user's home directory, or you can use Group Policy Objects within Active Directory to specify that specific folders should be excluded when the roaming profile is loaded.

Using Mandatory Profiles

A mandatory profile is a profile that can't be modified by the user. Only members of the Administrators group can manage mandatory profiles. You might consider creating mandatory profiles for users who should maintain consistent Desktops.

For example, suppose you have a group of 20 salespeople who know enough about system configuration to make changes but not enough to fix any problems they create. For ease of support, you could use mandatory profiles. This way, all the salespeople will always have the same profile and will not be able to change their profiles.

You can create mandatory profiles for a single user or a group of users. The mandatory profile is stored in a file named ntuser.man. A user with a mandatory profile can set different Desktop preferences while logged on, but those settings will not be saved when the user logs off.

NOTE You can use only roaming profiles as mandatory profiles. Mandatory profiles do not work for local user profiles.

There is a second type of mandatory profile called Super Mandatory Profile. Let's look at this other type of profile.

Using Super Mandatory Profiles

A super mandatory profile is a mandatory user profile with an additional layer of security. With mandatory profiles, a temporary profile is created if the mandatory profile is not available when a user logs on. However, when super mandatory profiles are configured, temporary profiles are not created if the mandatory profile is not available over the network, and the user is unable to log on to the computer.

The process for creating super mandatory profiles is similar to creating mandatory profiles, except that instead of renaming the user folder to Username.v2, you name the folder Username.man.v2.

Users and Security

PART III

Configuring Logon Scripts

Logon scripts are files that run every time a user logs on to the network. They are usually batch files, but they can be any type of executable file.

You might use logon scripts to set up drive mappings or to run a specific executable file each time a user logs on to the computer. For example, you could run an inventory management file that collects information about the computer's configuration and sends that data to a central management database. Logon scripts are also useful for compatibility with non–Windows 7 clients who want to log on but still maintain consistent settings with their native operating system.

To run a logon script for a user, enter the script name in the Logon Script text box on the Profile tab of the user's Properties dialog box.

Next we'll look at another item that you can configure on the Profile tab: home folders.

Setting Up Home Folders

Users usually store their personal files and information in a private folder called a home folder. In the Profile tab of the user's Properties dialog box, you can specify the location of a home folder as a local folder or a network folder.

To specify a local path folder, choose the Local Path option and type the path in the text box next to that option. To specify a network path for a folder, choose the Connect option and specify a network path using a Universal Naming Convention (UNC) path.

A UNC consists of the computer name and the share that has been created on the computer. In this case, a network folder should already be created and shared. For example, if you wanted to connect to a folder called \Users\Will on a server called SALES, you'd choose the Connect option, select a drive letter that would be mapped to the home directory, and then type \\SALES\Users\Will in the To box.

If the home folder you are specifying does not exist, Windows 7 attempts to create the folder for you. You can also use the variable %username% in place of a specific user's name.

Perform the following steps to assign a home folder to a user. These steps assume you have completed all the previous steps in this chapter.

1. Open the Admin Console MMC desktop shortcut and expand the Local Users and Groups snap-in.

2. Open the Users folder and double-click user WPanek. The WPanek Properties dialog box appears.

3. Select the Profile tab and click the Local Path radio button to select it.

4. Specify the home folder path by typing `C:\HomeFolders\WPanek` in the text box for the Local Path option. Then click OK.

5. Use Windows Explorer to verify that this folder was created.

6. Close the Local Users and Groups MMC.

Now that you understand how to create user accounts, in the next section I'll show you how to work with groups.

Create and Manage Groups

Groups are an important part of network management. Many administrators are able to accomplish the majority of their management tasks through the use of groups; they rarely assign permissions to individual users.

Windows 7 includes built-in local groups, such as Administrators and Backup Operators. These groups already have all the permissions needed to accomplish specific tasks. Windows 7 also uses default special groups, which are managed by the system. Users become members of special groups based on their requirements for computer and network access.

You can create and manage local groups through the Local Users and Groups utility. With this utility, you can add groups, change group membership, rename groups, and delete groups.

One misconception with groups is that they have to work with Group Policy Objects (GPOs). This is not correct. GPOs are a set of rules that allow you to set computer configuration and user configuration options that apply to users or computers. Group Policies are typically used with Active Directory and are applied as GPOs. GPOs are discussed in detail in Chapter 8.

In the following sections, you will learn about groups and all the built-in groups. Then you will learn how to create and manage these groups.

Using Built-in Groups

On a Windows 7 computer, default local groups have already been created and assigned all necessary permissions to accomplish basic tasks. In addition, there are built-in special groups that the Windows 7 system handles automatically. These groups are described in the following sections.

Using Default Local Groups   A local group is a group that is stored on the local computer's accounts database. These are the groups you can add users to and can manage directly on a Windows 7 computer. By default, the following local groups are created on Windows 7 computers:

- Administrators
- Backup Operators
- Cryptographic Operators
- Distributed COM Users
- Event Log Readers
- Guests
- IIS_IUSRS
- Network Configuration Operators
- Performance Log Users
- Performance Monitor Users
- Power Users
- Remote Desktop Users
- Replicator
- Users

I'll briefly describe each group, its default permissions, and the users assigned to the group by default.

The Administrators Group   The Administrators group has full permissions and privileges. Its members can grant themselves any permissions they do not have by default to manage all the objects on the computer. (Objects include the file system, printers, and account management.) By default, the Administrator account, which is disabled by default, and the initial user account are members of the Administrators local group.

Members of the Administrators group can perform the following tasks:

- Install the operating system.
- Install and configure hardware device drivers.

- Install system services.
- Install service packs, hot fixes, and Windows updates.
- Upgrade the operating system.
- Repair the operating system.
- Install applications that modify the Windows system files.
- Configure password policies.
- Configure audit policies.
- Manage security logs.
- Create administrative shares.
- Create administrative accounts.
- Modify groups and accounts that have been created by other users.
- Remotely access the Registry.
- Stop or start any service.
- Configure services.
- Increase and manage disk quotas.
- Increase and manage execution priorities.
- Remotely shut down the system.
- Assign and manage user rights.
- Reenable locked-out and disabled accounts.
- Manage disk properties, including formatting hard drives.
- Modify systemwide environment variables.
- Access any data on the computer.
- Back up and restore all data.

The Backup Operators Group   Members of the Backup Operators group have permissions to back up and restore the file system, even if the file system is NTFS and they have not been assigned permissions to access the file system. However, the members of Backup Operators can access the file system only using the Backup utility. To access the file system directly, Backup Operators must have explicit permissions assigned. There are no default members of the Backup Operators local group.

Users and Security

PART III

The Cryptographic Operators Group   The Cryptographic Operators group has access to perform cryptographic operations on the computer. There are no default members of the Cryptographic Operators local group.

The Distributed COM Users Group   The Distributed COM Users group has the ability to launch and run Distributed COM objects on the computer. There are no default members of the Distributed COM Users local group.

The Event Log Readers Group   The Event Log Readers group has access to read the event log on the local computer. There are no default members of the Event Log Readers local group.

The Guests Group   The Guests group has limited access to the computer. This group is provided so that you can allow people who are not regular users to access specific network resources. As a general rule, most administrators do not allow Guest access because it poses a potential security risk. By default, the Guest user account is a member of the Guests local group.

The IIS_IUSRS Group   The IIS_IUSRS group is used by Internet Information Services (IIS). The NT AUTHORITY\IUSR user account is a member of the IIS_IUSRS group by default.

The Network Configuration Operators Group   Members of the Network Configuration Operators group have some administrative rights to manage the computer's network configuration—for example, editing the computer's TCP/IP settings.

The Performance Log Users Group   The Performance Log Users group has the ability to access and schedule logging of performance counters and can create and manage trace counters on the computer.

The Performance Monitor Users Group   The Performance Monitor Users group has the ability to access and view performance counter information on the computer. Users who are members of this group can access performance counters both locally and remotely.

The Power Users Group   The Power Users group is included in Windows 7 for backward compatibility. The Power Users group is included to ensure that computers upgraded from Windows XP function as before with regard to folders that allow access to members of the Power Users group. Otherwise, the Power Users group has limited administrative rights.

The Remote Desktop Users Group   The Remote Desktop Users group allows members of the group to log on remotely for the purpose of using the Remote Desktop service.

The Replicator Group   The Replicator group is intended to support directory replication, which is a feature that domain servers use. Only domain users who will start the replication service should be assigned to this group. The Replicator local group has no default members.

The Users Group   The Users group is intended for end users who should have very limited system access. If you have installed a fresh copy of Windows 7, the default settings for the Users group prohibit its members from compromising the operating system or program files. By default, all users who have been created on the computer, except Guest, are members of the Users local group.

Another type of group that is used by Windows 7 is special groups. In the next section you will learn about special groups and how they work.

Using Special Groups

Special groups can be used by the system or by administrators. Membership in these groups is automatic if certain criteria are met. You cannot manage special groups through the Local Users and Groups utility, but an administrator can add these special groups to resources. Table 7.3 describes several of the special groups that are built into Windows 7.

Table 7.3: Special Groups in Windows 7

Group	Description
Anonymous Logon	This group includes users who access the computer through anonymous logons. When users gain access through special accounts created for anonymous access to Windows 7 services, they become members of the Anonymous Logon group.
Authenticated Users	This group includes users who access the Windows 7 operating system through a valid username and password. Users who can log on belong to the Authenticated Users group.

Users and Security

PART III

Table 7.3: Special Groups in Windows 7 *(continued)*

Group	Description
Batch	This group includes users who log on as a user account that is used only to run a batch job. Batch job accounts are members of the Batch group.
Creator Owner	This is the account that created or took ownership of the object and is typically a user account. Each object (files, folders, printers, and print jobs) has an owner. Members of the Creator Owner group have special permissions to resources. For example, if you are a regular user who has submitted 12 print jobs to a printer, you can manipulate your print jobs as Creator Owner, but you can't manage any print jobs submitted by other users.
Dialup	This group includes users who log on to the network from a dial-up connection. Dial-up users are members of the Dialup group.
Everyone	This group includes anyone who could possibly access the computer. The Everyone group includes all users who have been defined on the computer (including Guest), plus (if your computer is a part of a domain) all users within the domain. If the domain has trust relationships with other domains, all users in the trusted domains are part of the Everyone group as well. The exception to automatic group membership with the Everyone group is that members of the Anonymous Logon group are not included as a part of the Everyone group.
Interactive	This group includes all users who use the computer's resources locally. Local users belong to the Interactive group.
Network	This group includes users who access the computer's resources over a network connection. Network users belong to the Network group.
Service	This group includes users who log on as a user account that is used only to run a service. You can configure the use of user accounts for logon through the Services program, and these accounts become members of the Service group.
System	When the system accesses specific functions as a user, that process becomes a member of the System group.
Terminal Server User	This group includes users who log on through Terminal Services. These users become members of the Terminal Server User group.

Now that we have looked at the different types of groups, let's explore how to manage and work with these groups.

Working with Groups

Groups are used to logically organize users with similar rights require-ments. Groups simplify administration because you can manage a few groups rather than many user accounts. For the same reason, groups simplify troubleshooting. Users can belong to as many groups as needed, so it's not difficult to put users into groups that make sense for your organization.

For example, suppose Jane is hired as a data analyst to join the four other data analysts who work for your company. You sit down with Jane and create an account for her, assigning her the network permis-sions for the access you think she needs. Later, however, you find that the four other data analysts (who have similar job functions) sometimes have network access Jane doesn't have, and sometimes she has access they don't have. This is happening because all their permissions were assigned individually and months apart.

To avoid such problems and reduce your administrative workload, you can assign all the company's data analysts to a group and then assign the appropriate permissions to that group. Then, as data analysts join or leave the department, you can simply add them to or remove them from the group.

You can create new groups for your users, and you can use the Windows 7 default local built-in groups that were described in the pre-vious section. In both cases, your planning should include checking to see if an existing local group meets your requirements before you decide to create a new group.

For example, if all the users need to access a particular application, it makes sense to use the default Users group rather than creating a new group and adding all the users to that group.

To work with groups, you can use the Local Users and Groups util-ity. Let's see how to create new groups.

Creating New Groups

To create a group, you must be logged on as a member of the Administrators group. The Administrators group has full permissions to manage users and groups.

As you do in your choices for usernames, keep your naming conventions in mind when assigning names to groups. When you create a local group, consider the following guidelines:

- The group name should be descriptive (for example, Accounting Data Users).

- The group name must be unique to the computer, different from all other group names and usernames that exist on that computer.

- Group names can be up to 256 characters. It is best to use alphanumeric characters for ease of administration. Most special characters—for example, backslash (\)—are not allowed.

Creating groups is similar to creating users, and it is a fairly easy process. After you've added the Local Users and Groups MMC or use the Local Users and Groups through Computer Management, expand it to see the Users and Groups folders. Right-click the Groups folder and select New Group from the context menu. This brings up the New Group dialog box, as shown in Figure 7.10.

Figure 7.10: The New Group dialog box

The only required entry in the New Group dialog box is the group name. If appropriate, you can enter a description for the group, and you can add (or remove) group members. When you're ready to create the new group, click the Create button.

Perform the following steps to create two new local groups:

1. Open the Admin Console MMC Desktop shortcut you created and expand the Local Users and Groups snap-in.

2. Right-click the Groups folder and select New Group.

3. In the New Group dialog box, type `Data Users` in the Group Name text box. Click the Create button.

4. In the New Group dialog box, type `Application Users` in the Group Name text box. Click the Create button.

After the groups are created, you have to manage the groups and their memberships. In the next section we look at managing groups.

Managing Group Membership

After you've created a group, you can add members to it. As mentioned earlier, you can put the same user in multiple groups. You can easily add and remove users through a group's Properties dialog box, as shown in Figure 7.11. To access this dialog box from the Groups folder in the Local Users and Groups utility, double-click the group you want to manage.

Figure 7.11: A group's Properties dialog box

From the group's Properties dialog box, you can change the group's description and add or remove group members. When you click the Add button to add members, the Select Users dialog box appears, as shown in Figure 7.12.

Figure 7.12: The Select Users dialog box

In the Select Users dialog box, enter the object names of the users you want to add. You can use the Check Names button to validate the users against the database. Select the user accounts you want to add and click Add. Click OK to add the selected users to the group.

NOTE   Although the special groups that were covered earlier in the chapter are listed in this dialog box, you cannot manage the membership of these special groups.

To remove a member from the group, select the member in the Members list of the Properties dialog box and click the Remove button.

Perform the following steps to create new user accounts and then add these users to one of the groups you created in the previous steps:

1. Open the Admin Console MMC shortcut you created and expand the Local Users and Groups snap-in.

2. Create two new users: JDoe and DDoe. Deselect the User Must Change Password At Next Logon option for each user.

3. Expand the Groups folder.

4. Double-click the Data Users group.

5. In the Data Users Properties dialog box, click the Add button.

6. In the Select Users dialog box, type the username **JDoe**, then click OK. Click Add and type the username **DDoe**, then click OK.

7. In the Data Users Properties dialog box, you will see that the users have all been added to the group. Click OK to close the group's Properties dialog box.

Another task that might need to be completed is changing the name of a group, and I discuss this in the next section.

Renaming Groups

Windows 7 provides an easy mechanism for changing a group's name. For example, you might want to rename a group because its current name does not conform to existing naming conventions, or you may need to rename a group because the group's task or location may change.

For example, let's say you have a group called Sales but as the company grows, so do the office locations. You now might have to rename the group NHSales and then create other groups for the other locations.

NOTE   As happens when you rename a user account, a renamed group keeps all of its properties, including its members and permissions.

To rename a group, right-click the group and choose Rename from the context menu. Enter a new name for the group and press Enter.

Perform the following steps to rename one of the groups you created in the previous steps:

1. Open the Admin Console MMC Desktop shortcut and expand the Local Users and Groups snap-in.

2. Expand the Groups folder.

3. Right-click the Data Users group and select Rename.

4. Rename the group to **App Users** and press Enter.

There might come a point when a specific group is no longer needed. In the next section we look at how to delete a group from the Local Users and Groups utility.

Deleting Groups

If you are sure that you will never again want to use a particular group, you can delete it. Once a group is deleted, you lose all permissions assignments that have been specified for the group.

To delete a group, right-click the group and choose Delete from the context menu. You will see a warning that after a group is deleted, it is gone for good. Click the Yes button if you're sure you want to delete the group.

If you delete a group and give another group the same name, the new group won't be created with the same properties as the deleted group because as with users, groups are assigned unique SIDs at the time of creation.

Perform the following steps to delete the group that you created in the previous steps:

1. Open the Admin Console MMC shortcut you created and expand the Local Users and Groups snap-in.

2. Expand the Groups folder.

3. Right-click the App Users group and choose Delete.

4. In the dialog box that appears, click Yes to confirm that you want to delete the group.

Creating users and groups is one of the most important tasks that we as IT members can do. On a Windows 7 machine, creating users and groups is an easy and straightforward process.

8

Managing Security

IN THIS CHAPTER, YOU WILL LEARN TO:

Users and Security

PART III

O ne of the most important tasks that anyone can perform on a system is protecting and securing the machine. Windows 7 offers a wide variety of security options.

If the Windows 7 computer is part of a domain, you can apply security through a Group Policy Object using the Group Policy Management Console. If the Windows 7 computer is not part of a domain, you use Local Group Policy Objects to manage local security.

In the first part of this chapter, you will learn about the various Windows 7 environments and the utilities you can use to manage security.

You can use policies to help manage user accounts. Account policies control the logon environment for the computer, such as password and logon restrictions. Local policies specify what users can do after they log on and include auditing, user rights, and security options. You can also manage critical security features through the Windows Security Center.

In the final section of this chapter, I will show you how to encrypt the physical drive using BitLocker. I will also discuss how to encrypt removable media (USB drive) using BitLocker To Go.

Manage Security Configurations

The tools you use to manage Windows 7 computer security configurations depend on whether the Windows 7 computer is part of a Windows 2000, Windows 2003, or Windows 2008 domain environment.

If the Windows 7 client is not part of a domain, you apply security settings through Local Group Policy Objects (LGPOs). LGPOs are a set of security configuration settings that are applied to users and computers. LGPOs are created and stored on the Windows 7 computer.

If your Windows 7 computer is part of a domain, which uses the services of Active Directory, you typically manage and configure security through Group Policy Objects (GPOs). Active Directory is the database that contains all your domain user and group accounts together with all other domain objects. GPOs are policies that can be placed on either users or computers in the domain.

The Group Policy Management Console (GPMC) is a Microsoft Management Console (MMC) snap-in that is used to configure and manage GPOs for users and computers via Active Directory.

Windows 7 computers that are part of a domain still have LGPOs, and you can use LGPOs in conjunction with the Active Directory group policies.

> **Group Policy Objects**
>
> GPOs are covered in detail in *MCTS: Windows Server 2008 Active Directory Configuration,* by William Panek and James Chellis (Sybex, 2008).

The settings you can apply through the Group Policy Management Console (GPMC) utility are more comprehensive than the settings you can apply through LGPOs.

By default, LGPOs are stored in %systemroot% System32\ GroupPolicyUsers. Table 8.1 lists some of the options that you can set for GPOs within Active Directory and which of those options you can apply through LGPOs.

Table 8.1: Group Policy and LGPO Setting Options

Group Policy Setting	Available for LGPO?
Software installation	No
Remote Installation Services	Yes
Scripts	Yes
Printers	Yes
Security settings	Yes
Policy-based QOS	Yes
Administrative templates	Yes
Folder redirection	No
Internet Explorer configuration	Yes

Group Policy Objects and Active Directory

Most Windows 7 computers reside within a Windows Server 2000, Windows Server 2003, or Windows Server 2008 domain. GPOs are applied through Active Directory by using the Group Policy

Users and Security

PART III

Management Console (GPMC). It is much easier to globally manage GPOs through the GPMC than applying LGPOs at local levels of each Windows 7 machine.

To help you understand how GPOs and LGPOs work together, the following sections first provide an overview of Active Directory and then show you how GPOs and LGPOs are applied based on predefined inheritance rules.

Active Directory Overview

First off, the easiest way to explain Active Directory is to state that Active Directory is a database. That's it. Active Directory is just a database but it's the most important database in your domain because the Active Directory database contains all your usernames and passwords, groups, and other objects within the domain.

Within that Active Directory database, you have several levels of a hierarchical structure. A typical structure consists of domains and organizational units (OUs). Other levels exist within Active Directory, but this overview focuses on domains and OUs in the context of using GPOs.

The domain (for example, Panek.com) is the main unit of organization within Active Directory, as shown in Figure 8.1. Within a domain are many domain objects including security objects such as user and group accounts. Each domain security object can then have permissions applied that specify what rights that security object can have when it accesses resources within the domain.

Figure 8.1: Active Directory hierarchical structure

Within a domain, you can further subdivide and organize domain objects through the use of Organizational Units (OUs). This is one of the key differences between Windows NT 4 domains and Windows 2000, 2003, and 2008 domains. The NT domains were not able to store information hierarchically. Windows 2000, 2003, and 2008 domains, through the use of OUs, allow you to store objects hierarchically, typically based on function or geography.

For example, assume that your company is called Stellacon. You have locations in New York, San Jose, and Belfast. You might create a domain called Stellacon.com with OUs called NY, SJ, and Belfast. In a large corporation, you might also organize the OUs based on function. For example, the domain could be Stellacon.com and the OUs might be Sales, Accounting, and R&D. Based on the size and security needs of your organization, you might also have OUs nested within OUs. As a general rule, however, you want to keep your Active Directory structure as simple as possible.

Domains are logical grouping of objects. If you had the Stellacon .com domain, you would expect that everyone in the domain would belong to the organization named Stellacon. A domain does not have to be in one geographical location. Microsoft is a worldwide company and the Microsoft.com domain has locations all over the world.

If you need to set up physical locations, you would set up *sites*. Sites are physical representations of the domain. For example, let's say that you have a company with two buildings next to each other. You might want all the users in one building to access resources within that building and the same for the other building. You can set up two sites, one for each building. Then, users will always try to find resources in their own site first. If the resource in the site is not available, the user will automatically leave the site and try to find the resource in another site. Sites are an excellent way to keep your users local to their location.

Sites

Sites are covered in detail in *MCTS: Windows Server 2008 Active Directory Configuration,* by William Panek and James Chellis (Sybex, 2008).

Users and Security

PART III

Now let's take a look at GPO inheritance. In the next section, I explain how GPO inheritance works and what happens when multiple GPOs conflict with one another.

Understanding GPO Inheritance

When GPOs are created within the Active Directory using the GPMC, there is a specific order of inheritance. That is, the policies are applied in a specific order within the hierarchical structure of the Active Directory. When a user logs onto the Active Directory, depending on where within the hierarchy GPOs have been applied, the order of application is as follows:

1. Local

2. Site

3. Domain

4. OU

Each level of the hierarchy is called a container. Containers higher in the hierarchy are called parent containers; containers lower in the hierarchy are called child containers. Settings from these containers are inherited from parent container to child container. By default, child container policy settings override any conflicting settings applied by parent containers.

For example, if you set the wallpaper at the site level to be red and set the wallpaper at the OU level to be blue, if a user that belongs to both the site and the OU logs on, their wallpaper would be blue.

The local policy is, by default, applied first when a user logs on. Then the site policies are applied, and if the site policy contains settings that the local policy doesn't have, they are added to the local policy. If there are any conflicts, the site policy overrides the local policy. Then the domain policies are defined.

Again, if the domain policy contains additional settings, they are incorporated. The domain policy overrides the site policy or the local policy when settings conflict. Finally, the OU policies are applied. Any additional settings are incorporated; for conflicts, the OU policy overrides the domain, site, and local policies. If any child OUs exist, their GPOs are applied after the parent OU GPOs.

So as we have just stated, the child policy overrides the parent policy by default but this can be changed. As with any child/parent relationship, the parent can force the child to accept the policy that is being issued.

The enforce option allows you to override a child option. There is also the ability to block inheritance. Let's look at these two options:

Enforce (No Override)   The Enforce option is used to specify that child containers can't override the policy settings of higher-level containers. For example, if a site policy is marked as Enforce, it will not be overridden by conflicting domain or OU policies. If multiple Enforced policies are set, then the one from the highest container would take precedence.

The Enforce option would be used if you wanted to set corporate-wide policies without allowing administrators of lower-level containers to override your settings. This option can be set per container, as needed.

The Enforce option used to be known as the No Override option. When you created a GPO in Active Directory Users and Computers, this option was called No Override. Now that we use the Group Policy Management Console (GPMC), it's called Enforce.

Block Inheritance   The Block Inheritance option is used to allow a child container to block GPO inheritance from parent containers. This option would be used if you do not want to inherit GPO settings from parent containers and want only the GPO you have set for your container to be applied. For example, if you set Block Inheritance on an OU policy, only the OU policy would be applied; no parent container policies would be inherited.

If a conflict exists between the Enforce and the Block Inheritance settings, then the Enforce option would be applied. Now that we have looked at GPOs, let's look at some of the tools available for creating and managing GPOs.

Using the Group Policy Result Tool

When a user logs on to a computer or domain, a resulting set of policies to be applied is generated based on the LGPOs, site GPOs, domain GPOs, and OU GPOs. The overlapping nature of group policies can make it difficult to determine what group policies will actually be applied to a computer or user.

To help determine what policies will actually be applied, Windows 7 includes a tool called the Group Policy Result Tool, also known as the Resultant Set of Policy (RSoP). You can access this tool through the

Users and Security

PART III

GPResult command-line utility. The gpresult command displays the resulting set of policies that were enforced on the computer and the specified user during the logon process.

The gpresult command displays the RSoP for the computer and the user who is currently logged in. You can use several options with this command. Table 8.2 shows the different switches that you can use for the gpresult command.

Table 8.2: gpresult Switches

Switch	Explanation
/F	Forces gpresult to override the filename specified in the /X or /H command
/H	Saves the report in an HTML format
/P	Specifies the password for a given user context
/R	Displays RSoP summary data
/S	Specifies the remote system to connect to
/U	Specifies which user context under which the command should be executed
/V	Specifies that verbose information should be displayed
/X	Saves the report in XML format
/Z	Specifies that the super verbose information should be displayed
/?	Shows all the gpresult command switches
/scope	Specifies whether the user or the computer settings need to be displayed
/User	Specifies the username for which the RSoP data is to be displayed

Complete the following steps to run the gpresult command and place the data into a text file:

1. Click Start and type **cmd** in the Search Programs and Files box. Press Enter.

2. At the Command Prompt, type **gpresult /r >test.txt** and press Enter.

3. Find and open the test.txt file (which should be placed under the user account that the file was created in).

In the next section, I'll show you how to create and apply LGPOs to a Windows 7 machine.

Create and Apply LGPOs

As I discussed previously, policies that have been linked through the Active Directory will, by default, take precedence over any established local group policies. Local group policies are typically applied to computers that are not part of a network or are in a network that does not have a domain controller and thus do not use the Active Directory.

Previous versions of Windows (before Vista) contained only one LGPO that applied to all the computer's users unless NTFS permissions were applied to the LGPO. However, Windows 7 and Windows Vista changed that with the addition of Multiple Local Group Policy Objects (MLGPOs). Like Active Directory GPOs, MLGPOs are applied in a certain hierarchical order, as follows:

1. Local Computer Policy
2. Administrators and Non-Administrators Local Group Policy
3. User-Specific Group Policy

The Local Computer Policy is the only LGPO that includes computer and user settings; the other LGPOs contain only user settings. Settings applied here apply to all users of the computer.

The Administrators and Non-Administrators LGPOs were new to Windows Vista and are still included with Windows 7. The Administrators LGPO is applied to users who are members of the built-in local Administrators group. As you might guess, the Non-Administrators LGPO is applied to users who are not members of the local Administrators group. Because each user of a computer can be classified as an administrator or a non-administrator, either one policy or the other will apply.

User-Specific LGPOs are also included with Windows 7. These LGPOs make it possible for specific policy settings to apply to a single user.

Like Active Directory GPOs, any GPO settings applied lower in the hierarchy will override GPO settings applied higher in the hierarchy by default. For example, any user-specific GPO settings will override any conflicting administrator/non-administrator GPO settings or Local Computer Policy settings. And, of course, any AD GPO settings will still override any conflicting LGPO settings.

Users and Security

PART III

NOTE   Domain administrators can disable LGPOs on Windows 7 computers by enabling the Turn Off LGPOs Processing domain GPO setting, which you can find under `Computer Configuration\Administrative Templates\System\Group Policy`.

You apply an LGPO to a Windows 7 computer through the GPO Editor snap-in within the MMC. Figure 8.2 shows the Local Computer Policy dialog box for a Windows 7 computer.

Figure 8.2: Local Computer Policy dialog box

Perform the following steps to add the Local Computer Policy Snap-In to the MMC:

1. Open the Admin Console MMC shortcut by typing **MMC** in the Search Programs And Files box.

2. If the User Account Control dialog box appears, click Yes.

3. Select File ➢ Add/Remove Snap-in.

4. Highlight the Group Policy Object Editor Snap-in and click the Add button.

5. The Group Policy Object specifies Local Computer by default. Click the Finish button.

6. In the Add Or Remove Snap-ins dialog box, click OK.

7. In the left-hand pane, right-click the Local Computer Policy and choose New Windows From Here.

8. Choose File ➤ Save As and name the console **LGPO**. Make sure you save it to the Desktop. Click Save.

9. Close the MMC Admin console.

Now let's look at how to open an LGPO for a specific user account on a Windows 7 machine.

Perform the following steps to access the Administrators, Non-Administrators, and User-Specific LGPOs. The previous steps must be completed to perform this procedure.

1. Open the Admin Console MMC shortcut by typing **MMC** in the Search Programs And Files box.

2. Select File ➤ Add/Remove Snap-in.

3. Highlight the Group Policy Object Editor Snap-in and click Add.

4. Click Browse to look for a different GPO.

5. Click the Users tab.

6. Select the user that you want to access and click OK.

7. In the Select Group Policy Object dialog box, click Finish.

8. In the Add Or Remove Snap-ins dialog box, click OK. You can close the console when you are finished looking at the LGPO settings for the user you chose.

NOTE   Notice that the Administrators, Non-Administrators, and User-Specific LGPOs contain only User Configuration settings, not Computer Configuration settings.

Now let's look at the different security settings that you can configure in the LGPO.

Configuring Local Security Policies

Through the use of the Local Computer Policy, you can set a wide range of security options under Computer Configuration\Windows Settings\Security Settings.

This portion of the Local Computer Policy is also known as the Local Security Policy. The following sections describe in detail how to apply security settings through LGPOs, as shown in Figure 8.3.

Figure 8.3: Security Settings of the LGPO

The main areas of security configuration of the LGPO are as follows:

Account Policies   You can use Account policies to configure password and account lockout features. Some of these settings include Password History, Maximum Password Age, Minimum Password Age, Minimum Password Length, Password Complexity, Account Lockout Duration, Account Lockout Threshold, and Reset Account Lockout Counter After.

Local Policies   You can use Local policies to configure auditing, user rights, and security options.

Windows Firewall with Advanced Security   Windows Firewall with Advanced Security provides network security for Windows computers. Through this LGPO you can set Domain, Private, and Public profiles. You can also set this LGPO to authenticate communications between computers and inbound/outbound rules.

Network List Manager Policies   This section allows you to set the network name, icon, and location group policies. Administrators can set Unidentified Networks, Identifying Networks, and All Networks.

Public Key Policies   You can use the Public Key Policies settings to specify how to manage certificates and certificate life cycles.

Software Restriction Policies   Software Restriction Policies allow you to identify malicious software and control that software's ability to run on the Windows 7 machine. These policies allow an administrator to protect the Microsoft Windows 7 operating system against security threats such as viruses and Trojan horse programs.

Application Control Policies   You can use these policies to set up AppLocker. AppLocker allows you to configure a Denied list and an Accepted list for applications. Applications that are configured on the Denied list will not run on the system and applications on the Accepted list will operate properly.

IP Security Policies on Local Computer   You can use these policies to configure the IPSec policies. IPSec is a way to secure data packets at the IP level of the message.

Advanced Audit Policy Configuration   You can use Advanced Audit Policy configuration settings to provide detailed control over audit policies. This section also allows you to configure auditing to help show administrators either successful or unsuccessful attacks on their network.

NOTE   You can also access the Local Security Policy by running secpol.msc or by opening Control Panel and selecting ➤ Administrative Tools ➤ Local Security Policy.

Now that we have seen all the options in the security section of the LGPO, let's look at account policies and local policies in more detail in the following sections.

Using Account Policies

You use account policies to specify the user account properties that relate to the logon process. They allow you to configure computer security settings for passwords and account lockout specifications.

If security is not an issue—perhaps because you are using your Windows 7 computer at home—you don't need to bother with account policies. If, on the other hand, security is important—for example, because your computer provides access to payroll information—you should set very restrictive account policies.

Account Policies

Account policies at the LGPO level apply only to local user accounts, not domain accounts. To ensure that user account security is configured for domain user accounts, you need to configure these policies at the Domain GPO level.

To access the Account Policies folder from the MMC, follow this path: Local Computer Policy ➤ Computer Configuration ➤ Windows Settings ➤ Security Settings ➤ Account Policies. We look at all these folders and how to use them throughout the rest of this chapter.

In the following sections you will learn about the password policies and account lockout policies that define how security is applied to account policies.

Setting Password Policies

Password policies ensure that security requirements are enforced on the computer. It is important to understand that the password policy is set on a per-computer basis; it cannot be configured for specific users. Figure 8.4 shows the password policies that Table 8.3 describes.

Figure 8.4: The password policies

You can use the password policies in Table 8.3 as follows:

Enforce Password History   Prevents users from repeatedly using the same passwords. Users must create a new password when their password expires or is changed.

Maximum Password Age   Forces users to change their password after the maximum password age is exceeded. Setting this value to 0 will specify that the password will never expire.

Minimum Password Age   Prevents users from changing their password several times in rapid succession in order to defeat the purpose of the Enforce Password History policy.

Minimum Password Length   Ensures that users create a password and specifies the length requirement for that password. If this option isn't set, users are not required to create a password at all.

Password Must Meet Complexity Requirements   Passwords must be six characters or longer and cannot contain the user's account name or any part of the user's full name. In addition, passwords must contain three of the following character types:

- English uppercase characters (A through Z)
- English lowercase characters (a through z)
- Decimal digits (0 through 9)
- Symbols (such as !, @, #, $, and %)

Store Passwords Using Reversible Encryption   Provides a higher level of security for user passwords. This is required for Challenge Handshake Authentication Protocol (CHAP) authentication through remote access or Internet Authentication Services (IAS) and for Digest Authentication with Internet Information Services (IIS).

Table 8.3: Password Policy Options

Policy	Description	Default	Minimum	Maximum
Enforce Password History	Keeps track of user's password history	Remember 0 passwords	Same as default	Remember 24 passwords
Maximum Password Age	Determines maximum number of days user can keep valid password	Keep password for 42 days	Keep password for 1 day	Keep password for up to 999 days

Table 8.3: Password Policy Options *(continued)*

Policy	Description	Default	Minimum	Maximum
Minimum Password Age	Specifies how long password must be kept before it can be changed	0 days (password can be changed immediately)	Same as default	998 days
Minimum Password Length	Specifies minimum number of characters password must contain	0 characters (no password required)	Same as default	14 characters
Password Must Meet Complexity Requirements	Requires that passwords meet minimum levels of complexity	Disabled		
Store Passwords Using Reversible Encryption	Specifies higher level of encryption for stored user passwords	Disabled		

Perform the following steps to configure password policies for your computer. These steps assume that you have added the Local Computer Policy snap-in to the MMC completed in earlier steps.

1. Open the LGPO MMC shortcut that you created earlier.

2. Expand the Local Computer Policy Snap-in.

3. Expand the folders as follows: Computer Configuration ➤ Windows Settings ➤ Security Settings ➤ Account Policies ➤ Password Policy.

4. Open the Enforce Password History policy. On the Local Security Setting tab, specify that 5 passwords will be remembered. Click OK.

5. Open the Maximum Password Age policy. On the Local Security Setting tab, specify that the password expires in 60 days. Click OK.

Let's look at how to set and manage the Account Lockout Policies section.

Setting Account Lockout Policies

The account lockout policies specify how many invalid logon attempts should be tolerated. You configure the account lockout policies so that after x number of unsuccessful logon attempts within y number of minutes, the account will be locked for a specified amount of time or until the administrator unlocks the account.

Account lockout policies are similar to a bank's arrangements for ATM access code security. You have a certain number of chances to enter the correct PIN. That way, anyone who steals your card can't just keep guessing your access code until they get it right. Typically, after three unsuccessful attempts, the ATM takes the card. Then, you need to request a new card from the bank. Figure 8.5 shows the account lockout policies that Table 8.4 describes.

Figure 8.5: The account lockout policies

The Account Lockout Duration and Reset Account Lockout Counter After policies will be disabled until a value is specified for the Account

Lockout Threshold. After the Account Lockout Threshold is set, the Account Lockout Duration and Reset Account Lockout Counter After policies will be set to 30 minutes. If you set the Account Lockout Duration to 0, then the account will remain locked out until an administrator unlocks it.

NOTE The Reset Account Lockout Counter After value must be equal to or less than the Account Lockout Duration value.

Table 8.4: Account Lockout Policy Options

Policy	Description	Default	Minimum	Maximum
Account Lockout Duration	Specifies how long account will remain locked if Account Lockout Threshold is reached	Disabled, but if Account Lockout Threshold is enabled, 30 minutes	Same as default	99,999 minutes
Account Lockout Threshold	Specifies number of invalid attempts allowed before account is locked out	0 (disabled; account will not be locked out)	Same as default	999 attempts
Reset Account Lockout Counter After	Specifies how long counter will remember unsuccessful logon attempts	Disabled, but if Account Lockout Threshold is enabled, 30 minutes	Same as default	99,999 minutes

Perform the following steps to configure account lockout policies and test their effects. Make sure that all previous step procedures were completed before performing this procedure.

1. Open the LGPO MMC shortcut.

2. Expand the Local Computer Policy Snap-in.

3. Expand the folders as follows: Computer Configuration ➢ Windows Settings ➢ Security Settings ➢ Account Policies ➢ Account Lockout Policy.

4. Open the Account Lockout Threshold policy. On the Local Security Setting tab, specify that the account will lock after three invalid logon attempts. Click OK.

5. Accept the Suggested Value Changes for the Account Lockout Duration and Reset Account Lockout Counter After policies by clicking OK.

6. Open the Account Lockout Duration policy. On the Local Security Setting tab, specify that the account will remain locked for 5 minutes. Click OK.

7. Accept the Suggested Value Changes For The Reset Account Lockout Counter After policy by clicking OK.

8. Log off your Administrator account. Try to log on as one of the accounts that have been created on this Windows 7 machine and enter an incorrect password four times.

9. After you see the error message that states that the referenced account has been locked out, log on as an administrator.

10. To unlock the account, open the Local Users and Groups snap-in in the MMC, expand the Users folder, and double-click the user.

11. On the General tab of the user's Properties dialog box, click to remove the check from the Account Is Locked Out check box. Then click OK.

In the next section we discuss how to control a user or computer after the user has logged into the Windows 7 machine.

Using Local Policies

As you learned in the preceding section, account policies are used to control logon procedures. When you want to control what a user can do after logging on, you use local policies. With local policies, you can implement auditing, specify user rights, and set security options.

To use local policies, first add the Local Computer Policy snap-in to the MMC. Then, from the MMC, follow this path to access the Local Policies folders: Local Computer Policy ➢ Computer Configuration ➢ Windows Settings ➢ Security Settings ➢ Local Policies. Figure 8.6 shows the three Local Policies folders: Audit Policy, User Rights Assignment, and Security Options. We look at each of these in the following sections.

Figure 8.6: Accessing the Local Policies folders

Setting Audit Policies

You can implement audit policies to track success or failure of specified user actions. You audit events that pertain to user management through the audit policies. By tracking certain events, you can create a history of specific tasks, such as user creation and successful or unsuccessful logon attempts. You can also identify security violations that arise when users attempt to access system management tasks for which they do not have permissions.

When you define an audit policy, you can choose to audit success or failure of specific events. The success of an event means that the task was successfully accomplished. The failure of an event means that the task was not successfully accomplished.

By default, auditing is not enabled, and it must be manually configured. After you have configured auditing, you can see the results of the audit in the Security log by using the Event Viewer utility.

Figure 8.7 shows the audit policies that Table 8.5 describes.

Figure 8.7: The audit policies

Table 8.5: Audit Policy Options

Policy	Description
Audit Account Logon Events	Tracks when a user logs on or logs off either their local machine or the domain (if domain auditing is enabled)
Audit Account Management	Tracks user and group account creation, deletion, and management actions, such as password changes
Audit Directory Service Access	Tracks directory service accesses
Audit Logon Events	Audits events related to logon, such as running a logon script or accessing a roaming profile or accessing a server
Audit Object Access	Enables auditing of access to files, folders, and printers
Audit Policy Change	Tracks any changes to the audit policies, trust policies, or user rights assignment policies
Audit Privilege Use	Tracks users exercising a user right
Audit Process Tracking	Tracks events such as activating a program, accessing an object, and exiting a process
Audit System Events	Tracks system events such as shutting down or restarting the computer, as well as events that relate to the Security log in Event Viewer

Users and Security

PART III

After you set the Audit Object Access policy to enable auditing of object access, you must enable file auditing through NTFS security or print auditing through printer security.

Perform the following steps to configure audit policies and view their results. These steps assume that you have added the Local Group Object Policy snap-in to the MMC completed in earlier steps.

1. Open the LGPO MMC shortcut.

2. Expand the Local Computer Policy Snap-in.

3. Expand the folders as follows: Computer Configuration ➢ Windows Settings ➢ Security Settings ➢ Local Policies ➢ Audit Policy.

4. Open the Audit Account Logon Events policy. Check the boxes for Success and Failure. Click OK.

5. Open the Audit Account Management policy. Check the boxes for Success and Failure. Click OK.

6. Log off your Administrator account. Attempt to log back on as your Administrator account with an incorrect password. The logon should fail (because the password is incorrect).

7. Log on as an administrator.

8. Select Start, right-click Computer, and choose Manage to open Computer Management. Click Event Viewer.

9. From Event Viewer, open the Security log by selecting Windows Logs ➢ Security. You should see the audited events listed with a Task Category of Credential Validation.

Auditing

You might want to limit the number of events that are audited. If you audit excessive events on a busy computer, the log file can grow quickly. In the event that the log file becomes full, you can configure the computer to shut down through a security option policy, Audit: Shut Down System Immediately If Unable to Log Security Audits. If this option is triggered, the only user who will be able to log on to the computer will be an administrator until the log is cleared. If this option is not enabled and the log file becomes full, you have the option of overwriting older log events.

In the next section you'll learn how to configure the user rights on the Windows 7 machine.

Assigning User Rights

The user right policies determine what rights a user or group has on the computer. User rights apply to the system. They are not the same as permissions, which apply to a specific object (permissions are discussed later in this chapter, in the section "Managing File and Folder Security").

An example of a user right is the Back Up Files And Directories right. This right allows a user to back up files and folders, even if the user does not have permissions that have been defined through NTFS file system permissions. The other user rights are similar because they deal with system access as opposed to resource access.

Figure 8.8 shows the user right policies that Table 8.6 describes.

Figure 8.8: The user right policies

Table 8.6: User Rights Assignment Policy Options

Right	Description
Access Credential Manager As A Trusted Caller	Used to back up and restore Credential Manager.
Access This Computer From The Network	Allows a user to access the computer from the network.

Table 8.6: User Rights Assignment Policy Options *(continued)*

Right	Description
Act As Part Of The Operating System	Allows low-level authentication services to authenticate as any user.
Add Workstations To Domain	Allows a user to create a computer account on the domain.
Adjust Memory Quotas For A Process	Allows you to configure how much memory can be used by a specific process.
Allow Log On Locally	Allows a user to log on at the physical computer.
Allow Log On Through Terminal Services	Gives a user permission to log on through Terminal Services. Does not affect Windows 2000 computers prior to SP2.
Back Up Files And Directories	Allows a user to back up all files and directories, regardless of how the file and directory permissions have been set.
Bypass Traverse Checking	Allows a user to pass through and traverse the directory structure, even if that user does not have permissions to list the contents of the directory.
Change The System Time	Allows a user to change the internal time and date on the computer.
Change The Time Zone	Allows a user to change the time zone.
Create A Pagefile	Allows a user to create or change the size of a page file.
Create A Token Object	Allows a process to create a token if the process uses an internal API to create the token.
Create Global Objects	Allows a user to create global objects when connected using Terminal Server.
Create Permanent Shared Objects	Allows a process to create directory objects through the Object Manager.
Create Symbolic Links	Allows a user to create a symbolic link.
Debug Programs	Allows a user to attach a debugging program to any process.
Deny Access To This Computer From The Network	Allows you to deny specific users or groups access to this computer from the network. Overrides the Access This Computer From The Network policy for accounts present in both policies.

Table 8.6: User Rights Assignment Policy Options *(continued)*

Right	Description
Deny Log On As A Batch Job	Allows you to prevent specific users or groups from logging on as a batch file. Overrides the Log On As A Batch Job policy for accounts present in both policies.
Deny Log On As A Service	Allows you to prevent specific users or groups from logging on as a service. Overrides the Log On As A Service policy for accounts present in both policies.
Deny Log On Locally	Allows you to deny specific users or groups access to the computer locally. Overrides the Log On Locally policy for accounts present in both policies.
Deny Log On Through Terminal Services	Specifies that a user is not able to log on through Terminal Services. Does not affect Windows 2000 computers prior to SP2.
Enable Computer And User Accounts To Be Trusted For Delegation	Allows a user or group to set the Trusted For Delegation setting for a user or computer object.
Force Shutdown From A Remote System	Allows the system to be shut down by a user at a remote location on the network.
Generate Security Audits	Allows a user, group, or process to make entries in the Security log.
Impersonate A Client After Authentication	Enables programs running on behalf of a user to impersonate a client.
Increase a Process Working Set	Allows the size of a process working set to be increased.
Increase Scheduling Priority	Specifies that a process can increase or decrease the priority that is assigned to another process.
Load And Unload Device Drivers	Allows a user to dynamically unload and load device drivers. This right does not apply to Plug and Play drivers.
Lock Pages In Memory	Allows an account to create a process that runs only in physical RAM, preventing it from being paged.
Log On As A Batch Job	Allows a process to log on to the system and run a file that contains one or more operating system commands.
Log On As A Service	Allows a service to log on in order to run the specific service.

Users and Security

PART III

Table 8.6: User Rights Assignment Policy Options   *(continued)*

Right	Description
Manage Auditing And Security Log	Allows a user to enable object access auditing for files and other Active Directory objects. This right does not allow a user to enable general object access auditing in the Local Security Policy.
Modify An Object Label	Allows a user to change the integrity level of files, folders, or other objects.
Modify Firmware Environment Variables	Allows a user to install or upgrade Windows. It also allows a user or process to modify the firmware environment variables stored in NVRAM of non-x86-based computers. This right does *not* affect the modification of system environment variables or user environment variables.
Perform Volume Maintenance Tasks	Allows a user to perform volume maintenance tasks such as defragmentation and error checking.
Profile Single Process	Allows a user to monitor nonsystem processes through performance-monitoring tools.
Profile System Performance	Allows a user to monitor system processes through performance-monitoring tools.
Remove Computer From Docking Station	Allows a user to undock a laptop through the Windows 7 user interface.
Replace A Process Level Token	Allows a process, such as Task Scheduler, to call an API to start another service.
Restore Files And Directories	Allows a user to restore files and directories, regardless of file and directory permissions.
Shut Down The System	Allows a user to shut down the Windows 7 computer locally.
Synchronize Directory Service Data	Allows a user to synchronize Active Directory data.
Take Ownership Of Files Or Other Objects	Allows a user to take ownership of system objects, such as files, folders, printers, and processes.

Perform the following steps to apply a user right policy. These steps assume that you have added the Local Group Object Policy snap-in to the MMC completed in earlier steps.

1. Open the LGPO MMC shortcut.

2. Expand the Local Computer Policy Snap-in.

3. Expand the folders as follows: Computer Configuration ➢ Windows Settings ➢ Security Settings ➢ Local Policies ➢ User Rights Assignment.

4. Open the Log On As A Service user right.

5. Click the Add User or Group button. The Select Users Or Groups dialog box appears.

6. Click the Advanced button and then select Find Now.

7. Select a user. Click OK.

8. Click OK in the Select Users Or Groups dialog box.

9. In the Log On As A Service Properties dialog box, click OK.

Now let's look at how to define security options within the LGPO.

Defining Security Options

You can use security option policies to configure security for the computer. Unlike user right policies, which are applied to a user, security option policies apply to the computer. Figure 8.9 shows the security option policies that Table 8.7 describes.

Figure 8.9: The security option policies

PART III

Users and Security

Table 8.7: Security Options

Option	Description	Default
Accounts: Administrator Account Status	Specifies whether the Administrator account is enabled or disabled under normal operation. Booting under Safe Mode, the Administrator account is enabled, regardless of this setting.	Disabled.
Accounts: Guest Account Status	Determines whether the Guest account is enabled or disabled.	Disabled.
Accounts: Limit Local Account Use Of Blank Passwords To Console Logon Only	Determines whether a local user with a blank password will be able to log on remotely. If this policy is enabled, users with blank passwords will only be able to log on locally. This setting does not apply to domain logon accounts.	Enabled.
Accounts: Rename Administrator Account	Allows the Administrator account to be renamed.	Administrator account is named Administrator.
Accounts: Rename Guest Account	Allows the Guest account to be renamed.	Guest account is named Guest.
Audit: Audit The Access Of Global System Objects	Allows access of global system objects to be audited.	Disabled.
Audit: Audit The Use Of Backup And Restore Privilege	Allows the use of backup and restore privileges to be audited.	Disabled.
Audit: Force Audit Policy Subcategory Settings (Windows 7 Or Later) To Override Audit Policy Category Settings	Allows audit policy subcategory settings to override audit policy category settings at the category level.	Not defined.
Audit: Shut Down System Immediately If Unable To Log Security Audits	Specifies that the system shuts down immediately if it is unable to log security audits.	Disabled.
DCOM: Machine Access Restrictions On Security Descriptor Definition Language (SDDL) Syntax	Specifies the users who can access DCOM applications.	Not defined.

Table 8.7: Security Options *(continued)*

Option	Description	Default
DCOM: Machine Launch Restrictions On Security Descriptor Definition Language (SDDL) Syntax	Specifies the users who can launch DCOM applications.	Not defined.
Devices: Allow Undock Without Having To Log On	Allows a user to undock a laptop computer from a docking station by pushing the computer's eject button without first having to log on.	Enabled.
Devices: Allowed To Format and Eject Removable Media	Specifies which users can format and eject removable NTFS media.	Not defined.
Devices: Prevent Users From Installing Printer Drivers	If enabled, allows only administrators to install print drivers for a network printer.	Disabled.
Devices: Restrict CD-ROM Access To Locally Logged-On User Only	Specifies whether the CD-ROM is accessible to local users and network users. If enabled, only the local user can access the CD-ROM, but if no local user is logged in, then the CD-ROM can be accessed over the network. If disabled or not defined, then access is not restricted.	Not defined.
Devices: Restrict Floppy Access To Locally Logged-On User Only	Specifies whether the floppy drive is accessible to local users and network users. If enabled, only the local user can access the floppy, but if no local user is logged in, then the floppy can be accessed over the network. If disabled or not defined, then access is not restricted.	Not defined.
Domain Controller: Allow Server Operators To Schedule Tasks	Allows server operators to schedule specific tasks to occur at specific times or intervals. Applies only to tasks scheduled through the AT command and does not affect tasks scheduled through Task Scheduler.	Not defined.

Users and Security

PART III

Table 8.7: Security Options *(continued)*

Option	Description	Default
Domain Controller: LDAP Server Signing Requirements	Specifies whether a Lightweight Directory Access Protocol server requires server signing with an LDAP client.	Not defined.
Domain Controller: Refuse Machine Account Password Changes	Specifies whether a domain controller will accept password changes for computer accounts.	Not defined.
Domain Member: Digitally Encrypt Or Sign Secure Channel Data (Always)	Specifies whether a secure channel must be created with the domain controller before secure channel traffic is generated.	Enabled.
Domain Member: Digitally Encrypt Secure Channel Data (When Possible)	Specifies that if a secure channel can be created between the domain controller and the domain controller partner, it will be.	Enabled.
Domain Member: Digitally Sign Secure Channel Data (When Possible)	Specifies that all secure channel traffic be signed if both domain controller partners who are transferring data are capable of signing secure data.	Enabled.
Domain Member: Disable Machine Account Password Changes	Specifies whether a domain member must periodically change its computer account password as defined in the Domain Member: Maximum Machine Account Password Age setting.	Disabled.
Domain Member: Maximum Machine Account Password Age	Specifies the maximum age of a computer account password.	30 days.
Domain Member: Require Strong (Windows 2000 Or Later) Session Key	If enabled, the domain controller must encrypt data with a 128-bit session key; if not enabled, 64-bit session keys can be used.	Disabled.
Interactive Logon: Do Not Display Last User Name	Prevents the last username in the logon screen from being displayed.	Disabled.

Table 8.7: Security Options *(continued)*

Option	Description	Default
Interactive Logon: Do Not Require Ctrl+Alt+Del	Allows the Ctrl+Alt+Del requirement for logon to be disabled.	Not defined, but it is automatically used on stand-alone workstations, meaning users who log on to the workstation see a start screen with icons for all users who have been created on the computer.
Interactive Logon: Message Text For Users Attempting To Log On	Displays message text for users trying to log on, usually configured for displaying legal text messages.	Not defined.
Interactive Logon: Message Title For Users Attempting To Log On	Displays a message title for users trying to log on.	Not defined.
Interactive Logon: Number Of Previous Logon Attempts To Cache (In Case Domain Controller Is Not Available)	Specifies the number of previous logon attempts stored in the cache. This option is useful if a domain controller is not available.	10.
Interactive Logon: Prompt User To Change Password Before Expiration	Prompts the user to change the password before expiration.	14 days before password expiration.
Interactive Logon: Require Domain Controller Authentication To Unlock	Specifies that a user name and password be required to unlock a locked computer. When this is disabled, a user can unlock a computer with cached credentials. When this is enabled, a user is required to authenticate to a domain controller to unlock the computer.	Disabled.

Table 8.7: Security Options *(continued)*

Option	Description	Default
Interactive Logon: Require Smart Card	Specifies that a smart card is required to log on to the computer.	Disabled.
Interactive Logon: Smart Card Removal Behavior	Specifies what happens if a user who is logged on with a smart card removes the smart card.	No action.
Microsoft Network Client: Digitally Sign Communications (Always)	Specifies that the server should always digitally sign client communication.	Disabled.
Microsoft Network Client: Digitally Sign Communications (If Server Agrees)	Specifies that the server should digitally sign client communication when possible.	Enabled.
Microsoft Network Client: Send Unencrypted Password To Third-Party SMB Servers	Allows third-party Server Message Block servers to use unencrypted passwords for authentication.	Disabled.
Microsoft Network Client: Amount Of Idle Time Required: Before Suspending Session	Allows sessions to be disconnected when they are idle.	15 minutes.
Microsoft Network Server: Digitally Sign Communications (Always)	Ensures that server communications will always be digitally signed.	Disabled.
Microsoft Network Server: Digitally Sign Communications (If Client Agrees)	Specifies that server communications should be signed when possible.	Disabled.
Microsoft Network Server: Disconnect Clients When Logon Hours Expire	If a user logs on and then their logon hours expire, specifies whether an existing connection will remain connected or be disconnected.	Enabled.
Network Access: Allow Anonymous SID/Name Translation	Specifies whether an anonymous user can request the security identifier (SID) attributes for another user.	Disabled.
Network Access: Do Not Allow Anonymous Enumeration Of SAM Accounts	If enabled, prevents an anonymous connection from enumerating Security Account Manager (SAM) accounts.	Enabled.

Table 8.7: Security Options *(continued)*

Option	Description	Default
Network Access: Do Not Allow Anonymous Enumeration Of SAM Accounts And Shares	If enabled, prevents an anonymous connection from enumerating Security Account Manager (SAM) accounts and network shares.	Disabled.
Network Access: Do Not Allow Storage Of Credentials Or .NET Passports For Network Authentication	Specifies whether passwords, credentials, and .NET Passports are stored and available for use after a user is authenticated to a domain.	Disabled.
Network Access: Let Everyone Permissions Apply To Anonymous Users	Specifies whether Everyone permission will apply to anonymous users.	Disabled.
Network Access: Named Pipes That Can Be Accessed Anonymously	Specifies which communication sessions are allowed to anonymous users.	Defined.
Network Access: Remotely Accessible Registry Paths	Determines which Registry paths will be accessible when the winreg key is accessed for remote Registry access, regardless of the ACL setting.	Defined.
Network Access: Remotely Accessible Registry Paths And Sub-Paths	Determines which Registry paths and subpaths will be accessible when the winreg key is accessed for remote Registry access, regardless of the ACL setting.	Defined.
Network Access: Restrict Anonymous Access To Named Pipes And Shares	Specifies whether anonymous access is allowed to shares and pipes for the Network Access: Named Pipes That Can Be Accessed Anonymously and Network Access: Shares That Can Be Accessed Anonymously policies	Enabled.
Network Access: Shares That Can Be Accessed Anonymously	Specifies which network shares can be accessed by anonymous users.	Not defined.
Network Access: Sharing And Security Model For Local Accounts	Specifies how local accounts will be authenticated over the network.	Classic — Local Users Authenticate As Themselves

Users and Security

PART III

Table 8.7: Security Options *(continued)*

Option	Description	Default
Network Security: Do Not Store LAN Manager Hash Value On Next Password Change	Specifies whether LAN Manager will store hash values from password changes.	Enabled.
Network Security: Force Logoff When Logon Hours Expire	Specifies whether a user with a current connection will be automatically logged off when the user's logon hours expire.	Disabled.
Network Security: LAN Manager Authentication Level	Specifies the LAN Manager Authentication Level.	Send NTLMv2 Response Only.
Network Security: LDAP Client Signing Requirements	Specifies the client signing requirements that will be enforced for LDAP clients.	Negotiate Signing.
Network Security: Minimum Session Security For NTLM SSP Based (Including Secure RPC) Clients	Specifies the minimum security standards for application-to-application client communications.	No minimum.
Network Security: Minimum Session Security For NTLM SSP Based (Including Secure RPC) Servers	Specifies the minimum security standards for application-to-application server communications.	No minimum.
Recovery Console: Allow Automatic Administrative Logon	Specifies whether a password is required for Administrative logon when the Recovery Console is loaded. If Enabled, the password is not required.	Disabled.
Recovery Console: Allow Floppy Copy And Access To All Drives And All Folders	Allows you to copy files from all drives and folders when the Recovery Console is loaded.	Disabled.
Shutdown: Allow System To Be Shut Down Without Having To Log On	Allows the user to shut down the system without logging on.	Enabled.
Shutdown: Clear Virtual Memory Pagefile	Specifies whether the virtual memory pagefile will be cleared when the system is shut down.	Disabled.

Table 8.7: Security Options *(continued)*

Option	Description	Default
System Cryptography: Force Strong Key Protection For User Keys Stored On The Computer	Specifies whether a password is required to use a private key.	Not defined.
System Cryptography: Use FIPS Compliant Algorithms For Encryption, Hashing And Signing	Specifies which encryption algorithms should be supported for encrypting, hashing, and signing file data.	Disabled.
System Objects: Default Owner For Objects Created By Members Of The Administrators Group	Determines whether, when an object is created by a member of the Administrators group, the owner will be the Administrators group or user who created the object.	Object Creator.
System Objects: Require Case Insensitivity For Non-Windows Subsystems	By default, Windows 7 does not specify case insensitivity for file subsystems. However, subsystems such as POSIX use case-sensitive file systems, so this option allows you to configure case sensitivity.	Enabled.
System Objects: Strengthen Default Permissions Of Internal System Objects (for example, Symbolic Links)	Specifies the default discretionary access control list for objects.	Enabled.
System Settings: Optional Subsystems	Specifies the subsystems that are used to support applications in your environment.	POSIX.
System Settings: Use Certificate Rules On Windows Executables For Software Restriction Policies	Specifies whether digital certificates are required when a user or process runs an EXE file.	Disabled.
User Account Control: Admin Approval Mode For The Built-in Administrator Account	If Enabled, the built-in Administrator account will require approval for any operation that requires privilege elevation. If Disabled, the built-in Administrator account will use XP-compatible mode with full administrative privileges.	Disabled.

Users and Security

PART III

Table 8.7: Security Options *(continued)*

Option	Description	Default
User Account Control: Behavior Of The Elevation Prompt For Administrators In Admin Approval Mode	Specifies the method for approval of privilege elevation for administrators.	Prompt For Consent.
User Account Control: Behavior Of Fhe Elevation Prompt For Standard Users	Specifies the method for approval of privilege elevation for standard users.	Prompt For Credentials.
User Account Control: Detect Application Installations And Prompt For Elevation	Specifies how applications are installed and whether approval is required.	Enabled.
User Account Control: Only Elevate Executables that are Signed and Validated	Specifies whether PKI signature checks are required for applications that request privilege elevation.	Disabled
User Account Control: Only Elevate UIAccess Applications That Are Installed In Secure Locations	Requires that applications executing with a UIAccess integrity level reside in a secure file system location.	Enabled.
User Account Control: Run All Administrators In Admin Approval Mode	Enforces UAC policy for all users, including administrators.	Enabled.
User Account Control: Switch To The Secure Desktop When Prompting For Elevation	If Enabled, elevation requests will go to the Secure Desktop. If Disabled, elevation requests will appear on the users' desktop.	Enabled.
User Account Control: Virtualize File And Registry Write Failures To Per-User Locations	Allows standard users to run pre–Windows 7 applications that formerly required administrator-level access to write to protected locations.	Enabled.

Perform the following steps to define some security option policies and see how they work. These steps assume that you have added the Local Group Object Policy snap-in to the MMC completed in earlier steps.

1. Open the LGPO MMC shortcut.

2. Expand the Local Computer Policy Snap-in.

3. Expand the folders as follows: Computer Configuration ➢ Windows Settings ➢ Security Settings ➢ Local Policies ➢ Security Options.

4. Open the policy Interactive Logon: Message Text For Users Attempting To Log On. On the Local Policy Setting tab, type **Welcome to all authorized users**. Click OK.

5. Open the policy Interactive Logon: Message Title For Users Attempting To Log On. On the Local Security Setting tab, type **Welcome Message**. Click OK.

6. Open the policy Interactive Logon: Prompt User To Change Password Before Expiration. On the Local Security Setting tab, type **3 days**. Click OK.

7. Log off your Administrator account and see the Welcome Message text appear. Click OK.

8. Log on as an administrator.

In the next section we look at how users can install resources on Windows 7 without being an administrator by using the User Account Control.

Configure User Account Control

Most administrators have had to wrestle with the balance between security and enabling applications to run correctly. In the past, some applications simply would not run correctly under Windows unless the user running the application was a local administrator.

Unfortunately, granting local administrator permissions to a user also allows the user to install software and hardware, change configuration settings, modify local user accounts, and delete critical files. Even more troubling is the fact that malware that infects a computer while an administrator is logged in is also able to perform those same functions.

Limited user accounts in Windows XP were supposed to allow applications to run correctly and allow users to perform necessary tasks. However, in practical application, it did not work as advertised. Many applications require that users have permissions to write to protected folders and to the Registry, and limited user accounts did not allow users to do so.

Windows 7's answer to the problem is User Account Control (UAC). UAC enables nonadministrator users to perform standard tasks, such as install a printer, configure a VPN or wireless connection, and install updates, while preventing them from performing tasks that require administrative privileges, such as installing applications.

Managing Privilege Elevation

UAC protects computers by requiring privilege elevation for all users, even users who are members of the local Administrators group. As you have no doubt seen by now, UAC prompts you for permission when you perform a task that requires privilege elevation. This prevents malware from silently launching processes without your knowledge.

Privilege elevation is required for any feature that contains the four-color security shield. For example, the small shield shown on the Change Date and Time button in the Date and Time dialog box in Figure 8.10 indicates an action that requires privilege elevation.

Now let's look at how to elevate privileges for users.

Figure 8.10: Date and Time dialog box

Elevated Privileges for Users

By default, local administrators are logged on as standard users. When administrators attempt to perform a task that requires privilege escalation, they are prompted for confirmation by default. You can require administrators to authenticate when performing a task that requires privilege escalation by changing the User Account Control: Behavior Of The Elevation Prompt For Administrators In Admin Approval Mode policy setting to Prompt For Credentials. On the other hand, if you don't want UAC to prompt administrators for confirmation when elevating privileges, you can change the policy setting to Elevate Without Prompting.

Nonadministrator accounts are called standard users. When standard users attempt to perform a task that requires privilege elevation, they are prompted for a password of a user account that has administrative privileges. You cannot configure UAC to automatically allow standard users to perform administrative tasks, nor can you configure UAC to prompt a standard user for confirmation before performing administrative tasks. If you do not want standard users to be prompted for credentials when attempting to perform administrative tasks, you can automatically deny elevation requests by changing the User Account Control: Behavior Of The Elevation Prompt For Standard Users policy setting to Automatically Deny Elevation Requests.

The built-in Administrator account, though disabled by default, is not affected by UAC. UAC will not prompt the Administrator account for elevation of privileges. Thus, it is important to use a normal user account whenever possible and use the built-in Administrator account only when absolutely necessary.

Perform the following steps to see how UAC affects administrator and nonadministrator accounts differently:

1. Log on to Windows 7 as a nonadministrator account.

2. Select Start ➤ Control Panel ➤ Large Icons View ➤ Windows Firewall.

3. Click the Turn Windows Firewall On or Off link on the left side. The UAC box should prompt you for permission to continue, as shown in Figure 8.11. Click Yes. You should not be allowed access to the Windows Firewall Settings dialog box.

Users and Security

PART III

Figure 8.11: UAC dialog box

4. Log off and log on as the Administrator account.

5. Select Start ➢ Control Panel ➢ Large Icons View ➢ Windows Firewall.

6. Click the Turn Windows Firewall On or Off link.

7. You should automatically go to the Windows Firewall screen. Close the Windows Firewall screen

Now instead of just elevating privileges for users, let's look at elevating privileges for executable applications.

Elevated Privileges for Executables

You can also enable an executable file to run with elevated privileges. To do so, on a one-time basis, you can right-click a shortcut or executable and select Run As Administrator.

But what if you need to configure an application to always run with elevated privileges for a user? To do so, log in as an administrator, right-click a shortcut or executable, and select Properties. On the Compatibility tab, select the Run This Program As An Administrator check box. If the check box is unavailable, the program is blocked from permanently running as an administrator, the program doesn't need administrative privileges, or you are not logged on as an administrator.

Many applications that are installed on a Windows 7 machine need to have access to the Registry. Windows 7 protects the Registry from nonadministrator accounts. Let's look at how this works.

Registry and File Virtualization

Windows 7 uses a feature called Registry and file virtualization to enable nonadministrator users to run applications that previously required administrative privileges to run correctly. As discussed previously, some applications write to the Registry and to protected folders, such as `C:\Windows` and `C:\Program Files`. For nonadministrator users, Windows 7 redirects any attempts to write to protected locations to a per-user location. By doing so, Windows 7 enables users to use the application successfully while it protects critical areas of the system.

In the next section we look at other areas of security such as Windows Firewall and the Action Center.

Use the Advanced Security Options

In this section you'll learn about advanced security options that you can configure to protect a Windows 7 machine. The first section discusses the Windows Firewall and how to use the firewall to protect against intruders.

Next we'll look at the Action Center, shown in Figure 8.12. The Action Center is designed to allow you to monitor and configure critical settings through a centralized dialog box. Critical settings include Automatic Updating, Malware Protection, and Other Security Settings. Malware Protection includes virus protection and spyware protection (included through Windows Defender).

Figure 8.12: Windows Security Center dialog box

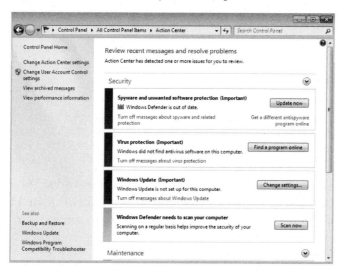

Users and Security

PART III

Let's start by looking at how to configure and maintain the Windows Firewall.

Configuring Windows Firewall

Windows Firewall, which is included with Windows 7, helps to prevent unauthorized users or malicious software from accessing your computer. Windows Firewall does not allow unsolicited traffic (traffic that was not sent in response to a request) to pass through the firewall.

To configure Windows Firewall, select Start ➤ Control Panel ➤ Large Icons View ➤ Windows Firewall, and then click Turn Windows Firewall On or Off. The Windows Firewall Settings dialog box appears, as shown in Figure 8.13.

Figure 8.13: Windows Firewall Settings dialog box

The Windows Firewall Settings dialog box allows you to turn Windows Firewall on or off for both private and public networks. The On setting blocks external sources except those that are specified on the Exceptions tab. The Off setting allows external sources to connect.

There is also a check box for Block All Incoming Connections. This feature allows you to connect to networks that are not secure. When Block All Incoming Connections is enabled, exceptions are ignored and no notification is given when an application is blocked by Windows Firewall.

The exceptions section of the Windows Firewall Allowed Programs dialog box, shown in Figure 8.14, allows you to define which programs and services should be allowed to pass through the Windows Firewall. You can select from a defined list of programs and services, or you can use the Add Another Program button to customize your exceptions.

Figure 8.14: Windows Firewall Allowed Programs dialog box

Take great care in enabling exceptions. Exceptions allow traffic to pass through the firewall, which could expose your computer to risk. Remember that the Block All Incoming Connections setting ignores all exceptions.

Now that you have looked at the basic Windows Firewall settings, let's discuss Windows Firewall with Advanced Security.

Windows Firewall with Advanced Security

You can configure more advanced settings by configuring Windows Firewall with Advanced Security (WFAS). To access Windows Firewall with Advanced Security, click Start ➤ Control Panel ➤ Large Icons View ➤ Windows Firewall and then click the Advanced Settings link. The Windows Firewall With Advanced Security On Local Computer dialog box appears, as shown in Figure 8.15.

Figure 8.15: Windows Firewall With Advanced Security On Local Computer dialog box

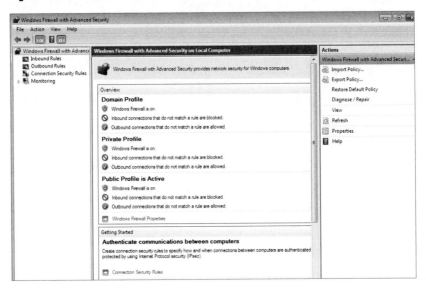

The scope pane to the left shows that you can set up specific inbound and outbound rules, connection security rules, and monitoring rules. The central area shows an overview of the firewall's status, as well as the current profile settings. Let's look at these in detail.

Inbound and Outbound Rules

Inbound and outbound rules consist of many preconfigured rules that can be enabled or disabled. Obviously, inbound rules monitor inbound traffic, and outbound rules monitor outbound traffic, as shown in Figure 8.16. By default, many are disabled. Double-clicking a rule brings up its Properties dialog box, as shown in Figure 8.17.

Figure 8.16: Inbound Rules dialog box

Figure 8.17: An inbound rule's Properties dialog box

You can filter the rules to make them easier to view. Filtering can be performed based on the profile the rule affects, on whether the rule is enabled or disabled, or on the rule group.

If you can't find a rule that is appropriate for your needs, you can create a new rule by right-clicking Inbound Rules or Outbound Rules in the scope pane and then selecting New Rule. The New Inbound (or Outbound) Rule Wizard launches and you are asked whether you want to create a rule based on a particular program, protocol or port, predefined category, or custom settings.

Perform the following steps to create a new inbound rule that will allow only encrypted TCP traffic:

1. Select Start ➤ Control Panel ➤ Large Icons View ➤ Windows Firewall.

2. Click Advanced Settings on the left-hand side.

3. Right-click Inbound Rules and select New Rule.

4. Choose a rule type. For this exercise, let's choose Custom so that we can see all the options available to us and then click Next.

5. Choose the programs or services that are affected by this rule. For this exercise, let's choose All Programs and then click Next.

6. Choose the protocol type, as well as the local and remote port numbers that are affected by this rule. For this exercise, let's choose TCP, and ensure that All Ports is selected for both Local Port and Remote Port. Click Next to continue.

7. Choose the local and remote IP addresses that are affected by this rule. Let's choose Any IP Address for both local and remote, and then click Next.

8. Specify whether this rule will allow the connection, allow the connection only if it is secure, or block the connection. Let's select the option Allow The Connection If It Is Secure, then click Next.

9. Specify whether connections should be allowed only from certain users. You can experiment with these options if you want. Then click Next to continue.

10. Specify whether connections should be allowed only from certain computers. Again you can experiment with these options if you want. Then click Next to continue

11. Choose which profiles will be affected by this rule. Select one or more profiles and click Next to continue.

12. Give your profile a name and description and then click Finish. Your custom rule appears in the list of Inbound Rules and the rule is enabled.

13. Double-click your newly created rule. Notice that you can change the options that you previously configured.

14. Disable the rule by deselecting the Enabled check box. Click OK.

Now let's look at setting up Connection Security Rules through the Windows Firewall with Advanced Security.

Connection Security Rules

You can use Connection Security Rules to configure how and when authentication occurs. These rules do not specifically allow connections; that's the job of inbound and outbound rules. You can configure the following connection security rules, as shown in Figure 8.18:

- Isolation: To restrict a connection based on authentication criteria

- Authentication Exemption: To specify computers that are exempt from authentication requirements

- Server-to-Server: To authenticate connections between computers

- Tunnel: To authenticate connections between gateway computers

- Custom

The final section that we look at for the Windows Firewall with Advanced Security is the Monitoring section.

Monitoring

The Monitoring section shows detailed information about the firewall configurations for the Domain Profile, Private Profile, and Public Profile settings, as shown in Figure 8.19. These network location profiles determine what settings are enforced for private networks, public networks, and networks connected to a domain.

Users and Security

PART III

Figure 8.18: Connection Security Rules

Figure 8.19: Monitoring section

In the next section we look at the Action Center and some of the functions it lets you perform.

Configure the Action Center

These days, having a firewall just isn't enough. Spyware and viruses are becoming more widespread, more sophisticated, and more dangerous. Users can unintentionally pick up spyware and viruses by visiting websites, or by installing an application in which spyware and viruses are bundled.

Even worse, malicious software cannot typically be uninstalled. Thus, antispyware and virus protection applications are also required to ensure that your computer remains protected. Let's take a look at some of the different ways that you can protect your Windows 7 computers using the Action Center.

Use Windows Defender

Windows 7 comes with an antispyware application called Windows Defender, formerly known as Microsoft AntiSpyware. Windows Defender offers real-time protection from spyware and other unwanted software. You can also configure Windows Defender to scan for spyware on a regular basis.

Like antivirus programs, Windows Defender relies on definitions, which are used to determine whether a file contains spyware. Out-of-date definitions can cause Windows Defender to fail to detect some spyware. Windows Update is used to regularly update the definitions used by Windows Defender so that the latest spyware can be detected. You can also configure Windows Defender to manually check for updates using Windows Update.

To access Windows Defender, as shown in Figure 8.20, click Start ➤ Control Panel ➤ Large Icons View ➤ Action Center ➤ Windows Defender. The status appears at the bottom of the screen, which includes time of the last scan, the scan schedule, the real-time protection status, and the definition version.

Users and Security

PART III

Figure 8.20: Windows Defender dialog box

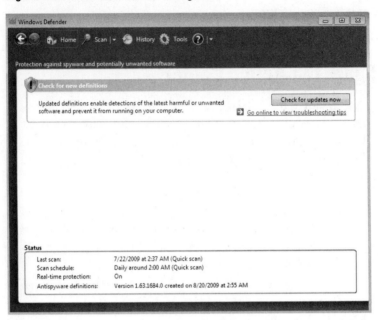

Let's look at how we can scan the system for spyware using Windows Defender.

Performing a Manual Scan

You can configure Windows Defender to perform a manual scan of your computer at any time. You can perform the following three types of scans:

- Quick Scan checks only where spyware is most likely to be found.

- Full Scan checks all memory, running processes, and folders.

- Custom Scan checks only the drives and folders that you select.

By default, Windows Defender performs a Quick Scan every morning at 2 a.m. You can change this setting by using the Tools menu option as shown in Figure 8.21.

Programs are classified into four spyware alert levels, as shown in Figure 8.22:

- Severe

- High

- Medium

- Low

Depending on the alert level, you can choose to have Windows
Defender ignore, quarantine, remove, or always allow software.

Figure 8.21: Windows Defender ➢ Tools menu dialog box

Figure 8.22: Spyware Alert Levels

In the next section we look at how to configure the many options of Windows Defender.

Configuring Windows Defender

Use the Tools menu to configure Windows Defender. As shown in Figure 8.23, you can access the following items through the Tools and Settings menu:

- Options
- Microsoft SpyNet
- Quarantined Items
- Allowed Items
- Windows Defender Website
- Microsoft Malware Protection Center

Figure 8.23: Windows Defender Tools and Settings menu

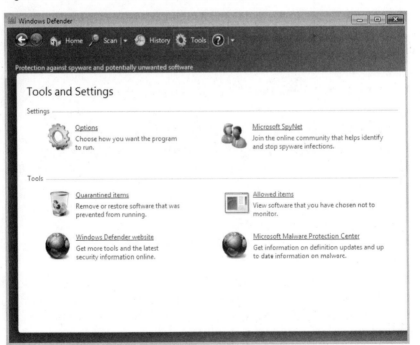

Let's look at each one of these Windows Defender Tools options in greater detail.

Options

Click Options on the Tools menu to enable you to configure the default behavior of Windows Defender. You can configure the following options:

Automatic Scanning   Automatic Scanning configures Windows Defender to automatically scan, how often automatic scans should occur, the time that scans will occur, and the type of scan to perform. You can also configure whether definitions should be updated before scanning, and whether the default actions should be taken on any spyware that is found.

Default Actions   Default Actions configures the actions Windows Defender should take on High, Medium, and Low Alert items. You can configure each level so that Windows Defender can take the default action for that level, always remove the item, or always ignore the item.

Real-Time Protection   Real-Time Protection configures whether real-time protection is enabled, which security agents you want to run, how you should be notified about threats, and whether a Windows Defender icon is displayed in the notification area.

Excluded Files And Folders   Excluded Files And Folders allow you to set up files and folders that are to be excluded during a scan.

Excluded File Types   Excluded File Types lets you configure certain file types that will be excluded from a scan, as shown in Figure 8.24. For example, you can exclude all DOC files if needed.

Advanced Options   Advanced Options configures whether archived files and folders, email, and removable drives are scanned; whether heuristics are used to detect unanalyzed software; and whether a restore point is created before removing spyware. You can also specify file locations that are exempt from scanning.

Administrator Options   Administrator Options configures whether Windows Defender is enabled, and whether you display items from all users on this computer.

The next option that we'll look at is Microsoft SpyNet.

Users and Security

PART III

Figure 8.24: Excluded File Types

Microsoft SpyNet

Microsoft SpyNet is an online community that can help you know how others respond to software that has not yet been classified by Microsoft. Participation in SpyNet is voluntary, as shown in Figure 8.25, and subscription to SpyNet is free. If you choose to volunteer, your choices will be added to the community so that others can learn from your experiences.

To join the SpyNet community, click Microsoft SpyNet on the Tools menu, and then choose either a basic or advanced membership. The level of membership will specify how much information is sent to Microsoft when potentially unwanted software is found on your computer.

By default, "I do not want to join Microsoft SpyNet at this time" is selected, but you can choose to participate in SpyNet by selecting the appropriate radio button. If you choose not to participate, no information will be sent to Microsoft, and Windows Defender will not alert you regarding unanalyzed software.

Figure 8.25: Microsoft SpyNet participation options

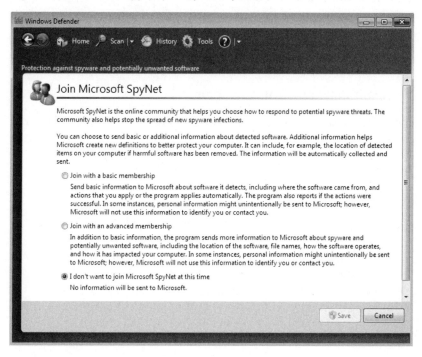

Quarantined Items

Software that has been quarantined by Windows Defender is placed in Quarantined Items. Quarantined software will remain here until you remove it. If you find that a legitimate application is accidentally removed by Windows Defender, you can restore the application from Quarantined Items.

Allowed Items

Software that has been marked as allowed is added to the Allowed Items list. Only trusted software should be added to this list. Windows Defender will not alert you regarding any software found on the Allowed Items list. If you find that a potentially dangerous application has been added to the Allowed Items list, you can remove it from the list so that Windows Defender can detect it.

Users and Security

PART III

Windows Defender Website

Clicking Windows Defender Website opens Internet Explorer and takes you to the Windows Defender website. Here you can find information on Windows Defender, spyware, and security.

Microsoft Malware Protection Center

Clicking Microsoft Malware Protection Center opens Internet Explorer and takes you to the Malware Protection Center website. Here, you can find information on antimalware research and responses.

History Menu Option

There is also a History option next to the Tools option. You can use the History option to see what actions have been taken by Windows Defender. Information is included about each application, the alert level, the action taken, the date, and the status. Information is retained until you click the Clear History button.

In the next section we look at using Windows BitLocker Drive Encryption and how it can help you protect your hard drive.

Use BitLocker Drive Encryption

To prevent individuals from stealing your computer and viewing personal and sensitive data found on your hard disk, some editions of Windows 7 come with a new feature called BitLocker Drive Encryption. BitLocker encrypts the entire system drive. New files added to this drive are encrypted automatically, and files moved from this drive to another drive or computers are decrypted automatically.

Only Windows 7 Enterprise and Ultimate include BitLocker Drive Encryption and only the operating system drive (usually C:) or internal hard drives can be encrypted with BitLocker. Files on other types of drives must be encrypted using BitLocker To Go.

BitLocker can use a Trusted Platform Module (TPM) version 1.2 or higher to store the security key. A TPM is a chip that is found in newer computers. If you do not have a computer with a TPM, you can store the key on a removable USB drive. The USB drive will be required each time you start the computer so that the system drive can be decrypted.

If the TPM discovers a potential security risk, such as a disk error, or changes made to BIOS, hardware, system files, or startup components, the system drive will not be unlocked until you enter the 48-digit BitLocker recovery password or use a USB drive with a recovery key.

TIP The BitLocker recovery key (also referred to as the recovery password) is very important. Do not lose it, or you may not be able to unlock the drive. Even if you do not have a TPM, be sure to keep your recovery key in case your USB drive becomes lost or corrupted.

BitLocker requires that you have a hard disk with at least two partitions, both formatted with NTFS. One partition will be the system partition that will be encrypted. The other partition will be the active partition that is used to start the computer; this partition will remain unencrypted. Windows 7 Ultimate and Professional automatically create the system partition and second partition at the time of clean install.

BitLocker Drive Preparation Tool

If you are using Vista Enterprise or Ultimate, you can also use BitLocker. There is a tool called the BitLocker Drive Preparation Tool that can help you set up these systems. In many originations, if you have Windows 7 and want to use BitLocker, you will most likely have Windows Vista machines that will also require BitLocker.

The BitLocker Drive Preparation Tool allows you to easily configure the hard disk drives in your computer to support BitLocker. This tool is available for free and can be downloaded at Microsoft's website (http://www .microsoft.com/downloads/details.aspx?familyid=320B9AA9-47E8-44F9-B8D0-4D7D6A75ADD0&displaylang=en).

The BitLocker Drive Preparation Tool will automatically complete the following three processes. These processes will configure the hard disk drive correctly:

1. If a secondary volume is not present, this tool will create the volume.

2. The preparation tool relocates the boot files to the correct volume and ensures that the operating system is correctly configured to find them at startup.

3. The preparation tool then configures the correct volume as the active partition on the drive for startup.

Users and Security

PART III

When the BitLocker Drive Preparation Tool finishes, you must restart the computer. The computer's hard disk drive will then be configured correctly to allow for the BitLocker application.

Before the BitLocker Drive Preparation Tool can be downloaded, the Windows system must require validation. This can be done at the time of the download.

Configuring BitLocker

Configuring BitLocker in Windows 7 is an easy and straightforward process. In the Windows 7 Control Panel is a BitLocker Drive Encryption icon that you'll click.

Complete the following steps to enable Windows 7 BitLocker Drive Encryption:

1. Open the Windows 7 Control Panel.

2. Change your view to Large Icons.

3. Double-click the BitLocker Drive Encryption icon.

4. Click the Turn On BitLocker link to enable BitLocker (see Figure 8.26).

5. At the Choose How You Want To Unlock This Drive screen, select the Use A Password To Unlock The Drive check box. Enter a password and then retype it. Click Next.

6. At the How Do You Want To Store Your Recovery Key? screen, choose Save The Recovery Key To A File.

7. Specify a filename and location.

8. At the Are You Ready To Encrypt? screen, click the Start Encrypting button.

9. If asked to reboot, reboot the system.

The drive will now become encrypted. After the drive is encrypted, all data is secure from physical theft. Now let's take a look at how to use BitLocker for removable media.

Figure 8.26: Enabling BitLocker

BitLocker To Go

BitLocker To Go allows you to use BitLocker on removable media. For example, say you have a USB drive that you want to use with a BitLocker encrypted internal hard drive. You would need to encrypt the USB drive to work with the internal drive. If you don't encrypt the USB drive using BitLocker To Go, you will not be able to move any encrypted files from the internal drive to the USB drive. This protects against other users just moving encrypted data to removable media.

There are two easy ways to encrypt a removable device:

- Choose to encrypt it when you connect the device to the system (a prompt will appear asking you to encrypt the new device).

- Right click the device and choose Turn On BitLocker (see Figure 8.27).

Now that the removable media is encrypted, you can move files from the BitLocker hard disk to the BitLocker removable media. There may be a time when you need to read a BitLocker encrypted file without having BitLocker. This is where BitLocker To Go Reader can help.

Figure 8.27: BitLocker To Go

BitLocker To Go Reader

There may be a time when you need to read a BitLocker encrypted removable drive on a Windows XP or Windows Vista machine.

Machines that are running Windows XP or Windows Vista do not automatically recognize removable drives that are BitLocker encrypted. With the BitLocker To Go Reader, users can unlock the BitLocker-protected drives by using a password or a recovery key. This gives these machines read-only access to the data on the BitLocker encrypted device.

The BitLocker To Go Reader is a free download from Microsoft's website. To download the application, visit http://www.microsoft.com/downloads/details.aspx?FamilyID=64851943-78C9-4CD4-8E8D-F551F06F6B3D&displayLang=en.

PART IV

Hardware and Networking

IN THIS PART ▶

9

Configuring Hardware and Printing

Hardware and Networking

PART IV

An important part of any computer system is its hardware. Think about using your computer without a keyboard, mouse, or printer. Computers allow us to connect many different types of hardware (cameras, scanners, MP3 players, etc.) and then use that hardware to make our life easier or more comfortable.

When you purchase and then install new hardware on today's operating systems, there are usually no problems. Because of Plug and Play technology, the initial installation and configuration will typically go smoothly and without error.

However, most of the time the software controlling the hardware (the drivers) will need to be updated over time and sometimes you may have to roll back a driver (to a previous version) in the event of an error with the new files. There may also be times when the drivers need to be installed manually for legacy hardware. You might also have to verify hardware configuration and make adjustments. The utility provided to perform these functions is Device Manager.

Device Manager displays all installed hardware, including input/output (I/O) devices like your mouse, keyboard, and monitor. It also displays information on storage, both removable and fixed, and communication devices like network interface cards and wireless and Bluetooth devices.

What you won't see for hardware in Device Manager are printers (unless they're USB; in that case, you'll see the USB port and thus the printer will be identified, but you won't be able to configure the printer from here). You'll use Devices And Printers for configuring and troubleshooting printers. New functionality in Windows 7 integrates some Device Manager functionality into Devices And Printers. This new functionality is known as Device Stage.

Configure Hardware

Device Manager in Windows 7 works the same way as it did in Vista and XP. Device Manager is designed to display information about the hardware installed on your computer, provides an interface to add new hardware, and lets you configure the hardware. Hardware today follows the Plug and Play standard, so simply connecting most hardware will allow Device Manager (well, the OS processes controlling devices that are displayed to you) to automatically configure them.

If you have devices that are not Plug and Play, you can install them manually from Device Manager as well. Windows 7 introduces a new functionality known as Device Stage, which is an enhanced graphic output that gives better details and functionality to installed devices such as cameras.

You can use Device Manager to ensure that all devices are working properly and to troubleshoot misbehaving devices. For each device installed, you can view specific properties down to the resources being used, such as the input/output (I/O) port and interrupt requests (IRQs). The specific actions that you can take with Device Manager include the following:

- Viewing a list of all hardware installed on your computer
- Determining which device driver is installed for each device
- Managing and updating device drivers
- Installing new devices
- Disabling, enabling, and uninstalling devices
- Using driver rollback to return to a previous version of a driver
- Troubleshooting device problems

Although many of the features of Device Manager in Windows 7 work similarly to Device Manager in older versions of Windows, a new feature has been added to make configuration and use of some devices easier: Device Stage.

Device Stage

Throughout the evolution of technologies and PCs, one of the greatest features is how PCs let you use such a wide array of devices. Device Manager lets you see all the hardware connected and make configuration changes, but utilizing the features of the devices themselves has been left up to alternate programs outside the Windows interface.

Windows 7 introduces a new specification for hardware vendors (knowing that most hardware comes with software for the user to interface with) that allows them to provide user access within Windows. The new feature is known as Device Stage. Windows 7 Devices And Printers is the interface for displaying and accessing hardware that supports Device Stage. The Windows 7 Devices And Printers screen is shown in Figure 9.1.

Take the example of a digital camera. When you connect the camera to the PC, the PC recognizes the device (which is Plug and Play) and typically displays the camera as a mass storage device. The user wanting advanced features like downloading or editing the photos uses another program.

Hardware and Networking

PART IV

Figure 9.1: Devices And Printers

When you plug in a device like a camera supporting Device Stage technology, Device Stage displays a single window that gives you easy access to common device tasks, such as importing pictures, launching the vendor-supplied editing program, or simply browsing all from one interface. With Windows 7, you'll be able to access all your connected and wireless devices from the single Devices And Printers screen as well as clicking the device that displays in the Windows 7 enhanced Taskbar and using the menu as shown in Figure 9.2. From this menu, you can work with your devices, browse files on them, or manage device settings.

Figure 9.2: Device options appear
in the Taskbar.

Device Stage–supported devices also include wireless and Bluetooth devices that make managing these resources for the end user more efficient than ever. As portable devices are disconnected and reconnected, the Device Stage–driven Devices And Printers screen updates in real time.

The following procedures will guide you through opening and viewing devices recognized on your Windows 7 machine.

Perform the following steps to find Devices And Printers in Control Panel:

1. Choose Start ➢ Control Panel ➢ Hardware And Sound.

2. Choose Devices And Printers from the main window.

3. Right-click a device to see functions specific to that device.

Perform the following steps to open Devices And Printers from the Start menu:

1. Click Start ➢ Control Panel ➢ Devices And Printers.

2. Right-click a device to see functions specific to that device.

Or you can do the following:

- Click the Start button and type **device** in the Start menu's search box, as shown in Figure 9.3, to launch Devices And Printers, the first applet in the search list.

Figure 9.3: Type the word device in the Start menu's search box.

Hardware and Networking

PART IV

Using Device Manager

Device Manager is this first-line component in Windows 7 to display the devices that are connected to your machine. More appropriately (and importantly) is the ability to see which devices Windows 7 has recognized. If you install or connect a new piece of hardware, you won't see it in Device Manager if Windows 7 doesn't recognize it. This would be an unusual occurrence given the sophistication of today's hardware vendors and the standards like Plug and Play that have been implemented. However, this is an important step in seeing just which devices are known to Windows 7.

In some cases, Windows 7 doesn't recognize a device but can tell what *type* of device it is. Device Manager adds an Unknown Device item with as much information about the device that it can present. Hopefully, this will give you enough information about the hardware so that you can manually install the device driver. Keep in mind that I have been using Device Manager for many versions of Windows, so what we're discussing is applicable to legacy versions as well. Device Manager has a fairly simple opening screen but a lot of functionality behind it. Open Device Manager in Windows 7 quickly by typing **Device Manager** in the Start menu's search bar and view the opening screen as shown in Figure 9.4.

Figure 9.4: Device Manager opening screen

On the opening screen, you get a good first feeling for the hardware installed and recognized, as well as a glimpse at any major issues such as a device that's recognized but does not have drivers installed or is not working correctly. How do you see that? A warning symbol is displayed over the misbehaving device. For example, say you have just installed a new network adapter but the device does not seem to be working. You can open Device Manager and click the Network Adapters option to start the troubleshooting.

> **NOTE**   When something occurs that's outside the normal functionality in a Windows interface, an additional notification icon appears. As shown in the following graphic, the yellow triangle with the exclamation point icon is the indicator that a device is experiencing difficulty. Informational notifications consist of a blue circle with a question mark. A critical error displays as a red circle with an X through it.

To continue troubleshooting a network adapter in Device Manager, right-click the misbehaving adapter and select Properties to open the dialog box shown in Figure 9.5. This is just the start to the functionality within Device Manager.

Figure 9.5: Device Manager network adapter properties window

There are many reasons to view the devices installed and configured on a machine. One reason is to verify hardware type and status.
Suppose someone in your organization has given you documentation
for a user's machine with the machine's hardware specifications. You're
concerned that the stated network adapter for the machine may not be
the one installed.

Follow these steps if you want Device Manager on the machine in
question to show you the recognized network adapters in the machine:

1. Choose Start ➢ Control Panel ➢ Hardware And Sound ➢ Device
   Manager (under Devices And Printers).

2. Click the triangle next to Network Adapters (or double-click
   Network Adapters) to expand Network Adapters.

Here's another way to launch Device Manager:

1. Click Start.

2. Type **Device Manager** in the Start menu's search box.

3. Press Enter.

Or you can:

1. Click Start and then right-click Computer.

2. Select Manage.

3. In the navigation pane of the Microsoft Management Console
   (MMC), select Device Manager.

The latter method puts Device Manager into a functional interface, MMC, that allows access to several administrative tools
from one location. (The MMC was covered in detail in Chapter 3,
"Configuring Disks.")

Device Properties Available Within Device Manager

After you open Device Manager and have access to the installed devices
on your machine, you might want to view the properties for the hardware.
The properties dialog box lets you view and change configuration parameters as necessary. The tabs in the dialog box vary from device to device.

Many device properties dialog boxes include an Advanced tab, as
shown in Figure 9.6.

Figure 9.6: You can click the Advanced tab to see additional properties specific to the device.

Configuring Network Adapter Advanced Properties

If you need to change the hardware configuration properties, Device Manager is the best way to access the parameters.

Perform the following steps to learn to access the advanced properties of your network adapter. Here you can make configuration changes as necessary:

1. Choose Start ➢ Control Panel ➢ Hardware And Sound ➢ Device Manager (under Devices And Printers).

2. Click the triangle next to Network Adapters (or double-click Network Adapters) to expand Network Adapters.

3. Right-click your network adapter and select Properties.

4. Choose the Advanced tab.

5. Select various properties and view the parameters.

After installing a new piece of hardware, you might need to update the drivers to a later version than those shipped with the hardware.

Hardware and Networking

PART IV

Installing and Updating Device Drivers

Device drivers are the controlling code that interfaces the hardware components with the operating system. The commands issued to a piece of hardware are specific to each piece of hardware and might be different commands, memory locations, or actions even within the same type of hardware.

For example, a network interface card (NIC) from one vendor might have a different set of instructions necessary for its operation than a NIC from a different manufacturer. This doesn't work well for an operating system or software vendor who would like to be able to issue a standard command and have the same functionality across the hardware, regardless of the vendor. This is where the driver comes in; the driver takes a standard instruction from the operating system and issues the device-specific command to the hardware to perform the desired function.

Why do we update drivers? There are cases where a command set for the driver might perform a function incorrectly. This might produce errors in some cases and has to be fixed. The hardware vendor will update the driver to fix the problem. It might also be the case that new or better functionality is desired and the hardware vendor needs to change the driver code to allow added functionality or provide better performance; this will also lead to an update.

Typical first-time installation of drivers today happens automatically, thanks to the Plug and Play specification. After installation of the hardware, Windows 7 will recognize the new hardware and will launch the driver installation program.

Take, for example, the connection of a digital camera to the USB port of your computer. Windows 7 will recognize that a device has been plugged in and will gather the information about the USB device. Windows 7 will then install the best driver it knows about (and if it doesn't know about the device, it will ask you how to proceed). Figure 9.7 shows the message that indicates the operating system found a driver and is installing it automatically.

Once the installation completes, the device becomes available in Device Manager. Figure 9.8 shows the digital camera as a hardware item you can now access as you did previously with the network adapter.

If you need to review the driver details for your newly installed device—the digital camera in our example—you can right-click the device in Device Manager and choose Properties. Figure 9.9 shows the right-click menu (also known as the context menu); note the top choice in this menu is a faster way to access the Update Driver Software command—rather than selecting Properties and clicking the Update Driver button—if that's what you're trying to do.

Figure 9.7: Automatic driver installation

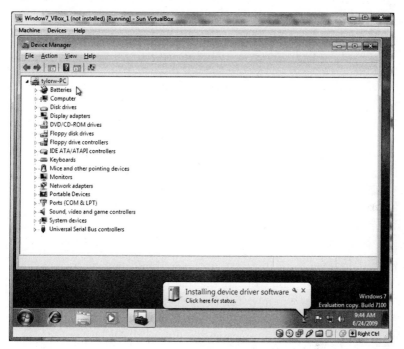

Figure 9.8: New device availability in Device Manager

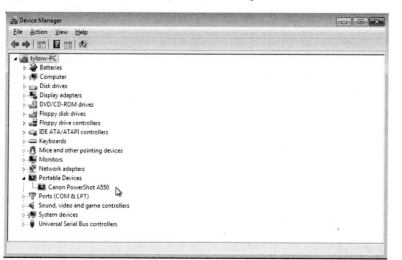

Hardware and Networking

PART IV

Figure 9.9: The right-click menu for a device in Device Manager

You might want to verify the driver general information such as the driver provider or version; you can see that information on the Driver tab of the Properties window. You can also choose to view the driver details, which are the supporting files and associated paths. Figure 9.10 shows the digital camera's Properties window with the Driver tab selected, along with the Driver File Details dialog box that opened when I clicked the Driver Details button.

Viewing Driver Details

When you're having issues with a hardware device, you can go online and read forums or query search engines for ideas. A lot of the time someone will say, "We had a terrible time with driver version 2.1.1 but version 2.1.2 fixed it," referencing your exact problem. When that happens, you can use the Device Manager to view your driver details.

Perform the following steps to see your device driver information:

1. Choose Start ➢ Control Panel ➢ Hardware And Sound ➢ Device Manager (or type **device manager** in the Start menu's search box).

2. Click the triangle next to the category you're interested in to expand the item list; you can also double-click the category name (for example, double-click the Portable Devices category to see the portable devices connected to the machine).

3. Right-click the hardware item and select Properties.

4. Select the Driver tab and view the Driver Version setting.

5. Click the Driver Details button to see the files associated with the hardware.

Figure 9.10: Verifying the driver details

Updating Drivers

Perform the following steps to update drivers:

1. Choose Start ➤ Control Panel ➤ Hardware And Sound ➤ Device Manager (or type **device manager** in the Start menu's search box).

2. Click the triangle next to the category you're interested in to expand the item list.

3. Right-click the hardware item and select Properties.

4. Select the Driver tab.

5. Click the Update Driver button; a window launches and asks how you want to update the driver.

6. Choose Search Automatically For Updated Driver Software to have Windows 7 search for you, or you can choose Browse My Computer For Driver Software if you already have the new drivers. Windows 7 searches for and updates the drivers or reports back that you have the most current version.

NOTE   You might install a new driver for new or updated functionality even if you're not having issues. You can receive notification from the manufacturer if you have let them know you're interested by registering your hardware. Otherwise, visit the manufacturer's website periodically to see if updates are available.

Rolling Back to a Previous Version of a Device Driver

Occasionally an update breaks a piece of functioning hardware or doesn't solve a problem. In that case, you'll want to go back to the previous version, or "roll back" the driver.

Perform the following steps to roll back to a previous version of an updated driver:

1. Choose Start ➤ Control Panel ➤ Hardware And Sound ➤ Device Manager (or type **device manager** in the Start menu's search box).

2. Click the triangle next to the category you're interested in to expand the item list.

3. Right-click the hardware item and select Properties.

4. Select the Driver tab.

5. Click the Roll Back Driver button. The previous driver will be installed and the hardware will return to its previous state of functionality.

NOTE   If the Roll Back Driver button is grayed out, there isn't a previous version available to roll back to.

The Driver tab for a piece of installed hardware in Device Manager also provides functionality for disabling and uninstalling a driver. Why would you want to disable a driver? There are several possibilities, but troubleshooting is in the forefront. Disabling the driver effectively disables the hardware; it will no longer function as designed. Uninstalling the device driver also has a similar effect, but if the hardware is still installed, you can uninstall it, perform a hardware scan to ensure the hardware is still recognized, and then reinstall.

Many times, I disable a device from Device Manager to eliminate one piece of a problem I am having with a system. If I'm confident the problem exists with the hardware, I'll uninstall the driver and let the operating system reinstall it as part of the troubleshooting procedure. This works much of the time.

Disabling a Device

There may be a time when you need to disable a device from working on a system. For example, let's say you have a webcam built into your kids' Windows 7 laptop but you do not want them using the camera, you can disable the camera from working on the system. Complete the following steps to disable a device:

1. Choose Start ➤ Control Panel ➤ Hardware And Sound ➤ Device Manager (or type **device manager** in the Start menu's search box).

2. Click the triangle next to the category you're interested in to expand the item list.

3. Right-click the hardware item and select Properties.

   You can select Disable directly from the context menu if you want.

4. Select the Driver tab.

5. Click the Disable button (this is a toggle button; it will say Disable if the device is enabled, or Enable if the device is disabled).

   The device driver and thus the device will be disabled and will no longer function. A down arrow appears on the item in Device Manager and the General tab will show the device as disabled.

Enabling a Device

After a device is disabled, you may want to go back and re-enable the device so that you can now use it. Perform the following steps to enable a device:

1. Choose Start ➤ Control Panel ➤ Hardware And Sound ➤ Device Manager (or type **device manager** in the Start menu's search box).

2. Click the triangle next to the category you're interested in to expand the item list.

3. Right-click the hardware item and select Properties. (Alternatively, select Enable from the context menu.)

4. Choose the Driver tab. (Alternatively, click Enable Device on the General tab).

5. Click the Enable button.

The device driver becomes enabled and the hardware will work as designed (barring any other issues).

It might be beneficial at times to uninstall and reinstall a device driver. By uninstalling and reinstalling a device driver, many times the default configuration parameters will be reset to their original specifications. Therefore, any changes you have made will need to be reconfigured. You might also consider using a different device driver than Windows 7 is set up to use via Plug and Play. Uninstalling the device driver and manually installing a different version might be a solution as well.

Keep in mind that uninstalling a device driver does not delete the driver files from the machine; uninstalling the device drivers removes the operating system configuration for the hardware. You might want to find the files and delete them manually in some cases. Remember, you can find the files (and thus the filenames) by clicking the Driver Details button on the Driver tab of the hardware device's Properties pages.

Uninstalling a Device Drive

If you have determined the device driver for a misbehaving hardware is potentially the problem, you can uninstall the device driver. Windows 7 will detect the device again (assuming that it found the device the first time) and reinstall the driver. You have the option of letting Windows 7 search and install the driver, or you can manually choose where to install it from.

Perform the following steps to uninstall a device driver:

1. Choose Start ➤ Control Panel ➤ Hardware And Sound ➤ Device Manager (or type **device manager** in the Start menu's search box).

2. Click the triangle next to the category you're interested in to expand the item list.

3. Right-click the hardware item and select Properties. (You can select Uninstall directly from the context menu if you want.)

4. Select the Driver tab.

5. Click the Uninstall button.

6. Click OK in the Confirm Device Uninstall dialog box. A progress box will appear as the device driver is uninstalled. Device Manager will no longer show the hardware.

Reinstalling a Device Driver Automatically

You can have Windows 7 automatically reinstall an uninstalled driver. To begin, from the Device Manager click Action ➤ Scan For Hardware Changes. Alternatively, you can right-click the machine name in Device Manager and select Scan For Hardware Changes from the context menu.

Windows 7 initiates the process of discovering the Plug and Play device and reinstalls the device driver configuration into the operating system. The hardware will be available again within Device Manager.

Some hardware manufacturers would like you to install the driver files and some software for their device before the operating system has a chance to discover it. This might be just so the software program controlling some of the hardware functionality will be installed first; that way, its configuration file can accurately reference the installed drivers.

Another reason might be to add the driver files to the driver configuration directories of the operating system before the OS discovers the device. This is usually done by inserting and running a setup program from a provided CD or DVD. Following the manufacturer's recommendations will most often produce a better result.

There are also situations I run into that require a manual installation of hardware. This might be for legacy hardware you are using, for drivers not supplied in the operating system distribution files, or for drivers that might perform different functions from the default drivers available. You can also perform a manual driver installation in Windows 7 by using the Add Hardware Wizard.

During the manual installation process, you can have Windows 7 access a Microsoft online database with available drivers to find a current driver, or you can specify a location of your choosing locally.

Hardware and Networking

PART IV

Installing a Device Driver Using the Add Hardware Wizard

From Device Manager, launch the Add Hardware Wizard by choosing Add Legacy Hardware from either the Action menu or the context menu of the machine. The next step is to tell Windows 7 where to look for the driver. The next screen of the Add Hardware Wizard shows the default selection, as shown in Figure 9.11.

Figure 9.11: Select this option to have the wizard install the hardware for you.

In order to choose a piece of hardware from a list of supplied drivers, or more importantly, to choose a specific path, you select the option Install The Hardware That I Manually Select For A List (Advanced) and click Next. This allows you to select a device or choose Show All Devices; if you choose Show All Devices, click Next to choose a location.

If you have a disk or have the appropriate drivers stored in an accessible location, click the Have Disk button, as shown in Figure 9.12, and browse to the driver files you need to install. If all goes as planned, the hardware device drivers will be installed and Device Manager will display the newly installed hardware.

The devices you use to get information into and out of your Windows 7 machine are your I/O devices. I/O devices include your keyboard, mouse, scanner, and printer. These devices are also configurable through Device Manager, as you'll learn in the next section.

Figure 9.12: Click the Have Disk button.

Manage I/O Devices

Your I/O devices might be connected to your computer by standard cabling or via USB, or you might use a wireless technology such as IrDA (infrared, the Infrared Data Association) or RF (radio frequency). Most of the time you will not have to (or want to) change the configuration of these devices. However, doing so is possible, and in this section I'll show you how to make changes.

Configuring the Keyboard

Most of the time you can leave the keyboard settings at their default values. There are ease-of-access properties as well as advanced keyboard options you can configure if desired. Accessing the ease-of-access features for the keyboard by choosing Start ➤ Control Panel ➤ Ease Of Access and clicking the Change How Your Keyboard Works link, as shown in Figure 9.13. You can also click the Ease Of Access Center link (from Ease of Access) and then choose Make The Keyboard Easier To Use. Either way, you get to the same window and can access the advanced properties from this window by selecting Keyboard Settings in the See Also section.

Figure 9.13: Keyboard Ease of Access Center

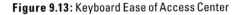

The advanced properties for the keyboard allow you to change the character repeat delay and the character repeat rate. The delay is how long Windows 7 waits before repeating characters when a key is held down, and the repeat rate is how quickly the characters repeat after the delay interval has expired. The keyboard properties also include a setting for the cursor blink rate. Figure 9.14 shows the Keyboard Properties window. The Hardware tab allows you to access the device driver properties (as found in Device Manager).

Figure 9.14: Keyboard Properties window

Changing the Repeat Delay for Your Keyboard

If you have an issue where your typing style has you hold down a key on your keyboard a little too long sometimes and the characters start to repeat, you can change the amount of time Windows 7 waits before repeating the character.

Perform the following steps to modify the repeat delay for your keyboard:

1. Choose Start ➤ Control Panel ➤ Ease Of Access.

2. Click Change How Your Keyboard Works.

3. Scroll down to the See Also section and choose Keyboard Settings to open the Keyboard Properties window.

4. Select the Repeat Delay slider and adjust the repeat delay to a longer value.

Configuring the Mouse

As with many I/O devices, you probably won't need to change the mouse configuration. Once you know you can, you might try out a few different options, just because you are able to. To check out the mouse options, open Control Panel, select Ease Of Access, and click Change How Your Mouse Works, as shown in Figure 9.15.

The Make The Mouse Easier To Use window opens, displaying several options we used to refer to as Accessibility options in previous versions of Windows. The Ease Of Access options include changing the color or size of the mouse pointer, controlling the mouse with the keyboard, managing windows with the mouse, as well as having access to the mouse properties dialog box. You access the mouse properties by choosing Mouse Settings in the See Also section at the bottom of the Make The Mouse Easier To Use window, as shown in Figure 9.16.

Figure 9.15: In Ease Of Access, click Change How Your Mouse Works.

Figure 9.16: The Make The Mouse Easier To Use window

After you select Mouse Settings, the Mouse Properties window opens, where you can configure more of your mouse functionality and display options. The Mouse Properties window provides five tabs of options for you work with. The first tab on the left, as shown in Figure 9.17, is labeled Buttons.

Figure 9.17: The Buttons tab of the Mouse Properties window

This tab allows you to switch the primary and secondary buttons. These are what we refer to as the left and right mouse buttons; the left is the primary and the right is the secondary. This is the default setup the way a person using the mouse on the right side (physically "right side" in lieu of the "correct side") would normally and intuitively think of the functions. If a user uses their mouse on the left side of the keyboard, it would be more reasonable to have the right and left (primary and secondary) functions reversed.

The Buttons tab also allows you to change the double-click speed and set up a function called ClickLock. With ClickLock enabled, a single click acts as a click and hold—like when you want to drag a window, you "click and hold" and then drag, releasing to drop. ClickLock has you click and release on a window, drag it to where you want it, and click a second time to drop it. You can modify the setting for the length of time you hold the initial click before the window is grabbed; that

Hardware and Networking

PART IV

way, a casual click to change cursor position will not attach the window to the mouse pointer.

The Pointers tab of the Mouse Properties window, shown in Figure 9.18, allows you to change the pointer properties. The pointer is the image we normally just refer to as the mouse.

Figure 9.18: The Pointers tab of the Mouse Properties window

You might not have considered the importance of the mouse pointer; it gives you feedback as to what is going on within the operating system. You can check out the Customize section of the Pointers tab to get an idea of just how many different feedback pointers there are. The pointers available do (or can) change with the user interface (UI) scheme, and you have the option to change them as a whole on the Pointers tab as well.

Figure 9.19 shows the Pointer Options tab of the Mouse Properties window. These options allow you to change the Motion parameters and Visibility options. There's an option to set up Snap To, which will automatically move the mouse to the default button in a dialog box.

Depending on the style of mouse you are using, you might have a scroll wheel. This wheel allows vertical scrolling as well as horizontal scrolling. The Mouse Properties dialog box's Wheel tab allows you to change the Vertical Scrolling and Horizontal Scrolling configuration, as you can see in Figure 9.20.

Figure 9.19: The Pointer Options tab of the Mouse Properties window

Figure 9.20: The Wheel tab of the Mouse Properties window

Reversing the Primary and Secondary Buttons from the Default

As a network administrator, you need to provide the best environment for your users to be productive. Sometimes this involves changing a user's I/O environment.

There are cases where the user will use their mouse on the left side of their keyboard instead of the right and might need to have the primary and secondary functions reversed. The user may also use a more condensed screen and need the mouse pointers to be a larger size so they can see them better. Because of the type of work being done on the machine, a user might also be better served having the scroll wheel scroll pages (screens) instead of lines for each roll of the wheel.

Perform the following steps to change the primary and secondary buttons to a keyboard left-style mouse:

1. Choose Start ➢ Control Panel ➢ Ease Of Access.
2. Click Change How Your Mouse Works.
3. Select Mouse Settings in the See Also section.
4. On the Buttons tab, click the Switch Primary And Secondary Buttons check box.
5. Click OK to close the Mouse Properties window.
6. Click OK to close the Change How Your Mouse Works window.
7. Close the Ease Of Access Center window.

Changing the Pointer to the Large-Sized Windows Aero Scheme

Perform the following steps to change the mouse pointer and Windows Aero scheme:

1. Choose Start ➢ Control Panel ➢ Ease Of Access.
2. Click Change How Your Mouse Works.
3. Click Mouse Settings in the See Also section.
4. On the Pointers tab, open the Scheme drop-down list.
5. Select the Windows Aero (Large) (System Scheme) option from the Scheme drop-down list.
6. Click OK to close the Mouse Properties window.
7. Click OK to close the Change How Your Mouse Works window.
8. Close the Ease Of Access Center window.

Changing the Mouse Wheel Function to Scroll Screens Rather than Lines

Follow these steps to change the mouse wheel functionality to scroll screens as opposed to lines:

1. Choose Start ➤ Control Panel ➤ Ease Of Access.

2. Click Change How Your Mouse Works.

3. Click Mouse Settings in the See Also section.

4. On the Wheel tab, select the One Screen At A Time radio button in the Vertical Scrolling section.

5. Click OK to close the Mouse Properties window.

6. Click OK to close the Change How Your Mouse Works window.

7. Close the Ease of Access Center window.

Today, we have to deal with removable storage devices being connected to machines; it's rare to have a user on a Windows machine who doesn't want to save something to a memory stick. Next, you'll learn how to configure removable storage devices.

Configuring Removable Storage Devices

Removable storage devices have been part of the computing world since the beginning. CDs, DVDs, and floppy disks are examples of removable storage. Today, we're using other types of removable storage as well, including flash-based electronics such as USB sticks, memory cards, USB or FireWire external rotating hard drives, cameras, phones, and so on. These devices (or media) are discovered automatically as the devices are connected.

NOTE In this section I'll concentrate on dynamically connected devices utilizing the USB/FireWire connectivity and memory cards. These devices present challenges to the administrative team because end users using the technology might not follow the guidelines (loss as well as security guidelines) for protecting their data.

Windows 7 includes improvements to the Safely Remove Hardware (Eject) menu. For example, it's now possible to eject just one memory card at a time and physically remove it, whereas previously ejecting

Hardware and Networking

PART IV

one card removed all the memory cards from the software interface. You have to physically reinstall any cards you still want to access (from a single hub) and keep the ports available for future use. Removable media is now listed under its own label through Devices And Printers, as shown in Figure 9.21, rather than just its drive letter, as it was in previous versions of Windows. This is also part of the new Device Stage functionality of Windows 7, where the hardware vendors can include configuration information about portable devices and give users more resources from one location.

Figure 9.21: Devices And Printers with USB stick installed

You must consider certain factors related to data access performance with the portable devices as well. To improve data access and make saves faster, it's possible to have the operating system cache the data and write it to the portable device later (when there's free processor time). However, this increases the possibility of a user removing the portable device before the write is made; this would mean a loss of data. Windows 7 defaults to writing the data immediately, which minimizes the chance of data loss and the cost of performance. The configuration for optimizing the portable device for Quick Removal or Better Performance is found on the Policies tab for the hardware in Device Manager.

Depending on how your portable storage device is used, you might want to change the write cache policy for better operating system performance.

Modifying the Write Cache Policy for a Portable Storage Device

Perform these steps to change the write cache policy for a USB memory stick attached to a Windows 7 machine:

1. Choose Start ➤ Control Panel ➤ Hardware And Sound ➤ Device Manager (under Devices And Printers) or type **Device Manager** in the Start menu's search box.

2. Click the triangle next to Disk Drives (or double-click Disk Drives) to expand that item.

3. Right-click USB Disk Hardware and select Properties.

4. Choose the Policies tab.

5. Select the Better Performance radio button and then click OK.

Removing a Portable Hardware Device

In my next example, I've changed the USB portable storage device write cache policy for better performance; this means writes to the portable device may be saved and written at a later time (when the processor has clock cycles available). To ensure no loss of data, it is fairly important to eject the device through Windows 7 before physically removing the device.

Click the icon in the Taskbar to eject the device which initiates a stop for the hardware, forcing any cached writes in memory to be written to the device.

Stopping the portable hardware device can also be done from the Devices And Printers window by choosing Eject from the context menu of the device. The device will close, meaning the writes have been made, and you are presented with a window saying it's safe to remove the hardware.

Another device that administrators have to deal with on a regular basis is the corporate printer. Next, I'll explore printer management.

Configure Printers

Printers have long been an issue for IT teams. Every new version of an operating system has new software intelligence to make the installation and maintenance easier, but printer technology continues to grow and hardware vendors continue to make changes. The driver base for all the different printers out there is huge, and even for the same printer, there are numerous variations. Each printer itself might have lots of options that can be made available, and this all has to be controlled by the operating system through the printer drivers.

Hardware and Networking

PART IV

Microsoft Definitions in the Printer World

When I use the term *printer* in the real world, I'm referring to the physical piece of hardware and the functions of that hardware. In the Windows world, we need to distinguish between the functionality of the hardware and of the software (both the driver software and the controlling software). In the Windows world, the physical device that has paper in it is the *print device,* not the printer. The *printer* is the software application on the local machine controlling the print device. The printer driver is the software shim between the operating system and the locally installed software (the printer).

You will find in most organizations that a print device is not attached to every computer. Print devices are shared between users. This is cost effective on many levels, but it tends to cause issues. I don't know very many users who do not have a need to print something once in a while, and so they send their documents or web pages to be printed to the print device. The print device might be connected to someone's machine and shared for others to use, or it might be a stand-alone. You might have a server on your network to which one or more print devices are attached and everyone sends their documents to a central location. Each user machine has a printer installed and the appropriate drivers to allow Windows 7 to send the document to the print device through the printer with the appropriate instructions.

Do you think the print device can physically print a document at the same speed the printer can send to the data to it? No, of course not. This is where a software component called the spool (spooler or print spool) comes in. You need a software component that can buffer the print job until the print device can complete it. In fact, there might be more than one user sending documents to be printed to the same print device at the same time—and yes, the spool handles this as well.

Installing Printers

You can install printers to a machine in two distinct ways; one where the print device is physically connected to the machine and one where it is not (it's connected over the network). There have to be software drivers in either case, and these can be located on a CD/DVD, on a network share, or even in the Windows distribution files. Printers in Windows 7 will be located in the Devices And Printers window and will allow the Device Stage configuration to accommodate a full range of functionality from this one location. To add a printer to a machine locally, you'll usually run the setup program on the CD/DVD (following the manufacturer's instructions). The manufacturer's setup program in a wizard format asks the appropriate questions. You can set up the printer through Windows 7 as well by using the Add Printer functionality of Devices And Printers. To add a printer using the Windows 7 functionality, choose Start ➤ Devices And Printers and then choose Add Printer. USB printers will be automatically detected and have their drivers installed (or at least searched for automatically).

Choosing Add Printer launches the Add Printer Wizard and brings up the screen where you make the choice of installing the printer and print device locally or installing the printer locally to access a print device remotely.

From the opening screen, you can follow the next example to install the printer for a physically connected print device to a machine. I'm going on the premise that the setup program on the CD/DVD (if one existed) was not run and you're installing the printer from the wizard associated with Windows.

Perform the following steps to install a printer on a local machine's parallel port (lpt1):

1. Choose Start ➤ Devices And Printers.

2. Choose Add Printers.

3. Select the Add A Local Printer option.

4. In the Add Printer window, choose the Use An Existing Port radio button and use the drop-down window to select LPT1: (Printer Port); then click Next.

5. Select the manufacturer of your print device and the printer model you want to install in the Install A Printer Driver window.

6. If there was a driver previously installed, you will be given the option to use the existing driver or replace it.

7. After choosing the appropriate device driver or using the existing driver and clicking Next, you choose the name of the printer. An intuitive name is always a good choice here. Enter the name and click Next.

Hardware and Networking

PART IV

8. You can make the print device available on the network by sharing it. The next page of the Add Printer Wizard gives you the opportunity to share it. For most of the options within the wizard, you can change the values or function from the properties pages (if, for example, you change your mind later). After making your choice, click Next.

9. On the final page of the Add Printer Wizard, select the Set As The Default Printer check box (to make this the default printer for any application on the machine) and click Print A Test Page. After the test page prints, click Finish and the wizard completes. The locally connected print device has its printer installed on the local machine.

NOTE   If you don't find your model in list, it wasn't included in the distribution files; you can select the Windows Update button to get more choices from Microsoft. If you still don't have your model available and you have the original disk, you can choose Have Disk and browse to the driver files. (OK, if you had the disk, wouldn't you have just run the setup? Ah, you didn't have the disk—you went onto the Internet and downloaded the drivers.) Use the Have Disk option to browse to the folder with the .inf file for the printer drivers.

NOTE   Do not remove this printer; we'll use it in a later example.

After you complete the Add Printer Wizard (or let the hardware vendor's setup program install your printer), you can open the Devices And Printers window and see the printer(s) available. The context menu gives you access to the properties pages, as well as some of the standard printing functions we've had in Windows past. As hardware vendors start implementing functionality for Windows 7, you'll have a full array of access to software components from the Devices And Printers window, at least for the vendors who are going to participate in the Device Stage specification.

What about installing a printer on a machine that needs to access a print device connected to another machine? That's fine—that is the functionality we want. You launch the Add Printer Wizard and go through the process of installing the printer, but point to a share or stand-alone network printer. Knowing that not all machines on any company's network are going to have print devices physically attached, there is functionality to allow sharing of networked devices and printers (software) to be installed on client machines.

Perform the following steps to install printer client software (and drivers) for a network printer:

1. Choose Start ➤ Devices And Printers.

2. Click Add Printers.

3. Click Add A Network, Wireless Or Bluetooth Printer.

4. The Add Printers Wizard searches the locally available network for print devices that are available.

5. Select the networked print device from the Select A Printer section. If the device is not listed, you can choose The Printer That I Want Is Not Listed and enter the parameters for the networked print device.

6. The print device is detected, the driver is discovered and installed, and you are able to use the printer. Open Devices And Printers and you'll see this print device is available.

Once the printer is installed for a print device physically connected on the local machine (or if it's a network-connected printer), you can view the configuration parameters and modify them if necessary from the properties dialog box. Access the properties dialog box from Devices And Printers. Right-click the printer, as shown in Figure 9.22, and select Properties for the hardware properties and Printer Properties for the software components.

Printer properties follow a standard Microsoft has in place, but the content is up to the manufacturer. Some vendors supply more information than others. Most printers provide a basic set of tabs, as follows:

General Tab   The printer name, location, and comment are displayed here. The model is typically shown, as well as the features of the specific print device and available paper. The Printer Preferences page is available by clicking the Preferences button, and you can print a test page by clicking the Print Test Page button.

Sharing Tab   The Sharing tab allows you to share a printer if it wasn't shared during its installation, or to stop sharing it if it were previously shared. You can also add drivers for other flavors of operating systems so the printer installed locally and shared can supply drivers for other machines attempting to connect and use the locally connected printer.

Hardware and Networking

PART IV

Ports Tab You can view available ports and print devices connected to them on the Ports tab. You can add a port, delete a port, and configure ports on this tab as well. You can also configure bidirectional support for print devices supporting this functionality (sending codes back from the print device to the printer for control) on the Ports tab. Printer pooling is also available here; printer pooling is the ability of the IT staff to configure multiple print devices (using identical drivers) to appear as one printer to connected users. The print jobs are printed on one of the devices in the pool (the first available prints the job). If a print device fails, the others keep working, which makes life better for the users.

Security Tab Group or user access permissions are controlled on the Security tab. You can specify advanced permissions here as well.

Advanced Tab The Advanced tab provides various configuration parameters to control the printer and print device functions. The time period a printer is available is a configuration parameter on the Advanced tab. You can install drivers for the print device as well as add a new driver (by launching an Add Printer Driver Wizard). Spool options include whether or not to spool, and whether to start printing immediately upon job submission or start printing after the last page is spooled.

Figure 9.22: Printer context menu from Devices And Printers

The following buttons are available on the Advanced tab:

Printing Defaults Button   Launches the Printer Properties window for the vendor as it applies to the documents.

Print Processor Button   Lets you choose whether to use the vendor-supplied print processor or the built-in Windows print processor and to choose the default data type to be sent to the print device.

Separator Page Button   Allows a specific page to be inserted between print jobs, making the separation of different documents easier.

Device Settings   Specific parameters for each print device are set up on the Device Settings tab. Items like form to tray assignment, font substitution, or other installable options for the print device are configurable here.

After the configuration is complete and the printer and print device are working in harmony, life is good. You can see the status of the document currently being printed as well as documents waiting to be printed (the print queue). The queue was previously viewed by selecting the Queue option from the context menu for the printer; Windows 7 now calls it See What's Printing, as shown in Figure 9.23.

Figure 9.23: See What's Printing

Selecting See What's Printing opens the window that shows you what's going on with your printer (as far as document/job control).

To take a better look at the functionality of Device Stage, you can select the context menu from Devices And Printers. To observe a

Hardware and Networking

PART IV

graphical view of Device Stage, double-click the printer in Devices And Printers and get a consolidated view and the popular (as decided by the vendor) menu choices.

We've installed printers in previous examples for both a locally connected and a network connected printer. Let's take a look at sending a print job to the locally connected printer from a previous example and view the document properties.

First, you might not actually have the print device available and the printer won't be able to send the job anywhere. We'll go to the Printer window and pause printing so the job will simply stay in the queue and not attempt to be sent to the print device. We'll use the Device Stage interface to perform our tasks.

Managing Printers

After a printer is installed, you may need to manage the printer while it is online or offline. Some of the tasks that you can perform are pausing a printer, testing a printer, viewing properties, and deleting a document.

Pausing a Printer

There may be times when you have to stop a printer from printing. Complete the Following steps to pause printing for a locally connected printer:

1. Choose Start ➢ Devices And Printers.

2. Double-click the printer previously installed as the locally connected printer.

3. To pause printing, open the Printer window; then double-click the See What's Printing area in the body of the window or single-click the Printer item in the top of the window.

4. Choose Printer ➢ Pause Printing.

5. View the status bar of the printer to verify the printer is paused; there will also be a check mark next to Pause Printing in the menu.

To restart the printer, just uncheck the pause printer menu item.

Sending a Test Document

If you think a printer is having problems, you may want to print out a test document. By printing a test document, you can verify that the drivers and devices are performing properly. Complete the following steps to send a document to a locally connected printer:

1. In the Printer window, select Printer ➤ Properties.

2. On the General tab of the Properties dialog box, click the Print Test Page button.

3. An information box appears stating a test page was sent to the printer; click the Close button.

4. Click OK in the printer's Properties window.

5. The Printer window displays the print job in the queue.

Viewing Document Properties from a Job in the Print Queue

You may need to view the properties of a document that is in the print queue. Follow these steps to view a document's properties from the print queue:

1. In the Printer window, click the specific document you want to view.

2. Choose Document ➤ Properties to view the document properties; you can also right-click the print job and select Properties from the context menu. The General tab shows you the document properties; the other tabs are vendor supplied to control additional printer functionality for the document.

3. Click OK or Cancel to close the Properties window. OK saves any changes made and closes the window; Cancel closes the window without saving any changes. If you have made any configuration changes, the Apply button becomes available; selecting Apply saves any changes that you made but it does not close the window.

Deleting a Document from the Queue

There might be times when managing a printer that you will need to delete a document from the print queue. Perform the following steps to delete a document from the printer:

1. In the Printer window, click the specific job you want to delete from the queue.

2. Choose Document ➤ Cancel from the Printer window menu structure to delete the document. You can also right-click the

document and select Cancel to delete the print job. Either method prompts a confirmation message box that asks Are You Sure You Want To Cancel The Document? Click Yes. The document will no longer appear in the queue in the Printer window.

3. Choose Printer ➤ Close to close the Printer window.

Removing a Printer

There might also be times when you want to delete a printer, either locally connected or a network printer, from your Windows 7 machine. This might be due to a replacement of an older print device, or perhaps you're moving a user to a new print device and the old one is no longer needed.

Follow these steps to remove a printer (to remove the software configuration in the operating system) from Windows 7:

1. Choose Start ➤ Devices And Printers.

2. Right-click the printer you want to remove and select Remove Device from the context menu; alternatively, choose Remove Device from the Devices And Printers menu to unpair the printer from the machine.

3. Click Yes when you see the prompt Are You Sure You Want To Remove This Device? You are presented with a status box during the removal process, and then the device is no longer available in Devices And Printers.

10

Configuring Network Connectivity

IN THIS CHAPTER, YOU WILL LEARN TO:

Hardware and Networking

PART IV

I n today's world of technology, it is very rare that a computer would remain a stand-alone system (not connected to any network). Even most home users have a small network setup using their Internet routers and all of their home computers. To allow this, you must understand how to set up network and networking devices.

To successfully establish network connectivity, you must have a properly installed and configured network interface card (NIC) and network protocol. The first step is to physically install and configure the network adapter that you will use and verify that Windows 7 recognizes the hardware.

Today, a big part of most networks is wireless connectivity, and that may present a whole new and interesting set of challenges. Not only does wireless connectivity present challenges in physical connectivity, but it also requires a thorough understanding of the physical connectivity to ensure a secure network.

The second step is to install, configure, and test a network protocol. In most home networks, network protocol connectivity seems automatic, but as an administrator, you need to understand the protocols like TCP/IPv4 as well as TCP/IPv6.

From here, you need to connect to other resources you have on your network, including shared resources on other machines, whether it's servers or other users' machines. You might also need to connect to printers, cameras, or other data-supplying devices needed for you or your users' productivity or pleasure. Setting up peer-to-peer networking is a big part of connecting to other devices as most users will want to be able to browse to the resources.

Connect Network Devices

NICs are hardware components used to connect computers or other devices to the network. NICs are responsible for providing the physical connection that recognizes the physical address of the device where they are installed.

Physical Addresses vs. Logical Addresses

The Open System Interconnect (OSI) model defines the encapsulation technique that builds the basic data structure for data transport across an internetwork. The OSI model provides interoperability between hardware vendors, network protocols, and applications. The physical address is the OSI address, or for Ethernet technologies, the Media Access Control address (MAC address). This is not the IP address, which is the OSI Layer 3 or Network Layer address, also generically defined as the Logical Address. I'll discuss logical addressing later in this chapter in the section "Basics of IP Addressing and Configuration."

The most common place you see network adapters installed are computers, but you also see NICs installed in network printers and specialized devices like intrusion detection systems (IDSs) and firewalls. You generically refer to the interface between your network devices and the software components of the machines as network adapters. Network adapters do not need to be separate cards; they can be built in, as is the case for most PCs today or other network-ready devices such as network cameras or network media players. These adapters (and all other hardware devices) need a driver to communicate with the Windows 7 operating system.

Installing a Network Adapter

Before you physically install a NIC or network adapter, it's important to read the vendor's instructions that come with the hardware. Most network adapters you get today should be self-configuring using Plug and Play capabilities. After you install a network adapter that supports Plug and Play, it should work following the installation procedure (which should be automated if the vendor says it is). You might have to restart, but operating systems are getting much better with this, and you might just get lucky and be all right immediately.

If you happen to have a network adapter that is not Plug and Play, the operating system should detect the new piece of hardware and start

Hardware and Networking

PART IV

a wizard that leads you through the process of loading the adapter's driver and sets initial configuration parameters. You can see your network connection and manage the network connection properties through the Network And Sharing Center. You'll explore this applet in the "Connect Wireless Devices" section later in this chapter.

Configuring a Network Adapter

After you have installed the network adapter, you configure it through its Properties dialog box. There are several ways to access the properties: by using the Network And Sharing Center, through the Computer Management MMC, or via Device Manager. We'll look at the Network And Sharing Center later in the section, "Viewing the Network And Sharing Center." Let's use the Device Manager applet for the network adapter configuration here. To access the Properties dialog box, choose Start and type **Device Manager** in the Start menu's search box to launch Device Manager. Alternatively, you can right-click Computer on the Start menu and choose Manage from the context menu to access Computer Management, which lets you access Device Manager, as shown in Figure 10.1.

Figure 10.1: Accessing Device Manager from the Computer Management MMC

Figure 10.1 shows the Network Adapters item expanded. Having Computer Management open is a great way to open Device Manager; this MMC has numerous other installed plug-ins available that might be helpful as you work with your machines.

Network Adapter Properties

Accessing the network adapter properties allows you to view and change configuration parameters of the adapter. You do this by right-clicking the adapter in Device Manager and selecting Properties from the context menu. Figure 10.2 shows the Properties dialog box and the tabs available for a network adapter. The available tabs depend on the hardware manufacturer:

Figure 10.2: Network adapter Properties dialog box

The General Tab   The General tab of the network adapter Properties dialog box (the tab open in Figure 10.2) shows the name of the adapter, the device type, the manufacturer, and the location. The Device Status box reports whether or not the device is working properly. If a device is not working, the Device Status box gives you an error code and a brief description of what Windows 7 identifies as the issue. You can perform an Internet search for the error code(s) if the text is not sufficient.

Hardware and Networking

PART IV

The Advanced Tab   The contents of the Advanced tab of a network adapter's Properties dialog box vary depending on the network adapter and driver that you are using. Figure 10.3 shows an example of the Advanced tab for a Fast Ethernet adapter. To configure options in this dialog box, choose the property you want to modify in the Property list box and specify the desired value for the property in the Value box on the right. I have selected the Connection Type property and opened the Value drop-down list to show you the options for this network adapter.

Figure 10.3: The Advanced tab of a network adapter's Properties dialog box

The Driver Tab   The Driver tab of the network adapter's Properties dialog box provides the following information about your driver:

- The driver provider
- The date the driver was released
- The driver version (useful in determining whether you have the latest driver installed)
- The digital signer (the company that provides the digital signature for driver signing)

The Driver tab for a typical adapter is shown in Figure 10.4. The information on this tab varies from driver to driver and even from vendor to vendor.

Figure 10.4: The Driver tab of a network adapter's Properties dialog box

Clicking the Driver Details button on the Driver tab opens the Driver File Details dialog box, which provides the following details about the driver:

- The location of the driver file (useful for troubleshooting)
- The original provider of the driver
- The file version (useful for troubleshooting)
- Copyright information about the driver
- The digital signer for the driver

The Update Driver button starts a wizard to step you through upgrading the driver for an existing device.

The Roll Back Driver button allows you to roll back to the previously installed driver if you update your network driver and encounter problems. In Figure 10.4, the Roll Back Driver button is unavailable because we have not updated the driver or a previous driver is not available.

Hardware and Networking

PART IV

The Disable button is used to disable the device. After you disable the device, the Disable button changes into an Enable button, which you can use to enable the device.

The Uninstall button removes the driver from your computer's configuration. You would uninstall the driver if you were going to remove the device from your system or if you wanted to completely remove the driver configuration from your system so that you could reinstall it from scratch either automatically or manually.

The Details Tab The Details tab of the network adapter's Properties dialog box lists the resource settings for your network adapter. Information found on the Details tab varies by hardware device. Figure 10.5 shows the Details tab for a typical adapter with the Property drop-down list open to show the options.

Figure 10.5: The Details tab of a network adapter's Properties dialog box

The Resources Tab The Resources tab of a network adapter's Properties dialog box lists the resource settings for your network adapter. Resources include interrupt request (IRQ), memory, and input/output (I/O) resources. This information can be important for troubleshooting, especially if other devices are trying to use the same resource settings. This is not normally the case as Windows 7 and the Plug and Play specification should set up nonconflicting parameters. If there are issues, the Conflicting Device list box at the bottom of the Resources tab shows the conflicts.

Navigating to the Advanced Tab and Assigning a Connection Type

There might be times when you, as a network administrator, need to manually assign a connection type for one of your servers' NICs. For example, suppose the hardware switch to which you are connecting does not seem to negotiate with the NIC in your server and you want to set up the best connection. When you view the NIC parameters, it seems to be set up for half duplex and you know the switch is set to full duplex.

Perform the following steps to navigate to the Advanced tab and assign the connection type to 100 Mbps and Full Duplex for the most efficient connection for your server and switch connection:

1. Click Start and type **Device Manager** in the Start menu's search box.

2. Double-click Network Adapters in Device Manager to expand the Network Adapters item.

3. Right-click your NIC in the Network Adapters list and select Properties from the context menu.

4. Click the Advanced tab of your NIC's Properties dialog box.

5. Choose Connection Type in the Property list box.

6. Click the drop-down list box and select the choice that allows you to have Full Duplex at 100 Mbps. This item will probably be set at Auto Sense by default, which is not working in this scenario.

7. Click OK to save your changes and close your NIC's Properties dialog box.

8. Close Device Manager.

Troubleshooting a Network Adapter

If your network adapter is not working, the problem might be with the hardware, the driver software, or the network protocols. I discuss the Layer 3 (network protocol) issues later in this chapter in the section, "Basics of IP Addressing and Configuration." Table 10.1 gives some common causes for network adapter problems related to Layer 1 and Layer 2.

Hardware and Networking

PART IV

Table 10.1: Layer 1 and Layer 2 Network Adapter Troubleshooting

Symptom	Solution
Network Adapter Not on the HCL	If the device is not on the Hardware Compatibility List (HCL), use Internet resources to see if others have discovered a solution or contact the hardware vendor for advice.
Outdated Driver	Make sure that you have the most current driver for your adapter. You can check for an updated driver by selecting the Driver tab of the adapter's Properties dialog box and clicking the Update Driver button. Windows 7 searches for a better driver or checks for the latest driver on the hardware vendor's website.
Network Adapter Not Recognized by Windows 7	Check Device Manager to see if Windows 7 recognizes the adapter.
	If you don't see your adapter, you can try to manually install it.
Improperly Configured Network Card	Verify that the settings for the network card are correct for the parameters known within your network and the hardware device the machine is connected to.
Cabling Problem	Make sure that all network cables are functioning and are the correct type.
	Make sure the connector is properly seated, the cable is straight or crossed (depending on where it's plugged into), and the cable is not broken.
	You can do this by looking at the little green light (LGL) for the link and activity on the NIC. This does not guarantee a good connection even if the LGLs are illuminated. A single conductor failure in a cable can still have a link light on but that doesn't mean data is passing.
Bad Network Connection Device	Verify that all network connectivity hardware is properly working. For example, on a Fast Ethernet network, make sure the switch and port being used are functioning properly.

Connecting to a Network Projector

Windows 7 includes network projector support. We use a projector to display presentations, and it's normally connected with a video cable. Today many projectors come with a network interface, wireless or wired, to provide a convenient way to get video output to the projector.

If the projector is configured properly for the network, you can use Windows 7 to provide the video to it as a networked display. The projector functionality is designed to use the Remote Desktop Protocol (RDP) to send the video stream of a machine to a remote device via the network.

Select Start and then type **Network Projector** into the Start menu's search box (you can also choose Start ➤ All Programs ➤ Accessories ➤ Connect To A Network Projector) to initiate the connection process. The Connect To A Network Projector Wizard launches, as shown in Figure 10.6.

Figure 10.6: The Connect To A Network Projector Wizard

Click Search For A Projector to locate a projector connected to your wired or wireless network. If no projectors are found, you can go back and enter the name or IP address of a projector. If you know the name or IP address, you can simply choose Enter The Projector Address during the initial wizard screens. You might also need a password for the projector if a password has been configured, as shown in Figure 10.7.

Figure 10.7: You might have to enter a projector password.

Connecting to a Network Printer

Adding a network printer to Windows 7 is even easier than it was in Vista (which was much easier than previous versions). There is new functionality in Windows 7 for devices and printers known as Device Stage (discussed in Chapter 9, "Configuring Hardware and Printing"). To add a network printer, select Start ≻ Devices And Printers. When the Devices And Printers item launches, choose the Add A Printer menu item.

Next, select Add A Network, Wireless Or Bluetooth Printer. Windows 7 searches for available printers and allows you to install them. If your printer isn't found, you can select The Printer That I Want Isn't Listed and browse for a printer, or you can select a printer by name or IP address.

Wired connections have been available since the beginning of networking. Today, many are transitioning to a wireless network infrastructure, and Windows 7 can ease that transition to the wireless world.

Connect Wireless Devices

Wireless technology has matured to the point of becoming cost-effective and secure. The use of wireless network adapters is increasingly popular, scaling well out of the home and into the workplace. Windows 7 supports wireless autoconfiguration, which makes wireless network connections easy to use. Windows 7 will automatically discover the wireless networks available and connect your machine to the preferred network. Although this connection is convenient, you must still take certain considerations, such as security, into account.

Configuring Wireless Network Settings

If you have a wireless network adapter that is compatible with Windows 7, it will be automatically recognized by the operating system. This can be a built-in adapter (used in most modern laptops), a wireless card installed in the machine, or even a wireless USB adapter. After it is installed, it is recognized and shown in Device Manager as well as the Network And Sharing Center in the View Your Active Networks section. You used Device Manager in the previous section for the network adapter configuration, so let's use the Network And Sharing Center for the wireless network configuration. Figure 10.8 shows the Network And Sharing Center with two active networks: the wireless network connection and the wired local area connection.

Figure 10.8: Network And Sharing Center

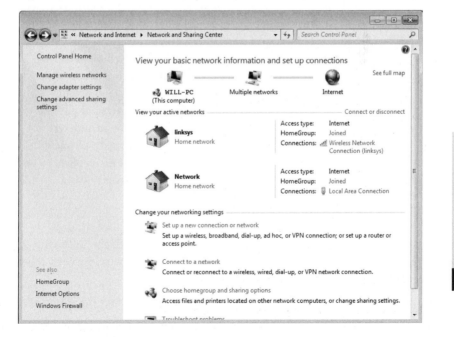

Hardware and Networking

PART IV

Viewing the Network And Sharing Center

Perform any of the following step to access the Network and Sharing Center:

- Choose Start and type **Network and Sharing Center** into the Start menu's search box.

- Choose Start ➤ Control Panel ➤ Network And Internet ➤ Network And Sharing Center.

- Choose Start, and then right-click Network and select Properties from the context menu.

NOTE The caveat to this choice is that the Network option on the Start menu is not available by default in Windows 7 (the same as in previous Windows versions) and must be added as a customized option to your Start menu using its Properties dialog box.

Viewing the Wireless Network Connection Status

From the Network And Sharing Center you have easy access to the Wireless Network Connection Status window. This window gives you an initial look at the status by providing the Layer 3 connectivity status (IPv4 and IPv6), media state, Service Set Identifier (SSID) being used, how long the connection has been active (Duration), the negotiated speed of the connection, and the signal quality. The Wireless Network Connection Status window is shown in Figure 10.9.

The Details button in the Wireless Network Connection Status window provides detailed information, including the physical address (Layer 2), logical address (Layer 3), dynamic addressing parameters (DHCP), name resolution items, and more. After you verify physical layer parameters, this area of properties and status is a great place to verify and troubleshoot logical (driver and software) issues.

Viewing Wireless Network Connection Details

If you have a wireless adapter in your machine, perform the following steps to view the network connection details for your wireless network connection:

1. Choose Start and type **Network and Sharing Center** into the Start menu's search box; press Enter.

2. Select the Wireless Network Connection option in the View Your Active Networks section.

3. Click the Details button.

4. Review the network connection details for this connection.

Figure 10.9: The Wireless Network Connection Status window

The Wireless Network Connection Status window has an Activity section showing real-time traffic (in bytes) being sent from and received by the wireless network. In this window, you also have access to the wireless network connection properties, which includes access to the wireless adapter configuration pages. You access the Properties dialog box by clicking the Properties button in the Activity section. The Wireless Network Connection Properties window is shown in Figure 10.10.

The Wireless Network Connection Properties window has a Networking tab that shows which network adapter is being used for this connection (which you can change if you have more than one available). There is also a tab to allow you to configure Internet Connection Sharing (ICS), which allows other users on your network to access resources through this machine's connection. The This Connection Uses

The Following Items section displays the various client, service, and protocols that are currently available for this connection.

Figure 10.10: Wireless Network Connection Properties window

You can install or uninstall network clients, network services, and network protocols by choosing the appropriate button. You can also view the client, service, or protocol properties if they are available by clicking the Properties button for the selected item (if the Properties button is gray, a properties window is not available for the item). From the Wireless Network Connection Properties window, you have access to the network adapters' hardware configuration properties pages. These would be the same pages you have access to from Device Manager.

Accessing the Wireless Network Adapter Properties Page from the Network And Sharing Center

Perform the following steps to access the network adapter properties from the Wireless Network Connection Properties window:

1. Choose Start and type **Network and Sharing Center** into the Start menu's search box; press Enter.

2. Select Wireless Network Connection in the View Your Active Networks section.

3. Click the Properties button in the Activity section.

4. Click the Configure button.

5. View the various tabs regarding the network adapter properties.

6. Choose Cancel to return to the Wireless Network Connection Status window.

Configuring Wireless Network Security

Wireless network security is a very large part of setting up our wireless networks. The focal point for this is the wireless access point or wireless router to which we connect.

Wireless Connection: Infrastructure or Ad Hoc?

You might not always be connecting to an access point or router; these connections are considered infrastructure mode connections. Infrastructure mode connections are similar to our wired connection of a PC to a switch. You might connect in an ad hoc fashion that could be a computer-to-computer connection to share information with other wireless network devices without another wireless device acting as an intermediary. Ad hoc connections exist in the wired environment, as well anywhere you would connect two PCs' NICs together using an Ethernet crossover cable. Securing data transfer in an ad hoc setup is as important as in infrastructure mode where the data is still traversing between devices using radio frequency (RF). Network sniffers today running the wireless adapter promiscuously (in monitor mode) have no problem viewing the RF data stream. If the data stream is not encrypted, the sniffers will have access to it.

Whether you are using a small wireless network or large wireless infrastructure, you should have a plan for ensuring secure communications and configuring wireless network security. There are several basic parameters you can configure on your network access devices that you should increase the security of your wireless network:

Disable SSID Broadcast   The SSID is the name of the wireless network. When SSID broadcast is disabled, the wireless network cannot be detected automatically until a user manually configures their wireless network card to connect to that SSID.

Hardware and Networking

PART IV

Create a MAC Address Filter   You can create a Media Access
Control (MAC) address filter list so only specifically allowed wireless devices are allowed to connect to the wireless network, or require
users attempting to connect to supply connection credentials.

Enable Encryption   You can enable encryption such as Wi-Fi
Protected Access (WPA) or WPA2.

For large implementations, several vendors supply wireless access
points under the control of a wireless director. This offers software-
based controllers that allow access points on the network, provides user
access control, and enforces encryption policies. For smaller implementations, this control functionality is done manually when the wireless
routers or access points are set up. The security policies are configured
on the wireless access device and the wireless client. The Windows 7 client components in our case must be set up to match the security settings
of the wireless network access devices.

During the setup of the most wireless access devices that hardware
vendors provide, the administrator will configure the security parameters. Configuring can be done during the setup program and/or when
accessing the wireless access device configuration pages through a web
browser. Most of our current devices have a built-in web server to allow
the HTTP connection from a web browser. Windows 7 also has the
ability to configure the wireless access device if the hardware vendor
makes it available. If there is no specific component written, you can
launch the web browser–based configuration from a convenient location: the Network And Sharing Center.

Configuring a Network And Sharing Center Wireless Access Device

Perform the following steps to see how to initiate a Windows 7 wireless
access point configuration:

1. Choose Start and type **Network and Sharing Center** in the Start
   menu search box; press Enter.

2. Choose the Set Up A New Connection Or Network option.

3. Choose Set Up A New Network to configure a new router or
   access point and then click Next.

4. Select the wireless access device you want to configure from the Set Up A Network window and click Next.

5. Depending on your device, you might be asked to enter a PIN or other identifying parameter to access the device. Enter the PIN and click Next.

6. On the next screen you will be able to configure the security settings dictated by the wireless security policy to be implemented. The settings defined here need to be configured for each client machine connecting to the wireless network. After making the setting choices, click Next.

7. The configuration of the wireless network device completes and you are shown a confirmation window. Click Finish to close the window.

Whether you had Windows 7 configure the wireless network connection or you performed the setup through the manufacturer's process, you still need to configure your Windows 7 client access. If you have performed the simplest configuration, and there are no security parameters configured—bad idea, by the way—Windows 7 will connect automatically with a quick window showing the wireless network it's connecting to and provide access without much user intervention. Even canceling through the screens will produce a successful (nonsecure) connection. This simple configuration process makes connecting a home or small network easy and straightforward for nontechnical users, but it is not a good solution.

If you have configured wireless network security (a good idea), then you need to configure the Windows 7 client with the correct settings. Once again, the configuration screens are available from a convenient location known as the Network And Sharing Center.

Configuring the Network And Sharing Center Wireless Network Client

Perform the following steps to access the Windows 7 client wireless network properties:

1. Choose Start and type **Network and Sharing Center** in the Start menu search box; then press Enter.

2. Choose Wireless Network Connection item in the View Your Active Networks section of the Network And Sharing Center.

Hardware and Networking

PART IV

3. Click the Wireless Properties button in the Connection area of the Wireless Network Connection Status window. The Wireless Network Properties dialog box opens, displaying the current setup for the wireless network.

Figure 10.11 shows the Connection tab of the Wireless Network Properties dialog box. Here, you have the ability to set or change the Windows 7 client configuration.

Figure 10.11: The Connection tab of the Wireless Network Properties dialog box

The Connection tab displays the following information:

Name   The name assigned to the wireless network.

SSID   The SSID of the wireless connection. This specifies a friendly name for the wireless network. This is normally an ASCII string and is usually broadcast by default, allowing a machine or users to select a wireless network with which to connect. Some wireless access devices will allow more than one SSID to be available (or broadcast) at the same time, thus creating more than one wireless network within the same device.

Network Type   Displays the mode in which the wireless network is operating. If the wireless network is in infrastructure mode, this parameter will be Access Point. If the wireless network is ad hoc, this field will display Computer-To-Computer.

Network Availability   Displays to whom the wireless network is available—All Users or Me Only, for example.

You can configure the following information:

Connect Automatically When This Network Is In Range
This option, when checked, allows automatic connection for this wireless network. If this option is deselected, the user has to select this wireless network for connection.

Connect To A More Preferred Network If Available
Windows 7 will attempt to connect to a preferred network (if the Connect Automatically option is selected). If there is more than one preferred network, Windows 7 might switch back and forth if they are both available at the same time. Clearing this option allows the currently connected network to stay connected until it is no longer available, possibly preventing data dropping or even dropped connections.

Connect Even If The Network Is Not Broadcasting Its Name (SSID)   If the wireless network you are attempting to connect to is not broadcasting its SSID, you must select this option to allow Windows 7 to automatically connect.

There is one more option on the Connection tab of the Wireless Network Properties tab: Copy This Network Profile To A USB Flash Drive. Selecting this link launches the Copy Network Settings Wizard, as shown in Figure 10.12.

After you insert a USB flash drive, Windows 7 saves the currently configured wireless network configuration in the form of a setupSNK .exe program and a folder named SMRTNTKY with the configuration parameters. Exercise caution to protect this information as all the configuration parameters (including security keys) are stored in clear text.

After the files and folder are created and saved on the flash drive, you are presented with a confirmation screen with simple instructions and a link for the detailed information about wireless network configuration. The confirmation page is shown in Figure 10.13.

Hardware and Networking

PART IV

Figure 10.12: Copy Network Settings Wizard for the wireless connection

Figure 10.13: Wireless connection copy confirmation window

The second tab of the Wireless Network Properties dialog box is the Security tab. This tab allows you to configure the security parameters as defined in your security policy and configured on your wireless network access devices. Figure 10.14 shows the Security tab with the Security Type and Encryption Type drop-down lists open. You can also see the Network Security Key entry as clear text as the Show Characters option is enabled.

Figure 10.14: Wireless Network Properties, Security tab

Join and Share HomeGroups in Windows 7

Have you ever wanted to share your music or pictures and found it difficult? HomeGroup is a new functionality of Windows 7 that simplifies the sharing of music, pictures, and documents in your small office or home network between Windows 7 PCs. HomeGroup allows you to share USB connected printers, too.

If you have a printer installed on a Windows 7 computer and it's shared by HomeGroup, it is automatically installed onto the other HomeGroup-enabled Windows 7 PCs. This even extends to domain-joined computers; they can be part of a HomeGroup as well.

The first step in the process of using HomeGroup for sharing is to create a new HomeGroup or join an existing one. If the Windows 7 Network Discovery feature is not enabled, you will be asked to create a HomeGroup. In the Network And Sharing Center select Choose Homegroup And Sharing Options and then click the Create A Homegroup button (both items are shown in Figure 10.15).

Figure 10.15: Creating a HomeGroup

With Windows 7 Network Discovery turned on (the default), HomeGroup is created automatically. You still need to join the HomeGroup to make use of the other shared resources and to share yours. In the Network And Sharing Center, you can join an existing HomeGroup by clicking the Join Now button, as shown in Figure 10.16.

Part of joining a HomeGroup setup is to define the resources that you want to make available to the other members of HomeGroup. The next screen in the setup, as shown in Figure 10.17, lets you choose which resources you want to share.

Figure 10.16: Joining an existing HomeGroup

Choose homegroup and sharing options
Access files and printers located on other network computers, or change sharing settings.

◀ ▶ ▾ 📶 ▸ Control Panel ▸ Network and Internet ▸ HomeGroup   ▾ 🔍 | Search Control Panel   🔎

Share with other home computers running Windows 7

tylorw on WINDOWS7-PC-1 has created a homegroup on the network.

With a homegroup, you can share files and printers with other computers running Windows 7. You can also stream media to devices. The homegroup is protected with a password, and you'll always be able to choose what you share with the group.

Tell me more about homegroups

Change advanced sharing settings...

Start the HomeGroup troubleshooter

[Join now]   [Cancel]

Figure 10.17: HomeGroup sharing selections

📶 Join a Homegroup

Share with other home computers running Windows 7

Windows detected a homegroup on your network. With a homegroup, you can share files and printers with other computers running Windows 7. You can also stream media to devices.

Tell me more about homegroups

Select what you want to share:

☑ Pictures   ☐ Documents

☑ Music   ☑ Printers

☑ Videos

[Next]   [Cancel]

Hardware and Networking

PART IV

The next step is to enter the HomeGroup password. Windows 7, by default, will recognize a HomeGroup on the network. However, the other Windows 7 machines will not have access to the resources. Allowing any Windows 7 machine connecting to the network to automatically have shared resource access would be a huge security hole. To protect the Windows 7 user resources, a password must be entered to join HomeGroup. Figure 10.18 shows the screen where you enter the password.

Figure 10.18: HomeGroup password screen

The password for the HomeGroup can be found or changed on the machine that established the HomeGroup. After other machines have joined, each machine has the ability to view or change the password, but they must join the HomeGroup first. The initial machine in the HomeGroup will create a random secure password.

To view and/or print the HomeGroup password, select Choose HomeGroup And Sharing Options in the Network And Sharing Center and then choose View Or Print The HomeGroup Password, as shown in Figure 10.19. Again, this can be done from any Windows 7 machine that is already a member of the HomeGroup, but not from one that wants to join.

Figure 10.20 shows the View And Print Your HomeGroup Password screen. I changed the password to **password** (not recommended for your network) for this illustration.

Figure 10.19: Changing the HomeGroup settings

Figure 10.20: View And Print Your HomeGroup Password screen

Remember that Windows 7 initially creates a random secure password for the HomeGroup, and you need to visit the View And Print Your HomeGroup Password screen to find out what it is. You will probably want to change it. To change the password, choose the Change The Password option on the Change HomeGroup Settings screen and then select Change The Password on the Change Your HomeGroup Password screen, as shown in Figure 10.21. When you change the HomeGroup password, you need to go to each of the other Windows 7 machines that are members of the HomeGroup and change the password if you still want the others to share resources.

Figure 10.21: Changing the HomeGroup password

After the HomeGroup is set up, you can see the other members' resources by choosing the HomeGroup option in Windows Explorer. You can also add the HomeGroup option to your Start menu, as shown in Figure 10.22.

Choosing the HomeGroup option from the Start menu (or choosing Computer and selecting HomeGroup in the Explorer window) allows you to access the other members of your HomeGroup. Figure 10.23 shows the HomeGroup item expanded and the resources of another Windows 7 machine that has joined the HomeGroup.

Figure 10.22: HomeGroup in the Start menu

Figure 10.23: Viewing HomeGroup resources from Explorer

HomeGroups are a great option for users in the Windows 7 environment for sharing resources. But what if you still have non–Windows 7 machines? The legacy function of simply sharing resources and setting permissions still works for Windows 7 and allows older operating systems to have access to resources shared on Windows 7 machines. It also allows users running Windows 7 to have access to the shared resources on Vista and XP.

To connect to other network devices, having a network protocol configured correctly is a key process. TCP/IP is the default network protocol for Windows 7.

Understand Network Protocols

Network protocols function at the OSI model Layer 3 (the Network layer) and Layer 4 (the Transport layer). Network protocols are responsible for transporting data across an internetwork. They are responsible for reliable communication as well. The only network protocol installed by default in Windows 7 is TCP/IP, both version 4 and version 6 (called IPv4 and IPv6).

A solid understanding of TCP/IP and the configuration required for network communication is a substantial piece of the Windows 7 setup.

Overview of TCP/IP

Transmission Control Protocol/Internet Protocol (TCP/IP) is the most commonly used network protocol. It is a suite of protocols that have evolved into the industry standard for network, intranet, and Internet connectivity. The main protocols providing basic TCP/IP services include Internet Protocol (IP), Transmission Control Protocol (TCP), User Datagram Protocol (UDP), Address Resolution Protocol (ARP), Internet Control Message Protocol (ICMP), and Internet Group Management Protocol (IGMP).

Benefits of Using TCP/IP

TCP/IP as a protocol suite was accepted as an industry standard in the 1980s and continues to be the primary internetworking protocol today. For a default installation of Windows 7, IPv4 and IPv6 are both installed by default. TCP/IP has the following benefits:

- TCP/IP is the most common protocol and is supported by almost all network operating systems. It is the required protocol for Internet access.

- TCP/IP is dependable and scalable for use in small and large networks.

- Support is provided for connectivity across interconnected networks, independent of the operating systems being used at the upper end of the OSI model or the physical components at the lower end of the OSI model.

- TCP/IP provides standard routing services for moving packets over interconnected network segments. Dividing networks into multiple subnetworks (or subnets) optimizes network traffic and facilitates network management.

- TCP/IP is designed to provide data reliability by supplying a connection at the transport layer and verifying each data segment is received and passed to the application requiring the data by retransmitting lost information.

- TCP/IP allows for the classification of data in regard to its importance (quality of service). This allows important time-sensitive streams of data to get preferential treatment (like Voice over IP).

- TCP/IP is designed to be fault tolerant. It is able to dynamically reroute packets if network links become unavailable (assuming alternate paths exist).

- Protocol applications can provide services such as Dynamic Host Configuration Protocol (DHCP) for TCP/IP configuration and Domain Name System (DNS) for hostname-to-IP address resolution.

- Windows 7 continues to support Automatic Private IP Addressing (APIPA) used by small local connection–only networks without a DHCP server to allow Windows 7 to automatically assign an IP address to itself.

- Support for NetBIOS over TCP/IP (NetBT) is included in Windows 7. NetBIOS is a software specification used for identifying computer resources by name as opposed to IP address. We still use TCP/IP as the network protocol, so we map the NetBIOS name to an IP address.

- The inclusion of Alternate IP Configuration allows users to have a static and a DHCP-assigned IP address mapped to a single network adapter, which is used to support mobile users who roam between different network segments.

- IPv6 incorporates a much larger address space and, more importantly, incorporates many of the additional features of TCP/IP into a standardized protocol. This is important because if a vendor says they support TCP/IP, they only have to support the 1980s version and may not support additional features like the Internet protocol security features of IPSec. IPv6 as a standard includes these features and is thus a more robust network protocol.

Features of TCP/IP

One of the main features of TCP/IP is that it allows a common structure for network communications across a wide variety of diverse hardware and operating systems and a lot of applications, specifically written to configure and control it. Several of the features of TCP/IP included with Windows 7 are:

- TCP/IP connectivity tools allowing access to a variety of hosts across a TCP/IP network. TCP/IP tools in Windows 7 include clients for HTTP, FTP, TFTP, Telnet, and finger, among others. Server components for the tools are available.

- Inclusion of a Simple Network Management Protocol (SNMP) agent that can be used to monitor performance and resource use of a TCP/IP host, server, or network hardware devices.

- TCP/IP management and diagnostic tools are provided for maintenance and diagnostic support. TCP/IP management and diagnostic commands include ipconfig, arp, ping, nbtstat, netsh, route, nslookup, tracert, and pathping.

- Support for TCP/IP network printing, allowing you to print to networked print devices.

- Logical and physical multihoming, allowing multiple IP addresses on a single computer for single or multiple network adapters.

Multiple network adapters installed on a single computer are normally associated with routing for internetwork connectivity.

- Support for internal IP routing, which allows a Windows 7 computer to route packets between multiple network adapters installed in one machine.

- Support for virtual private networks, which allows you to transmit data securely across a public network via encapsulated and encrypted packets.

Basics of IP Addressing and Configuration

Before you can configure TCP/IP, you should have a basic understanding of TCP/IP configuration and addressing. Let's review TCP/IP addressing. To configure a TCP/IP client, you must specify an IP address (also known as the logical address), subnet mask, and default gateway (if you're going to communicate outside your local network). Depending on your network, you might want to configure a DNS server, domain name, or maybe even a WINS server.

You can see the Windows 7 TCP/IP version 4 properties window in Figure 10.24. I will go through the configuration steps and show you how to access this window later in this section.

Figure 10.24: Windows 7 TCP/IP version 4 properties

Hardware and Networking

PART IV

IPv4 Address Types

There are three types of IPv4 addresses: broadcast, multicast, and unicast.

A broadcast address is read by all hosts that hear it (the broadcast will not go across a router, so only local devices hear the broadcast). The IPv4 broadcast address is 255.255.255.255; every single bit is a one.

A multicast address is a special address that one or more devices will listen for by joining a multicast group. Not all the local devices respond and process the data in the multicast packet; only the devices configured to listen for it respond. A multicast address will have a value between 224 and 239 in the first octet (the leftmost number in the dotted decimal representation). A multicast example is 224.0.0.5.

A unicast IP address uniquely identifies a computer or device on the network. An IPv4 unicast address is a four-octet, 32-bit address represented as dotted decimal (an example is 131.107.1.200). Each number in the dotted decimal notation is a decimal representation of 8 bits, and the value of each is going to be between 0 and 255 (255 is the numerically largest value that 8 bits can represent). A portion of the IPv4 unicast address is used to identify the network the device is on (or the network of a destination device), and part is used to identify the individual host on the local network or the unique host on a remote network. The IPv4 address scheme is the only address space that the Internet uses today, and TCP/IP is the only network protocol that the Internet uses today.

IPv4 Address Classes

When the TCP/IP suite was accepted as a standard in the 1980s, three classes of unicast IP addresses were defined. Depending on the class you use, different parts of the address show the default network portion of the address and the host address. Network administrators still refer to these addresses by class, but they no longer utilize this class structure; I'll explain shortly.

Table 10.2 shows the three classes of network addresses and the number of networks and hosts available for each network class as defined by the original TCP/IP version 4 standard.

The values are based on the number of bits that can be changed (or used) by the network portion for the number of networks available or by the host portion for the number of hosts available. A quick example: if you have 8 bits to work with, 2 raised to the 8th power equals the total number of different combination (of 8 bits) you can make. Now, 2 raised to the 8th power is 256. So, if you have 8 bits available to you in the host portion of an IP address, you can have 256 possible addresses. The catch here is that the first address in the range is not assignable to a host (typically, the first address defines the network ID) and the last address is not assignable to a host (the last address is the subnetwork broadcast address). If you have 8 bits to use, you can only assign 254 to unique unicast IPv4 addresses to devices. It just so happens that the original IPv4 specification for a Class C address space allocated 24 bits to the network portion and 8 bits for the host portion. How many unique addresses are available? Yes: 254.

Table 10.2: IPv4 Class Assignments

Network Class	Address Range of First Octet	Number of Unique Networks Available	Number of Unique Hosts Per Network
A	1–126	126	16,777,214
B	128–191	16,384	65,534
C	192–223	2,097,152	254

IPv4 Subnet Mask

The subnet mask is used to specify which portion of the unicast IPv4 address defines the network value and which portion of the unicast IPv4 address defines the unique host value. The subnet mask can be shown as dotted decimal, as with 255.255.255.0, or as slash notation, as in /24. The 1980s standard for classful network addressing defined subnet masks for each class, as shown in Table 10.3.

Table 10.3: IPv4 Classful Subnet Masks

Class	Default Mask	Slash Notation
Class A	255.0.0.0	Slash 8 (/8)
Class B	255.255.0.0	Slash 16 (/16)
Class C	255.255.255.0	Slash 24 (/24)

Hardware and Networking

PART IV

The slash notation is easier to use as it defines the same information in a more convenient format. If you look at the Class A default (or natural) mask or 255.0.0.0, you can say that 255 is 8 ones (converting a decimal 255 to binary yields 1111 1111). Slash 8 simply means there are 8 ones in the subnet mask (or 255.0.0.0). By using 255, you are selecting the octet or octets (or, in some cases, the piece of an octet) used to identify the network address. For example, in the Class B network address 192.168.2.1, with the default subnet mask for a Class B space being 255.255.0.0, then 192.168 is the network address and 2.1 is the unicast host address.

Network Infrastructure

TCP/IP subnetting is discussed in detail in *MCTS: Windows Server 2008 Network Infrastructure Configuration Study Guide* by William Panek, Tylor Wentworth, and James Chellis (Sybex, 2008).

IPv4 Default Gateway

To communicate with other devices, each machine evaluates the network portion of the IP address it desires to communicate with (the destination device) and the network portion of its IP address. If the two network values are the same, the machine attempts to communicate directly with the destination machine. If the network portions of the two IP addresses are different, then the local machine sends the packet to the default gateway. The default gateway will then decide where the destination is by evaluating the network portion of the IP address and send it to the next device. You configure a default gateway if the network contains routers (the default gateway is a router). A router is a device that connects two or more network segments (IP subnetworks) together. Routers function at the Network layer of the OSI model.

You can configure a Windows 7 computer or Windows Server 2008 to act as a router by installing two or more network cards in the server, attaching each network card to a different network segment, and then configuring each network card for the segment to which it will attach. You can also use third-party routers, which typically offer more features than Windows 7 computers or Windows Server 2008 configured as a router. Many times in our network we use the first available IP address as the address of our default gateway (for example, 131.107.1.1).

You do not send packets to the default gateway; the network protocol does by getting the physical address (MAC) or the default gateway and inserting it as the destination MAC address with the actual destination IP or the remote device.

DNS Servers

Domain Name System (DNS) servers are used to resolve hostnames to IP addresses. Name resolution makes it easier for people to access other IP hosts. For example, do you know what the IP address is for Google? No? Do you know the hostname of Google server? Yes, you would use www.google.com. From your computer, pinging www.google.com actually sends the request to 66.102.1.147, the IP address returned by your DNS server. You can understand why many people might not know the IP address but would know the domain hostname. Windows 7 asks the DNS server configured on the machine for the resolution of the hostname to an IP address. Most companies and Internet service providers (ISPs) have their own DNS servers that know how to resolve any valid request. There are public DNS servers that can be used as well.

Fully Qualified Domain Name

The name you use to access the Stellacon server, www.stellacon.com, is an example of a fully qualified domain name (FQDN). This notation has a domain component, which is stellacon.com. The "dot com" is the top-level domain that parents most company names. You will see .gov for government agencies and .edu for educational institutions, along with a lot more. The stellacon of the stellacon.com domain is the organization that is logically responsible for the resource. Finally, the www is the unique identifier within the organization for the resource. We have become very familiar with this notation, but it is not guaranteed to be the name (nor does it have to be). You might well have seen your browser go to www1.acme.com or even willpanek.com. As long as the name resolves to the correct IP address, all is good.

If you do not have access to a properly configured DNS server or simply don't want your machine to resolve an IP address dynamically, you can statically configure a hostname to an IP address by editing the HOSTS file on your Windows 7 machine. Why would you do this? Perhaps there is more than one server available with the same name (do

Hardware and Networking

PART IV

you think there is only one Google server?), and you want to use one of the addresses specifically. You can edit your local host's file, as shown in Figure 10.25, with a FQDN and the configured IP address will be used.

Figure 10.25: HOSTS file location in Windows 7

WINS Servers

Windows Internet Name Service (WINS) servers are used to resolve NetBIOS (Network Basic Input/Output System) names to IP addresses. Windows 7 uses NetBIOS names in addition to hostnames to identify network computers. This is mainly for backward compatibility with legacy Windows operating systems, which used this addressing scheme extensively. When you attempt to access a computer using the NetBIOS name, the computer must be able to resolve the NetBIOS name to an IP address. This address resolution can be accomplished by using one of the following methods:

- Through a broadcast (if the computer you are trying to reach is on the same network segment)

- Through a WINS server

- Through an LMHOSTS (LAN Manager HOSTS) file, which is a static mapping of IP addresses to NetBIOS computer names

Dynamic Host Configuration Protocol (DHCP)

Each device that will use TCP/IP on your network must have a valid, unique IP address. This address can be manually configured or better yet can be automated through Dynamic Host Configuration Protocol (DHCP). DHCP is implemented as a client-server application. The server is configured with a pool of IP addresses and other IP-related configuration settings, such as subnet mask, default gateway, DNS server address, and WINS server address. The client is configured to automatically request IP configuration information from the DHCP server and use it for a given period of time (the lease length). Figure 10.26 shows the TCP/IP version 4 properties pages set up to use DHCP.

Figure 10.26: TCP/IP properties using DHCP

DHCP works in the following manner (remember DORA):

1. When the client computer starts up, it sends a broadcast DHCP*DISCOVER* message, requesting a DHCP server. The request includes the hardware address of the client computer.

2. Any DHCP server receiving the broadcast that has available IP addresses will send a DHCP*OFFER* message to the client. This message offers an IP address for a set period of time (called a *lease*), a subnet mask, and a server identifier (the IP address of the DHCP server). The address that is offered by the server is marked as unavailable and will not be offered to any other clients during the DHCP negotiation period.

3. The client selects one of the offers and broadcasts a DHCP*REQUEST* message, indicating its selection. This allows any DHCP offers that were not accepted to be returned to the pool of available IP addresses.

Hardware and Networking

PART IV

4. The DHCP server that was selected sends back a DHCP*ACK* message as an acknowledgment, indicating the IP address, subnet mask, and duration of the lease that the client computer will use. It might also send additional configuration information, such as the address of the default gateway and the DNS server address.

Using Deployment Options for TCP/IP Configurations

Windows 7 has four methods available for configuring TCP/IP:

- Static IP addressing
- Dynamic Host Configuration Protocol (DHCP)
- Automatic Private IP Addressing (APIPA)
- Alternate IP configuration

Although DHCP is the most common method for configuring an IP address on the machines in a network, the other methods are used as well.

Configuring Static IP Addressing

You can manually configure IP addressing if you know your IP address and subnet mask. If you are using optional components such as a default gateway or a DNS server, you will need to know the IP addresses of the computers that host these services as well. This option is not typically used in large networks because it is time consuming and prone to user error.

Statically Configuring a Windows 7 IPv4 address and DNS Server

Perform the following steps to manually configure a static IP address for a Windows 7 machine:

1. Select Start and type **Network and Sharing Center** into the Start menu search box.

2. In the Network And Sharing Center window, click Local Area Connection in the View Your Active Networks section.

3. Click the Properties button in the Activity section of the Local Area Connection Status box.

4. In the Local Area Connection Properties dialog box, select Internet Protocol Version 4 (TCP/IPv4) and click the Properties button.

5. Choose Use The Following IP Address in the Internet Protocol Version 4 (TCP/IPv4) Properties dialog box.

6. In the IP Address box, enter 131.200.1.200; in the Subnet Mask box, enter 255.255.0.0; and in the Default Gateway box, enter 131.107.1.1.

7. Choose Use The Following DNS Server Addresses in the Internet Protocol Version 4 (TCP/IPv4) Properties dialog box.

8. Enter 4.2.2.2 in the Preferred DNS Server box. You can leave the Alternate DNS Server box blank.

9. If you have entered valid information in steps 6 and 8, you can click OK to save your settings and close the dialog box; otherwise, click Cancel to revoke your changes.

Use a Valid Address for Your Network

The example in step 6 is likely not a valid IP address on your network. You can substitute a valid address, subnet mask, and default gateway if you know them. If you click OK and see this is not a valid IP address for your network, you will lose connectivity!

Accessing Advanced Configuration TCP/IPv4 Properties

Clicking the Advanced button in the Internet Protocol Version 4 (TCP/IPv4) dialog box opens the Advanced TCP/IP Settings dialog box. In this dialog box, you can configure advanced IP, DNS, and WINS settings.

You can edit or add multiple addresses to the same machine in the Advanced TCP/IP Settings windows as well as edit or add default gateways here. You also have access to the advanced DNS and WINS tabs, where you can modify specific parameters for both hostname resolution (DNS) and NetBIOS name resolution (WINS).

Hardware and Networking

PART IV

Table 10.4 shows the DNS advanced configuration properties and outlines the functionality.

Table 10.4: Advanced DNS TCP/IP Settings Options

Option	Description
DNS Server Addresses, In Order Of Use	Specifies the DNS servers that are used to resolve DNS queries. Use the arrow buttons on the right side of the list box to move a server up or down in the list.
Append Primary And Connection Specific DNS Suffixes	Specifies how unqualified domain names are resolved by DNS. For example, if your primary DNS suffix is iq.com and you type **ping bob**, DNS will try to resolve the address as bob.iq.com.
Append Parent Suffixes Of The Primary DNS Suffix	Specifies whether name resolution includes the parent suffix for the primary domain DNS suffix, up to the second level of the domain name. For example, if your primary DNS suffix is maine.iq.com and you type **ping bob**, DNS will try to resolve the address as bob.maine.iq.com. If this doesn't work, DNS will try to resolve the address as bob.iq.com.
Append These DNS Suffixes (In Order):	Specifies the DNS suffixes that will be used to attempt to resolve unqualified name resolution. For example, if your primary DNS suffix is iq.com and you type **ping bob**, DNS will try to resolve the address as bob.iq.com. If you append the additional DNS suffix Corp.com and type **ping bob**, DNS will try to resolve the address as bob.iq.com and bob.Corp.com.
DNS Suffix For This Connection:	Specifies the DNS suffix for the computer. If this value is configured by a DHCP server and you specify a DNS suffix, it will override the value set by DHCP.
Register This Connection's Addresses In DNS	Specifies that the connection will try to register its addresses dynamically using the computer name that was specified through the System Properties dialog box (accessed through the System icon in Control Panel).
Use This Connection's DNS Suffix In DNS Registration	Specifies that when the computer registers automatically with the DNS server, it should use the combination of the computer name and the DNS suffix.

Table 10.5 shows the WINS advanced configuration properties and outlines the functionality.

Table 10.5: Advanced WINS TCP/IP Settings Options

Option	Description
WINS Addresses, In Order Of Use	Specifies the WINS servers that are used to resolve WINS queries. You can use the arrow buttons on the right side of the list box to move a server up or down in the list.
Enable LMHOSTS Lookup	Specifies whether an LMHOSTS file can be used for name resolution. If you configure this option, you can use the Import LMHOSTS button to import an LMHOSTS file to the computer.
Default: Use NetBIOS Setting From The DHCP Server	Specifies that the computer should obtain its NetBIOS-over-TCP/IP and WINS settings from the DHCP server.
Enable NetBIOS Over TCP/IP	Allows you to use statically configured IP addresses so that the computer is able to communicate with pre–Windows XP computers (NetBIOS was discontinued with XP).
Disable NetBIOS Over TCP/IP	Allows you to disable NetBIOS over TCP/IP. Use this option only if your network includes only Windows XP clients, Windows Vista clients, Windows 7 clients, or DNS-enabled clients.

Setting Up DHCP

Dynamic IP configuration assumes that you have a DHCP server on your network that is reachable by the DHCP clients. DHCP servers are configured to automatically provide DHCP clients with all their IP configuration information, including IP address, subnet mask, and DNS server. For large networks, DHCP is the easiest and most reliable way of managing IP configurations. By default, a Windows 7 machine is configured as a DHCP client for dynamic IP configuration.

Perform the following steps if your computer is configured for manual IP configuration and you want to use dynamic IP configuration:

1. Select Start and type **Network and Sharing Center** into the Start menu search box.

2. In the Network And Sharing Center window, click Local Area Connection in the View Your Active Networks section.

Hardware and Networking

PART IV

3. Click the Properties button in the Activity section of the Local Area Connection Status box.

4. In the Local Area Connection Properties dialog box, select Internet Protocol Version 4 (TCP/IPv4) and click the Properties button.

5. Choose Obtain An IP Address Automatically on the General tab of the Internet Protocol Version 4 (TCP/IPv4) Properties dialog box.

6. Choose Obtain DNS Server Address Automatically on the General tab.

7. To use this configuration, click OK to accept the selection and close the dialog box. To exit without saving (if you had a valid static configuration), click Cancel.

Using APIPA

Automatic Private IP Addressing (APIPA) is used to automatically assign private IP addresses for home or small business networks that contain a single subnet, have no DHCP server, and are not using static IP addressing. If APIPA is being used, clients will be able to communicate only with other clients on the same subnet that are also using APIPA. The benefit of using APIPA in small networks is that it is less tedious and has less chance of configuration errors than statically assigning IP addresses and configuration.

APIPA is used with Windows 7 under the following conditions:

- When the client is configured as a DHCP client, but no DHCP server is available to service the DHCP request.

- When the client originally obtained a DHCP lease from a DHCP server, but when the client tried to renew the DHCP lease, the DHCP server was unavailable and the lease period expired.

APIPA uses a Class B network address space that has been reserved for its use. The address space is the 169.254.0.0 network where the range of 169.254.0.1–169.254.255.254 is available for hosts to assign to themselves.

The process that APIPA uses is as follows:

1. The Windows 7 client attempts to use a DHCP server for its configuration, but no DHCP servers respond.

2. The Windows 7 client selects a random address from the 169.254.0.1–169.254.255.254 range of addresses and uses

a subnet mask of 255.255.0.0. The client uses a duplicate-address detection method to verify the address it selected is not already in use on the network.

3. If the address is already in use, the client repeats steps 1 and 2.

If the address is not already in use, the client configures its network interface with the address it randomly selected. If you note the number of the address the APIPA client can select from (65,536 addresses), the odds of selecting a duplicate is very slim.

4. The Windows 7 network client continues to search for a DHCP server every five minutes. If a DHCP server replies to the request, the APIPA configuration is dropped and the client receives new IP configuration settings from the DHCP server.

You can determine if your network interface has been configured using APIPA by looking at your IP address. Do so easily from the command prompt using ipconfig /all.

Perform the following steps to view your IP address this way:

1. Click Start and enter **cmd** in the Start menu search box.

2. Type **ipconfig /all** in the command interpreter.

3. Look at the Local Area Connection IP address. If your IP address is in the range of 169.254.0.1 – 169.254.255.254 and the text Autoconfiguration Enabled is present, you are using APIPA.

Using Multiple IP Addresses

Windows 7 allows you to configure more than one network adapter in a single computer, an approach known as multihoming. You can also configure multiple IP addresses on the same network adapter in Windows 7, an approach known as logical multihoming. Use logical multihoming if you have a single physical network logically divided into subnets and you want your computer to be connected with more than one subnet.

Perform the following steps to configure multiple IP addresses for a single network adapter:

1. Select Start and type **Network and Sharing Center** in the Start menu search box.

2. In the Network and Sharing Center window, click Local Area Connection in the View Your Active Networks section.

Hardware and Networking

PART IV

3. Click the Properties button in the Activity section of the Local Area Connection Status box.

4. In the Local Area Connection Properties dialog box, select Internet Protocol Version 4 (TCP/IPv4) and click the Properties button.

5. You will need to have a static IP address to use multihoming. Choose Use The Following IP Address in the Internet Protocol Version 4 (TCP/IPv4) Properties dialog box.

6. In the IP Address box, enter 131.200.1.200; in the Subnet Mask box, enter 255.255.0.0; and in the Default Gateway box, enter 131.107.1.1.

7. Click the Advanced button to access the Advanced TCP/IP Settings dialog box. On the IP Settings tab in the IP Addresses section, click the Add button.

8. You add additional IP addresses by entering them into the TCP/IP address window launched in step 5 along with their subnet mask and then clicking Add. You can repeat this step to add additional IP addresses.

9. If you need to assign more than one default gateway to your IP configuration, use the Default Gateways section of Advanced IP Settings.

Use a Valid Address for Your Network

The example in step 6 is likely not a valid IP address on your network. You can substitute a valid address, subnet mask, and default gateway if you know them. If you click OK and see this is not a valid IP address for your network, you will lose connectivity!

Using Alternate Configuration

Alternate Configuration is designed to be used by laptops and other mobile computers to manage IP configurations when the computer is used in multiple locations and one location requires a static IP address and the other location(s) require dynamic IP addressing. For example, a user with a laptop might need a static IP address to connect to their broadband ISP at home, and then use DHCP when connected to the corporate network.

Alternate Configuration works by allowing the user to configure the computer so that it will initially try to connect to a network using DHCP; if the DHCP attempt fails (for example, when the user is at home), the alternate static IP configuration is used. The alternate IP address can be an APIPA or a manually configured IP address.

Perform the following steps to configure Alternate Configuration:

1. Select Start and type **Network and Sharing Center** in the Start menu search box.

2. In the Network and Sharing Center window, click Local Area Connection in the View Your Active Networks section.

3. Click the Properties button in the Activity section of the Local Area Connection Status box.

4. In the Local Area Connection Properties dialog box, select Internet Protocol Version 4 (TCP/IPv4) and click the Properties button.

5. Select the Alternate Configuration tab in the Internet Protocol Version 4 (TCP/IPv4) Properties dialog box.

6. The Automatic Private IP address radio button is selected by default. To create a static configuration if the DHCP server is unavailable, choose the User Configured radio button and enter the values for your Alternate Configuration.

7. Click OK to save your Alternate Configuration or reset to the default Automatic Private IP Address radio button and click OK, or click Cancel to abandon your changes and close the window.

Using IPv6 Addresses

Through most of this section, I've been referencing TCP/IP as the network protocol, but you should remember that it is really a suite of protocols running in Layer 3 and Layer 4 of the OSI model. Internet Protocol (IP) is the Layer 3 protocol responsible for assigning end devices globally unique addresses (and I mean from the whole company for private addresses to the whole Internet for public addresses). Back in the 1980s, it was unimaginable that anyone would ever need more than 4 billion addresses, but we do. They (the keepers of the Internet) realized in the 1990s that there was going to be a problem and decided that a new Layer 3 would be needed. This was not an easy task, and integration into the existing infrastructure was going to be long as well. An interim solution was devised for use while the new Layer 3 protocol became standardized. The interim solution, known as NAT and PAT, allowed more than one device to use the same IP address on a private network as long as there was one Internet address available. Cool enough, but it was not the real solution.

IPv6 is the solution to the IPv4 address depletion. As time has progressed from the IPv4 standard acceptance in the 1980s, we have needed new and better functionality. However, given the way the standards process works around the world, you can add functionality, but it may or may not be supported in any vendor's TCP/IPv4 network stack. What happened in IPv6 is not only did the address space increase in size, but the additional functionality that may or may not have been included before has become part of the IPv6 standard. For example, IPv4 is defined as having a variable-length header, which is cumbersome as you need to read an additional piece of data to see how big the header is. Most of the time it stays the same, so why not just fix its length and add perhaps an extension to the header if you need to carry more information? IPv6 uses a fixed-length IP header with the capability of carrying more information in an extension to the header known as an *extension header.*

What about the Layer 4 piece, TCP and UDP? Those don't need to change; we're only changing Layer 3. What about the MAC address and the Ethernet specification? Those don't need to change, either; we're only changing Layer 3. (You'll have to add a new identifier for the Layer 2 header so you know to hand the data to IPv6.)

Microsoft has included IPv6 in its operating systems since NT 4.0; it just was not enabled by default. Windows 7 natively supports both IPv4 and IPv6 (as did Vista). The main differences you will notice between IPv4 and IPv6 is the format and size of the IP address. IPv6 addresses are 128 bits (IPv4 is 32 bits) and typically written as eight groups of four hex characters. IPv4, as you saw earlier, is four decimal representations of 8 bits. Each of the eight groups of characters is separated by a colon. An example of a valid IPv6 address is 2001:4860:0000:0000:00 12:10FF:FECD:00EF.

Leading zeroes can be omitted, so you can write the example address as 2001:4860:0:0:12:10FF:FECD:EF. Additionally, a double colon can be used to compress a set of consecutive zeroes, so you can write the example address as 2001:4860::12:10FF:FECD:EF. The IPv6 address is 128 bits; when you see a double colon, it's a variable that says fill enough zeros within the colons to make the address 128 bits.

NOTE You can only have one set of double colon—two variables in one address will not work.

Will you see IPv6 take over the Global Address space soon? Even with IPv4's lack of address space, you are going to continue to use it for many years. The integration of IPv6 into the infrastructure is going to happen as a joint venture, with IPv4 and IPv6 running at the same time in the devices and on some networks.

There are many mechanisms for enabling IPv6 communications over an IPv4 network, including the following:

- Dual Stack, which involves a computer or device running both the IPv4 and IPv6 protocol stacks at the same time

- ISATAP (Intra-Site Automatic Tunnel Addressing Protocol)

- 6to4, which is an encapsulation technique for putting IPv6 addresses inside IPv4 addresses

- Toredo Tunneling, which is another encapsulation technique for putting IPv6 traffic inside an IPv4 packet

Some IPv6-to-IPv4 dynamic translation techniques require that a computer's IPv4 address be used as the last 32 bits of the IPv6 address. When these translation techniques are used, it is common to write the last 32 bits as you would typically write an IPv4 address, such as 2001:4850::F8:192.168.122.26.

Testing IP Configuration

After you have installed and configured the TCP/IP settings, you can test the IP configuration using the ipconfig, ping, and nbtstat commands. These commands are also useful in troubleshooting IP configuration errors. You can graphically view connection details through the Local Area Connection Status of the Network And Sharing Center.

Using the ipconfig Command

The ipconfig command displays your IP configuration. Table 10.6 lists the command switches that you can use with the ipconfig command.

Hardware and Networking

PART IV

Table 10.6: ipconfig Switches

Switch	Description
/?	Shows all the help options for `ipconfig`
/all	Shows verbose information about your IP configuration, including your computer's physical address, the DNS server you are using, and whether you are using DHCP
/allcompartments	Shows IP information for all compartments
/release	Releases an IPv4 address that has been assigned through DHCP
/release6	Releases an IPv6 address that has been assigned through DHCP
/renew	Renews an IPv4 address through DHCP
/renew6	Renews an IPv6 address through DHCP
/flushdns	Purges the DNS Resolver cache
/registerdns	Refreshes DHCP leases and re-registers DNS names
/displaydns	Displays the contents of the DNS Resolver Cache
/showclassid	Lists the DHCP class IDs allowed by the computer
/setclassID	Allows you to modify the DHCP class ID

Perform the following steps to use ipconfig to view your IP address configuration:

1. Select Start and type **cmd** into the Start menu search box or choose Start ➢ All Programs ➢ Accessories ➢ Command Prompt.

2. In the Command Prompt window, type **ipconfig** and press Enter. Note the IPv4 address as well as the IPv6 address.

3. In the Command Prompt dialog box, type **ipconfig /all** and press Enter. You now see more information such as the Ethernet address, IPv6 tunnel parameters, and their interface identifiers. Close the Command Prompt window when you have finished viewing the information by typing **exit** or closing the window.

Using the *ping* Command

The ping command is useful for verifying connectivity between two IP devices. The command sends an Internet Control Message Protocol (ICMP) Echo Request message to a remote machine and receives an ICMP Echo Reply message back if the remote device is able to respond.

You can ping a computer based on the computer's IPv4 address, IPv6 address, hostname (DNS resolves), or NetBIOS name (WINS resolves). The following list shows examples of ping:

```
ping 131.107.1.200
ping 2001:4860::12:10FF:FECD:EF
ping www.google.com
ping windows7-pc-1
```

If you are having trouble connecting to a host on another network, ping could help you verify that a valid communication path exists. You might ping the following addresses:

- The IPv4 loopback address, 127.0.0.1
- The IPv6 loopback address, ::1
- The local computer's IP address
- The local router's (default gateway's) IP address
- The remote computer's IP address

If ping fails to get a reply from any of these addresses, you have a starting point for troubleshooting the connection error. Table 10.7 lists common error messages that can be returned from a ping request.

Table 10.7: ping Command Error Messages

Error	Description
Request Timed Out	Means that the Echo Reply message was not received from the destination computer within the time allotted. By default, destination computers have 4 seconds to respond.
TTL Expired In Transit	Means the packet exceeded the number of hops specified to reach the destination device. Each time a packet passes through a router, the Time To Live (TTL) counter is decremented and reflects the pass through the router as a hop. If the TTL reaches 0, this message is returned.
Destination Host Unreachable	Generated when a local or remote route path does not exist between the sending host and the specified destination computer. This error could occur because the router is misconfigured or the target computer is not available.

Hardware and Networking

PART IV

Table 10.7: ping Command Error Messages *(continued)*

Error	Description
Ping Request Could Not Find Host	Indicates the destination host name couldn't be resolved. You should verify the destination host name was properly specified, that all DNS and WINS settings are correct, and that the DNS and WINS servers are available.

Using the *nbtstat* Command

NBT is NetBIOS over TCP/IP, and the nbtstat command is used to display TCP/IP connection protocol statistics over NBT. Table 10.8 lists the command-line options that you can use.

Table 10.8: nbtstat Command-Line Options

Switch	Option	Description
/?	Help	Shows all the help options for `nbtstat`
-a	Adapter Status	Shows adapter status and lists the remote computer's name, based on the hostname you specify
-A	Adapter Status	Shows adapter status and lists the remote computer's name, based on the IP address you specify
-c	cache	Displays the NBT cache of remote computers through their names and IP addresses
-n	names	Shows a list of the local computer's NetBIOS names
-r	resolved	Shows a list of computer names that have been resolved through either broadcast or WINS
-R	Reload	Causes the NBT remote cache name table to be purged and reloaded (must be logged on as an administrator with privilege elevation)
-S	Sessions	Shows the current sessions table with the destination IP addresses
-s	sessions	Shows the current sessions table and the converted destination IP address to the computer's NetBIOS name
-RR	Release Refresh	Sends a Name Release packet to the WINS server and then starts a refresh

TCP/IP Troubleshooting

If you are having trouble connecting to network resources, you might want to check the following:

- If you can access resources on your local subnet but not on a remote subnet, you should check the default gateway settings on your computer. Pinging a remote host and receiving a Destination Unreachable message is also related to default gateway misconfiguration.

- If you can access some but not all resources on your local subnet or remote subnet, you should check your subnet mask settings, the wiring to those resources, or the devices between your computer and those resources.

- Use the ipconfig command to ensure you are not configured with an APIPA address. If so, determine why you are not receiving IP settings from your DHCP server.

- If you can access a resource (for example, by pinging a computer) by IP address but not by name, you should check the DNS settings on your computer.

PART V

Applications

IN THIS PART ▶

11

Configuring Internet Explorer 8

IN THIS CHAPTER, YOU WILL LEARN TO:

E8 tries to inform the user of potential issues through security enhancements while allowing administrators to enforce security with the least amount of inconvenience to the end users.

Internet Explorer 8 (IE8) is available for Windows XP, Windows Server 2003 with at least SP2, Windows Vista, Windows 7, and Server 2008 in both the 32-bit and 64-bit versions. It is automatically being shipped with Windows 7 (both 32-bit and 64-bit).

IE8 is loaded with new user features to provide end users with a better and simpler way to get the information they desire from their browsing experience.

Use New IE8 Features

The new features added to IE8 are designed to give end users an easy way to browse the Internet for the information they're looking for while providing a secure environment for the network by recognizing potentially bad sites (those attempting to sneak viruses or Trojans into the network), phishing sites (those who attempt to steal private information about the user), or invasive sites that users may go to either on purpose or inadvertently. I will explore the security and safety features of IE8 later in this chapter.

Let's look at the user experience additions to IE8 first. Microsoft has added accelerators to give users a faster way to access online services; Web Slices, which let users see if parts of a website have changed that they might be watching, such as a stock quote; and Compatibility View, which ensures older web pages display appropriately in IE8.

Defining IE8 Accelerators

IE8 includes a new feature that allows you to gain access to Internet services with a click. By highlighting a word on a web page and clicking the accelerator icon, you have access to a various range of services by default and can add more accelerators if you desire. In Figure 11.1, you can see the word *cryptographic* highlighted and the accelerator icon selected. Click the accelerator icon to bring up a list of currently available services.

Figure 11.1: Accelerator icon

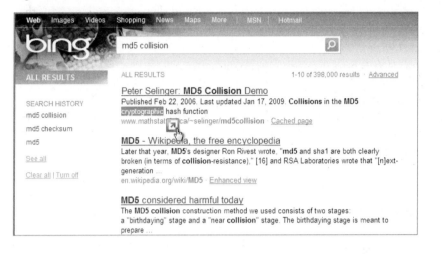

The default set of accelerator services are shown in Figure 11.2 and are available to launch a web page to provide information about the selected text. In our example, let's search Bing for the term *cryptographic* by choosing Search With Bing.

Figure 11.2: Choosing the Search With Bing accelerator

Figure 11.2 shows the default set of accelerator services installed by default in IE8, but there are several more currently available and more to be available as time goes on. You add more accelerators from the same menu by selecting All Accelerators and then clicking Find More Accelerators, as shown in Figure 11.3.

Figure 11.3: Clicking Find More Accelerators

Adding accelerators to your IE8 will certainly provide a more feature-rich and efficient browsing experience. Most of the time when browsing, a second browser or new tab is opened to do further research about the page you are currently viewing. Sometimes this is just for a quick look at a new piece of information or to look up something. If you're used to going to a certain page to find the "extra" information, this would be a great candidate to add to your accelerators.

Adding the Define With Bing Accelerator to IE8

Perform the following steps to add an accelerator to IE8 from a currently open web page:

1. Open IE8 and open a web page.

2. Select a word or phrase and click the accelerator icon.

3. Choose All Accelerators, and then click Find More Accelerators.

4. Review the available accelerators and select the Define With Bing accelerator, as shown in Figure 11.4. (This might not be available on the first page of accelerators.)

Figure 11.4: The Define With Bing accelerator

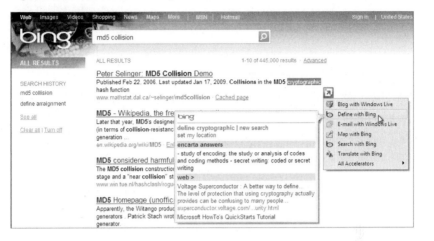

5. A confirmation box appears that asks if you're sure you want to add this accelerator and if you want to make it the default for this accelerator category. Select the check box to make it the default and click Add.

6. You can verify the installation of the Define With Bing accelerator by returning to the web page (or going to any web page), highlighting a word or phrase, and clicking the accelerator icon. The Define With Bing option is now available.

You can also add the Define With Bing accelerator directly from the IE8 menus, which is also where you can manage any of the accelerators you have installed (which includes deleting them).

Managing IE8 Accelerators

Perform the following steps to manage the installed accelerators or add new accelerators directly from the IE8 program interface:

1. Open IE8.

2. Click Tools ➤ Manage Add-ons.

3. In the Manage Add-ons window, select Accelerators in the Add-on Types section.

4. Select the accelerator in the right pane you would like to manage or click Find More Accelerators in the bottom left of the Manage Add-ons window to add more accelerators to IE8.

Handling Accelerators in IE8

Let's take a look at some of the various capabilities of the accelerators in IE8. In the previous section, you installed the Define With Bing accelerator. I showed you how to add the Define With Bing accelerator as a quick launch of Bing with define search functionality implemented in a new tab of IE8. But the accelerator provides an even more useful function by giving you a preview of the search without opening a new tab.

If you select a word in a web page you are viewing and would like a definition of the word, you can open the Accelerators menu by clicking the icon and simply pausing over the Define With Bing option. IE8 will use Bing and display a quick definition in the current window, as shown in Figure 11.5.

Figure 11.5: Viewing a quick definition using an accelerator

If you think this is cool, hold on—it gets even better. The default Map With Bing accelerator works like Define With Bing and will open a new tab in IE8 with a highlighted location address entered and searched with Bing. The Map With Bing accelerator also has the preview capability and will show you an insert in your current page with the map of the address if you hover over the address, as shown in Figure 11.6 (where we searched for the latitude and longitude of a lighthouse in Maine).

As with accelerators, there are more new services available in IE8, such as Web Slices, as you'll see in the next section.

Figure 11.6: Quick map from an accelerator

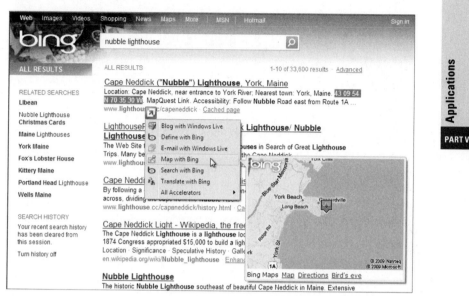

Defining IE8 Web Slices

Web Slices in IE8 allows the browser to check for updates to web page content that you may frequently want to have. How many times in the course of the day do you check your local weather or stock quotes or watch an auction item on eBay? Most of the time you either keep a tab open and refresh it periodically or return to the website with the content you would like to review. With Web Slices, you can add the piece of the web page with the content you're looking for to the new Favorites toolbar and IE8 will check it for you and give you a visual clue when the content changes. You can control how often IE8 checks for changes as well as have IE8 play a sound when Web Slice content is found on a page—and even when an update to content is discovered.

Web Slice content is being added to provider pages continually and its functionality will grow over time. Even at the time Windows 7 and IE8 were released, the available content made this new feature a welcome addition. If Web Slice content is available on a web page, the green Web Slice icon becomes active on the Favorites toolbar; it also becomes visible as you hover over available Web Slice content in the page itself. Figure 11.7 shows the Web Slice icon in the IE8 new Favorites toolbar.

Figure 11.7: Web Slice icon in the Favorites toolbar

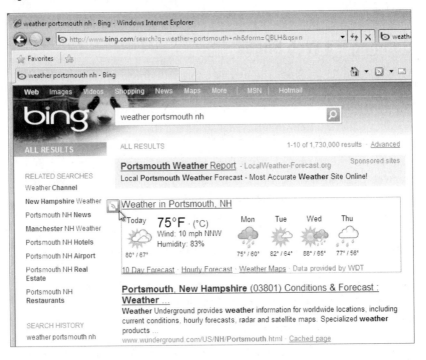

Figure 11.8 shows a Bing query for a weather forecast for Portsmouth, New Hampshire, and the option icon available to add the forecast content as a Web Slice to the IE8 Favorites toolbar. Click the down arrow associated with the Favorites toolbar's Web Slice icon to display all the Web Slices available on the current web page. On eBay, for example, all the items that match your search will be individual Web Slices you can pick from, allowing you to watch just one (or more if you add more than one Web Slice) item.

Figure 11.8: Web Slice icon within a web page

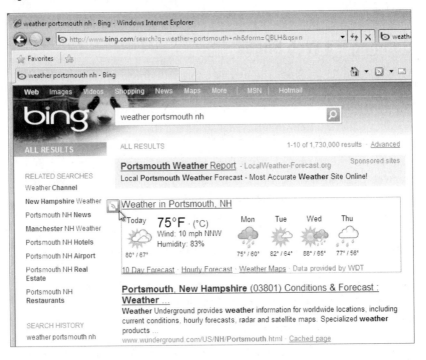

Clicking the Web Slice icon on web page content presents the user with a confirmation box for adding the Web Slice to the Favorites toolbar. Once accepted, the Web Slice is available to be viewed at any time, even if you browse away from the originating page. Figure 11.9 shows the Web Slice content for the weather forecast added.

Figure 11.9: Web Slice content from the Favorites toolbar

After you add a Web Slice to IE8, the browser periodically checks the source of the content for changes. If there are changes to the content, the Web Slice favorite text changes to bold and the background color flashes a color that indicates an update has been detected. Adding a Web Slice to your browser is a simple task you will find extremely convenient.

Adding a Stock Quote Web Slice to IE8

You might like to monitor a company's stock prices throughout the course of the day.

Perform the following steps to add Microsoft's stock quote to your IE8 interface:

1. Open IE8 and browse to `www.bing.com`.

2. Enter `msft` into the search box in Bing and click the search button.

3. Choose the drop-down arrow from the Web Slice icon in the IE8 new Favorites toolbar and select Microsoft Corp Web Slice.

4. Select the Add To Favorites Bar button in the Internet Explorer confirmation window.

5. Verify that the Web Slice is available in the IE8 Favorites toolbar.

6. Click the down arrow of the Bing Microsoft Corp Web Slice and you are presented with the current information from the Web Slice of the original page, with updated information if it's available.

You could have also added a Web Slice by clicking the Web Slice icon associated with the content on the page. After you add the Web Slice, you can change certain parameters associated with it, such as how often the content is checked for updates, or to add a sound association with Web Slices.

After you add Web Slices to IE8, you might want to tweak the properties to allow a more frequent update check. The default update interval for a Web Slice is dependent on the website content developer. The eBay interval shows up as 3,600+ seconds for an item expiring a long time from when the Web Slice was added.

The weather Web Slice from Bing defaults to 360 seconds. You can change the properties for the Web Slice timing by adjusting the values from the properties pages of the Web Slice. Right-click (alternate mouse click) the Web Slice from the Favorites toolbar and select Properties to open the properties dialog box, as shown in Figure 11.10.

Figure 11.10: Web Slice Properties dialog box

Managing IE8 Web Slices

Perform the following steps to change the update time interval for a Web Slice:

1. Perform the tasks in the earlier section "Adding a Stock Quote Web Slice to IE8" if you have not done so.

2. Right-click (alternate mouse click) the Bing Microsoft Corp Web Slice in the Favorites toolbar and select Properties.

3. Click the Use Custom Schedule radio button.

4. Click the down arrow to open the Frequency drop-down list and choose a new interval.

5. Click OK to close the Properties box and save your changes.

You can set other properties for a Web Slice from the Properties dialog box as well by clicking the Settings button in the Update Schedule section, as shown in Figure 11.11. You can set sound options and display options for the Web Slices from the Feed And Web Slice Settings page.

Figure 11.11: Feed And Web Slice Settings

If you have to enter credentials for a Web Slice, you can add or modify the information on the Web Slice's Properties dialog box by clicking the Settings button next to the User Name And Password field. You can change the display text as well as the URL for the Web Slice in the Properties dialog box.

After you finish with a Web Slice, remove it from the Favorites toolbar by right-clicking it and selecting Delete from the context menu; you are asked to confirm the deletion. The alternate click context menu also provides shortcuts to Web Slice properties, such as choosing to bold a new entry and modifying the text or icons shown on the Favorites toolbar. You will find Web Slices a fast and convenient way to keep up-to-date with content you review periodically throughout the day; it can also help you keep track of web content that may need to be addressed as it changes.

As IE continues to advance, content providers can make use of the new features, but there might be older pages that don't display correctly. IE8 adds Compatibility View, thus allowing IE8 to present older content correctly.

Browsing with IE8's Compatibility View

IE8 is a new release of Microsoft's web browser included in Windows 7 and some websites may not be updated to use the new features of IE8 or display their content correctly. Problems might include displaying misaligned images or text. By using Compatibility View, IE8 will display a web page the way it would have been displayed in IE7 (which should correct any display issues). To display a page in Compatibility View, click the Compatibility View button in the IE8 address bar, as shown in Figure 11.12.

Figure 11.12: Compatibility View

Once you choose Compatibility View for a website, you will not need to make the choice again; IE8 displays the site in Compatibility View the next time you browse to the same website. If the website is updated in the future or you decide you would prefer to see it in the native IE8 standard mode, you can simply click the Compatibility View button again to return to the standard view.

You can also enable this option by choosing Tools ➤ Compatibility View. In addition, a Compatibility View Settings option in the Tools menu lets you manage the sites currently set to Compatibility View. You can add or delete sites using the Add and Remove buttons, as shown in Figure 11.13. Many companies today have an extensive website for their users who may take time to update to IE8 features. The Compatibility View Settings page has the default setting for all intranet sites to be displayed in Compatibility View. You also have the choice to display all websites in Compatibility View.

Figure 11.13: Compatibility View Settings

Compatibility View helps in the transition to the new IE8 that allows users to view pages in a consistent manner. The new features—accelerators, Web Slices, and Compatibility View—are all a definite plus in the overall browsing experience. IE8 also includes a wide range of enhancements and updated features.

Use Updated Features of IE8

Windows Internet Explorer has included features through all releases that provide users with a simple way to get information from the Internet as well as browse more efficiently. IE8 takes much of the existing functionality and adds to it. Updated features include the Smart Address Bar, enhanced tab browsing, tab grouping, and better Find On Page functionality.

Exploring Address Bar and Tab Updates

The address bar now offers information to the user rather than just waiting for input and processing the data. IE8 adds intelligence to the address bar and refers to it as a Smart Address Bar. Once upon a time, you had to open separate browsers if you wanted to surf to more than one website at a time.

Earlier versions of IE added a tab functionality to allow more than one website or multiple pages of the same website to be open at the same time within one browser. This multisite single-browser capability lets users open separate tabs for each session. This is good, but in previous versions of IE, the view was just a tab with a site and didn't offer much information to an end user. Windows IE8 has added enhanced tab browsing and grouping by giving users more information while surfing the Web. Let's start by taking a look at the Smart Address Bar.

Browsing with the Smart Address Bar

Windows IE8 shows you options for places to browse as you type the address of a site. Previous versions of the Internet Explorer address bar have presented the user with history options, but the Smart Address Bar enhances the input by displaying the history with a different color text as you type in a new address. The Smart Address Bar also offers as-you-type options that allow you to open the new page in a new tab, as shown in Figure 11.14.

Figure 11.14: Smart Address Bar

In previous versions of IE, the address bar would also show you each page you browsed to in a specific site; if you browsed to 20 pages in a news website, you'd have 20 history entries in your address bar. The new IE8 Smart Address Bar only displays the main site address. IE8 populates the Smart Address Bar by searching across your history, favorites, and the RSS (Really Simple Syndication) feeds you have subscribed to. If you mistyped a website, it will also show up in the Smart Address Bar, but you can select and delete the unwanted entry.

Another feature enhanced in IE8 is the tabs users open instead of multiple browsers. It's easy to get overwhelmed while browsing if you have too many tabs open. IE8 now gives you enhanced tab browsing, which sets up tab groups. If a second tab is opened from a page in another tab, the second tab is placed next to the originating tab in the tab bar and then color-coded so each related tab is the same color. This way, you can quickly see the tabs that have related content. If you close a tab but there are still related tabs, IE8 will open the related tabs rather than just drop you into unrelated content.

IE8 offers improved functionality in the way tabs are managed as well. By right-clicking a tab, you open the context menu shown in Figure 11.15, allowing you to close the individual tab, close the whole tab group, or close the other tabs (except the selected tab). Another nice feature, as shown in Figure 11.15, is the Refresh All option, which refreshes all the available tabs.

Figure 11.15: Tab group context menu

Also, part of enhanced tab browsing are the options IE8 presents when you open a new tab. IE7 displayed a thumbnail view of your browsing history, but IE8 provides a whole new layer of functionality. When you open a new tab in IE8, you can choose to make it an InPrivate session (which I will discuss in the "Use IE8's Enhanced Security and Safety Features" section later in this chapter). IE8 lets you reopen your last browsing session (maybe you closed the whole session by mistake) or reopen specific previously opened websites. The user can choose to launch an accelerator directly into a new tab as well.

Opening a New Tab and Launching the Search With Bing Page

Perform the following steps to open a new tab and start a search in Bing:

1. Open IE8.

2. Click the New Tab area of the tab bar, or press Ctrl+T to open a new tab.

3. In the Use An Accelerator section of the new tab, choose Search With Bing.

4. The Bing page opens and you can enter your search criteria.

Using Find On Page and Improved Zoom

When you view web pages, there are many times when you would like to be able to search for a word or phrase on a page, assuming you can see the small words. You can use the improved Find On Page functionality in IE8 and then use the improved zoom feature to better read or see the information.

Searching with the Improved Find On Page

IE8 has a redesigned Find On Page that adds a new Find On Page toolbar. You can activate the Find On Page toolbar by pressing Ctrl+F or by selecting Edit ➤ Find On Page. The Edit menu itself might be a problem for you as IE8 does not display the classic Windows menus by default. In order to see the Windows menus, you need to press the Alt key.

Perform the following steps to activate the better Find on Page toolbar:

1. Open IE8 and browse to a page with text available for you to search through.

2. Press the Alt key to activate the Windows classic menus.

3. Click Edit ➤ Find On This Page. Alternatively, press Ctrl+F.

4. Enter text to search for in the Search box of the Find On Page toolbar. You should notice the matching characters become highlighted as you type them into the search box.

As you type characters into the Find On Page toolbar, you should also notice the next and previous buttons are now part of the toolbar, not located in a dialog box in the page (which has always been an annoyance). The toolbar also shows you a hit count on the number of times the search criteria has been met on the current page. Each instance of a match for the criteria is highlighted for easier location on the web page. You can toggle the highlighting feature on and off by clicking to toggle the highlighting button in the Find On Page toolbar. You also have the option to search on the whole word or to match case using the Options drop-down box.

Say you've searched for text on a web page and found the item you're looking for but would like to zoom in to see it better. This is where the improved zoom functionality of IE8 comes into play.

Applications

PART V

Viewing Web Content with Improved Zoom

Choosing the Zoom button or the Zoom drop-down list box in the lower-right corner of IE8, as shown in Figure 11.16, lets you zoom into or out of a web page. You can also press Ctrl++ (plus sign) or Ctrl+− (minus sign) to zoom in or out, respectively.

Figure 11.16: Zoom options in IE8

Zoom In	Ctrl +
Zoom Out	Ctrl -
400%	
200%	
150%	
125%	
● 100%	
75%	
50%	
Custom...	

The IE8 zoom has been enhanced from previous versions with an adaptive Page Zoom feature. In previous versions, the page just zoomed to the upper-left corner of the current page, requiring the user to use the scroll bars to find the data they had centered on their screen. Unless the data you want is in the upper-left corner (not very likely), scrolling is necessary and not friendly or enjoyable. The improved feature zooms around the content you are viewing in the page, so you may not have to move the content you have zoomed in to but will have to scroll only in order to view more data than you can see initially.

These new and enhanced user features aren't the only great improvements to IE8; there are numerous new and improved security and safety features as well.

Use IE8's New Security and Safety Features

IE8's new security and safety features are designed to help protect users from malicious attacks or attempts to get personal information without their knowledge. Because we all use the Internet and our corporate intranets to provide information every day, online crime has risen dramatically. The new type of criminals we face are known as cybercriminals and are using extremely deceptive and sophisticated methods for getting information from users.

Malware is one type of method in which a cybercriminal will try to steal private information through software pretending to be an expected website. This malware could be a program running on your PC that reads everything you type (including login information from a web browser) and reports the information back to a cybercriminal.

Phishing is another technique used by cybercriminals to gain personal information from users. Phishing can be perpetrated by the cybercriminal pretending to be a legitimate website, such as the user's banking site or credit card site, and convincing the user to enter information into a fraudulent page.

New features of IE8 help to identify malware and phishing schemes and make it easier for users to quickly identify potential issues. This in turn allows administrators to spend less time fixing the network and fixing user-compromised data. Domain highlighting, the Cross-Site Scripting (XSS) filter, click-jacking prevention, SmartScreen filters, InPrivate browsing, and InPrivate filtering are new additions to IE8.

Understanding Domain Highlighting

When a user surfs to a website, they normally type in a URL in the form of www.bing.com. This URL displays in the address bar of the browser, and the user can see it during the entire browsing session. This may or may not be apparent to the user as it is nondescript text and nothing jumps out at the user. In IE8, the displayed URL is shown to the user with the domain highlighted, such as www.bing.com. As the user continues to surf to other pages within Bing, the domain portion, bing.com, remains clear (the other text softens to gray). That way, if the user is redirected to another site, there is a visual clue that jumps out at the user.

Domain highlighting and user education are a good starting place for security and safety, but are there features that can be added to proactively help the user? The answer is yes. One of the common phishing/malware activities is XSS, where the user inadvertently runs a script in a website link exploiting a flaw in a website, or click-jacking where a user clicks a link that says one thing on the page but sends them somewhere else. IE8 has proactive software to help identify these types of phishing/malware attacks before they can happen.

Defending Against XSS and Click-Jacking

XSS attacks attempt to exploit vulnerabilities that exist in the websites you use. XSS attacks are set up by inserting a malicious website address in a link a user might click in an email. The data in the link direct the browser to a legitimate website that has been compromised to contain malicious code that can capture keystrokes, therefore letting the cyber-criminal capture a user's login credentials. IE8 includes an XSS filter that attempts to detect these types of attacks and disable the harmful scripts.

Users surfing to a website that has been compromised can be detected and IE8 can modify the request, avoiding the potential risk. A message appears at the top of the IE8 page that indicates to the user "Internet Explorer has modified this page to help prevent cross-site scripting." Figure 11.17 shows the message displayed when issuing a malformed query to a search engine. The user can click the message to get further information about the compromise.

Figure 11.17: Cross-site scripting filter message

As with all technology and cybercrime, it's a cat and mouse game between the administrators and users with the cybercriminals. Every time the good guys find a way to block or mitigate an attack, the bad guys (good/bad, I guess, depends on your point of view...) find a different way to perpetrate an exploit. Click-jacking is a growing threat to our online community; a savvy cybercriminal can create a website where a real page is placed in a frame in the attacker's page.

Clicking an item in the attacker's page allows the attacker to manipulate your input and have you view an advertisement at best or change your browser parameters at worst. IE8 includes code that allows developers not to let their websites be inserted into a frame in the IE8 interface, helping to mitigate the click-jacking event. The XSS filter and click-jack prevention code offer protection against malicious code in the website.

There is also a set of tools included in IE8 that help prevent the user from visiting a website that has been reported as unsafe or from downloading content that has been reported as unsafe. This protection is known as SmartScreen filtering.

Working with SmartScreen Filters

Microsoft maintains a database of unsafe websites that is checked while a user is browsing through websites. If the user chooses an unsafe website, IE8 blocks the user's request and presents a page that displays that the page has been identified as unsafe, as shown in Figure 11.18, and changes the background color of the address bar to reflect the same.

The user can continue to the web page if they are confident of the safety of the website by choosing More Options and continuing to the website. This functionality is part of the IE8 suite of technologies helping to protect users from the deceptive practices of cybercriminals. The SmartScreen filters also have the ability to block malware or phishing from within initially safe sites by including specific pages as unsafe in the Microsoft unsafe website database.

Another new feature related to SmartScreen filters is the ability to protect the user from unsafe downloads. If a user attempts to download a file and the file has been reported as unsafe (and accepted into the Microsoft database as unsafe), an Unsafe Download Security Warning dialog box is generated and the user is prevented from downloading the file. As with the unsafe website filter, the user can still continue the download if they are confident the file they are requesting is safe, as shown in Figure 11.19.

Figure 11.18: SmartScreen filter of an unsafe website

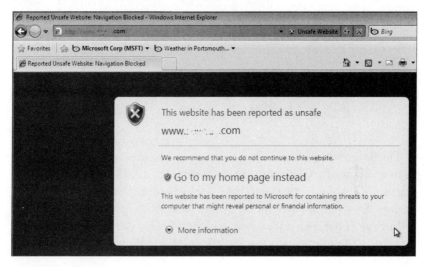

Figure 11.19: SmartScreen filter of an unsafe download

Administrators do have the option of configuring Group Policy for IE8 to disable the ability of the users to download unsafe files, if this is desired. You can manage SmartScreen Filtering functionality from the Safety menu of IE8. Figure 11.20 shows the option Turn Off SmartScreen Filter. Using the SmartScreen filter menu, you can check whether the current site has been reported as unsafe. (For instance, say you turned off SmartScreen filtering but would like to check a specific site.)

Figure 11.20: SmartScreen Filter options

The SmartScreen filter feature also gives you the ability to report a website as unsafe. Once your report is submitted, Microsoft will review the site and add it to their database if they determine it meets the criteria they have put in place for an unsafe website.

Microsoft has also added two new features for the safety of users by protecting their personal information: InPrivate browsing and InPrivate filtering.

Browsing with InPrivate Browsing and InPrivate Filtering

InPrivate browsing provides a level of privacy to IE8 users. The privacy maintained with InPrivate browsing relates to current browsing where an InPrivate session has been enabled. The InPrivate session prevents the browsing history from being recorded, nor will temporary Internet files be retained. Cookies, usernames, passwords, and form data will not remain in IE8 following the closing of the InPrivate session, thus leaving no footprints or data pertaining to the InPrivate browsing session.

This is a good method of protecting user data if you are not surfing from your own machine or are surfing from a public location (always a bad place to leave personal information). InPrivate browsing can also be used if you don't want anyone to be able to see data from your Internet browsing session.

There are several ways to launch an InPrivate IE8 browsing session. One way is to open a new tab and select the Open An InPrivate Browsing Window option from the Browse With InPrivate section. This opens a new tab, and the tab is an InPrivate session. You can also choose to open IE8 and start an InPrivate session directly by clicking Safety ➤ InPrivate Browsing, or open a new IE8 browser and press Ctrl+Shift+P. Figure 11.21 shows an InPrivate session launched with Ctrl+Shift+P; you are taken to `login.live.com`. This ensures that none of your login and browsing information is saved to this computer.

Figure 11.21: InPrivate browsing session

InPrivate browsing keeps information from being saved to the local machine while you're in the session, but don't get lulled into a false sense of security; malware, phishing, and other compromises that send data out of the local machine are still valid and can provide personal information to a cybercriminal.

InPrivate filtering takes a slightly different approach in providing security and safety to the user who is surfing using IE8. Many websites gather content from different sources as they present a web page to you. Some of these sources are websites outside the main location and provide third-party companies with tracking information about where you surf and what you look at.

This information can then be used to provide statistics as well as advertisements back to you. InPrivate filtering provides an added layer of control for the user to decide what information third-party websites have access to while browsing, thus limiting the ability for third-party websites to track your browsing usage.

InPrivate filtering is not enabled by default and must be enabled per browsing session. InPrivate filtering is enabled from the Safety menu in IE8, as shown in Figure 11.22. You can alternatively use Ctrl+Shift+F to enable InPrivate filtering.

Figure 11.22: Enabling InPrivate filtering

After you choose InPrivate Filtering, you are given the option to have IE8 automatically block some third-party content or choose to let the user select which third-party providers receive the user's browsing information, as shown in Figure 11.23. You can always go back and change the options later or turn off InPrivate filtering if you desire.

Figure 11.23: InPrivate Filtering options

After you enable InPrivate filtering, you can see which pages have been blocked as third-party queries from the InPrivate Filtering Settings dialog box. The InPrivate Filtering Settings dialog box is an alternate location for enabling (or disabling) InPrivate filtering, as shown in Figure 11.24. You open InPrivate Filtering Settings from IE8's Safety menu.

Figure 11.24: You can enable (or disable) InPrivate filtering here.

Along with the new security and safety features of IE8, there are several enhancements to existing features as well, which we'll discuss in the next section.

Use IE8's Enhanced Security and Safety Features

Among the enhancements to the security and safety features of IE8 are data execution prevention and an updated Automatic Crash Recovery function, as well as an enhanced Delete Browsing History feature.

Protecting Users with Data Execution Prevention

Data execution prevention (DEP) is enabled by default in IE8 and is a security feature of the browser. DEP helps to prevent malicious code from being run (or executed) in memory when it should not. Viruses, Trojans, and other dangerous software might try to execute code when they should not be able to. DEP prevents certain types of applications that are known to be malicious from writing to executable memory space. The various types of malicious code that are prevented are constantly being updated, and IE8 provides the latest information for the best layer of protection.

Along with DEP, IE8 includes an enhanced Automatic Crash Recovery feature to give the user a more seamless surfing experience, even when something goes wrong.

Dealing with Automatic Crash Recovery

When dealing with legacy Internet Explorer versions, users would have multiple browsers open at the same time. With the new implementations, you use the same instance of Internet Explorer running with individual tabs open for multiple websites. In the legacy implementation, if one IE instance crashes due to an application fault, the other browsers would remain active.

If all the sites you are browsing to are in one application, the potential for an all-out failure is present. Automatic Crash Recovery uses tab isolation so only a single tab is affected in case of an application or browser add-in failure. If a tab experiences a fault, the main IE8 browser application remains stable, as do the other tabs. IE8 also uses a better crash recovery model; if one (or more) of the tabs closes or crashes unexpectedly, the remaining tabs are automatically reloaded and you are returned to the site(s) you were on before the fault. This provides the user with a cleaner experience and less to think about in times of peril.

Another enhancement to the security and safety functionality of IE8 is the update to the Delete Browsing History functionality.

Controlling Browsing with Enhanced Delete Browsing History

With previous versions of Internet Explorer, you had the ability to delete your web browsing history and individual components (such as temporary Internet files, cookies, form data, and passwords) on an individual basis or delete them all at once. IE8 provides better control of what you want to delete (and keep, for that matter) with a check box selection. You access this option on IE8's Safety menu or by pressing Ctrl+Shift+Del. You are then presented with the Delete Browsing History dialog box, as shown in Figure 11.25, where you can decide what to delete and what not to delete.

Figure 11.25: Enhanced Delete Browsing History dialog box

The IE8 Delete Browsing History dialog box adds two new features that complement the new functionality in IE8 by including InPrivate filtering data as a component and allows you to delete (or keep) browsing history specific to your Favorites website data. This is a welcome addition to IE8 that gives users better control and an easier experience to keep their personal data out of the eyes of others. With all of the new and enhanced features of IE8, it is still the same browser you have become used to. IE8 should just be more helpful as you continue to use and configure it as you have done in previous versions.

Configure IE8

IE8 is used to surf the Internet as well as corporate intranets using HTTP, HTTPS, and FTP on a day-to-day basis. We have become used to surfing, but utilizing the browser's enhancements might not be something we're all familiar with. IE8 provides many features included in legacy Microsoft browsers that you might find useful if you have not discovered them. A search box tied to an Internet search engine, automatic Really Simple Syndication (RSS) feed detection and updating, add-on support providing third-party utilities, and a Pop-up Blocker are available to provide a better surfing experience. IE8 also includes Protected Mode functionality to help shield the user from malicious code.

Taking Advantage of the Instant Search Box

The Instant Search box of IE8 provides quick access to Internet search capabilities without the need to install a third-party toolbar or open more tabs to load a search engine page. The Instant Search box is located in the upper-right corner of IE8 and defaults to Bing as its search provider, as shown in Figure 11.26. By clicking the down arrow associated with the search box, you can configure other search providers as well as choose a different default, if you so desire.

Figure 11.26: Instant Search box in IE8

After you have more than one search provider listed, you can simply choose which provider you want to use, enter the search term, and hit Enter. You will also notice that as you add characters and words to the Instant Search box, IE8 will make suggestions and show visuals of potential search responses, allowing you a preview and the ability to select a previewed search result.

Adding a New Search Provider to the Instant Search Box

There might be times when you want to choose between two search providers when you are looking for something on the Internet.

Perform the following steps to add a new search provider to the Instant Search box:

1. Open IE8.

2. Choose the drop-down arrow from the Instant Search box in the upper-right corner of IE8.

3. Click the Find More Providers option.

4. Choose a search provider from the Microsoft Add-ons Gallery: Search Providers page (Wikipedia Visual Search, for example).

5. Click the Add button in the Add Search Provider dialog box.

6. Choose the drop-down arrow from the Instant Search box and note that you can now use the new provider to perform an Internet search.

Managing Search Providers

If you have included more than one search provider, you might want to manage them by changing the search order and having the search providers preview content.

Perform the following steps to change the search order of the search providers:

1. Open IE8 and add a search provider to the Instant Search box, if you haven't already done so (see "Adding a New Search Provider to the Instant Search Box" earlier).

2. Click the down arrow associated with the Instant Search box located in the upper-right corner of IE8.

3. Select the Manage Search Providers option.

4. In the Manage Add-ons window, select Search Providers in the Add-on Types section.

5. Select a search provider in the right side of the Manage Add-ons window.

6. Use the Move Up or Move Down text item below the Search Providers box to change the order of the search providers.

You also have the ability in IE8 to use RSS feeds and get a visual when there is updated content for you to read.

Configuring RSS

RSS is a content syndication technology that enables a website to syndicate content via an RSS file formatted in XML (known as a feed). As you visit sites that have an RSS feed available, you can subscribe to the feed and any updates to the content will be automatically downloaded to the host machine.

IE8 monitors and downloads the content and makes it available. Microsoft has added RSS support across many of its websites to enable users to automatically get updates and information about Microsoft products whenever new information is published. TechNet and the MSDN Microsoft sites use RSS feed to distribute information to users via RSS.

In IE8, any website that has an RSS feed is indicated by an orange Feeds icon. Clicking the orange icon lets the user pick from any of the feeds available on the page and keeps the content updated by checking periodically to see whether the data has changed. This is similar to the way Web Slices work (as described earlier in this chapter). The timing and other options for the RSS feed and Web Slice updates are found in the same configuration pages. Figure 11.27 shows two RSS feeds that are available on the TechNet home page (note that no Web Slices are available in the page).

Figure 11.27: RSS feed availability in a website

Subscribing to an RSS Feed

Perform the following steps to subscribe to a Microsoft TechNet RSS feed:

1. Open IE8.

2. Enter technet.microsoft.com in the address bar and press Enter.

3. Click the down arrow associated with the RSS feed icon in the tab bar.

4. Click the Featured TechNet Downloads RSS Feed option.

5. In the TechNet Featured Download page, you are given the option to subscribe to the feed. Click the subscribe link.

6. Click the Favorites star to open the Favorites window.

7. Select the Feeds tab to see that you have subscribed to the TechNet feed; by selecting the TechNet option, you can view the feed data.

Managing an RSS Feed

After you subscribe to an RSS feed, you can configure several options for the feed, such as how often the feed is checked for updates, whether attachments associated with the feed are downloaded, or how many updates should be saved.

Perform the following steps to modify the properties of an RSS feed:

1. Open IE8 and click the Favorites star to open the Favorites window.

2. Click the Feeds tab and right-click an RSS feed that you have subscribed to (if you need to subscribe to a feed, see the previous section, "Subscribing to an RSS Feed").

3. View the properties of the RSS feed and modify as desired.

As with the Instant Search box and RSS feeds, there are other features that might enhance your browsing experience but that are not specifically provided by Microsoft. These features might come in the form of an add-on.

Installing Add-ons to IE8

IE8 provides the ability to install add-ons to extend the functionality of the browser. Add-ons can improve the user experience by providing a simpler approach to resources, enhancing security, or simply providing enjoyment (a joke-of-the-day add-on, for example). Add-ons can be created by Microsoft, but many times you will find third-party add-ons to be equally as useful.

To enable, disable, or install add-ons, select Tools ➤ Manage Add-ons. This opens the Manage Add-ons dialog box. In the Add-on Types pane, select Toolbars And Extensions, and you can change the properties for installed add-ons in the right pane. By selecting an item, you can toggle it from enable to disabled, or vice versa, by clicking the button in the lower right. In Figure 11.28, you can see that the Shockwave Flash Object add-on is selected and enabled; the button in the lower left would be used to disable this add-on.

Figure 11.28: Manage Add-ons dialog box

If you were looking for more add-ons for your IE8, you could click Find More Toolbars And Extensions in the lower left of the Manage Add-ons windows. You can install and manage toolbars as well as search providers and extensions from the Manage Add-ons window.

Another feature of many websites is the pop-up windows the website developers include. IE8 includes functionality to block pop-ups dynamically.

Controlling Pop-ups

IE8 includes a Pop-up Blocker feature, which prevents pop-up pages from being displayed. Most of the time, advertisers and marketers use these pop-up pages to get users to view content in an attempt to convince them to click and buy. Not all pop-ups are malicious or advertisement-related and some may actually provide useful information. IE8's Pop-up Blocker is enabled by default, but does inform the user anytime a pop-up page is blocked. When a pop-up is blocked, the user has the option immediately to allow the pop-up to display. Figure 11.29 shows the message in IE8; as you can see, the user could allow the pop-up to be displayed.

Figure 11.29: Pop-up Blocker message

You can also allow a pop-up to be displayed from a website where it was blocked by IE8 by selecting Tools ➤ Pop-up Blocker ➤ Temporarily Allow Pop-ups or from the Pop-up Blocker selection of the Tools menu. The option Always Allow Pop-ups From This Site is also available, as well as the ability to open the Pop-up Blocker Settings page, as shown in Figure 11.30. The Pop-up Blocker Settings dialog box allows you to manage which sites will not have pop-ups blocked.

Figure 11.30: Pop-up Blocker Settings dialog box

In addition to providing the ability to create and maintain a list of sites approved for pop-ups, the Pop-up Blocker Settings dialog box lets you configure notification options. You can enable or disable the playing of a sound when a pop-up is blocked or control whether or not the information bar is displayed. The Blocking Level drop-down list gives you better control of which pop-ups are blocked and provides three levels of control:

- High: Block All Pop-ups (press Ctrl+Alt to override)
- Medium: Block Most Automatic Pop-ups
- Low: Allow Pop-ups from Secure Sites

By default, IE8 has the Blocking Level set to Medium.

Changing the Blocking Level for Pop-up Blocker

Perform the following steps to change the Blocking Level to Low for Pop-up Blocker.

1. Open IE8.
2. Select Tools ➢ Pop-up Blocker Settings.
3. Click the down arrow next to the Blocking Level drop-down list box.
4. Click the Low: Allow Pop-ups From Secure Sites option.
5. Click the Close button to exit the Pop-up Blocker Settings dialog box.

Adding a Website to the Allowed Sites for Pop-up Blocker

Perform the following steps to manually add a site for IE8 to allow pop-ups:

1. Open IE8.
2. Select Tools ➢ Pop-up Blocker Settings.
3. Enter a website for which you want to allow pop-ups to be displayed in the Address Of Website To Allow text box.
4. Click the Add button to include the desired website in the Allowed Sites text box.
5. Click the Close button to exit the Pop-up Blocker Settings dialog box.

Using Protected Mode

Protected Mode is a feature of Windows 7 for IE8 that forces IE8 to run in a protected, isolated memory space, thus preventing malicious code from writing data outside the Temporary Internet Files directly unless the program trying to write the information is specifically granted access by the user. Protected Mode is enabled by default and displayed in the lower-right corner of the IE8 window.

You can install software through IE8, but you will need to explicitly allow the modification of the file structure of Windows 7 if the software is going to install outside the protected directory. You can switch out of Protected Mode using the Security tab of IE8's Internet Options dialog box. To access this dialog box, select Tools ➤ Internet Options; or type **internet options** in the Start menu Search box in Windows 7. You also have the option of double-clicking Protected Mode: On at the bottom right of the IE8 interface to open just the Security tab of Internet Options, as shown in Figure 11.31.

Figure 11.31: Security tab of IE8's Internet Options

To change the Protected Mode settings, click to select or deselect the Enable Protected Mode (Requires Restarting Internet Explorer) check box. Microsoft recommends that Protected Mode remain active as it provides a greater level of security and safety for the user and does not prohibit an action (installing a program from IE8); it just requires interaction from the user to allow the modification.

Configuring IE8 Options

In addition to the security and usability options that you can configure in IE8, you can configure other options for managing the browser. Many of the configurations I have discussed in this chapter used the Safety or Tools options to quickly change individual parameters. The ability to change the individual parameters is also available from within the Internet Properties tabbed dialog box. This dialog box offers general parameters, security parameters, privacy configurations, content control, connection settings, program options, and advanced settings available for Internet options.

General Parameters in Internet Properties

You can open the Internet Properties dialog box by selecting Tools ➢ Internet Properties or by typing **internet options** in the Start menu Search box in Windows 7. The General tab, as shown in Figure 11.32, allows you to change the default home page that displays when IE8 is launched. An interesting feature here is that you can have more than one default home page. By entering more than one page in the Home Page text box, every time IE8 is launched each of these pages will open in its own tab.

Figure 11.32: General tab of IE8's
Internet Properties

The General tab also allows you to control your browsing history settings, search settings, tabs, and the appearance (including accessibility options) of the IE8 interface.

Security Parameters in Internet Properties

The Security tab of the Internet Properties dialog box not only gives you access to control Protected Mode (as seen earlier in this section), but also gives you the ability to set security settings on the specific zones you may browse to. The zones are the Internet, Local Intranet, Trusted Sites, and Restricted Sites. You can set the behavior of IE8 individually for each zone and even individual sites within each zone.

Privacy Configurations in Internet Properties

The Privacy tab, as shown in Figure 11.33, allows you to manage privacy settings for the Internet zone; this is the cookie management for specific sites.

You can also control the settings for the Pop-up Blocker and your InPrivate filtering and InPrivate browsing here.

Figure 11.33: Privacy tab of Internet Properties

Content Control in Internet Properties

Figure 11.34 shows the Content tab of the Internet Properties dialog. Parental controls let you manage which sites are available through web filtering and monitoring of website access using the Activity Monitor. There has to be a privileged account with a password set to enforce parental controls. InPrivate browsing is not allowed when parental controls are in place.

Figure 11.34: Content tab of Internet Properties

You can enable Content Advisor settings on the Content tab. Content Advisor displays rated sites as users browse to different locations. Certificate management for secure browsing is managed through the Content tab as well. You have the ability to manage AutoComplete functionality and manage RSS feeds and Web Slice data here, too.

Connection Settings in Internet Properties

The Connections tab of the Internet Properties dialog box allows you to manage the way IE8 gains access to the network. You can initiate the Connect To The Internet Wizard on this tab as well as set up a virtual private network. If you are using dial-up networking, you can also configure this connection from the Connections tab. Local area network (LAN) general settings are configured on this tab. You can specify a proxy server if you need to use one (this is typical across many corporate sites as well as to provide a better level of anonymity for Internet surfing).

Program Options in Internet Properties

The Programs tab of the Internet Properties dialog box allows you to control which browser you are using as your default web browser. You can manage add-ons specific to IE8 on the Programs tab as well. You can set up an application to allow for HTML editing and set up default programs to be used for Internet services such as email.

Advanced Settings in Internet Properties

The Advanced tab, shown in Figure 11.35, allows you to configure advanced configuration settings for IE8. Some of the advanced configuration items include accessibility settings, browsing settings, international browsing settings, encoding settings, multimedia parameters, printing parameters, and general security settings. You can control whether links are underlined, whether pictures should be displayed, which versions of the secure communication protocols or SSL are used, background colors, and many other parameters.

Figure 11.35: Advanced tab of Internet Properties

In addition to being able to change the advanced settings, you also have the option to restore advanced settings to their original configurations or reset the Internet Explorer settings (clicking this option resets all IE8 settings, not just the advanced settings, to the default configuration).

IE8, with all of its new and exciting features for user browsing, safety, and security, provides a solid foundation for users to enjoy Internet surfing and gives administrators comfort with the knowledge that their users will be on the network safely. Many of the enhancements provide administrators with more peace of mind about the integrity of the network, as well as being able to suppress the intentions of cybercriminals without dramatically affecting the surfers.

12

Installing and Configuring Applications

IN THIS CHAPTER, YOU WILL LEARN TO:

N ow that you have installed and configured Windows 7, it's time to install and use applications. Windows 7 introduced Live Essentials, a new downloadable program suite, to use some of the built-in programs from Vista.

Previous versions of Windows introduced applications like Mail, Calendar, Contacts, a Getting Started welcome center, Fax and Scan, Media Player, and Media Center. These applications gave users quick access to features they would use on a day-to-day basis, but only on the local machine.

Windows 7 utilizes Live Essentials for Mail and Calendar to make online access to those applications available, but it also allows offline access to users' data, which enhances and simplifies application use. It is still fairly straightforward to install, repair, change, and uninstall other commercial applications as well.

Having everyday applications available in Windows 7 allows efficient productivity for users as well as administrators because users spend less time installing and updating applications. With the new online collaboration of Live Essentials, functionality previously available only in Windows Vista is now available from any Internet-accessible location.

Windows 7's built-in applications also allow you to use your PC as a hub for multimedia by providing functionality to access audio and video that is stored on your PC from the Internet. You can also send the same audio and video to other media-capable devices within your local network.

Use Getting Started in Windows 7

Windows Vista provided you with a welcome center that launched automatically by default after you logged in. This window displayed the edition of Windows Vista that's installed, the CPU, the amount of RAM, the video card, and the computer name. Windows 7 also features a welcome center, where you are presented with a Getting Started window, as shown in Figure 12.1.

The Getting Started window does not show you the hardware configuration of your PC or which version of Windows 7 you have, but it does offer several links to the following features of Windows 7 that are commonly set up when you first get started:

- Go Online To Find Out What's New In Windows 7
- Use A Homegroup To Share With Other Computers In Your Home

- Back Up Your Files

- Personalize Windows

- Choose When To Be Notified About Changes To Your Computer

- Add New Users To Your Computer

- Transfer Files And Settings From Another Computer

- Go Online To Get Windows Live Essentials

- Change The Size Of The Text On Your Screen

Figure 12.1: Getting Started in Windows 7

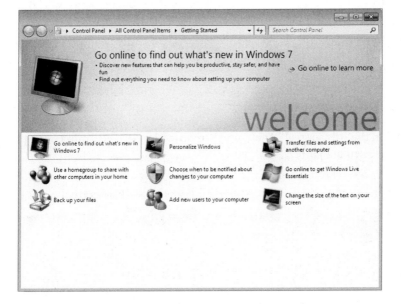

All of the items in the Getting Started window are available from various locations in the Windows 7 interface, and you can even launch them individually from the Start menu Search box. Rather than search around, use Getting Started to gain access by typing **Getting Started** in the Search box.

You can also open the Getting Started window with these steps:

1. Click Start ➢ Control Panel.

2. Choose System And Security.

3. On the left side of the System And Security screen, click Control Panel Home, as shown in Figure 12.2.

Figure 12.2: Select Control Panel Home.

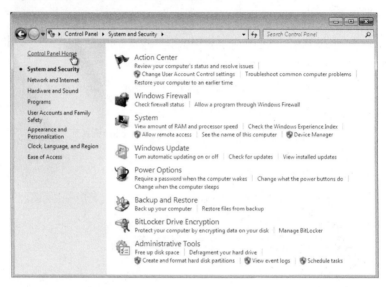

4. In the All Control Panel Items window, choose Getting Started, as shown in Figure 12.3.

Figure 12.3: Choose Getting Started in the All Control Panel Items window.

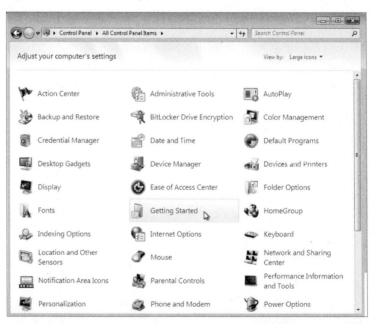

If you need to access the hardware configuration of your PC or version of Windows 7, you can still do so from the System window in Control Panel. The easiest way is to type **system** in the Start menu Search box and select System from the Control Panel section, as shown in Figure 12.4.

Figure 12.4: Choosing System from Windows 7 search results

The System window that shows the hardware configuration is shown in Figure 12.5.

You can also choose Start ➢ Control Panel ➢ System And Security ➢ System or choose Start, right-click Computer in the Start menu, and select Properties to access the System window.

Although Getting Started gives you access to many of the common initial configuration tasks, you should note that there is no task to configure email. In fact, in Windows 7 no email client is available from the distribution—you must download it, which I discuss in the next section.

Figure 12.5: Windows 7 System window

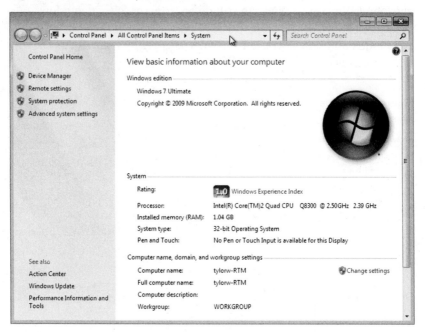

Access Email in Windows 7

Windows Mail was introduced in Vista as the replacement for Outlook Express. Windows Mail added new functionality, such as junk email filters. In Windows 7, the Windows Mail program is not available (nor is Outlook Express). Microsoft has opted to include the email program in its Live Essentials download. Why did Microsoft do this? The company seems to have decided that having the users install the more collaborative applications after the fact will give the users better control over which applications they install.

The basic installation of Windows 7 has become so streamlined that you barely have to stop and make any decisions. After the installation, users can simply install or uninstall programs as desired. If they have to go online to get their applications, users will be more inclined to use Windows Live, a set of collaborative servers. Again, what does this mean? Live Messenger includes a set of contacts, so why not use the same contacts list for email? Many of the web-based email providers

(Yahoo! and Google, for example) also provide contacts, messaging, and email.

Your Windows Live account, Live Mail, Live Messenger, and other collaborative programs that might become available in the future can share your collected information across the applications.

Microsoft Live Essentials

You can get the Essentials bundle from http://download.live.com. After the web page loads, you might want to take a few minutes to review the available items. Once you decide, click the Download button and either save the file to run later or run the downloaded file directly. After you run the downloaded file, you will be shown the installation options.

Installing Live Mail

To use Live Mail in Windows 7, you must download and run the installation of the Live Essentials programs. You can choose which applications associated with Live Essentials you want to install. Selecting the Mail option will install Live Mail. Setting up an email account is the first task you'll undertake after you install Live Mail.

Setting Up Email Accounts Using Live Mail

After you install Live Mail, you will set up an email account for access. Assuming you have an SMTP server account, you set up the configuration just as you would with Windows Mail or Outlook Express. With your login credentials, SMTP server, and POP3 server parameters, you are able to compose and read email. In the Windows Live Mail window shown in Figure 12.6, you click Add E-mail Account to launch a wizard that prompts you for configuration parameters.

Perform the following steps to set up a new email account:

1. Open Live Mail by choosing Start ➢ Windows Live Mail.

2. If this is the first time Live Mail has been opened, the Add E-mail Account wizard starts. If this is not the first time Live Mail has been opened, you must select Add E-mail Account in the main window, as shown in Figure 12.6.

3. Type the email address of the account you are adding, the email account password, and the display name for the account.

Figure 12.6: Click Add E-mail Account in Live Mail.

4. Select the check box in the bottom left of the wizard to manually configure server settings for the email account, and then click Next.

5. Enter the parameters for your email account incoming and outgoing mail server type, along with their authorization parameters, and click Next.

6. Choose Finish, and your new email account is added to Live Mail.

There are several other parameters that you can use to configure the way Live Mail behaves. Next, I'll show you how to use the Options dialog box to customize Live Mail's actions.

Configuring Options in Live Mail

Live Mail will work as soon as you configure an email account, but you might want to tweak it for a personalized experience. To access the Options dialog box, press the Alt key to activate the standard menu bar. Click Tools ➢ Options to open the Options dialog box, as shown in Figure 12.7.

Figure 12.7: Accessing Live Mail Options dialog box

The General tab of the Options dialog box (see Figure 12.8) lets you configure general options, specify how messages are to be sent and received, and select default messaging programs. New options are available in Live Mail that allow you to automatically log on to Windows Live Messenger and to participate in the Windows Live improvement program by allowing Microsoft to collect information about your system and how you use the program (this option is not selected by default).

Figure 12.8: The General tab of Live Mail's Options dialog box

The Read and the Receipts tabs, as shown in Figure 12.9, allow you to configure the behavior of Windows Mail when messages are read and received. You can also use the Read tab to specify newsgroup behavior and to select the default font and encoding method to be used for reading messages. Use the Receipts tab to configure whether read receipts are requested or sent. You can also configure Secure receipts.

Figure 12.9: The Read and Receipts tabs of Live Mail's Options dialog box

Use the Send tab to configure the behavior of Live Mail when messages are sent. You can also use this tab to configure whether mail and newsgroup messages are sent in HTML or plain text. The Compose tab lets you configure the default font, stationery, and business card that are used for sending mail and newsgroup messages. The Send and Compose tabs are shown in Figure 12.10.

Applications

PART V

Figure 12.10: The Send and Compose tabs of Live Mail's Options dialog box

The Signatures tab, shown in Figure 12.11, lets you add, remove, and configure signatures. Signatures are the text automatically added to the bottom of outgoing messages. They are configured as straight text or added as a file.

On the Spelling tab (see Figure 12.12), you configure whether Windows Mail will check for spelling errors either before sending or while you are typing the message (the latter is a new feature of Live Mail). The Spelling tab features options for automatically correcting common capitalization and spelling mistakes as well as checking spelling in the current input language. The Spelling tab also lets you choose to ignore spelling when words are in uppercase or contain numbers, and whether the original text is checked for spelling.

Figure 12.11: The Signatures tab of Live Mail's Options dialog box

Figure 12.12: The Spelling tab of Live Mail's Options dialog box

The Connection tab (see Figure 12.13) lets you configure dial-up and Internet connection behavior. Live Mail uses the same Internet Connection settings that Internet Explorer uses. The Connection tab also lets you sign in to your Windows Live account or tell Live Mail to stop signing you in.

Figure 12.13: The Connection tab of Live Mail's Options dialog box

The last tab in the Options dialog box is the Advanced tab, as shown in Figure 12.14. You use the Advanced tab to configure IMAP settings, message threads, replies, and forwards. You can also click the Maintenance button to open the dialog box shown in Figure 12.15, which lets you configure maintenance tasks—such as whether deleted items are emptied on exit and how the database is compacted. The Maintenance dialog box also lets you clean up your newsgroup messages and change the location of your message storage, known as the Store Folder. You can configure the troubleshooting logs from the Maintenance window as well.

Figure 12.14: The Advanced tab of Live Mail's Options dialog box

Figure 12.15: Click the Maintenance button to open this dialog box.

The security configuration for virus protection features, such as whether an application attempts to send an email on your behalf, was formerly found on the Security tab in Windows Mail's Options window. In Live Mail, these configurations are found in the Safety window.

Setting Up Safety Parameters in Live Mail

Live Mail includes enhanced safety features to help protect users and give them a better email experience by:

- Identifying and handling junk email
- Setting up blocked sender and safe sender lists
- Configuring disallowed top-level domains (international countries and entities)
- Filtering phishing email
- Adding security features

You configure these features in the Safety Options dialog box of Live Mail. To access this window, activate the standard menu bar by pressing Alt and then select Tools ➤ Safety Options. This dialog box includes individual tabs for configuring the safety parameters.

The Options tab of the Safety Options dialog box, as shown in Figure 12.16, allows you to configure the junk mail settings for Live Mail.

Figure 12.16: The Options tab of Live Mail's Safety Options dialog box

The Options tab lets you choose the level of junk mail:

- No Automatic Filtering

- Low

- High

- Safe List Only

Two options at the bottom of this tab are "Permanently delete suspected junk e-mail instead of moving it to the Junk E-mail folder" and "Report junk e-mail to Microsoft and its partners (recommended)."

The Safe Senders and Blocked Senders tabs are shown in Figure 12.17. These tabs allow you to configure a list of addresses you want to always allow or block.

Figure 12.17: The Safe Senders and Blocked Senders tabs of Live Mail's Safety Options dialog box

The International tab allows you to choose which top-level domains you would like to block and which character sets may be present in an email you choose to block. Figure 12.18 shows the

International tab as well as the Blocked Top-Level Domain List and Blocked Encodings List dialog boxes.

Figure 12.18: The International, Blocked Top-Level Domain List, and Blocked Encodings List tabs of Live Mail's Safety Options dialog box

Accessing Email on the Web Using Live Mail Online

One great feature of Live Mail is the ability to integrate your local email with a web-based email that gives you access to your email from any location with Internet access. The email you access on the Web will initially be your Live email account, but you can even add your other accounts to the web-based version. Using web-based email has proven to be convenient for many users. Live Mail will boost your productivity and user experience to new levels of usefulness by integrating your web-based email with your local email program.

Live Mail conveniently integrates your email contacts and messaging. Also, having a calendar available for keeping track of appointments as well as setting up free time will make Live Mail one step closer to a complete collaborative solution.

Using the Live Mail Calendar

Windows Vista includes a program called Windows Calendar that allows you to create events and appointments in a local calendar and then publish the local calendar and perhaps even share it. In Windows 7, the calendar functionality is appropriately part of Live Mail. This calendar is stored in your Live account, making it available anytime you log in. You may want to use it only locally like the Vista version, but having it online makes the calendar even more functional.

Calendar is available from within the Live Mail program; you launch the Calendar program from the lower-left pane. You are presented with the Calendar window shown in Figure 12.19. A toolbar is available that lets you change your view from month to week or to the day.

Figure 12.19: Live Mail Calendar

The toolbar also gives you the ability to add new events or create new calendars, as shown in Figure 12.20. By creating new calendars, you can have multiple calendars all tied to Live Mail. You can also create a new email message, photo email, news message, or contact by using the New menu.

Figure 12.20: Live Mail Calendar's New menu

Applications

PART V

So far we've looked at a local implementation of Calendar, but if you have a Live account, you can sign up for a Live.com mail account and your calendar will then be available any time you log into Live. You can share any of the calendars you have created with friends or colleagues, and you can have one collaborative location. Be assured that you do not have to share all or any of your calendars if you choose not to.

In addition to integrating your email and calendar functionality with a web presence as well as local access, Live Mail provides you with the ability to add friends and colleagues to a common database accessible from your local machine or online.

Using Live Mail Contacts

Live Mail Contacts is a component in the Live suite that is used to store contact information for individuals. You can access Contacts by selecting Contacts in the lower-left pane in Live Mail. The Contacts window, shown in Figure 12.21, lets you create, modify, and delete contacts and contact groups. You can also use your default email program to compose an email message to the selected contact.

Figure 12.21: Live Mail Contacts window

Adding a new contact is as simple as clicking New ➤ Contact, as shown in Figure 12.22.

Figure 12.22: Choose New ➤ Contact to add a new contact.

Within each contact, you can record a great deal of information by clicking the Quick Add button (as shown in Figure 12.23). This information includes the following:

- First name
- Last name
- Personal email
- Home phone
- Company

Figure 12.23: Click the Quick Add button.

You can go even further with your contact information by adding many personal items to the contact information, such as the following:

- Additional contact information

- Personal information

- Work information

- Internet Messaging (IM) information

- Notes

- Digital IDs

As with Live Mail and Calendar, the contact information can also be made available to your Live account so your contacts are never more than an Internet connection away. Live Mail provides a set of applications available to you as a Windows 7 user and administrator. Some applications come installed in Windows 7 by default that provide more features and functionality to the users, such as Windows Fax and Scan.

Integrate Windows Fax and Scan

Windows Fax and Scan enables you to send and receive faxes without a fax machine. You can also use Windows Fax and Scan to scan documents so that you can fax or email them. To configure fax support and set fax properties, select Start ➤ All Programs ➤ Windows Fax And Scan. The Windows Fax and Scan application starts, as shown in Figure 12.24.

Figure 12.24: Windows Fax and Scan

Configuring Fax Support

Windows 7 allows you to add and configure fax support. You can add fax support to your computer even if a fax machine is not available. You configure fax support through the Windows Fax and Scan application.

Adding a Fax Account

Before you can send or receive faxes, you must first create an account. To create an account, click Tools ➤ Fax Accounts and then click Add to create an account. You are prompted to connect to a fax modem on your computer or to a fax server.

Setting Fax Properties

To configure fax settings, click Tools ➤ Fax Settings. The Fax Settings dialog box displays and has four tabs with options and information for your fax support, as follows:

General   The General tab displays the device name and provides the ability to configure the device parameters to send and receive faxes.

Tracking   From the Tracking tab, you can set up notification options for fax events and configure the Fax Monitor to display progress when faxes are sent or received. You can also configure sound options in the Tracking tab.

Advanced   The Advanced tab enables you to configure which folder is used for receiving faxes. Sent faxes will also be stored in the specified folder. It also allows you to include a banner with the fax. The Advanced tab lets you configure the number of redials to perform, and the start and end times for sending faxes.

Security   Settings on the Security tab enable you to configure which users or groups can send and receive faxes and who can manage fax configuration.

Starting the Fax Service

After you configure fax support, you need to start the Fax Service in Windows 7. Perform the following steps to start the service:

1. Right-click Computer on the Start menu and select Manage from the context menu.

2. Expand Services and Applications and then Services.

3. Double-click Fax Service and click the Start button.

4. Select Automatic as the Startup Type and click OK.

5. Close the Computer Management window.

Managing Imaging Devices

A scanner is a device that can read text or graphics that are on paper and translate the information to digital data that the computer can understand. After you install a scanner on a Windows 7 computer, you can manage the device through the Windows Fax and Scan application.

If the scanner is a USB scanner, simply connecting the device to the computer should install the appropriate driver, and the scanner will be available in the Windows Fax and Scan application. To configure a scanner that is attached to your computer, click Scan in the lower-left corner of the Windows and Fax application, and then click Tools ➤ Scan Settings, which opens the Scan Profiles dialog box.

If you have a scanner installed on your computer, perform the following steps to view and configure its properties:

1. Select Start ➤ All Programs ➤ Windows Fax And Scan.

2. In the Windows Fax and Scan application, click Scan in the lower-left corner.

3. Select the scanner to modify and then click the Edit button.

4. Modify the settings as desired and then click Save Profile.

5. Click Close to close the Scan Profiles dialog box.

6. Close the Windows Fax and Scan application.

Windows 7 has even more applications installed and available for your convenience, such as Media Player for listening to audio and viewing video.

Use Windows Media Player 12

Windows Media Player 12, shown in Figure 12.25, enables you to play digital media, organize your media files, burn CDs and DVDs, synchronize files to a portable music player, and shop for digital media online.

To open Windows Media Player 12, choose Start ➤ All Programs ➤ Windows Media Player.

Figure 12.25: Windows Media Player 12

Understanding the Windows Media Player 12 Interface

The new version of Windows Media Player in Windows 7 has a different look and feel than previous versions. Microsoft is following their goals of making the user experience easier by rearranging menu items to a more logical placement. Windows Media Player 12 has two views you can toggle between:

- The Library view (the default view when opening Windows Media Player 12 from the Start menu)
- The Now Playing view

Toggle between the Library and Now Playing views by clicking the icon in the lower right of the Library view or the upper right of the Now Playing view, as shown in Figure 12.26.

Figure 12.26: Windows Media Player 12
Now Playing view

Windows Media Player 12 organizes your media into several categories available in the Library view. The categories include:

Playlists   Choosing Save List from your list of songs saves the list as a playlist, which makes it available for future access.

Music   Any digital music Windows Media Player 12 has discovered on your PC is located in this category. Media files discovered include MP3, WMA, WAV, and so forth.

Videos   Any videos you have saved from cameras or have downloaded are saved in this category. Media files discovered for this category include AVI, MPEG, WMV, DivX, and so forth.

Pictures   Media Player saves digital pictures on your PC in this category and can display them to you. File types discovered for this category include JPEG, GIF, and so forth.

Recorded TV   If your PC has the hardware installed to capture TV, any recorded programs are saved into the Recorded TV category.

Other Libraries   The Other Libraries category holds media that is stored on other Windows 7 machines in the same HomeGroup as your PC. This category might also hold items you've added that Windows Media Player 12 doesn't recognize.

The following tabbed menu items are available in the Library view of Windows Media Player 12:

Play   Used to play a CD or DVD, create and clear playlists, and see what's currently being played.

Burn Used to burn music to a CD or data to a CD or DVD. You can burn at various speeds, apply volume leveling to audio CDs, and convert music to a different bit rate.

Sync Used to perform two-way synchronization of data between your computer and a portable media device, a flash memory device, or a Portable Media Center.

You can use Windows Media Player 12 as a launching spot to shop online for digital media. Select the drop-down list box in the lower-left corner, as shown in Figure 12.27, to access the Browse All Online Stores option.

Figure 12.27: Media options in Windows Media Player 12

When you play, burn, or sync a protected file, Windows Media Player checks to see whether you have valid media usage rights. If you have valid rights, you are allowed to play, burn, or sync the file. Normally, media usage rights are automatically downloaded for you. So why can't you play your file if you've got a connection to the Internet? Check to see if Download Usage Rights Automatically When I Play Or Sync A File is selected on the Privacy tab of the Options dialog box. If it is enabled, you might have to restore your media usage rights from the online store where you purchased your digital media. Playing a music CD in Windows Media Player 12 can be as simple as inserting the CD into your PC.

Playing Music CDs in Windows Media Player 12

Playing an audio CD in Windows 7 should be straightforward, because Windows Media Player 12 recognizes the insertion of a music CD into your PC and launches the Player view automatically. Some CDs that contain digital music might prompt Windows 7 to display a dialog box that asks you what you want to do. This happens sometimes when you create your own music CDs and Windows 7 simply sees the music as files. The dialog box offers you the option to play the audio CD, which launches Windows Media Player 7.

If by some chance another program plays your audio CD, then Windows Media Player 7 might not be the default program for playing audio CDs. Perhaps the file format on the CD is captured by another program. You can close the other program and launch Windows Media Player 12 from the Start menu and choose to play an audio CD.

Playing music CDs in Windows 7 using Windows Media Player 12 is fairly simple, but what about movies? Windows Media Player 12 also recognizes DVDs.

Playing DVDs in Windows Media Player 12

Windows Media Player 12 will react similarly to DVDs as it does for CDs: It will launch automatically into the Now Playing view when you insert a video DVD in your PC's DVD drive. Being able to play multiple media formats without user intervention is another way Microsoft is trying to make the music and movie experience simple.

To play your DVD movie in full-screen view, press and hold the Alt key and then press Enter. Return to the windowed view by pressing the same keystrokes. While in full-screen view, moving your mouse cursor will bring up the play controls, but they will disappear after a few moments of not moving the cursor.

You can play other video files in the same interface as the DVD movie screen as well. You can double-click movies that you have captured on a digital camera or from an Internet source in the Videos library and control them just as you would a DVD movie. What if you have a TV tuner built in or added to your PC? Windows 7's Media Center lets you control this added input.

Control Digital Media with Windows Media Center

Windows Media Center is included in the Home Premium, Professional, and Ultimate editions of Windows 7. Windows Media Center adds the ability to watch, pause, and record live TV (as long as you have the appropriate TV tuner hardware installed). You can also view online entertainment within Windows Media Center from around the world. Windows Media Center plays CDs, DVDs, music, and video much the same way Windows Media Player does, but with more controls available to the user.

When you launch Windows Media Center for the first time, you are prompted to go through a setup wizard. Windows Media Center is a little more intense than most. There is an express mode, but it will still take you a few minutes for the install application to go through your PC looking for music, videos, and so forth; to ask you questions about your home network and Internet connections; to ask which area of the world you live in (for a TV programming guide); and even ask you for the provider for your TV programming (if you have the TV tuner installed). If you don't know all the answers, you can guess and go back later to change any incorrect parameters if you need to. Changing the parameters after the fact is your first exercise in using the Windows Media Center menu structure.

Using Windows Media Centers Menus

Windows Media Center offers a lot of options for users, and creating access to the options in a convenient manner was an obvious challenge. The Microsoft team seems to have found a great solution by using both vertical and horizontal scrolling for the menu structure. Keep in mind that Windows Media Center is designed to be at home equally on a TV screen as well as a PC monitor. Figure 12.28 shows Windows Media Center as it might appear upon launching if the last thing you were doing was browsing music.

Figure 12.28: Windows Media Center's main screen

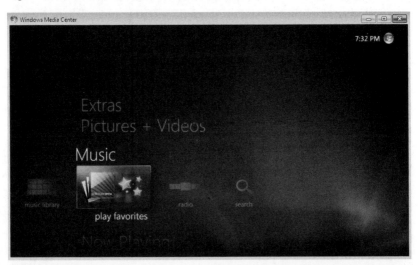

To browse through the various categories offered by Windows Media Center, you use the vertical scrolling options. You access the up and down arrows to scroll through the categories by moving your mouse cursor to a position above or below the categories, and the scroll arrows appear as shown in Figure 12.29.

Figure 12.29: Windows Media Center category selection scroll arrows

After you find the category you are looking for, you can scroll through the items within that category by scrolling horizontally. Access the horizontal scroll arrows by moving your mouse cursor to the left or right of the category item, and Windows Media Center will display the appropriate arrow. Figure 12.30 shows the left scroll arrow displayed for the Extras category.

Figure 12.30: The left scroll arrow displayed for the Extras category

You can scroll through the following categories in the Windows Media Center:

Extras   The Extras category displays miscellaneous items such as an Extras library where you can find Windows 7 games, Explore option, Internet TV, News, a Learn How item for interactive help, and new hardware Extenders for Windows Media Center allowing access to your audio and video content on your local network.

Pictures + Videos   Pictures + Videos gives you access to your picture library, video library, and favorites lists.

Music   The Music category gives you access to your music library, favorites music lists, the ability to search for music, and a radio option that has the ability to capture radio signals being carried by your TV provider (if you have the tuner installed).

Now Playing   If you want to go back to what you were listening to or watching before you accessed the menu structure, you can return by selecting the Now Playing category.

Movies   The Movies category allows you to access your movie library, which is where you will find any recorded video you have, movie guides, and movie trailers. You can even play a DVD.

TV   The TV category follows the Movies category in structure, allowing you access to recorded video, TV guides and schedules, live TV setup, and search functionality (by title, actor, director, and so forth).

Sports   If you're looking for sports scores, team player information, or sports league information, the Sports category is where you would look.

Tasks   The Tasks category is where you visit (or revisit) to change your setup options. Figure 12.31 shows the Tasks category with the Settings option selected. Click the Settings box to access the setup parameters and make changes if necessary.

Figure 12.31: The Tasks category with the Settings option

Along with the standard categories of files you can access on your local machine with Windows Media Center, you can also access other devices on your network and enjoy available media stored elsewhere.

Accessing Other Devices on Your Network with Windows Media Center

You can have one of your machines set up to use a TV and sound system for viewing and listening to your digital media, utilizing the functionality of Window Media Center. If you have some of your media resources stored on other devices in your network, Media Center provides a central location for accessing the resources and playing them for you. Media Center has the ability to connect to your networked Xbox 360, displaying its library of music, photos, and movies. You can use the Windows 7 HomeGroup functionality to allow other Windows 7 machines on your network to supply music, photos, and video as well.

Windows Media Center, Windows Media Player, and Windows Fax and Scan are programs installed in Windows 7 by default. Live Essentials is a package downloaded and installed via the Web. What if you have purchased a software program and need to install it? Relax, we've come a long way and Windows 7 will protect itself while allowing applications to be installed and then cleanly uninstall themselves when required.

Install and Uninstall Applications in Windows 7

Using the built-in applications in Windows 7 is all well and good, but there will certainly be other applications that will need to be installed. Microsoft might be the author of the applications, or it might be other software vendors. You may install from a CD or DVD or download the installation files from a website and then install the application. No matter which way you get the application, you will more than likely have to go through an installation process.

Installing an Application from a Disk

One of the operating system protection features of Windows 7 is that in order to install an application, you must have administrator privileges on the machine. You must be able to enter the username and password of an administrator of the local machine in order for the application to install and make the necessary configuration changes. This requirement applies to any installation location, not just from a CD or DVD disk.

Launching the Installation Program

Most commercial programs you purchase will be delivered via DVD or CD media and should come with a set of installation instructions. Just like everything else in our computing world, program installation is designed to be simple and seamless, and most written instructions state that you should insert the DVD or CD into the drive and follow the onscreen instructions.

To start an application installation, follow these steps:

1. Close any programs you might be running on your machine. This step is not required, but it's always a good idea.

2. Insert the application installation media into the appropriate disk drive.

3. Wait for the automated installation program to launch (this might take a moment or two).

4. Follow the onscreen instructions.

Normally the onscreen instructions are in the form of a wizard and will walk you through a series of questions (the fewer the better) as you click the Next button to continue. It's nice that most vendors include a default set of answers where possible so that many times you can just "next through the installation" and make changes to the configuration later if necessary. When all is done, you're normally presented with a confirmation screen saying all is well and you can click the Finish button to exit the installation.

There might be times when the automated start does not occur when you insert the installation disc. Why? Well, some users disable the Autorun feature so they don't get prompted each time a disc is inserted.

If your installation does not start automatically, perform the following steps to start the installation.

1. Choose Start ➤ Computer to open the computer window where you can access the drives in your PC.

2. Double-click the drive where you inserted the installation disc to start the automated setup program.

You might be one more step away from launching the application installation if the automated installation does not launch from the previous steps. You might need to locate the setup application and launch it manually.

Perform the following steps to manually launch an application installation.

1. Choose Start ➤ Computer to open the computer window where you can access the drives in your PC.

2. Right-click the drive where you inserted the installation disc and select Explore from the context menu.

3. Locate the application installation program, normally named setup.exe, and double-click the file; this should launch the setup program, thus allowing the installation to commence.

After the installation starts, you normally are presented with an installation wizard that provides a series of installation prompts as you progress through the installation.

Dealing with the Standard Installation Prompts

There are several standard prompts you might encounter as you install your application. You will be prompted for the following in most wizard-based installations:

A Serial Number, Registration Number, or Product Key   Most current commercial installation programs require some sort of validation that you have purchased a license to run the application. This is in the form of a serial number, registration number, or license key that is unique to your installation. The installation wizard prompts you for this parameter and will not continue without it. In some cases you can continue and use the application on a trial basis without entering a value, but you will most certainly need to purchase the license to fully use the product or continue beyond a trial period.

An End-User License Agreement (EULA)   Almost all commercial and most shareware/freeware applications want you to read and agree to a legal document outlining your rights to the program as well as retained rights from the vendor to the use of their program. The EULA is this agreement, and you won't be able to continue with the installation unless you agree to abide by its terms. Most of the time, you will not read this document as it is long and boring, but you *really* should. It may also outline multiple machine usage, copying of the disk for backup, and even whether you can sell the program to someone else when you're done with it.

Type of Application Installation   The goal of most vendors is to make the installation as simple as possible, but there might be times when you want to add your input to the installation by configuring advanced options. Most programs offer two types of installation: Express, where most (if not all) of the installation questions are answered by default for you by the software vendor, and Advanced, where you are given the opportunity to answer most of the configuration questions as the application installation wizard progresses.

Where to Install the Program Icon   After the installation, you want to run the application (that's why you are installing it). Most setup programs give you the option of adding the program icon to the desktop and/or adding it to the Start menu. It will be added to your program menu even if you don't choose either of the two options.

Installation Summary   Most current installation programs present the user with an installation summary at the completion of the installation, with any parameters you configured displayed.

After you install the program, you can run it by clicking the desktop icon (if you added it), choosing Start and selecting the application (if you added it to the Start menu), or choosing Start ➤ All Programs and finding the application in its All Programs folder. Even though you provided answers to configuration questions (or were provided with defaults), many programs will still ask you application-specific questions when you initially launch the program.

Occasionally files associated with an application might become corrupted or an application file might get inadvertently deleted; in this case, you may need to repair the installation.

Repairing or Changing an Application

In some cases, you might need to revisit an application's installation options. If you chose one type of installation—Express, for example—and then realize there are more components that you need, you might want to change the installed application items. Because these components were part of the install, you need to go through the installation process again to change them. You can use the Change option for your application from Control Panel.

Perform the following steps to access the Change option for an application.

1. Choose Start, type **control** in the Search box, and press Enter (you can also select Control Panel from the Start menu).

2. In Control Panel, select Programs.

3. In the Programs window, select Programs And Features.

4. In the Programs And Features window, select the application you want to change and then choose Change from the menu.

After you perform the previous steps, a new instance of the application installation program starts and you can change the original options to meet your needs. Figure 12.32 shows the choices for step 2, 3, and 4 selections that were used in the previous task.

Figure 12.32: Accessing the Change menu from Control Panel

This process works well to add options, but maybe you just need the installation to rerun because one of the application files has been deleted or because one of the application files has been corrupted. In this case you would want to repair the installation. You can follow the previous step to access the Repair option, but choose Repair instead of Change.

Bear in mind that with the Repair and Change options, the progression will change from application to application. In fact, some application installations won't offer the Change or Repair option. In most cases, repairing or changing an application will require you to have the original installation media (so you'll have the original files). If you simply don't need the application any longer, you may choose to uninstall the application.

Uninstalling an Application

If you no longer need an application, you can stop using it and even delete the icon from your desktop, but the application will still be installed using disk space and maybe using memory and CPU resources (if the application launches any components as Windows 7 starts). If you know you are not going to use the program anymore, uninstalling the application is the best course of action.

Perform the following steps to uninstall an application:

1. Choose Start, type **control** in the Search box, and press Enter (you can also select Control Panel from the Start menu).

2. In Control Panel, select Programs.

3. In the Programs window, select Programs And Features.

4. In the Programs And Features window, select the application you want to change and then choose Uninstall from the menu.

Finding an application in Control Panel Programs And Features window assumes the application vendor followed Windows 7 guidelines and included it there. If the program does not appear in the Programs And Features window, you might still be able to uninstall it conventionally by finding the application's uninstall program in its program directory (choose Start ➤ All Programs). Find the application you want to uninstall in All Programs, right-click, and choose Uninstall, or you can locate the uninstall program in the application's All Programs folder.

Some applications or services you use within Windows 7 are not actually installed after the fact—they are Windows features. You have the ability to change these features as well.

Modifying Windows 7 Features (Built-in Programs)

Windows 7 comes with many programs and services that enhance the functionality of Windows 7 and are known as Windows features. You can turn on features, turn off features, and change some of the features options from the Windows Features dialog box.

Perform the following steps to access the Windows Features dialog box:

1. Choose Start, type **control** in the Search box, and press Enter (you can also select Control Panel from the Start menu).

2. In Control Panel, select Programs.

3. In the Programs window, select Programs And Features.

4. In the Programs And Features window, select the Turn Windows Features On Or Off from the menu in the left column to launch the Windows Features dialog box.

5. In the Windows Features dialog box, select the Windows Feature check box you would like to activate, or deselect to turn off a feature. You can also click the plus sign to expose more subfeatures to turn on or off, as shown in Figure 12.33.

Figure 12.33: Windows Features selection window

I've gone through quite a few examples in this chapter about programs and features available in Windows 7. I discussed the new and exciting features of many existing programs, as well as the introduction of Live Essentials as a web-based collaboration of programs and utilities. The best way to fully understand Windows 7 is to experience it. Get into the operating system, look around, and enjoy.

PART VI
Recovery

IN THIS PART ▶

Recovery

PART VI

13

Maintaining and Optimizing Windows 7

IN THIS CHAPTER, YOU WILL LEARN TO:

▶ **OPTIMIZE WINDOWS 7** (Pages 534 – 558)

▶ **USE WINDOWS 7 TOOLS TO DISCOVER SYSTEM INFORMATION** (Pages 559 – 571)

▶ **MAINTAIN WINDOWS 7 WITH BACKUP AND RESTORE** (Pages 571 – 576)

Recovery

PART VI

f you want an optimized Windows 7 installation, you must monitor its reliability and performance. Windows 7 comes with many tools to track memory, processor activity, the disk subsystem, and the network subsystem, as well as other computer subsystems. Tools are available to provide baseline statistics for each of the subsystems so that you can track changes over time and better evaluate issues that pertain to the Windows 7 machine and make changes to proactively affect declining performance.

Windows 7 also has a full backup and restore application to allow you to maintain a backup copy of any of the Windows 7 component files and data files that are considered critical to the operation of your day-to-day business. You can use the backup of the files to restore them if they become unusable (corrupted, deleted, or even modified) and you want to go back to the original.

You'll also learn about system recovery and troubleshooting. In this chapter, we'll show you how to safeguard your computer and how to recover from a disaster. The benefit of having a disaster recovery plan is that when you expect the worst to happen and are prepared for it, you can easily recover from most system failures.

Optimize Windows 7

Optimizing Windows 7 is a good practice; it helps administrators keep end-user machines running at peak performance. The Performance Monitor provides tools that measure the performance of a local or a remote computer on the network. Performance Monitor enables you to do the following:

- Collect data from local or remote computers. You can collect data from a single computer or multiple computers concurrently.

- View data as it is collected in real time, or historically from collected data.

- Have full control over the selection of what data will be collected by selecting which specific objects and counters will be collected.

- Choose the time interval that you want to use for collecting data points and the time period that will be used for data collection.

- Determine the format in which data will be viewed: inline, histogram bar, or report views.

- Create HTML pages for viewing data.

- Create specific configurations for monitoring data that can then be exported to other computers for performance monitoring.

Viewing Performance Monitor on Remote Machines

To view data on remote computers, you need to have administrative rights to the remote computer, the Remote Registry Service must be enabled and running on the remote computer, and Windows Firewall must be set to allow the connection. This option is useful when you do not want the overhead of the Performance Monitor graphics running on the computer you are trying to monitor. Although Microsoft has minimized the effect of running Performance Monitor, even without the graphical display, there will be minimal impact of running the data collection of Performance Monitor within the counter statistics. You can connect to another machine by selecting Connect To Another Computer in the context window of Performance within the Performance Monitor window.

Recovery

PART VI

Through Performance Monitor, you can view current data or data from a log file. When you view current data, you are monitoring real-time activity. When you view data from a log file, you are importing a log file from a previous session.

To access Performance Monitor, choose Start ➢ Control Panel ➢ System And Security ➢ Administrative Tools, and then double-click Performance Monitor; or you can type **perfmon** in the Start menu Search box. Figure 13.1 shows the main Performance Monitor window when it is initially opened without configuration.

When you first start Performance Monitor, the Overview Of Performance Monitor page is displayed. This page gives a quick snapshot of what resources are being used in your computer in the System Summary pane. Notice the four initial resources tracked are Memory, Network Interface, Physical Disk, and Processor Information. You can view detailed information about each resource by clicking the Open Resource Monitor link.

Figure 13.1: Windows 7's Performance Monitor

Using Resource Monitor

The Resource Monitor was integrated into the Reliability and Performance utility of Windows Vista, but has been given its own dialog box in Windows 7. Figure 13.2 shows the Resource Monitor dialog box (which you can open from Performance Monitor or by typing **Resource Monitor** (or **resmon**) into the Start menu Search box.

Overview The Overview tab of the Resource Monitor dialog box opens by default and gives you a fair amount of detail. The main window provides an overview of the four major subsystems monitored by default (CPU, Disk, Network, and Memory). You expand or compress each of the four items by clicking the arrow in the left of the item title bar, as shown in Figure 13.3. For example, if you want to view details about the memory being used by the processes of Windows 7, click the arrow to expand Memory and you can view each process, process ID, and memory allocation by physical, shared, and private allotment. The other tabs of the Resource

Monitor dialog box offer detailed information about each of the major subsystems of Windows 7.

Figure 13.2: Windows 7 Resource Monitor

Figure 13.3: Expand or collapse Resource Monitor items.

CPU   The CPU tab displays the individual processes currently running on the machine, the process IDs (PIDs), a brief description, the running status of the process, how many threads the process is running, current CPU utilization, and average CPU utilization. You can also expand the Services, Associated Handles, and Associated Module items for more detail on each of these items. The CPU tab, shown in Figure 13.4, also offers a graphical representation of real-time statistics for CPU total usage by percentage and Service CPU usage as a percentage on the right of the screen.

Figure 13.4: The CPU tab of Resource Monitor

Memory   The Memory tab of Resource Monitor shows the process information as displayed on the CPU tab with an overview of memory allocation in the form of a graphical representation. The right side of the display also shows you real-time information of the physical memory and the currently allocated memory, called the Committed Charge and Hard Faults/Sec (the number of memory accesses that are not actually in RAM, but in a page file waiting to be used). The Memory tab is shown in Figure 13.5.

Disk   The Disk tab of Resource Monitor (Figure 13.6) is used to display the disk activity of your machine. The items available to view are Processes With Disk Activity, Disk Activity, and Storage. The Disk tab includes a real-time graphical representation of disk transfer in KB/sec and disk queue length (the amount of transfer currently waiting for transfer to RAM for processing).

Figure 13.5: The Memory tab of Resource Monitor

Figure 13.6: The Disk tab of Resource Monitor

Network   The Network tab of Resource Monitor (Figure 13.7) shows network utilization as well as network protocol information. The items available for detailed information include Processes With Network Activity, Network Activity, TCP Connections, and Listening Ports. We've had this information available to us in previous versions of Windows, but this is one convenient location for a slew of useful network information. The Network tab offers a huge amount of useful network information (we have opened the Listening Ports item in the figure) as well as the real-time graphical information for network data transfer, open TCP connections, and local area connection usage as a percentage. You can view any of these counters in Resource Monitor as well as Performance Monitor. The key counter value guidelines (what's good/what's not good) are included in the "Key Counters" sections later in this chapter.

Figure 13.7: The Network tab of Resource Monitor

For monitoring system activity other than what is provided by the Resource Overview and Resource Monitor, you must use more of the Performance Monitor features.

Utilizing Customized Counters in Performance Monitor

You can add numerous counters from any of the subsystems within Windows 7. To access the configurable Performance Monitor window, select the Performance Monitor item in the left pane, as shown in Figure 13.8.

Figure 13.8: Customizable Performance Monitor window

Customizable counters are listed at the bottom of the Performance Monitor window. By default, only the % Processor Time counter is tracked for the local computer. The fields just above the counter list will contain data based on the counter that is highlighted in the list, as described in Table 13.1.

Table 13.1: Performance Monitor Counter Data Fields

Data Field	Description
Last	Displays the most current data
Average	Shows the average of the counter

Table 13.1: Performance Monitor Counter Data Fields *(continued)*

Data Field	Description
Minimum	Shows the lowest value that has been recorded for the counter
Maximum	Shows the highest value that has been recorded for the counter
Duration	Shows how long the counter has been tracking data

Before we add counters to Performance Monitor, let's discuss the three Performance Monitor views.

Selecting the Appropriate View

Click the Change Graph Type button on the Performance Monitor toolbar to see your data in one of three views, as shown in Figure 13.9.

Figure 13.9: Change Graph Type button

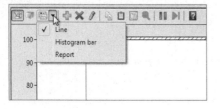

Line View   The line view is the Performance Monitor default view. It's useful for viewing a small number of counters in a graphical format. The main advantage of line view is that you can see how the data has been tracked during the defined time period.

Histogram View   The histogram view, shown in Figure 13.10, shows the Performance Monitor data in a bar graph. This view is useful for examining large amounts of data. However, it shows performance only for the current period. You do not see a record of performance over time, as you do with the line view.

Report View   The report view, shown in Figure 13.11, offers a logical text-based report of all the counters that are being tracked through Performance Monitor. Only the current session's data is displayed. The advantage of report view is that it allows you to easily track large numbers of counters in real time. It is important to note that when you view data in real-time format, the data can appear skewed as applications and processes are started. It is typically more useful to view data as an average over a specified interval.

Figure 13.10: Performance Monitor histogram view

Figure 13.11: Performance Monitor report view

Adding Counters

As mentioned previously, you can add customized counters to Performance Monitor to track data.

Follow these steps to add counters:

1. In Performance Monitor, click the Add button on the toolbar, which looks like a green plus sign (+). This brings up the Add Counters dialog box.

2. In the Add Counters dialog box, ensure that the Select Counters From The Computer drop-down list displays <Local Computer> so that you can monitor the local computer. Alternatively, to select counters from a specific computer, pick a computer from the drop-down list.

3. Select a performance object from the drop-down list. All Windows 7 system resources are tracked as performance objects, such as Cache, Memory, Paging File, Process, and Processor.

4. To view information about a specific counter, select the counter from the list, and then select the Show Description check box beneath the list on the left. Performance Monitor displays detail text regarding the highlighted counter. For example, the PhysicalDisk performance object has a % Disk Time counter, which will tell you how busy a disk has been in servicing read and write requests. PhysicalDisk also has % Disk Read Time and % Disk Write Time counters, which show you what percentage of disk requests are read requests and what percentage are write requests, respectively.

5. Select the counter or counters within the performance object that you want to track. Each performance object has an associated set of counters.

6. Select <All Instances> to track all the associated instances or pick specific instances from the list box.

7. Click the Add button to add the counters for the performance object.

8. Repeat steps 2 through 7 to specify any additional counters you want to track. When you finish, click OK.

Using Instances within Performance Monitor

An instance is a mechanism that allows you to track the performance of a specific object when you have more than one item associated with a specific performance object. For example, suppose your computer has two physical drives. When you track the PhysicalDisk performance object, you can track one or both of your drives. If a counter has more than one instance, you can monitor the sum of all of the instances by selecting the _Total option.

After you've added counters, you can select a specific counter by highlighting it in Performance Monitor. To highlight a counter, click it and then click the Highlight button (which looks like a highlighter) on the Performance Monitor toolbar, or select the counter and press Ctrl+H.

To stop showing data for a counter, deselect the check box under Show for that counter. To remove a counter, highlight it in Performance Monitor and click the Delete button on the toolbar. The Delete button looks like a red X.

Managing Performance Monitor Properties

To configure the Performance Monitor properties, click the Properties button on the Performance Monitor toolbar and the Performance Monitor Properties dialog box opens, as shown in Figure 13.12.

Figure 13.12: Performance Monitor Counter Properties dialog box

The Performance Monitor Properties dialog box has the following five tabs:

General Tab   The General tab of the Performance Monitor Properties dialog box, as shown in Figure 13.13, contains the following options:

- The display elements that will be used—legend, value bar, and/or toolbar

- The data that will be displayed—default (for reports or histograms, this is current data; for logs, this is average data), current, minimum, maximum, or average

- How often the data is updated, in seconds

Figure 13.13: The General tab of the Performance Counter Properties dialog box

Source Tab   The Source tab, shown in Figure 13.14, allows you to specify the data source. This can be current activity, or it can be data that has been collected in a log file or database. If you import data, you can specify the time range that you want to view.

Figure 13.14: The Source tab of the Performance
Counter Properties dialog box

Data Tab   The Data tab (the default tab that is active when the
properties window opens, as shown in Figure 13.12) lets you specify
the counters that you want to track. You can add and remove counters by clicking the Add and Remove buttons. You can also select a
specific counter and define the color, scale, width, and style that are
used to represent the counter in the graph.

Graph Tab   The Graph tab, shown in Figure 13.15, contains the
following options, which you can apply to the line or histogram
bar view:

- Whether the data will scroll or wrap (line view only)

- A title

- A vertical axis label

- Whether you will show a vertical grid, a horizontal grid, vertical scale numbers, and/or time axis labels

- The minimum and maximum numbers for the vertical scale

Appearance Tab   The Appearance tab of the Performance Monitor
Properties dialog box, shown in Figure 13.16, has options for customizing the colors and fonts used in the Performance Monitor display.

Figure 13.15: The Graph tab of the Performance Counter Properties dialog box

Figure 13.16: The Appearance tab of the Performance Counter Properties dialog box

After you have set counters and viewed them in real time, you might be interested in collecting the data over time and saving it to a file for maintaining baseline data for comparison. You do this in Performance Monitor by using data collector sets.

Managing Performance Monitor Data with Collector Sets

The Data Collector Sets portion of Performance Monitor is shown in Figure 13.17. Data collector sets are used to collect data into a log so that the data can be reviewed and saved for comparison at a later date (a process called baselining). You can view the log files with Performance Monitor, as described in the previous section, "Managing Performance Monitor Properties."

Figure 13.17: Configuring Performance Monitor data collector sets

To create a data collector set, right-click User Defined and choose New Data Collector Set from the context menu to launch the Create New Data Collector Set Wizard. You can let Windows 7 use a standard data collector set or you can define data logs from the following options:

- Performance counters
- Event trace data
- System configuration information

There are two built-in data collector sets that track multiple counters for system diagnostics and system performance. You can also create your own user-defined data collector sets and save them for later use. You can view the reports from these data collector sets within the Reports folder in Performance Monitor.

Creating a User-Defined Data Collector Set

Performance counter logs record data about hardware usage and the activity of system services. You can configure logging to occur manually or on a predefined schedule.

Perform the following steps to create a data log:

1. Expand Data Collector Sets, right-click User Defined, select New, and select Data Collector Set from the pop-up menu.

2. In the Create New Data Collector Set dialog box that opens, type a name for the collector set and choose whether to create the set from a template or to create it manually; then click the Next button.

3. If you chose to create the set from a template, follow the prompts to create the set. After the set is created, you can modify it.

   If you chose to create the set manually, you are asked whether you want to create data logs or a performance counter alert. Data logs can consist of the following types of data:

   - Performance counters
   - Event trace data
   - System configuration information

   After you select the data you want to collect, click Next.

4. Add the performance counters you want to collect and click Next after each data type.

5. You are asked where to save the data. Browse to the location, click OK, and then click Next.

6. You are asked under which user account the data collector set should run, and whether the data collector set should be edited, started, or saved. After you make your selections, click Finish.

Creating an Alert

Alerts can be generated when a specific counter rises above or falls below a specified value. You can configure alerts to log an entry in the application event log and/or start a data collector set. Creating an alert is similar to creating a performance counter data log except you are required to specify the alert conditions. You create an alert by creating a user-defined collector set and manually specifying counters. In the Create New Data Collector Wizard, you select the Performance Counter Alert radio button. For example, you might configure a performance counter alert that will log an entry whenever the % Free Space counter for C: falls below 5 percent. After you create the alert, you can modify the alert parameters by right-clicking the data collector and selecting Properties.

After you create the data collector sets and set the alerts, you will want to run the sets and save the logs periodically. Reviewing the logs gives you a proactive approach to managing your Windows 7 performance.

Simply creating the logs and saving them is not enough; you need to evaluate the data using previous logs to determine trends that allow you to manage your system's performance.

Managing System Performance

By analyzing data, you can determine whether any resources place an excessive load on your computer and result in a system slowdown. The following list gives some of the causes of poor system performance:

- A resource is insufficient to handle the load that is being placed upon it, and the component might need to be upgraded, or additional components might be required.

- If a resource has multiple instances, the resources might not be evenly balancing the workload, and the workload might need to be balanced over the multiple instances more effectively.

- A resource might be malfunctioning. In this case, the resource should be repaired or replaced.

- A specific program might be allocated resources improperly or inefficiently, in which case the program needs to be rewritten or replaced by another application.

- A resource might be configured improperly, causing excessive resource usage and requiring reconfiguration.

Recovery

PART VI

You should monitor four main subsystems. Configure counters in your data collector set for each of the following:

- The memory subsystem
- The processor subsystem
- The disk subsystem
- The network subsystem

Each subsystem should be examined over time to evaluate Windows 7 performance.

Monitoring and Optimizing Memory

When the operating system needs a program or process, the first place it looks is in physical memory. If the required program or process is not in physical memory, the system looks in logical memory (the page file). If the program or process is not in logical memory, the system then must retrieve the program or process from the hard disk. It can take thousands of times longer to access information from the hard disk than to get it from physical RAM. If your computer is using excessive paging, that is an indication that your computer does not have enough physical memory.

Insufficient memory is the most likely cause of system bottlenecks. If you have no idea what is causing a system bottleneck, memory is usually a good place to start checking. To determine how memory is being used, examine the following two areas:

Physical Memory   The physical RAM you have installed on your computer. You can't have too much memory as long as you are below your operating system's maximum. It's a good idea to have more memory than you think you will need just to be on the safe side. As you've probably noticed, each time you add or upgrade applications, you require more system memory.

Page File   Logical memory exists on your hard drive. If you are using excessive paging (swapping between the page file and physical RAM) or hard page faults, it's a clear sign that you need to add more memory.

The first step in memory management is determining how much memory your computer has installed and what the appropriate memory requirements are based on the operating system requirements and the applications and services you are running on your computer.

Key Counters to Track for Memory Management

The following are the three most important counters for monitoring memory:

Memory ➤ Available MBytes Memory ➤ Available MBytes measures the amount of physical memory that is available to run processes on the computer. If this number is less than 20 percent of your installed memory, it indicates that you might have an overall shortage of physical memory for your computer, or you possibly have an application that is not releasing memory properly. You should consider adding more memory or evaluating application memory usage.

Memory ➤ Pages/Sec Memory ➤ Pages/Sec shows the number of times the requested information was not in memory and had to be retrieved from disk. This counter's value should be below 20; for optimal performance, it should be 4 or 5. If the number is above 20, you should add memory or research paging file use more thoroughly. Sometimes a high Pages/Sec counter is indicative of a program that is using a memory-mapped file.

Paging File ➤ % Usage Paging File ➤ % Usage indicates the percentage of the allocated page file that is currently in use. If this number is consistently over 70 percent, you might need to add more memory or increase the size of the page file. You should track this counter in conjunction with Available MBytes and Pages/Sec.

These counters work together to show what is happening on your system. Use the Paging File ➤ % Usage counter value in conjunction with the Memory ➤ Available MBytes and Memory ➤ Pages/Sec counters to determine how much paging is occurring on your computer.

Along with memory counters, processor (or CPU) counters are valuable in evaluating Windows 7 performance.

Managing Processor Performance

Processor bottlenecks can develop when the threads of a process require more processing cycles than are currently available. In this case, the process will wait in a processor queue and system responsiveness will be slower than if process requests could be immediately served. The most common causes of processor bottlenecks are processor-intensive applications and other subsystem components that generate excessive processor interrupts (for example, disk or network subsystems).

Recovery

PART VI

In a workstation environment, processors are usually not the source of bottlenecks; however, you should still monitor this subsystem to make sure that processor utilization is at an efficient level. There are several standard counters you should monitor to track processor utilization.

Key Counters to Track for Processor

You can track processor utilization through the Processor and System objects to determine whether a processor bottleneck exists. The following are the most important counters for monitoring the system processor:

Processor ➤ % Processor Time   Processor ➤ % Processor Time measures the time that the processor spends responding to system requests. If this value is consistently above an average of 85 percent, you might have a processor bottleneck. The Processor ➤ % User Time and Processor ➤ % Privileged Time counters combine to show the total % Processor Time counter. You can monitor these counters individually for more detail.

Processor ➤ Interrupts/Sec   Processor ➤ Interrupts/Sec show the average number of hardware interrupts received by the processor each second. If this value is higher than 3,000, you might have a problem with a program or hardware that is generating spurious interrupts (this value will vary in optimization based on the processor type; you'll need to do a little research for your specific processor to see the appropriate value).

System ➤ Processor Queue Length   System ➤ Processor Queue Length is used to determine whether a processor bottleneck is due to high levels of demand for processor time. If a queue of two or more items exists for an extended period of time, a processor bottleneck might be indicated. If you suspect that a processor bottleneck is due to excessive hardware I/O requests, you should also monitor the System ➤ File Control Bytes/Sec counter.

Tuning and Upgrading the Processor

If you suspect that you have a processor bottleneck, you can try the following solutions:

- Use applications that are less processor-intensive.
- Upgrade your processor.
- If your computer supports multiple processors, add one.

The memory and processor subsystem objects are important counters to evaluate in determining your Windows 7 performance. You should look at the hard drive or disk subsystem to look for issues as well.

Managing the Disk Subsystem

Disk access is the amount of time your disk subsystem takes to retrieve data that is requested by the operating system. The two factors that determine how quickly your disk subsystem will respond to system requests are the average disk access time on your hard drive and the speed of your disk controller.

Key Counters to Track for the Disk Subsystem

You can monitor the PhysicalDisk object, which is the sum of all logical drives on a single physical drive, or you can monitor the LogicalDisk object, which represents a specific logical disk. Here are the more important counters for monitoring the disk subsystem:

PhysicalDisk ➤ % Disk Time and LogicalDisk ➤ % Disk Time PhysicalDisk ➤ % Disk Time and LogicalDisk ➤ % Disk Time shows the amount of time the disk is busy because it is servicing read or write requests. If your disk is busy more than 90 percent of the time, you will improve performance by adding another disk channel and splitting the disk I/O requests between the channels.

PhysicalDisk ➤ Current Disk Queue Length and LogicalDisk ➤ Current Disk Queue Length PhysicalDisk ➤ Current Disk Queue Length and LogicalDisk ➤ Current Disk Queue Length indicates the number of outstanding disk requests that are waiting to be processed. On average, this value should be less than 2.

LogicalDisk ➤ % Free Space LogicalDisk ➤ % Free Space specifies how much free disk space is available. This counter should be at least 15 percent.

Tuning and Upgrading the Disk Subsystem

When you suspect that you have a disk subsystem bottleneck, the first thing you should check is your memory subsystem. Insufficient physical memory can cause excessive paging, which in turn affects the disk subsystem.

Recovery

PART VI

If you do not have a memory problem, try the following solutions to improve disk performance:

- Use faster disks and controllers.

- Confirm that you have the latest drivers for your disk adapters.

- Use disk striping to take advantage of multiple I/O channels.

- Balance heavily used files on multiple I/O channels.

- Add another disk controller for load balancing.

- Use Disk Defragmenter to consolidate files so that disk space and data access are optimized.

After you evaluate the first three subsystems—memory, processor, and disk—you also need to look at the network subsystem to optimize your Windows 7 performance.

Optimizing the Network Subsystem

Windows 7 does not have a built-in mechanism for monitoring the entire network. However, you can monitor and optimize the traffic that is generated on your Windows 7 machine. You can monitor the network interface (your network card) and the network protocols that have been installed on your computer.

Network bottlenecks are indicated when network traffic exceeds the capacity that can be supported by the local area network (LAN). Typically, you would monitor this activity on a network-wide basis — for example, with the Network Monitor 3.4 (available for download at www.microsoft.com).

Key Counters to Track for the Network Subsystem

If you are using the Performance Monitor item to monitor local network traffic, the following two counters are useful for monitoring the network subsystem:

Network Interface ➤ Bytes Total/Sec   Network Interface ➤ Bytes Total/Sec measures the total number of bytes sent or received from the network interface and includes all network protocols.

TCPv4 ➤ Segments/Sec   TCPv4 ➤ Segments/Sec measures the number of bytes sent or received from the network interface and includes only the TCPv4 protocol.

Tuning and Upgrading the Network Subsystem

You can use the following guidelines to help optimize and minimize network traffic:

- Install only the network protocols you need.
- Use network cards that take advantage of your bus speed.
- Use faster network cards—for example, 100Mbps Ethernet or 1Gbps Ethernet instead of 10Mbps Ethernet.

Microsoft added a feature to Windows Vista's Performance Monitor called Reliability Monitor (hence the Windows Vista tool named Reliability and Performance Monitor). In Windows 7, Microsoft has removed the tool from Performance Monitor and Reliability Monitor is a separate tool.

Using Reliability Monitor

Reliability Monitor (see Figure 13.18) is a stand-alone feature in Windows 7 that provides an overview of the stability of your Windows 7 computer. You can access Reliability Monitor by typing **reliability monitor** in the Start menu Search box and selecting View Reliability Report from the resulting list.

Figure 13.18: Windows 7 Reliability Monitor

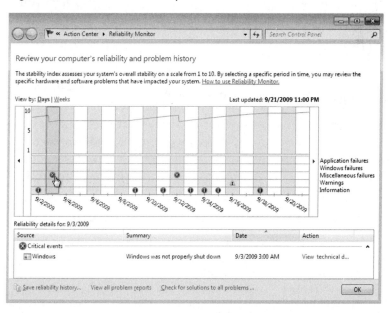

If a problem is causing system instability, Reliability Monitor can provide details about it. The data is collected and stored in the following five categories in the lower half of the display window, as described in Table 13.2.

Table 13.2 Windows 7 Reliability Monitor Categories

Category	Description
Application Failures	Programs that hang or crash
Windows Failures	Includes operating system and boot failures
Miscellaneous Failures	Includes unexpected shutdowns
Warnings	Items that are detrimental, but not failures
Information	Information messages that Windows 7 issues

The upper half of the graphical display indicates the relative reliability of your Windows 7 machine on a scale of 1 to 10 (with 10 representing completely reliable). To display the tracked reliability items in the time view (which you can change to display by days or weeks), click View By: Days | Weeks in the upper left of the Reliability Monitor window. You can view the details about failures, warnings, and informational messages by clicking the icon in the graphical window for the time period displayed.

If you notice a recurring problem, choose Check For Solutions To All Problems at the bottom of the window and let Windows 7 check the issues and report potential solutions. You can view all the problems Reliability Monitor has detected by choosing View All Problem Reports, also located at the bottom of the window. By selecting Save Reliability History, you can save the current report in XML format.

Using Performance Monitor, Reliability Monitor, and Resource Monitor to manage your Windows 7 computer will make your administrative tasks simpler. Several other tools are also available for you to learn about your system information.

Use Windows 7 Tools to Discover System Information

Windows 7 contains many other tools to discover system information about your computer. In this section, we'll explore three of them:

- System Information
- Task Manager
- Performance Information and Tools

Getting System Information

You can use the System Information utility, shown in Figure 13.19, to learn details about your hardware, software, and resources. Type **msinfo32** in the Start menu Search box to launch this utility.

Figure 13.19: System Information dialog box

A great deal of your system's information is available within this application. Click the fields in the left pane and details are displayed in the right pane. You can also search for a term by typing it in the Find What field at the bottom of the page. This utility has been available in many releases of the Windows product.

Using Task Manager

The Task Manager utility shows the applications and processes that are currently running on your computer, as well as CPU and memory usage information. To access Task Manager, press Ctrl+Alt+Delete and click Start Task Manager. Alternatively, right-click an empty area in the Taskbar and select Task Manager from the context menu, or type **task manager** in the Start menu search box. The Task Manager dialog box has the following six main tabs:

- Applications
- Processes
- Services
- Performance
- Networking
- Users

Managing Application Tasks in Task Manager

The Applications tab of the Task Manager dialog box, shown in Figure 13.20, lists all the applications that are currently running on the computer. For each task, you will see the name of the task and the current status (Running, Not Responding, or Stopped).

- To close an application, select it in Task Manager and click the End Task button at the bottom of the dialog box.
- To make the application window active, select it and click the Switch To button.
- If you want to start an application that isn't running, click the New Task button and specify the location and name of the program you wish to start.

Managing Process Tasks in Task Manager

The Processes tab of the Task Manager dialog box, shown in Figure 13.21, lists all the processes that are currently running on the computer. This is a convenient way to get a quick look at how your system is performing. For each process, you will see the Image Name (the name of the process), the User Name (the user account that is running the process), CPU (the amount of CPU utilization for the process), Memory (Private Working Set) (the amount of memory that is being used by the process), and Description (a description of the process).

Figure 13.20: Applications tab in Task Manager

Figure 13.21: Processes tab in Task Manager

Using the Processes tab, you can organize the listing and control processes as follows:

Organizing Processes   To organize the processes, click the column headings. For example, if you click the CPU column, the listing will start with the processes that use the most CPU resources. If you click the CPU column a second time, the listing will be reversed so that the processes that use the least CPU resources are listed first.

Managing Processes   To manage a process, right-click it and choose an option from the context menu. You can choose to end the process, end the process tree, debug the process, specify virtualization, create a dump file, or set the priority of the process (to Realtime, High, Above Normal, Normal, Below Normal, or Low). If your computer has multiple processors installed, you can also set processor affinity (the process of associating a specific process with a specific processor) for a process.

Customizing Counters   To customize the counters that are listed, select View ➤ Select Columns. This brings up the Select Columns dialog box where you can select various information you want to see listed on the Processes tab.

Showing Processes of Other Users in Task Manager

By default, only your processes are shown. To display processes from all users, including System, Local Service, and Network Service, click Show Processes From All Users.

On the Processes tab in Task Manager, you can also stop a process and manage process priority:

Stopping Processes   You might need to stop a process that isn't executing properly. To stop a specific process, select the process you want to stop in the Task Manager's Processes tab and click the End Process button. Task Manager displays a Warning dialog box. Click the End Process button to terminate the process. If you right-click a process, you can end the specific process or you can use the option End Process Tree. The End Process Tree option ends all processes that have been created either directly or indirectly by the process.

Managing Process Priority   To change the priority of a process that is already running, use the Processes tab of Task Manager.

Right-click the process you want to manage and select Set Priority from the context menu. You can select from Realtime, High, Above Normal, Normal, Below Normal, and Low. As you might expect, applications launch at Normal priority by default.

Perform the following steps to set a process priority and end a process from within Task Manager. I'll use the Calculator for this example.

1. Right-click an empty space on your Taskbar and select Task Manager from the context menu.

2. On the Applications tab, click the New Task button.

3. In the Create A New Task dialog box, type **calc** and click OK.

4. Click the Processes tab. Right-click calc.exe and select Set Priority, then select Low. In the Warning dialog box, click the Change Priority button to continue.

5. Right-click calc.exe and select End Process. In the Warning dialog box, click the End Process button.

Managing Services in Task Manager

The Services tab of the Task Manager dialog box, shown in Figure 13.22, lists all the services that can run on the computer. For each service, you will see the Name (the name of the service), the PID (the associated process identifier), Description (a description of the service, Status (whether a process is Running or Stopped), and Group (the service group).

Figure 13.22: Services tab of Task Manager

To start a stopped service, click the service and select Start Service. To stop a running service, click the service and select Stop Service. You can also open the Services tool by clicking the Services button. The Services tool allows you to specify whether a process starts automatically, automatically with a delayed start, or manually, or is disabled.

Managing Performance Tasks in Task Manager

The Performance tab of Task Manager, shown in Figure 13.23, provides an overview of your computer's CPU and memory usage. This information is similar to the information tracked by Performance Monitor.

Figure 13.23: Performance tab of Task Manager

The Performance tab shows the following information:

- CPU usage, in real time and in a history graph
- Memory usage, in real time and in a history graph
- Physical memory statistics
- Kernel memory statistics
- System totals for handles, threads, processes, uptime, and the pagefile

Click the Resource Monitor button to launch the Resource Monitor that you can also find in Performance Monitor.

Managing Networking Tasks in Task Manager

The Networking tab of Task Manager, shown in Figure 13.24, provides an overview of your networking usage. Statistics for each adapter are displayed at the bottom of the tab.

Figure 13.24: Networking tab of Task Manager

Managing Users in Task Manager

The Users tab of Task Manager, shown in Figure 13.25, shows the active and disconnected users on your computer. For each user, you will see the User (the name of the user), the ID (the current user ID), Status (whether Active or Disconnected), Client Name, and Session (whether the user is connected via the console session or by another method, such as Remote Desktop).

To send a message to a user, select the user and click the Send Message button. To connect to a user session, right-click the user and select Connect. To disconnect a user session, select the user and click the Disconnect button. To log off a user, select the user and click the Logoff button.

Figure 13.25: Users tab of Task Manager

If there are issues that occur within Windows 7, you use a different utility, called Event Viewer, to view these events.

Using Event Viewer

Event Viewer, shown in Figure 13.26, enables you to view event logs that are created by the operating system. This utility is useful when troubleshooting problems that occur on your computer.

Whenever an error occurs, an event is usually placed in one or more event logs. To open Event Viewer, click Start ➣ Control Panel ➣ System And Security ➣ Administrative Tools ➣ View Event Logs, or you can type **event viewer** in the Start menu Search box.

Whereas old versions of Event Viewer contained only the Application, Security, and System logs, the Windows 7 version of Event Viewer contains the following logs:

- Application
- Security
- Setup
- System
- Forwarded Events

Figure 13.26: Windows 7 Event Viewer

The Application log is used to log events relating to applications, such as whether an application, driver, or service fails. The Security log is used to log security events, such as successful or failed logon events. The Setup log is used only by domain controllers, so it doesn't have much practical use in Windows 7. The System log is used to log events concerning the operating system and related services. The Forwarded Events log is used to collect events that have been forwarded from other computers.

To configure log settings, right-click the log that you want to configure and select Properties. The Log Properties dialog box appears. The Application log properties are shown in Figure 13.27.

The Log Properties dialog box shows the following information:

- The full name of the log
- Where the log is stored
- The size of the log
- When the log was created, modified, and accessed
- Whether logging is enabled for the log
- The maximum log size in KB
- The action that occurs when the log reaches the max size

Figure 13.27: Event Viewer Application log properties

The left pane of Event Viewer is where you find the Windows logs noted previously, but it also contains other logs and views that can be helpful when troubleshooting a specific application. The Custom Views section can be used to create a view that contains only the information you want to see, such as only events in a particular log or only Critical events. One custom view, Administrative Events, is created for you by default, as shown in Figure 13.28.

The Administrative Events view contains Critical, Error, and Warning events from all logs, enabling you to easily view only the most important events. Another section in the left pane contains logs that relate to Applications and Services, as shown in Figure 13.29.

The Microsoft folder within the Application and Services Log contains many other logs related to specific Microsoft components and applications.

The Subscription folder enables you to receive event logs from other computers. Having multiple machines send events to one machine is useful as it provides a central location for viewing events from multiple locations. To use subscriptions, you must start the Windows Event Collector Service.

Figure 13.28: Event Viewer Custom Views section: Administrative Events

Figure 13.29: Event Viewer Application and Services Logs

The center pane of Event Viewer displays the events and information that relates to those events. You can also view a summary of your administrative events, which contains a count of Critical, Error, Warning, Information, Audit Success, and Audit Failure events. A count of these events is displayed for the last hour, day, and week, and the total number of events is also provided. Each event is assigned an event level of Critical, Error, Warning, Information, or Verbose.

The right pane of Event Viewer enables you to perform actions related to items you have selected in the left and center panes. You can save logs, open saved logs, create or import views, clear logs, filter logs, and find logs with certain keywords. You can also attach a task to an event. Clicking Attach Task To This Event opens the Create Basic Task wizard in Task Scheduler so that you can easily create a task related to the selected event.

Perform the following tasks to view events in Event Viewer and set log properties:

1. Select Start ➤ Control Panel ➤ System And Security ➤ Administrative Tools ➤ View Event Logs, or type **event viewer** in the Start menu Search box.

2. Open Windows Logs and click System in the left pane of the Event Viewer window to display the System log events.

3. Double-click the first event in the center pane of the Event Viewer window to see its Event Properties dialog box.

4. After you view the event properties, click the Close button to close the dialog box.

5. Right-click System in the left pane of the Event Viewer window and select Properties.

6. Configure the System log to archive the log file when it is full by clicking Archive The Log File When Full; Do Not Overwrite Events. Click OK to close the dialog box.

7. Right-click System in the left pane of the Event Viewer window and select Filter Current Log.

8. Select the Critical and Error check boxes; then click OK (you will see only Critical and Error events listed in the System log).

9. Right-click System and select Clear Log.

10. A dialog box appears that asks if you want to save the System log before you clear it; click the Save And Clear button.

11. Specify the path and filename for the log file, and then click the Save button (the events will be saved in an .evtx file, and the events will be cleared from the System log).

Event Viewer is one of the first places to look when you suspect Windows 7 is not behaving correctly. But what if you know Windows 7 is having a problem and you need to restore the configuration or restore files? You need to use Windows 7 Backup and Restore.

Maintain Windows 7 with Backup and Restore

The Windows 7 Backup and Restore utility allows you to create and restore backups. Backups protect your data in the event of system failure by storing the data on another medium, such a hard disk, CD, DVD, or network location. If your original data is lost due to corruption, deletion, or media failure, you can restore the data using your saved backup.

To access Backup and Restore (shown in Figure 13.30), type **backup and restore** in the Start menu Search box or select Start ➢ Control Panel ➢ System And Security ➢ Backup And Restore.

Recovery

PART VI

Figure 13.30: Windows 7 Backup and Restore

Creating a Backup

You can see in Figure 13.30 that no backups of this Windows 7 machine have been taken. To set up a backup, choose the Set Up Backup link to launch a wizard that takes you through the process of creating a backup. The Backup wizard first asks you for a location to save your backup. This location can be a hard disk (removable or fixed), a CD, a DVD, or even a network location (if you have Windows 7 Premium or Ultimate).

Next you are asked to either let Windows 7 choose the files and folders to back up or let you manually select the resources you want to back up. In manual selection, you can choose just the data libraries of Windows 7 for you as a user, or other users. You can also choose to create a backup of the Windows 7 systems files. If you want to choose other files and folders, you have the option of selecting any resources individually on your hard disk(s).

The final page of the wizard allows you to view the items you have selected as well as set up a schedule for your backups to occur. If you're happy with the setup, click the Save Settings And Run Backup button. The backup commences and you are able to restore the resources if necessary in the future. Figure 13.31 shows this author's Windows 7 machine right after he chose to save settings and run the backup. You can see the backup in progress and the history of his backups.

Figure 13.31: Windows 7 initial backup in progress

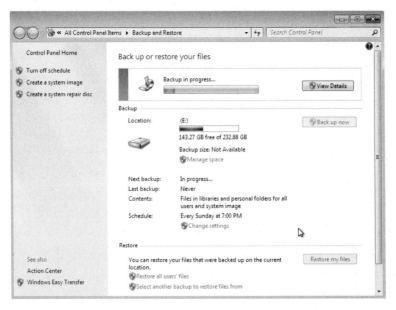

After you have created your backup, you can restore systems files and user data files with the restore utility.

Restoring Files from a Backup

If you have lost or destroyed files that you still want on your Windows 7 system, you can restore them from your backup. To restore files to your computer, launch the Backup and Restore program by typing **backup and restore** in the Start menu Search box. Assuming the media where your backup was saved is available, you can click the Restore My Files button, as shown in Figure 13.32.

Figure 13.32: Click the Restore My Files button to launch a restore wizard.

Clicking the Restore My Files button launches a restore wizard that prompts you to search for the files you want to restore. You can select multiple files and folders to restore. When you have selected all the files and folders you want to restore, click Next and you will have one final option: to restore to the original location or to pick an alternate location for restoration. After you make the restore location decision, click Restore and the restore operation commences and your original files and folders are available for you from the backup media.

You also have options in the Backup and Restore window to restore all users' files and to select another backup to restore files from. You would use this second option if you have saved your backup to multiple locations, and the last one (the one listed in the backup section) is not the set of backup files you want to use in your current session. Other than just files and folders, you have the choice to use other advanced backup options.

Using Advanced Backup Options

In the main backup and restore window, you have options in the left pane (as shown in Figure 13.33): Turn Off Schedule, Create A System Image, and Create A System Repair Disc.

Figure 13.33: Other backup options

Choosing Turn Off Schedule lets you take your backup out of the current backup scheduling as seen in Task Scheduler. Create A System Image lets you back up critical operating system files for restoration later if your operating system has become corrupted. Create A System Repair Disc allows you to create a bootable disc that will store a limited setup, repair utilities, and the ability to restore your backup files if necessary.

There's one more option for restoring your Windows 7 configuration: System Protection.

Using System Protection

System Protection is a feature of Windows 7 that creates a backup and saves the configuration information of your computer's system files and settings on a regular basis. System Protection saves previous versions of saved configurations rather than just overwriting them. This makes it possible to return to multiple configurations, known as restore points, in your Windows 7 history. These restore points are created before most significant events, such as installing a new driver. Restore points are also created automatically every seven days. System Protection is turned on by default in Windows7 for any drive formatted with NTFS.

You manage System Protection and the restore points from the System Protection tab of the System Properties dialog box. You access this tab directly by typing **restore point** in the Start menu Search box, as shown in Figure 13.34.

Clicking the System Restore button launches the System Restore wizard, which walks you through the process of returning Windows 7 to a previous point in time. Also on the System Protection tab of the System Properties dialog box, you'll find the Protection Settings section where you can configure any of your available drives. Select the drive on which you would like to modify the configuration and click the Configure button. The System Protection configuration dialog box for the drive appears, as shown in Figure 13.35.

Figure 13.34: The System Protection tab of the System Properties dialog box

Figure 13.35: Drive Protection properties in System Protection

The System Protection for the selected disk properties box allows you to enable or disable system protection for the drive. When you enable protection, you can opt for previous versions for files or previous versions of files and system settings. You also have the ability to set the maximum usage your restore points will use for storage. One final function of the System Protection dialog box for the selected disk is to delete all restore points (including system setting and previous versions of files) by clicking the Delete button.

Index

Note to the Reader: Throughout this index **boldfaced** page numbers indicate primary discussions of a topic. *Italicized* page numbers indicate illustrations.

N